Literary Journalism across the Globe

Literary Journalism across the Globe

Journalistic Traditions and Transnational Influences

Edited by
JOHN S. BAK AND BILL REYNOLDS

University of Massachusetts Press
Amherst and Boston

LC 2011006673
ISBN 978-1-55849-877-8 (paper); 978-1-55849-876-1 (library cloth)

Set in Adobe Garamond Pro
Printed and bound by Thomson Shore, Inc.

Library of Congress Cataloging-in-Publication Data

Literary journalism across the globe : journalistic traditions and transnational influences /
edited by John S. Bak and Bill Reynolds.
    p. cm.
Includes bibliographical references and index.
ISBN 978-1-55849-877-8 (pbk. : alk. paper) —
ISBN 978-1-55849-876-1 (library cloth : alk. paper)
1. Reportage literature—History and criticism. 2. Journalism and literature.
I. Bak, John S. II. Reynolds, Bill.
PN3377.5.R45L57 2011
070.9—dc22
                              2011006673

British Library Cataloguing in Publication data are available.

To IALJS

The art and craft of reportage—journalism marked by vivid description, a novelist's eye to form, and eyewitness reporting that reveals hidden truths about people and events that have shaped the world we know.

— *Granta*, England

Reportage Literature is an engagement with reality with a novelist's eye but with a journalist's discipline.

— Pedro Rosa Mendes, Portugal

I think one of the first things for literary reportage should be to go into the field and to try to get the other side of the story. Reportage should give a fresh vision of a topic.

— Anne Nivat, France

A good reportage must not necessarily be linked with topical or political events which are taking place around us. I think the miracle of things lies not in showing the extraordinary but in showing ordinary things in which the extraordinary is hidden.

— Nirmal Verma, India

Journalism that would read like a novel . . . or short story.

— Tom Wolfe, United States

Contents

Part III: Transnational Influences

Acknowledgments

This book has been a long time in the making. Its editors owe thanks not only to those scholars who have contributed to its pages but also to those literary journalists discussed in the sixteen essays who have waited decades or centuries for their work to be recognized to its fullest extent as literary journalism or literary reportage.

Many people have had a direct or indirect hand in this book's production. Among them we thank David Abrahamson, John C. Hartsock, Alice Donat Trindade, Isabel Soares, Thomas B. Connery, and Jan Whitt for their invaluable advice and support. A special thanks goes to Norman Sims, who not only helped steer this project along at University of Massachusetts Press but also added precious commentary to the book's introduction.

At University of Massachusetts Press, we thank director Bruce Wilcox and editors Brian Halley, Carol Betsch, and Amanda Heller for their continued support and sound advice.

An additional note of gratitude is extended to all members of the International Association for Literary Journalism Studies (IALJS) past and present, to whom this book is gratefully dedicated. They have enriched every essay here through their invigorating and cordial debate and dialogue.

All of the essays were originally written for this book, but two (chapters 1 and 13) were subsequently published elsewhere in a slightly different format before this book was published. We thank Timothy S. Murphy, editor at *Genre: Forms of Discourse and Culture,* and the editors at Palgrave Macmillan for graciously allowing them to be reprinted here.

Finally, we are grateful to our families for their continued support in this quixotic adventure called academia: Nathalie, Margaux, and James, and Laura and Justine.

Literary Journalism across the Globe

Introduction

John S. Bak

At the end of the nineteenth century, several countries were developing journalistic traditions similar to what we identify today as literary journalism or literary reportage. Throughout most of the twentieth century, however, and in particular after World War I, that tradition was overshadowed and even marginalized by the general perception among democratic states that journalism ought to be either "objective," as in the American tradition, or "polemical," as in the European one. Nonetheless, literary journalism would survive and at times even thrive. How and why is a story unique to each nation.

While many students, scholars, and practitioners of literary journalism have long acknowledged the form's Anglo-American roots, this book takes a broader approach to examining the ways literary journalism has been practiced and read throughout the world. From China to Brazil, Scotland to Australia, and Finland to New Zealand, international literary journalism has established itself as one of the most significant and controversial forms of writing of the last century—significant because it often raises our sociopolitical awareness about a disenfranchised or underprivileged people; controversial because its emphasis on authorial voice jeopardizes our faith in its claims of accuracy. In the age of electronic news, however, when concerns about word count and article length have almost become a thing of the past, literary journalism seems poised to revolutionize the way we read journalism and appreciate literature. This book aims to assess the extent to which literary journalism over the past century has influenced reporting in various nations—some of which have only recently known democracy, while others are still under full or partial state control—and how it might shape journalistic heuristics and literary aesthetics in the twenty-first century.

Several essays in this collection proclaim that, among the many nations today, literary journalism has proved itself a responsible and respectable voice of print media, one that struggles daily with the problem of maintaining a foundational readership. And if scholars of international media find these nations opting more for literary journalistic stories to attract readers—narrative pieces that recount the factual news of the day in dramatic or emotive ways—literary aesthetes too are rediscovering the powerful and typically neglected form of literary journalism, which has earned its place among the traditional belles lettres of many nations. In short, there exists a rich international contingent of literary journalism and literary journalism scholars, and this book brings both together for the first time under one cover.

Sixteen essays from the world's leading scholars of literary journalism have been assembled here to exhibit how the form has been viewed, read, written, and studied throughout the world. Because not all nations are alike in their journalistic traditions, we cannot expect their literary journalism to be precisely the same. This book offers a look at how and where literary journalism varies (or does not), whether it is written in English, French, Portuguese, Spanish, Slovene, Finnish, Dutch, German, Polish, Russian, or Mandarin. These essays, divided into three parts whose topics range from the taxonomic to the historical to the critical, provide both a window onto the past and a looking glass into the future of print media in North and South America, in Europe, and in Australia and Asia.[1] They reexamine literary journalism's historical roots in England and in America, but more from transnational perspectives of how writers in both nations—men and women alike—have influenced journalists abroad or were themselves influenced. They also look at the role that literary journalism has played in the building of nationhood or in the establishment of a national canon. Above all, they reveal how literary journalism, no matter in which language it appears, has remained loyal to its commitment to inform the world accurately and honestly about the magical in the mundane, the great in the small, and above all, the *us* in the *them*.

E Pluribus Veritas

Literary journalism has a long and complex international history, one built on a combination of journalistic traditions and transnational influences. Recovering these two dimensions of literary journalism as it is practiced throughout the world is complicated by several factors that need clarification. These obstacles suggest that scholars of international literary journalism need to adopt a phenomenological view of the form. Accepting literary journalism as a legitimate global form is not enough; we also need to exercise intercultural sensitivity to accompany our interdisciplinary awareness.

If examples of an American-style New Journalism can be found in today's international dailies and magazines worldwide, the reasons for that imitative strain are hard to isolate. Given the various continents' and countries' vastly incongruent histories, societies, and cultures, how could we expect what is deemed literary journalism in, say, Japan to be similar, let alone identical, to that produced in Argentina?² Consequently, the permutations that international literary journalism has undergone over the past century have been exponential. Two world wars have created environments entirely inhospitable for the form to have evolved in eastern Europe as it has in the West. While it is true, for example, that the late nineteenth century witnessed the near simultaneous birth of an Anglo-American literary journalism and a European literature reportage—whose similarities and differences this book attempts to account for—claims of a shared ancestry are readily countered by the marked differences between the two forms as they developed in response to those two wars. Literary journalism thus *is* and *is not* literary reportage. Emphasizing their differences is elementary; reclaiming their shared past, however, is much more challenging. This book is a response to that challenge.

Building on the few efforts that have promoted international literary journalism,³ this collection attempts to define the form through a celebration of its ancestral roots. Such a task has remained the mission of the International Association for Literary Journalism Studies (IALJS) since its inception in July 2006, following its first annual congress in the eastern French city of Nancy. Since then, the IALJS has promoted the definition of international literary journalism as journalism *as* literature, as opposed to journalism *about* literature. This book maintains that distinction but also recognizes its limitations within a global context.

What happens, for instance, when what constitutes "literature" and "journalism" varies from one nation to the next, or when what passes for "truth" in the world press belies a universal understanding, let alone praxis? National tastes in literature can blur the fact-fiction divide so much that literary journalism has been squeezed out by factographic fiction, a point Maria Lassila-Merisalo makes in her essay on Finnish literary journalism; or, inversely, it has been accorded preferential status over fiction because it captures reality better, which is what Peiqin Chen explains in her essay on Chinese literary reportage. Even in terms of journalistic practices, while the inverted pyramid news structure has held sway in the dailies of most democratic countries since the opening decades of the twentieth century, not every nation has filled that pyramid with the same heuristics or the same degree of accuracy. Consequently, journalism is neither taught nor valued equally worldwide, and the ramifications of that truism reverberate loudly in the production of literary journalism. Without a comparable understanding of literature and a mutual respect for the goals and ethics of responsible journalism, how can we ever expect to have a "literary journalism" on an international scale? This question lies at the heart of every essay in this book.

Comparative literatures and comparative journalisms are further complicated by an even simpler problem: if we search the world media over, the journalistic standard of truth we repeatedly find is based more on iron pyrite than on gold. Facts and truths are the luxuries of democracies, or so we have been led to believe. But there are as many lies, intentional or arbitrated through political alignments, printed in the free press as there are truths, some even disguised, in the censored press. In the introductions to several books on American literary journalism published over the last two decades or more, a postmodern incredulity toward objective reality reigns. Thomas B. Connery refers to it as "patterns of reality"; John C. Hartsock, "our phenomenal world"; Norman Sims, factual "triangulat[ion]"; Barbara Lounsberry, "themes" of literature; Edd Applegate, "the kernel of traditional journalism"; and Richard Keeble, a "rhetoric of factuality."[4]

Even before postmodernism began challenging metanarratives and their questionable truth-values, claims of objectivity bothered many. As Hartsock points out in his essay for this collection, postrevolutionary Russia considered objective reality to be the product of bourgeois thinking, manufactured to give the masses a semblance of truth and thus the illusion of freedom. Though a convenient argument to justify the Cheka's iron-fisted control of the Bolshevik news agencies, its theoretical implications appealed to the American Communist Party in the 1930s and had resounding effects on the form's evolution at home.[5] Joseph North's fellow travelers found their voices in pieces for *The New Masses* or *The Anvil,* and "three-dimensional reporting" had been given the Leninist flavor it was missing in the yellow journalism and muckraking journalism of previous decades.[6] In what proved to be one of its most significant, though by no means first, transnational mutations, literary journalism temporarily fused with literary reportage. But a second world war soon divided the world, and American plutocracy denuded literary reportage of its Marxist agenda. Literary journalism would continue to fight against objective reality, but now without the political ideologies of its European sibling, which would soon migrate east to China, as Chen explains in her essay. As two ideologies clashed for nearly half a century for control over the hemispheres, so too would their literary journalisms compete for international recognition.

The problem in determining who respects truth the most, then, is not as simple as dismissing state-run journalism for manipulating facts or manufacturing truths in favor of a democratic press's crusade for worldwide journalistic transparency. Surely questions concerning who decides *what* truth is and *how* it is to be reported have long preoccupied journalism scholars, and dividing the world between democratic truths and autocratic half-truths serves little in our desire to define an international literary journalism. Yes, freedom of the press does matter, but it is not simply an "us and them" scenario, a West versus East dialectic. Even in democratic strongholds such as Australia or France, where I write these words today, there is no constitutional right protecting the freedom of the press as there is in the United States or the Netherlands. Of course, French reporters are not gunned down in their apartment elevators for having revealed the secrets behind a dirty war, or hacked to death in their rented bungalows by a group of undisguised radicals for having defended the rights of that nation's women—only two of the countless atrocities committed against the world's journalists for reporting what they believe people should know and their governments have not told them. Then again, French reporters do know on which political side their baguette is *beurrée* when they publish a piece in *Le Monde* or *La Libération*. Perhaps critiquing state-controlled presses for squashing unsavory truths or spinning damning facts is to ignore the wider issue that, culturally speaking, we all just value truth and fact differently.

The friction caused in pursuing comparative international journalism is relieved to a certain extent in comparative international literary journalism. Take, for example, Edvaldo Pereira Lima's comment in his history of Brazilian literary journalism: "Freedom of expression and democracy are instrumental to literary journalism's prosperity." Though undoubtedly true, the statement's corollary that nations with state-controlled presses have had no literary journalism is not, as authors Peiqin Chen, Sonja Merljak Zdovc, and Soenke Zehle make clear in their essays for this book. If anything, literary journalism and literary reportage have both been equally productive during times of social and political crises that a given government did or did not want its body politic to know about. There are, for instance, striking examples of how journalists from various autocratic nations have circumvented state dictators, entrenched juntas, and armed warlords to produce pieces that are on a par with those by the literary journalists of freer nations.

In Chile, for instance, Gonzalo Saavedra Vergara describes how the Chilean press before and after the cruel regime of Augusto Pinochet used literary journalism as a salve to heal the nation's gaping political wounds:

> All TV channels and newspapers were under control. But there [were] a number of magazines that tried to investigate the other side of the official truth, and they suffered from censorship several times. In these magazines one often found the best written journalism available. . . . Among the most important pieces of that period is Verdugo's *Los zarpazos del puma* [The Claws of the Puma], about the so-called Death Caravan, a group of army officials who traveled through the country on board a Puma helicopter in the weeks that

followed Pinochet's *coup d'état* on September 11, 1973, and executed more than 120 opponents of the regime. The book was published in 1989, and, for the first time, it told this story with its macabre details—sixteen years after it had occurred! In the years that followed Chile's return to democracy, journalists slowly began to do their job better. But it was a difficult task, because many of them were simply not used to asking the tough questions, and newspapers were still being written in the traditional inverted pyramid way.[7]

And in Romania, Cristian Lupsa explains how journalism suffered under the Nicolae Ceausescu regime, but its literary journalism provided the nation with a tradition already in place that post-regime journalists could build upon:

> Romanian literary journalism is largely traced back to Filip Brunea-Fox, a newspaper reporter with a knack for social observation, whose work in the 1920s and 1930s chronicled the life of the unseen: from pretend beggars to circus performers (such as the fattest man in Romania) to the inhabitants of a leper colony on the banks of the Danube. Dubbed "the prince of reportage," Fox infused his writing with calls for social justice. A contemporary of Fox, Geo Bogza, is well known for travel reportage. The communist years diluted Romanian literary journalism, and the media of the post-communist years emphasized melodrama and opinionating overreporting. More recently, some glossy magazines have taken the lead in executing more thoroughly reported narrative pieces, where storytelling takes precedence over the author's personal observations.[8]

Oppression has fueled the production of literary journalism as much as, if not more than, freedom has. The right to know and to tell something is arguably trumped by the need for both. Having been denied the freedom to express the truth, censored journalists simply experimented with literary techniques to couch the truth in subversive ways. One must surely feel impunity to ramble on like a Tom Wolfe or to bite the hand that reads you like a Norman Mailer. More subtle voices, those driven by understatement or allusion as opposed to self-aggrandizement, are the hallmarks of an international literary journalism, as many of the essays in this collection argue. One way for these literary journalists to tell their stories was to call fact "fiction," though many readers in the know understood the piece to be working on two levels of truth. As Merljak Zdovc writes, "analytical factographic reporting was not possible" in communist-controlled Slovenia, so journalists "had to adopt indirect ways of commenting on the current state of affairs, such as disguising them as stories." This type of indirect journalism/reportage is potentially more effective as a sociopolitical weapon than the adoption of more traditional journalistic techniques, since it is precisely its literary quality that helps to deliver the truth while contributing a certain amount of beauty to the piece.

History has taught many war-torn nations to be wary of those promising to speak the truth, and centuries of civil wars, pogroms, and revolutions have made many European, African, South American, and Asian reporters more than a little gun-shy about truth-seeking and whistle-blowing. Perhaps we are all divided by history, past and recent, and that alone binds us and our efforts to produce a literary journalism which speaks as much to the New Zealander and it does to the Scot. Without a shared sense or value of truth and immersion reporting, though, how can we ever expect to agree on a set of rules or traits governing the body of international literary journalism? As I have tried to demonstrate here, the answer is less important than the question itself. Whatever that answer may be, one thing is certain: the question of international literary journalism cannot be formulated from one perspective alone.

Toward a Definition of International Literary Journalism

Nearly every book on literary journalism over the last twenty-five years at least has begun with an introduction that defines or characterizes "literary journalism." This book will not be any different, if only for the reason that international literary journalism still needs to establish its boundaries. Part I sets out to do just that: address several, and solve some, of the problems associated with defining a form that is more culturally bound than literature and more politically sensitive than journalism, and continually evolving even as I write these words.

A first concern involves determining what constitutes international literary journalism and what does not. If scholars of Anglo-American literary journalism have struggled with this problem for decades and have still not reached a consensus, we are logically a long way from determining what makes a literary journalism in the Netherlands negotiable to the form's Spanish or Portuguese heritage. And this book makes no promises about providing the definitive answer to that query. Whatever answer scholars of international literary journalism finally come to accept, we can be certain that it will only loosely resemble an Anglo-American version of the form.

One reason for this inevitable difference is that Anglo-American literary journalism makes clear distinctions among creative nonfiction, literary reportage, and feature writing, just as the English language distinguishes among the various hues of the color yellow, such as amber and gold. The international literary journalism represented in this book does not make such precise distinctions for the simple reason that many nations have not enjoyed a journalistic heritage that contains side-by-side examples of literary reportage, narrative journalism, creative nonfiction, and New Journalism, or the various media in which to publish them. What American scholars of the form deem a feature story, then, may appear in the international press as literary journalism, since it too upends the inverted pyramid and supplies a narrative voice. Within an international context, those who would define literary journalism cannot be persnickety.

With this in mind, Part I of this book is devoted to defining international literary journalism broadly, and does so from various interdisciplinary angles: historical, pedagogical, geographical, theoretical, and speculative. John C. Hartsock's essay on transnational and cross-cultural fertilization of literary journalism opens the debate. Providing a history of Russian literary reportage and literary journalism through German, Chinese, and post–World War I American sources, Hartsock sets up the problem facing all of the authors in this book: namely, literary reportage and literary journalism are defined today more by how they have evolved and interacted transnationally than by how they were initially perceived. This "elasticity" of form has made tracing the roots of literary journalism difficult to say the least. As Hartsock writes, "there can be a polemical literary reportage discursive in nature, a narra-descriptive literary reportage frozen in the tendentiousness of the distanced image of the absolute past, and a narra-descriptive literary reportage, much like American literary journalism, which embraces the inconclusive present of a fluid phenomenal world that grants free interpretive possibilities to the author and reader." Can one, then, use the terms "literary reportage" and "literary journalism" interchangeably? Yes and no. Hartsock adds that "[European] literary reportage and [American] literary journalism are much the same when they both emphasize narrative and descriptive modalities and eschew discursive polemic." Beyond these two cases, literary reportage and literary journalism differ historically for political reasons that cannot reconcile indefinitely the twins' ancestral parents.

If Hartsock shows how European reportage and American literary journalism have lived separate lives despite their comparable, though not exactly identical, DNA, Jenny McKay questions whether one is not the other's offspring. Like many unwanted children who emigrate and develop a new identity in the host environment, English literary reportage shed part of its polemical past and became literary journalism. It flourished because the foreign environment nourished it along. Reportage in the United Kingdom, however, has subsequently withered and nearly dried up. McKay examines some of the evidence for this neglect, which includes the difficulty writers have had in finding a market for their reportage, the problems publishers have had in categorizing it, and as a consequence, the difficulty potential readers have had in even locating it on the shelves of public or university libraries or bookstores. McKay's discussion touches on aspects of literary canon formation and the status of journalism as vocational training and an object of academic study in the U.K.'s system of higher education. Despite the grim descriptions, the essay concludes on the optimistic note that leading British journalists believe literary reportage can develop an understanding and communication between people of different societies and nations, which may ensure its future in an increasingly heterogeneous Great Britain.

While McKay explores the sorry state of affairs of literary journalism in the U.K., Bill Reynolds looks at how geographical elitism continues to control the definition, creation, and execution of literary journalism in Canada. Recent work from the nation's West Coast, and in particular by four writers and one editor from Vancouver, stands out in contrast to established norms in Toronto, the epicenter of the Canadian magazine industry. Distance reinforces this starkly different outlook on what constitutes literary journalism—in the formulation of story ideas, the development of themes, and the points of view. Vancouver, far from the corridors of national power, with its confluence of "sea, sky, and mountains," creates a variegated mindset in its writers. Stories emphasize travel, foreign languages, a sense of looking outward, and a struggle to understand the human condition. Rather than deliver a play-by-play analysis of who has gained and—stoking the reader's schadenfreude—lost money or power, West Coast literary journalists see themselves as part of a continuum that happily places Ryszard Kapuściński alongside *The Jungle,* Charles Bowden alongside *Don Quixote.*

David Abrahamson's essay moves the book out of the taxonomic and into the theoretical to establish a methodology in defining international literary journalism. Viewing literary journalism in a worldwide context, his essay appropriates, as Reynolds's does, a geophysical construct but, for purely heuristic purposes, employs it to describe a global phenomenon in literary journalism. Positing the existence of an imaginary "Counter-Coriolis Effect," Abrahamson argues that in general, much of what is celebrated as literary journalism or narrative nonfiction from the North (or the developed, industrialized West) tends to be written from a perspective that can be characterized as progressive, secular, and reformist, while the efforts of many writers of similar nonfiction from the South (or the developing world) are often conservative and traditionalist. The essay speculates on possible explanations for this proposed phenomenon and claims that, in an increasingly interconnected world, it is both likely and laudable that the effect will diminish.

Like Abrahamson, Norman Sims looks speculatively at the global trends in literary journalism by examining the specific challenges facing literary journalism in the United States today that could have ramifications on the form's future abroad. Sims believes that we are at a new turning point in the history of the form, at least in American literary journalism. The challenges may be more economic than literary, however. While some newspapers, American and international alike, have adopted narrative approaches to news, they are still severely limited in time and space, and the magazines that have been a traditional home for literary journalism have grown more interested in policy analysis. Although author advances have shrunk, books remain a haven for literary journalism. The Internet has not yet overcome its problems with length and with the lack of financial remuneration for literary journalists. Despite these difficulties, Sims optimistically concludes, the position of literary journalism in history seems as secure as ever, and it may even be expanding in Europe and Asia. Literary journalism has continued and will continue to provide the intimacy, subtlety, and artistry we need to understand the world and our times.

Together these five essays represent historical, pragmatic, and theoretical efforts to establish what it is that unites international literary journalism despite its seemingly irreconcilable differences. Arguably, what brings international forms of literary journalism closer together remains more on the theoretical than on the pragmatic level for now, but these essays are proof that any definition of international literary journalism must be elastic enough to account for its cultural variances. Comparisons using American standards or definitions alone limit our perspective on how nations have acquired literary journalism and how their environments have shaped its production and reception over the course of time. Part II takes up this issue and examines in more detail these nations' traditions in literary journalism.

Journalistic Traditions

Half of this book's subtitle, *Journalistic Traditions,* is aimed at tracing global literary histories and finding common journalistic ground. Since journalism in America and in Europe evolved from different traditions, it is only natural that their literary journalism should have done so as well. But the picture of a U.S.-led literary journalism and a European-produced literary reportage is not as clearly demarcated as one would think or hope. As noted earlier, the two world wars forced European cultures to evolve in a world divided between American and Soviet superpowers. Certain journalistic traditions in Europe that evolved before 1914 or 1939 were consequently altered, and western European presses leaned chauvinistically, if not propagandistically, toward the United States, while eastern European nations were forced to accept the state-controlled *pravda* (truth) of the Soviet-influenced press.

The result has been that the forms of literary journalism of various nations evolved in vastly different ways in the twentieth century than if the wars and the divided world had not forced them to do so. How they evolved is as interesting as where.

Research in the field of literary journalism has informed us that since the breakup of the Soviet bloc, more and more nations discovering or rediscovering a certain freedom of the press swallowed the New Journalistic pill and, logorrhea-like, spat out one story after another that, historical references aside, seem as if they were all written in the 1960s. American-style counterculture with its icons in music, literature, and literary journalism seemed an appropriate antidote to their stolid and controlled lives. But this reverence for the irreverent is not simply the case of an international equivalent to the American undergraduate who, on discovering the anarchic pleasures of a Hunter S. Thomson, expresses, willy-nilly, his or her invectives against the powers that be. For these nations only *seemed* young, given that communist rule had anaesthetized them for fifty years or more. Yet these nations had had a literary journalistic tradition dating back to the nineteenth century or the early decades of the twentieth, a tradition influenced more directly by European journalists than by American ones. As several of the essays in this part of the book posit, many nations looked to the United States for journalistic inspiration following the political thaw if only because they now could.

The six essays in Part II thus provide a panorama of literary journalism as it evolved on three continents over the past hundred-plus years. In the first essay, Clazina Dingemanse and Rutger de Graaf discuss the European pamphlet as a proto-literary journalism that had direct influence on later European-style literary reportage. Since the Renaissance, the pamphlet had served as the primary mass medium for political debate and local news in most European countries. They write, "Although there were papers that advocated political neutrality, many newspapers became involved with a political party or ideology, serving not so much as an objective news platform but more as a political signpost, telling readers what to think of current events and putting the news in a larger ideological perspective." Pamphleteers used a wide variety of literary genres and devices to get their political messages across. By the end of the nineteenth century, however, the prominence of the pamphlet had been taken over by the flourishing newspaper. Many of the century-old pamphleteering techniques and genres found their way into the columns of the changing newspaper, while the use of literary techniques and inventive genres in pamphlets decreased. This reinvention of century-old journalistic practices, referred to today as "remediation," supplies the basic theory for this essay, which explores the remediation of literary pamphlet genres into the newspaper in order to shed light on the historical evolution of literary journalism.

Like the Dutch pamphlet in the nineteenth century, Portuguese newspapers in these early days of reporting underwent a remediation that "ranged from the astounding increase in the number of periodicals in circulation to the varied topics being covered by journalists: political debates, sports events, international affairs, and so on." In the closing decades of the nineteenth century, four Portuguese journalists—Eça de Queirós, Batalha Reis, Ramalho Ortigão, and Oliveira Martins—participated in this remediation by importing the "new" journalism made popular by W. T. Stead and Henry Mayhew for a Portuguese-speaking public on both sides of the Atlantic. Their visions of London depicted images and concerns similar to those portrayed by England's pioneering literary journalists. London was a city of social horrors and darkness, of contrasts, an immense "modern Babylon," to quote Stead in the pages of the *Pall Mall Gazette*. Isabel Soares makes a strong case for the argument that journalistic change in Portugal was already in progress before contact with England's fin-de-siècle "new" journalism was made. Yet she also emphasizes the importance of a transnational influence at work on these Portuguese writers as they learned *how* to bring about change more fully through their having read the British journalists.

Like its neighbor Portugal, which also saw its free press stymied by a totalitarian regime in the first half of the twentieth century, Spain in the early days of reporting rarely printed evidence of hard news in its papers, which were filled mostly with literary pieces. Sonia Parratt explores how journalism and literature in Spain remained close allies for years, as many Spanish poets and novelists made their living working at dailies and later on as journalists publishing nonfiction. Franco's dictatorship, however, destroyed Spain's economy in the 1930s, and publishing possibilities became scarce. By the 1960s, America's New Journalism injected renewed life into the Spanish press, and today, literary journalism in Spain has not simply evolved but flourished. It has even extended its influence to more traditional methods of news writing, and it is common today to read breaking news being reported in the Spanish press in a style that used to be reserved for longer interpretative stories. Thanks to this literary news writing, or "*reportagization*," in Spanish newspapers, readers are finding stories that contain deeper insights and more detailed background than either television or the Internet mass media can report.

Just as it took a civil war in Spain to spark an interest in literary journalism, the Second Sino-Japanese War in China reignited a politically conscious literary reportage in China. Although Chinese literary reportage, *baogao wenxue*, has its roots in the nineteenth century, the war effectively elevated the literary form in the 1930s, when it was seen as a means to expose social evils in the country and to incite people to take action against them. Peiqin Chen's essay explores the evolution of literary reportage in China from the Reform Movement of 1898 to the new Enlightenment Movement of the 1980s. By situating the major classics of literary reportage within their social backgrounds, Chen argues that the development of Chinese literary reportage has flourished at moments of sharp social conflicts. She points out how Chinese literary reportage first had German roots, then later American influences drawn from Upton Sinclair and Edgar Snow. Reportage in China had to have a social edge to it, she writes—a sword cutting through the ills of society—because Chinese fiction lacked the punch of reality to accomplish the feat on its own. After a period of decline, Chinese reportage has once again found its soul and is poised to regain its place among the most respected examples of Chinese letters.

Civil wars and periods of social disruption have had an immense impact on the development of literary journalism in Europe, just as it had in America, and in the case of Brazil the situation is not much different. Edvaldo Pereira Lima examines how Brazil's bloody civil war at the end of the nineteenth century precipitated the nation's first piece of literary journalism. Writing as a war correspondent for *O Estado de S. Paulo,* Euclides da Cunha captured a voice and a literary style that a few years later would also distinguish the writings of João do Rio, who elevated the Brazilian *crônica,* a local genre that mixed literary and journalistic forms, to higher levels. Literary journalism, however, never knew a constant growth in the country, owing in part to the nation's illiteracy and totalitarian regimes. As the counterculture stormed the United States in the 1960s, the same years brought a flurry of nonfiction in Brazil. Between 1955 and 1960, under the administration of President Juscelino Kubitscheck de Oliveira, Brazil experienced its first full period of widespread democracy, which contributed in a meaningful way to several innovative advances in literary journalism. That freedom was short-lived, however, as a military junta recaptured power in 1964. Literary journalism again struggled, but the efforts of the magazine *Realidade,* influenced by America's New Journalism, sparked a golden age of Brazilian literary journalism that the country is now trying to recover.

If American influences can be detected in Brazilian literary journalism of the 1960s, it can also be found in Finnish literary journalism of the same era. As Maria Lassila-Merisalo points out, Finnish journalists borrowed literary techniques from fiction through the ages but did so, if not unconsciously, at least unsystematically. Her essay distinguishes three phases in the development of Finnish literary journalism over the past century. In the first phase, journalism became professionalized, and reportage was a genre that allowed for the strong presence of a narrator and the use of fictional techniques. The second phase, midway through the twentieth century, was the time for new heroes, antiheroes, and storytellers. In the 1980s a third phase took place when urban city culture and gonzo journalism arrived in Finland and inspired Finnish journalists to express themselves freely. If literary journalism in Finland today has not released its potential, this is due mostly to the lack of formal training that writers are given in the production of literary journalism, which in Finland would be acceptable, given the country's tradition of the realist novel. But Lassila-Merisalo argues that the opposite has proved to be true: because Finnish fiction is so fact-based, there has been little room for literary journalism to grow.

Together these six essays sketch out the landscape of literary journalism and literary reportage as they developed in parts of Europe, in China, and in Brazil. The emerging portrait of an international literary journalism shows that journalists most often turn literary when their nations are at war, be it with others or with themselves. Like a balm, the literary quality of the writing soothes the pain inflicted by the journalistic facts delivered in the piece or the dispatch, with literary journalism emerging as the byproduct. Another key notion apparent in these essays is the importance of transnational journalistic and literary borrowings. No nation's literary journalism or literary reportage (and I would argue that this includes America as well) fully blossomed independently; while many nations had developed a form of literary journalism concurrent with America or England, the form in each of these nations evolved essentially through a process of cross-cultural pollination. Part III looks more specifically at individual literary journalists across the globe in order to study how their reporting was influenced by journalistic traditions outside their own.

Transnational Influences

Part III contains five case studies of literary journalists (three male and two female) from varying nations during three different decades of the twentieth century. The different climes and times alone are ample proof of literary journalism's extended reach in the world of letters, but they also demonstrate the influence that immersion reporting has had over the last century on exposing and, ideally, correcting certain social ills. Each of these essays looks closely at the notion of transnational influence explored more holistically in the book's previous section on the literary journalistic traditions of select nations over the last century. Individually they tell stories of writers obsessed with the truth and frustrated with the "house style" in which they were supposed to relate it. Together they chronicle the necessary transnational influence that literary journalism has exerted from one nation to the next as journalists became increasingly aware of their shared destinies in a world growing smaller and in a discipline facing challenges from more dominant styles of journalism.

Nikki Hessell opens Part III by describing how Robin Hyde became one of New Zealand's most significant literary figures in the 1930s, the formative decade of that nation's literary canon. Hyde's career as a journalist brought her into contact with the works of some of the major figures in literary journalism, including Upton Sinclair and George Orwell, whose concern for the interests of the dispossessed infused her own writing. Among her many journalistic pieces, Hyde produced feature articles, often about the aboriginal Māori people, for the *New Zealand Railways Magazine* between 1935 and 1937, traveling the country and reporting on her experiences. Like other seminal literary texts from the late 1930s, such as Allen Curnow's volume of poems *Not in Narrow Seas* (1939) and John Mulgan's novel *Man Alone* (1939), Hyde's stories responded to the mounting call for a coherent national identity and a distinct national literature. Her literary journalism from different locations around New Zealand aimed to remind readers of the distinctive qualities of their country's landscape, people, and culture, qualities that were reinforced and enhanced by her use of a distinctively local voice and register. Hessell argues that Hyde contributed to the emerging form of New Zealand literary journalism and to the emerging discourse about what it meant to be a New Zealander.

Hyde's Marxist leanings were not uncommon for literary journalists of the 1930s, even for those writing in the Southern Hemisphere, as David Abrahamson argues in his essay in Part I. James Agee, whose *Let Us Now Praise Famous Men* (1941) made him a canonical figure in American literary journalism, was also keenly influenced by Marxist thought. William Dow explores how these political leanings gave shape to Agee's vision and voice as expressed in two of his short pieces for *Fortune* magazine, "Saratoga Springs" (1935) and "Havana Cruise" (1937)—published during the same years as Hyde's railway pieces. Dow signals the importance of seeing Agee as an intellectual consciously attempting to preserve a role as cultural critic against the growing power of mass culture in 1930s America. Considering himself to be an intellectual first and a journalist second, Agee pioneered new forms of literary journalism that relied on an observer-narrator perspective, a complex reader-narrator relation, and explorations of the nature of social class as a cultural indicator. Dow suggests that Agee's compassion for social suffering and injustice emerged from the sovereignty of his own will and understanding within the peculiar politicization of the 1930s.

If both Hyde and Agee were literary journalists who chose to be influenced transnationally by Marxist ideology, in communist Slovenia, Željko Kozinc was given little choice but to profess it in his writings. Sonja Merljak Zdovc examines how Kozinc, writing in the 1960s and 1970s, might have been influenced by America's New Journalists had they been translated and made available to the public, but given the nation's political policies against the West, Kozinc had to look to eastern European writers for influence. He discovered the Prague-born journalist Egon Erwin Kisch. Journalistic pieces experimenting with the narrative techniques of realistic fiction began appearing in the late 1960s in Slovenia, a time when journalism itself started to become more democratic in the country. Nevertheless, for a long time journalists like Kozinc could address the country's state of affairs only indirectly, and some of the more innovative journalists couched their criticism and their opinion of the political system in stories. With the aid of narrative techniques, they told their readers about the system's injustices or anomalies that they had witnessed; and despite the media's ties to politics, Kozinc was able to provide quality journalism to his readers while avoiding censorship. Neither before nor after that period, however, has the Slovene press published so much outstanding journalistic writing. Accordingly, Merljak Zdovc proposes that literary journalism might well be a way for Slovenia to regain its journalistic bearings.

If Kozinc figuratively looked "east" for his influences, Australian writer Helen Garner looked "west" to the *New Yorker,* in particular to Janet Malcolm and to U.S. authors such as Ernest Hemingway, F. Scott Fitzgerald, and Raymond Carver. But the transnational influence she drew from Malcolm did not prepare her for the problems she faced in writing long-form nonfiction when subjects refused to open themselves up to immersion reporting. As Willa McDonald demonstrates in her essay, Garner's nonfiction, *The First Stone: Some Questions about Sex and Power* (1995) and *Joe Cinque's Consolation: A True Story of Death, Grief and the Law* (2004), caused a furor because Garner applied fictional techniques to the nonfictional subject matter in both. McDonald examines the reactions of academic critics to Garner's literary journalism and proposes that Garner, despite the occasional flaws in her approach, has a unique and valid voice in nonfiction. McDonald argues that had Garner been properly trained to write literary journalism and to understand the ethics behind immersion reporting, she would not have had so much bad press.

Helen Garner is, of course, not alone in embellishing her nonfiction with imaginative details—a point so contentious among scholars of the form that it alone could threaten the future of international literary journalism. Perhaps for that very reason, literary journalism has often been marginalized as the bastard child of literature and journalism. Soenke Zehle examines another celebrated literary journalist, Ryszard Kapuściński, and his frustration with the limits of factology where the border between journalistic reportage and literary expression is as vague as the fronts between countries at war. Kapuściński's obsession with borders and their transgression becomes Zehle's focus in this philosophical piece on the Polish journalist, a reporter who witnessed civil wars and revolutions and traveled freely about the land to cover the story. It is "a threshold between different forms of experience" that has made Kapuściński as much a lightning rod of contemporary journalistic criticism as Tom Wolfe and Hunter S. Thompson were in the 1960s and 1970s. Whether revered or despised by his colleagues, Kapuściński, a polemical and controversial writer, nonetheless remains for many Western readers one of the best literary journalists writing in the second half of the twentieth century.

Five essays, five literary journalists, five distinct and often incongruous journalistic traditions. Attempts to situate them collectively under the same rubric seem pointless, as their differences far outweigh their similarities. And yet they do demonstrate the importance of the form's evolution over the last century and help account for the spread of literary and journalistic traditions throughout the world. Just when it appears that the authorities have succeeded in trampling it out of existence in one culture, it goes underground, metamorphoses, and takes root in another. What grows in the different soil, and amid the new microclimatic changes, can never be exactly the same as it was prior to dislocation. But that it continues to reproduce elsewhere provides hope enough that international literary journalism, no matter how or where it blossoms, will ensure its longevity for the century to come.

The Future of International Literary Journalism Studies

The sixteen essays collected in this book—written *by* many of the leading men and women working in the field of literary journalism studies *about* many of the leading men and women writing literary journalism the world over—are by no means heterogeneous, either in their adoption of one transcendental literary journalism or in their depiction of how literary journalism arrived on their native soil. To be honest, there cannot be such a book written today. And that is not a bad thing. To define international literary journalism in strict terms would be to transform what is essentially an organic process, one that is in constant flux, into a packaged product. For this reason, debates about international standards of truth, concepts of the literary mode, access to the facts, and objective versus phenomenological journalism risk forever miring international literary journalism, and its corresponding field of academic studies, in institutional quibbles unless a certain number of covenants are established, of which I humbly offer three.

First, we should not treat New Journalism like the Ten Commandments of literary journalism and hold up the world's production of the form in comparison, since many international forms predate it. If anything, we should pit international literary journalists against Wolfe's manifesto at times, if only to demonstrate that a European, African, or Asian literary journalism is not like an American literary journalism but that it nonetheless advances our understanding and appreciation of the form.

Second, we should stop referring to literary journalism as a genre (Wolfe, Connery), or even as a form (Sims, Hartsock), and start calling it what it is: a discipline. Doing so would move us beyond Ben Yagoda's view of literary journalism as a "profoundly fuzzy term" and help situate it alongside literature and journalism and their respective fields of inquiry.[9] As Sonia Parratt points out, the very notion of literary journalism is impossible to separate, since both literature and journalism evolved out of the same political principle of informing the public. Continually calling it a genre locks literary journalism into a subcategory of literature, alongside poetry and drama. Referring to it as a journalistic form sandwiches it somewhere between fiction and journalism. Suggesting that it is a subcategory of nonfiction dangerously sets it on even ground with biography, travelogues, policy analysis, history, cultural studies, and memoirs, some of which can be literary journalism but are not by definition that alone. Raising literary journalism to the level of a discipline would institute a moratorium on the barrage of definitions and defenses that have hindered the advancement of literary journalism studies and allow international scholars to work together on equal footing to promote their discipline, as literature professors and journalism professors frequently do at congresses such as the Modern Language Association (MLA) and the Association for Education in Journalism and Mass Communication (AEJMC) in America, or the European Society for the Study of English (ESSE) in Europe. The IALJS and its many sibling learned societies worldwide, academic or professional alike, have made considerable progress toward accomplishing this goal, but we are a long way still from finding disciplinary programs of literary journalism studies of the kind offered at the University of California–Irvine under the direction of Barry Siegel. Achieving disciplinary status would certainly reduce the pedagogical problems facing international literary journalism, as underlined here by McKay, Parratt, Lassila-Merisalo, and Merljak Zdovc.

Finally, we should stop fretting over the publishing industry's or the academy's legitimation of literary journalism or literary journalism studies. Continued research into the history and practice of literary journalism across the globe will serve to create that legitimation, as well as the market that literary journalism and literary journalism studies sorely need. Books about sexuality were traditionally lost among the many titles catalogued under sociology or anthropology, but once gender studies flexed its academic muscle, GLBT studies found shelf space of its own. The steady production of strong criticism, theory, and pedagogy will eventually coalesce the literary journalism that is out there now and create the discipline's niche at Waterstone's or Barnes & Noble. In sum, we have to stop writing definitional manifestos that show by default that literary journalism lacks cohesion, take charge of the discipline ourselves, conduct the research that needs to be conducted, and wait for the rest to catch up with us. They will, eventually. This book is betting on that.

NOTES

1. The discussion of literary journalism in Africa, which does not figure in this collection, is rich in possibilities and offers an adventurous scholar an abundance of material from which to work.

2. Matthew Stretcher contends that Japanese literary journalists emerged in Japan in the 1980s and 1990s as an "opposition press" to the Japanese media, which colluded to engineer and maintain the metanarrative of Japan as a "peaceful, stable, and prosperous society," and which "support[ed], rather than critique[d], society's status quo." Matthew C. Stretcher, "Who's Afraid of Takahashi O-Den? 'Poison Woman' Stories and Literary Journalism in Early Meiji Japan," *Japanese Language and Literature* 38 (2004): 26. If the Japanese usage of the term "literary journalism" follows the definition of the International Association for Literary Journalism Studies (IALJS), the Argentines retain the British understanding of literary journalism as a critical discourse about literature published in journals (what is commonly referred to as literary criticism). See, in addition to Stretcher, Francine Masiello, "Argentine Literary Journalism: The Production of a Critical Discourse," *Latin American Research Review* 20.1 (1985): 27–60.

3. No scholarly work as yet written in English addresses literary journalism as it is practiced, taught, and studied throughout the world. A few books, however, have dealt with literary journalism (its history, its practitioners, and its study) beyond the Anglo-American phenomena. One collection of essays on literary journalism outside of a strict U.S. context is *The Journalistic Imagination*, ed. Richard Keeble and Sharon Wheeler (Abingdon: Routledge, 2007), but it too examines almost exclusively British authors (one chapter is devoted to America's New Journalism) and adheres to the British usage of literary journalism as "journalism *about* literature."

Charles Laughlin, *Chinese Reportage: The Aesthetics of Historical Experience* (Durham: Duke University Press, 2002), is one example of an extended study of literary journalism in an international context. And Ian Jack, *The Granta Book of Reportage,* 3rd ed. (London: Granta Books, 2006), has been proactive in publishing international literary journalism, just as the Lettre Ulysses Award was (and perhaps one day will again be) instrumental in rewarding international literary journalism of the highest caliber.

4. Thomas B. Connery, ed., *A Sourcebook of American Literary Journalism: Representative Writers in an Emerging Genre* (New York: Greenwood Press, 1992), 5–12; John C. Hartsock, *A History of American Literary Journalism: The Emergence of a Modern American Form* (Amherst: University of Massachusetts Press, 2000), 15–17; Norman Sims, *True Stories: A Century of Literary Journalism* (Evanston: Northwestern University Press, 2007), 11–12, 14–18; Barbara Lounsberry, *The Art of Fact: Contemporary Artists of Nonfiction* (New York: Greenwood Press, 1990), xvi; Edd Applegate, *Literary Journalism: A Biographical Dictionary of Writers and Editors* (Westport, Conn.: Greenwood Press, 1996), xv–xvi; Keeble and Wheeler, *The Journalistic Imagination,* 9–11.

5. Here, and elsewhere throughout this book, key foreign terms—as well as book, journal, newspaper, essay, and story titles—are reproduced in their original languages. The reasons for this editorial decision are twofold: first, because many foreign works translated into English could be easily confused with existing titles in English; and second, because a polyglottal edition demonstrates this book's commitment to practice cultural sensitivity and reach out to an international audience. As the book's chosen lingua franca, English best allows for scholars from all over the world to access the rich literary journalistic traditions examined in the following pages. While an argument could be made for the use of English titles when they were made available in translation, such a practice was decided against lest the visual and oral aesthetics of the native language be sacrificed for semantics alone. Translations of foreign titles *are* provided, however, in subsequent references when a published translation in English exists (except in the case of newspaper names, which are considered here as proper nouns).

6. Joseph North, "Reportage," in *American Writers' Congress,* ed. Henry Hart (New York: International, 1935), 121.

7. Gonzalo Saavedra Vergara, personal e-mail, November 11, 2008.

8. Cristian Lupsa, personal e-mail, January 8, 2009.

9. Ben Yagoda, preface to *The Art of Fact: A Historical Anthology of Literary Journalism,* ed. Kevine Kerrane and Ben Yagoda (New York: Simon and Schuster, 1997), 13.

Part I

Toward a Theory of
International Literary Journalism

Chapter 1

Literary Reportage
The "Other" Literary Journalism

JOHN C. HARTSOCK

GIVEN THE SIMILARITIES in terms, it would be easy to assume that "literary reportage" and "literary journalism" are one and the same genre. But consider the following: journalists Svetlana Alexievich and Anna Politkovskaya, who derive from the same Soviet and post-Soviet cultural milieu, have both been described as writers of "literary reportage" and its variant "reportage literature." Yet they pose a riddle in genre studies because as journalists, they have produced work that is strikingly different, as even a cursory examination will reveal. Alexievich's work is one in which the narrative and descriptive modalities dominate in what has been characterized as a "narra-descriptive journalism" more in keeping with the American tradition of literary journalism.[1] Indeed, one anthology has firmly placed Alexievich as an author of literary journalism.[2] Politkovskaya's work, by contrast, is clearly one in which a discursiveness—expository and argumentative in nature—dominates. How, then, can both journalists be described as writers of literary reportage but only one be characterized as a writer of literary journalism?

My purpose is to explore the origins of the literary reportage tradition in which both writers have worked in an effort to account for those differences. Alexievich and Politkovskaya, I would suggest, have engaged in a genre that is, to be sure, reflective of their native Russian tradition, but a genre that is also very much a cosmopolitan one and transcends national boundaries. What ultimately emerges is that "literary reportage" of European origin is a much more "elastic" form than American literary journalism.

Such an examination is necessary if the comparative study of journalistic forms claiming to reflect the aesthetics of experience is to mature, a study that is long overdue.[3] This is especially the case because literary reportage is little recognized and understood in the United States, but is or has been extant elsewhere not only as a national expression but as a transnational one as well. The result of such an examination, I hope, is that we will be able to develop a more nuanced understanding of the overlapping traditions and concerns of the two widely acknowledged generic characterizations.

Defining "Literary Reportage" and "Literary Journalism" in an International Context

"Literary reportage," or "reportage literature," depending on which of the terms serves as the modifier, is a problematic terminology from the outset. One reason is that at times the noun "reportage" alone has been applied for the whole, which raises issues of instability, given a standard American English dictionary definition of "reportage" as "the act or process of reporting news."[4] Definitions of reportage of the "literary" kind discussed here, whether the term stands alone for the whole or serves as the modified or the modifier, can bear distinct similarities to that of literary journalism in the United States. Probably the most durable definition of literary journalism was articulated by the American practitioner of the form Tom Wolfe, when he defined it as a "journalism that would read like a novel," or, elsewhere, like a "short story."[5]

In concert with Wolfe, the Portuguese writer and journalist Pedro Rosa Mendes notes, "Reportage literature is an engagement with reality with a novelist's eye but with a journalist's discipline."[6] The British publication *Granta*, for the last thirty years or so a mainstay of the genre as "literary journalism" and as "reportage" of the literary kind, has provided the following definition: "The art and craft of reportage—journalism marked by vivid description, a novelist's eye to form, and eyewitness reporting that reveals hidden truths about people and events that have shaped the world we know."[7]

Should there be any doubt, some scholars have unambiguously equated literary journalism and literary reportage as the same thing. Rudolph G. Wagner, the German scholar of the Chinese version, observed in his 1992 study that "literary reportage" is "now called 'new journalism,'"[8] the latter referring to the movement of the 1960s involving the work of Wolfe, Gay Talese, Joan Didion, and Truman Capote, among others, that today we can see as one chapter in the long history of a narrative literary journalism. Peter Monteath takes a similar position in his 1990 study of the aesthetics of reportage on the subject of the Spanish civil war.[9]

But there are still other characterizations of literary reportage that push at such boundaries and hint at the difficulties of defining the reportage version. Alexievich, for one, engages in a characterization that, while potentially applicable to literary journalism, suggests broader possibilities: "Documentary prose ought to transcend the strict boundaries between the formats of literature and journalism. The person of the author, his mentality, his philosophy and his sensitivity must be unified by a good writing style. Documentary work means using reality as the raw material to create a new reality."[10] But what are the formats of literature? Can poetry be included? Drama? What is a good writing style? Is the creation of a "new reality" possibly the creation of fiction in the conventional sense?

The German-language Czech journalist Egon Erwin Kisch characterized literary reportage as a "milieu study."[11] But a milieu study can leave much to the imagination. It could be literary journalism, or an expository sociological or anthropological study.

Then there is a dictionary definition for the Chinese version, strongly influenced, as we will see, by the European. It is called *baogao wenxue,* which translates as "reportage literature"[12]:

> Reportage literature is a literary genre, a type of prose; also an umbrella term for sketches and the *texie* [often synonymous with *bagao wenxue* and first used in 1930s China to mean "close up," a term borrowed from cinematography].[13] It is a fast and timely representation with adequate artistic processing, of real people and real events that are drawn directly from and regarded as typical of real life. As such it serves the current political agenda and is said to be the "light cavalry" of literary production.[14]

But the definition leaves questions unanswered, among them: What is "adequate artistic processing"? And how is it the "light cavalry" of literary production?

The Russian term for such writing, *ocherk,* is merely defined as "essay," although a secondary definition gleaned from context can be "sketch."[15]

Given all of this, the British journalist Isabel Hilton has characterized the form as "elastic." One of Britain's most highly esteemed journalists, she has served as a juror on the Lettre Ulysses Award committee, the international award for literary reportage. As she puts it, "though reportage was widely practiced and its best examples long remembered, its boundaries seemed elastic."[16] And while she embraces the Wolfean definition, winners of the prize do not always fit that description: witness first-place winner Politkovskaya in 2003 and second-place winner Erik Orsenna in 2006.[17] Both are fundamentally expository polemicists.

What accounts, then, for these differing versions—and visions—of literary reportage, indeed *elastic,* as Hilton suggests? It would be easy to dismiss such differences as reflecting different national cultures. Yet when we approach it as a cosmopolitan genre, what remains remarkable is the degree to which the translated terms "literary reportage," "reportage literature," and "reportage" have been consistently applied transnationally.

Ocherki: Early Russian Literary "Sketches"

As exemplars of a more "elastic" reportage that is "literary" and constitutes "literature," Alexievich's and Politkovskaya's variations have at least two sources. First, there has been since the nineteenth century a tradition of Russian literary reportage, and to some extent a literary (narra-descriptive) journalism that was not explicitly polemical. Second, there is a transnational tradition that emerged in the early 1920s as part of the international communist movement, one that had far-reaching consequences for leftist writers around the world. Alexievich and Politkovskaya arose out of those traditions and provide a departure point for exploring those origins. I briefly sketch an outline of the Russian tradition, because it would be a mistake to suggest that there are not individual cultural distinctions. But once the individual cultural model has been acknowledged, we can begin to identify cross-cultural influences and transnational borrowings.

The Russian tradition can be traced at least as far back as the first half of the nineteenth century and was one that most likely evolved out of the ubiquitous travelogue.[18] This is an experience mirrored in many cultures and societies, such as in China or Finland, for example.[19] One of the earliest examples of a literary reportage was a collection of *ocherki,* or sketches, by various writers in the volume *Fiziologiya Peterburga* (Physiology of Petersburg) published in 1845 and edited by the poet and critic Nikolai Nekrasov.[20] The "physiology" was based on western European models and could be synonymous with "sketch." Indeed, a compound term for such writing in Russian is "physiological sketch," as reflected in the subtitle to Alexander Tseitlin's volume *Stanovlenie Realisma v Russkoi Literature: Ruskiy Fiziologicheski Ocherk* (The Formation of Realism in Russian Literature: The Russian Physiological Sketch).[21] The year before the appearance of *Physiology of Petersburg,* Charles Dickens's *Sketches by Boz, Illustrative of Every-Day Life and Every-Day People* was translated and published in Russian. (The sketches were originally published serially in England and came out in book form in 1836.)[22] But as a genre, the Russian "physiology" goes back still earlier to the 1820s and was based on the French model of "physiologies" then current, which were often satirical sketches that could be either true or fictional but, if fictional, were designed to provide a description of a type, consistent again with the later twentieth-century Chinese definition of "real people and real events that are drawn directly from and regarded as typical of real life."[23]

The second and more influential *ocherki* were Ivan Turgenev's *Zapiski Okhotnika* (A Hunter's Sketches), collected and published in 1852, but which he began publishing in the literary journal *Sovremennik* (The Contemporary) in 1847, for which Nekrasov served as editor. (It should be noted that *Zapiski Okhotnika* translates more closely as "a hunter's notes," though the standard English translation has usually been *A Hunter's Sketches* or *A Sportsman's Sketches*.) The sketches are fundamentally narrative and descriptive in their modalities and provide an empathetic portrait of Russian serfs. This empathy for what were understood as a kind of *Untermensch* by the upper levels of Russian society at the time so angered Tsar Nicholas I that he fired the censor who permitted them to be published and ordered Turgenev arrested and exiled from Moscow.[24]

Physiology of Petersburg and *A Hunter's Sketches* should be treated with some caution, however, because they are more a kind of proto-literary journalism and reportage. This was a time when the divide between fiction and nonfiction was not always clear.[25] That said, there can be little doubt that some were true, such as "Khor and Kalinich" in *A Hunter's Sketches,* which was the first and probably the most notable piece in Turgenev's collection. The real life Khor, a Russian serf, often read the tale with delight to visitors. Such veracity is also the case with "A Living Relic," which Turgenev described as "all a true incident."[26]

Some of Russia's greatest writers of realistic fiction, besides Turgenev, wrote narrative *ocherki*. Starting in 1855, Leo Tolstoy published the first of what eventually would be collected as *Sebastopol'skie rasskazy* (The Sebastopol Sketches), his firsthand account of the siege of that Crimean city by the British and French during the Crimean War.[27] In 1862 Fyodor Dostoevsky published *Zapiski iz myortvogo doma* (Notes from a Dead House), an account of his exile and imprisonment in Siberia in the early 1850s that established a tradition in which Alexander Solzhenitsyn would follow.[28] Among other notable examples, Anton Chekhov published *Ostrov Sakhalin,* or *The Island: A Journey to Sakhalin,* in 1895, an account of penal colonies on that remote island outpost of the Russian Empire.[29] Chekhov's is both a personal account of the experience as well as an expository examination of the medical conditions of convicts. (Chekhov was a doctor.)

The Russian revolutionary writer Maxim Gorky, starting in the 1890s, engaged in the *ocherk* with accounts of vagabonds, many of which were later collected in the volume *Through Russia*.[30] After 1900 his work became more political and more colored by his revolutionary sympathies. One example is "The Ninth of January," an account of the 1905 massacre in St. Petersburg when imperial troops opened fire on a peaceful demonstration.[31] Gorky's work would span both the pre- and postrevolutionary periods.

Another author whose work spans the two periods and provides for continuity is Vladimir Arsenyev, whose *Dersu Uzala,* or *Dersu the Trapper,* is one of a number of accounts of his travels while mapping the Russian Far East before World War I. *Dersu the Trapper* describes Arsenyev's relationship with an old native tribesman who served as his guide in the Ussuri region from 1902 through 1907. The book was published in 1923 and is thus a bridge from the nineteenth-century Russian tradition to the Soviet one. Tendentiousness is altogether absent, and yet the volume was highly regarded by the Soviet literary establishment. "The story of Dersu inspires a sense of love for the backwoods, the deep rivers and the blue hills of the Ussuri Territory," wrote Gorky, adding, "I am fascinated and swept away by its expressive impact."[32] Arsenyev's Ussuri writings were often cited "as superior to much of Soviet fiction and as a proof that fiction was dying out."[33]

All of these examples up to the beginning of the communist era provide national predecessors for one strain of what would become "literary reportage" or "reportage literature" in the Soviet Union, a tradition from which the works of Alexievich and Politkovskaya descended. Moreover, these early examples are to varying degrees narra-descriptive journalism. While Gorky's piece "The Ninth of January" is to some extent polemical within its historical context, *A Hunter's Sketches* is accidentally so because of how it was received by the tsar's government, and *Dersu the Trapper* is altogether free of political cant.

Egon Erwin Kisch and the *Neue Sachlikeit*

Another answer as to why Alexievich and Politkovskaya both can be said to engage in a literary reportage (or reportage literature) but why Alexievich comes closer to American literary journalism in practice lies in the rise of the literary reportage movement that was part of the larger international communist movement during and immediately after World War I, but which is largely unknown in the United States, perhaps because of a half-century of cold war politics that has now consigned the genre to the losing side in that historical struggle. The movement helps to account for how literary reportage became the cosmopolitan genre it did, so that two very different writers such as Alexievich and Politkovskaya can be described as engaging in the same genre. One central strand to the history of that genre derives from Germany and in no small part from the efforts of Egon Erwin Kisch. The other derives from the Soviet Union. Between the two there was considerable cross-fertilization, and then the movement continued to spread internationally, ensuring the creation of a genre that breached the boundaries of national cultures.

As Siegfried Kracauer, the German critic and sociologist, noted in 1930, "for a number of years now, reportage has enjoyed in Germany the highest favor of representation, since it alone is said to be able to capture life unposed." It was, he said, a reaction against the abstractness of German idealism.[34] In the aftermath of defeat following World War I, the desire to understand that defeat beyond imperial illusionism is understandable. The "reportage" Kracauer refers to, however, is not that of the conventional practice of journalism as understood in the United States. Instead it was a journalistic practice that reflected the *neue sachlikeit,* or "new objectivity," which emerged in aesthetic circles in Germany after the war. Unlike the concept of journalistic "objectivity" as it took shape in the United States at the same time, the German version emphasized first-person witness as the only kind of journalism that could make a claim to epistemological integrity. Undoubtedly its foremost advocate was Kisch, the communist writer and journalist.

Kisch was a Prague Jew who wrote in German like his compatriots Franz Kafka and Joseph Roth, the latter also a practitioner of literary reportage, although he is perhaps remembered more today as a novelist. Kisch's example, and his aggressive promotion of "literary reportage," served as a catalyst for others, and was drafted for purposes of showing the conditions of the struggling proletariat as well as to demonstrate the construction of socialist society. But before he became a committed leftist at the end of World War I, Kisch had engaged in a literary reportage that was fundamentally narrative and descriptive in its modalities without the heavy hand of ideology. Hence it was also a literary journalism. It can be detected in his earliest work in Prague. In 1906 he went to work for *Bohemia,* one of Prague's two German-language newspapers, as a local reporter. Crime news and news about the dark underside of Prague life became his specialty, including, for instance, a sketch about a Slovenian girl's descent into prostitution. In 1908 Kisch began writing sketches under the title "Prague Walks" for the feuilleton section of the Sunday paper. Among examples are sketches about an insane asylum and about a shelter for the homeless. In 1912 he began contributing to a series called "Prager Novellen," or "Prague Novellas," longer, more ambitious efforts that continued to examine society's dark side. "Christmas in a Court Prison" is one example.[35] "As the title suggests," Danica Kozlová and Jiří Tomáš note of the "Prague Novellas," Kisch "attempted a story form, largely on the borderline between artistic journalism and belles lettres."[36]

The origins of Kisch's reportage, then, can be traced back at least in part to the feuilleton of French origin in the nineteenth century. Derived from the French word for "leaf," meaning a page in a book, the feuilleton was an eclectic collection of articles (not infrequently running in a series, thus providing an early example of a multipart journalistic series or installments) usually for the purpose of entertainment as opposed to providing strictly news.[37] The contents of the feuilleton could be highly polemical broadsides, art criticism, or meditative essays, or they could be physiologies and sketches, narrative and descriptive in modal disposition, fictional and nonfictional, and often accompanied by illustrations. There was no single dominating discourse, and the result was very much a heterogeneous collection of different rhetorics and media (often including block prints to illustrate the articles). One can detect here early evidence of a proto-"reportage" that was more than just narrative and descriptive in its modalities. This was a nature inherited from the feuilleton, which helps to account for why it flourished in the international communist movement: any and all rhetorical means of production were to be drafted in the interests of the revolutionary enterprise.

During World War I, Kisch served in the Austro-Hungarian army on the Serbian front, an experience that helped to radicalize him politically. By the beginning of the 1920s, Kisch's conception of a literary reportage had reached maturity. As Harold B. Segel observes, Kisch "is credited with defining reportage as a literary genre."[38] In his exuberance for the form, and perhaps his hubris, Kisch proclaimed in 1929 that such a journalism with literary ambition would replace the novel as the dominant literary genre of the twentieth century:

> Novel? No. Reportage!
> What to think about the reportage? I think it is the literary sustenance of the future. To be sure, only the reportage of the highest quality. The novel has no future. I say there will be no novels produced; meaning no books with imagined plots. The novel is the literature of the last century. . . . Thus, there is a special kind of reportage work that has appeared; I would call it the pure reportage, the reportage itself.
> What's more, after the war [World War I] this reportage became the general, important mode. . . . Psychological novels? No! Reportages!
> The future belongs to the really true and courageous far-seeing reportage.[39]

The passage is noteworthy for a number of reasons, not the least of which is Kisch's hesitancy to attach "literary" as a modifier or to convert "reportage" into a modifier attached to "literature." Hence we see that *Granta*'s reference to a "reportage" that stands alone is not simply a case of synecdoche. Moreover, this is how John Carey interprets the term—"reportage" in isolation—in his collection *The Faber Book of Reportage,* which was published in the United States as *Eyewitness to History.*[40] While French and American definitions of "reportage" do not cite first-person witness, it perhaps comes as no surprise, given Kisch's influence in Germany, that the German definition does: "eyewitness account, running commentary."[41] One measure of his long-term cultural influence is that when the German magazine *Stern* founded one of the most distinguished awards for journalism in West Germany in the 1970s, it was named for Kisch, no small matter given his communist credentials during this period of cold war and a divided Germany. Moreover, officially he had been a citizen of Czechoslovakia after the collapse of the Austro-Hungarian Empire and remained so at his death in Prague in 1948. Nonetheless, that the award was named for him speaks to the regard in which he was held by the German-speaking world.[42]

Kisch's discussion of "reportage" is also noteworthy because as a characterization of the genre, it is still to some degree "elastic." It seems to suggest a relationship between the novel and reportage, but that relationship is not clearly delineated the way it is by American proponents of a "literary journalism," in other words, a "journalism that would read like a novel" or a "short story."

One reason why the form prospered among proletarian writers is that communists distrusted the idea of a bourgeois "objective" journalism whose rise during the 1920s became the professional standard for the capitalist media, particularly in the United States. From the Marxist perspective, a dispassionate "objective" journalism was an ideological ruse for concealing the true depths of the miseries of the struggling proletariat.[43] To some extent, such a viewpoint is consistent with literary journalism theory. It has been observed that the purpose of literary journalism is to engage in an "exchange of subjectivities," or at the least to engage in a narrowing of the distance between subject and object.[44] In other words, one should come away from such material with greater empathy for others, and in the case of Kisch, for the struggles of the proletariat. One can do so only if one engages one's subjectivity with the experiences of others.

Eyewitness (and thus personal) accounts provided, in the communist vision, a truer picture of the world—as long as they were ideologically correct. The ends justified the means, or in this instance the genre—except that the genre was rhetorically many-faceted. Such texts could be largely narra-descriptive in the developing tradition of American literary journalism, and Kisch often wrote in that vein. Or they could engage largely in discursive—and inflammatory—polemics, as in the case of Politkovskaya eight decades later.

Kisch's (literary) reportage was published in book form and received wide international circulation in leftist circles. Examples include, among others, *Zaren, Popen, Bolschewiken* (*Tsars, Priests, and Bolsheviks*, 1927); *Paradies Amerika* (*Paradise America*, 1929); *Asien gründlich verändert* (*Changing Asia*, 1932); *China geheim* (*Secret China*, 1933); and *Landung in Australien* (*Australian Landfall*, 1937).[45] As the titles suggest, he was very much a peripatetic world traveler, which not only gave him his material but also provided him the opportunity to spread his gospel about the virtues of a "reportage" that would replace the novel.

The Transnational Influence of Kisch

Kisch's influence internationally in the development of a cosmopolitan genre is reflected in what at first might appear to be two polar opposites geographically and culturally: the United States and China. One example from the United States is that of Joseph North, editor of the communist publication *The New Masses,* which was an important American venue for a literary reportage that reads much like literary journalism, but one that could be highly polemical in the service of political ideology. North was not just an editor but a practitioner of the form. In his autobiography he cites Kisch and American John Reed as his inspirations.[46] In what became an ideal for such a reportage, North observed: "Reportage is three-dimensional reporting. The writer not only condenses reality, he helps the reader feel the fact. The finest writers of reportage are artists in the fullest sense of the term. They do their editorializing through their imagery."[47] Such a prescription clearly can be applied to literary journalism, and recalls the dictum that has echoed down through generations of American creative writing workshops: "Show, don't tell."

Similarly, Kisch's influence ranged to the opposite side of the world. As Chinese journalist Xiao Qian recalled: "How our *texie* eventually developed I cannot say exactly. I only remember that, during the 1930s, the Czech writer Kisch came to China, and he promoted his literary form of *texie* in our country."[48] Kisch visited China in early 1932 and out of that came his volume *Secret China,* which received international distribution. It was initially published in German in 1933. Chapters were published in Chinese in 1935 and the whole in Chinese in 1938. The first English version appeared in 1935.[49]

But knowledge of Kisch's literary reportage preceded his visit to China. As Charles A. Laughlin notes in his study of the Chinese version, *baogao wenxue,* the League of Left-Wing Writers, a few months after its formation in 1930, issued a declaration calling for reportage on behalf of the proletarian political struggle: "From the midst of intense class struggle, from militant strikes, the smoldering village struggles, through community night schools, through factory newsletters, wall newspapers, through all kinds of inflammatory propaganda work let us create our reportage! Only thus can our literature be liberated."[50] Given the cosmopolitan—and "fraternal"—nature of the international proletarian writers' movement, whose members were in frequent communication with one another, the use of the term is hardly surprising.

One of the earliest references to reportage literature in Chinese came from an article published in early 1930 and translated from Japanese, "A Newly Emerging Literature in Germany." Of Kisch the article notes that "from a long life as a journalist [he] created a new literary form. . . . This literary form has expanded the realm of literature."[51] In a revealing insertion, "reportage" is spelled out in Roman characters within parentheses between the Chinese ideograms and logograms.[52]

Perhaps the most indicative measure of Kisch's international influence is to be found in a 1935 issue of the communist journal *Internationale Literatur,* which was published in German in Moscow by the International Union of Proletarian Writers. The issue, observing Kisch's fiftieth birthday, celebrated his contributions to the genre. It included forty-four messages to Kisch from what amounted to a who's who of the literati and artistic community in the world leftist movement. Praise for Kisch came from such notables as French journalist and novelist Henri Barbuse, the American communist writer Michael Gold (who was also the editor of *The Masses* and *The New Masses* before North took over), the Soviet man of letters Sergei Tretyakov, the German playwright Bertolt Brecht, the Hungarian Marxist philosopher and literary critic Georg Lukács, and the renowned leftist Chinese poet Emi Siao.[53] Kisch, "they all maintained, had made literary reportage into a work of art, neither forfeiting its militancy nor relinquishing artistic standards."[54]

Yet among such proletarian and "militant" belletrists (if that is not invoking an oxymoron) the form was not perceived as exclusively narra-descriptive in line with the Wolfean definition of "literary journalism." Again, perceptions harkened back to the rhetorical heterogeneity of the feuilleton, and herein again lies the form's elasticity. In the same issue of *Internationale Literatur,* the leftist critic Theodore Balk wrote: "Let us compare all that today is denoted as 'reportage.' Someone writes a biography of Madame du Barry and he calls it grand reportage historique. Someone makes a trip around the world and publishes his diary: 'A Reportage from all the World.' Someone collects the reports of an Arctic expedition—it is reportage. . . . Diary, biography, reports—everything is reportage."[55]

It is evident from his work that Kisch preferred writing a narra-descriptive discourse. Yet he not infrequently digresses into other rhetorics. But for doing so his preferred approach is to contextualize such material as a part within a larger narra-descriptive frame. One can detect this in his chapter "Stalinabad—A Capital in the Making" in the volume *Changing Asia,* which is an account of socialist construction in the newly created capital of Soviet Tajikistan. In part the chapter reviews the accomplishments of the communist Revolution, noting, for example, how many students were now attending school in a land where prior to the Revolution the vast majority of Tajiks were illiterate. The chapter "Cotton Statistics" is what the title suggests, a report on cotton farming. Both chapters are contained within a narrative and descriptive framing device.[56]

While Kisch may have been credited by some as the founder of the literary reportage form, he was not. Rather, it is more accurate to suggest that he was its foremost international booster during this period, all but leading a campaign to encourage the form. As he acknowledged, *his* influences were John Reed, Larissa Reissner,[57] and Maxim Gorky.[58] Even though Kisch had engaged in such writing on his own since at least 1908, Gorky still could have influenced Kisch in the latter's youth. But Reed and Reissner would have been much later influences contemporary with the Russian Revolution and civil war in the 1910s and 1920s. Given that Kisch had long engaged in a literary reportage that was narra-descriptive by the time Reed and Reissner published, their influences were likely more in the nature of suggesting and reinforcing ways to politicize the aesthetics of experience.

Perhaps the cosmopolitan and transnational nature of the proletarian writer's movement to encourage literary reportage is captured most clearly in an anecdote about John Spivak, the American communist writer:

> When [Spivak] and Kisch met in Paris in the late thirties and became good friends, he gave the Czech a book inscribed "To the Greatest Living Reporter." Kisch laughed at the inscription and said it meant the book didn't belong to him but to the Soviet writer Ilya Ehrenburg [also a writer of literary reportage]. Kisch reinscribed the book under Spivak's inscription, and the two took it around to Ehrenburg, who was in Paris on a visit. The Russian read the inscription and said, "No, this does not belong to me. It belongs to [American communist writer] Agnes Smedley." He signed the book and sent it off to Smedley, who was recuperating in Seattle after making the Long March with Mao Tse-tung's forces. Smedley decided the book didn't belong to her either and signed it over to her friend Anna Louise Strong. Strong read all the inscriptions, said "Oh, thank you," and kept the book.[59]

Strong was another leftist American journalist.

Kisch's work and example served, then, as an important influence, but one in which many other influences converged within him.

Sergei Tretyakov and Russian Literary Reportage

Kisch traveled to the Soviet Union twice, once in 1925–26, and again in 1930 to a writer's conference in Kharkov. If he had not done so earlier, he likely would have met Sergei Tretyakov during the later visit at the conference while he was continuing to spread the gospel of "reportage." The connection is important because Tretyakov has been described as an "ardent advocate" for a "factual literature" during the early Soviet years.[60] Moreover, he was one of the most vocal of Soviet critics to take a similar position as Kisch in claiming that reportage would replace the traditional novel.

We do not know much about the relationship between Kisch and Tretyakov other than that they both attended the conference and were acquainted, because when Tretyakov wrote his reminiscences of writers, he said that he did not include Kisch because he didn't know him as an intimate friend the way he knew other writers he did describe.[61] But there is no doubt that he regarded Kisch highly, given that he contributed to the 1935 issue of *Internationale Literatur* which honored Kisch's accomplishments.

Among Tretyakov's works are *Vyzov* (*The Challenge,* 1930) and *Tysiącha u odin trudoden* (*A Thousand and One Workdays,* 1934), which are accounts of farm collectivization. He characterized such work as "factographic" writing.[62] Perhaps his most famous work is *Den Shi-Hua* (*A Chinese Testament: The Autobiography of Tan Shih-hua as told to S. Tretyakov*), published in Russian in 1930 and in English in 1934.[63] While lecturing on Russian literature at the National University in Beijing in 1924–25, Tretyakov interviewed one of his students, Tan Shih-hua, every day for six months, viewing the young man (who was not a communist) as representative of young intellectuals committed to reforming and modernizing China. But Tretyakov's account is not simply memoir or biography because of the cultural tapestry he and Tan provide of early revolutionary China. Such cultural revelation has been described as one of the defining characteristics of literary journalism, and one that clearly can be attributed to literary reportage that also emphasizes descriptive narrative.[64] At this juncture they are one and the same.

Reportage, and Tretyakov's reportage in particular, drew the admiration of critic Walter Benjamin. Benjamin saw in the form as practiced by Tretyakov one possible avenue for the future of literature. "I admit, he is only one example; I hold others in reserve," Benjamin writes. "Tretiakov distinguishes the operating from the informing writer. His mission is not to report but to struggle; not to play the spectator but to intervene actively." Benjamin adds, "I did intentionally quote the example of Tretiakov in order to point out . . . how comprehensive is the horizon within which we have to rethink our conception of literary forms or genres, in view of the technical factors affecting our present situation, if we are to identify the forms of expression that channel the literary energies of the present. There were not always novels in the past, and there will not always have to be."[65] Thus the critic similarly questions the future of the novel as had Kisch and Tretyakov.

Benjamin has written elsewhere that conventional newspapers in bourgeois societies have a tendency to "paralyze" the imaginations of readers because of journalistic objectification.[66] Literary journalism, as I suggested earlier, attempts to engage in an "exchange of subjectivities," or at least tries to narrow the distance between subject and object in an empathetic engagement.[67] That is what Tretyakov attempted as an "operating" or engaged writer, according to Benjamin.

Furthermore, Wolfe wrote that the "new" journalism of his era required the journalist to engage in "saturation" reporting. Scholar Norman Sims would later characterize such engagement as "immersion" reporting.[68] Such an immersion or saturation in the experience of others would invariably lead to the literary journalist engaging his or her subjectivity with those he or she is writing about. That is what Tretyakov attempted to do. When writing his books about collective farms, he lived and worked with the communities he wrote about. In different historical periods and societies, critics, scholars, and writers then and more recently arrived at similar theoretical conclusions about a narra-descriptive literary reportage or literary journalism.

As Maxim Gorky observed in 1931, postrevolutionary reportage of the kind Tretyakov wrote had become widespread in the Soviet Union: "The broad flow of sketches is a phenomenon such as has never before existed in our literature. . . . The sketchers tell the multimillioned reader about everything that his energy is creating over the whole huge expanse of the Soviet Union, at all points where the creative energy of the working class is being applied."[69] While prerevolutionary Russia had a tradition of literary reportage in the form of the *ocherk,* what had not existed before was the "broad flow," influenced by Kisch and others such as Reed, Reissner, Gorky, and Tretyakov.

One of the most internationally recognized Soviet examples of such "factography" from this period was Valentin Kataev's *Vremya, vpered!,* or *Time, Forward!,* a 1933 account of a twenty-four-hour period during which construction workers attempted to set a world record for pouring concrete at the construction site of Magnitogorsk, one of the large-scale industrialization projects sponsored at the direction of Stalin.[70] As Marc Slonim notes, "its cinematographic style of flashbacks, rapidly shifting scenes, terse dialogue, and black-and-white character portrayal projected against roughly sketched backgrounds is definitely a departure from psychological realism [then dominant in Western fiction] and is somewhat reminiscent of American expressionists, particularly of the early Dos Passos."[71]

The reference to Dos Passos is revealing because of his leftist sympathies early in his writing career. When Joseph North, Granville Hicks, Michael Gold, and other leftists produced their anthology *Proletarian Literature in the*

United States in 1933, they included one fictional and one literary reportage piece by Dos Passos, thus providing more evidence of a transnational and cosmopolitan aesthetic that had developed as a result of the international communist movement.[72]

Another Soviet example is *Belomorsko—Baltiyskiy Kanal imeni Stalina* (Belomor, or The White Sea Canal). Published in 1934, *Belomor* is an account of the construction of the canal connecting the White Sea and the Baltic Sea (*byelo* in Russian means "white" and *mor* means "sea"). It was edited by a troika of editors, of whom the chief was Gorky.[73]

As one might expect, such works often descended into unambiguous propaganda because their purpose was to promote the construction of socialism (although Tretyakov's account of Tan Shih-hua is relatively free of such tendentiousness). In *Belomor,* for example, engineer Zubrik had been a "wrecker," or saboteur of Soviet industry. He had risen from the ranks of the proletariat to that of the bourgeoisie before the Revolution. The concluding paragraph to the chapter notes:

> Engineer Zubrik honestly earned his right to return again to the bosom of the class in which he was born. Engineer Zubrik earned this right by making a second vital exertion at Belomorstroy [where he contributed to the construction of a difficult dam project]—the most important exertion of his life. He cast aside all his former [meaning "bourgeois"] views, illusions, and prejudices—all that with which the bourgeoisie had once poisoned this young proletarian, sprung from the very heart of an oppressed class.[74]

In such polemics, then, the story becomes an ideological morality play on behalf of socialist construction. What is not mentioned is that Engineer Zubrik performs his duties under duress: he is a slave laborer within the vast system of penal labor camps known as the Gulag.

In principle, the early advocates of "literary reportage" and the like opposed explicit propaganda on the grounds that descriptive facts of the conditions of the peasants and workers should speak for themselves and the inevitability of world revolution. Kisch was emphatic about it.[75] But in the heat of class struggle the result was that such an approach was observed more in the breach. Despite his own formal opposition to explicit propaganda, Kisch himself was not above ideological pandering, as evident in *Changing Asia,* where it is apparent that his purpose is to promote socialist construction. We see this in the chapter "A Visit to the City of Garm" when he concludes with a moral lesson: "But to us Khassyad Mirkulan tells the story of how, out of a mere article of female 'goods,' a free woman was made: one of the thousand and one stories of the Soviet Republic of Tajikistan." One sees it again in the

chapter on cotton, when he draws a comparison between Tajik cotton farmers and American sharecroppers: "And we think of Dixie, the cotton belt of
America, where there are slaves, actually, just as before the time of Lincoln.
We think of that country, where we saw figures in rags, hungry, plundered
figures."[76] This was after he had toured the United States in 1928 and 1929, out
of which came his ironically titled volume *Paradise America*.[77]

Such propagandizing, in both Kisch's and the Soviet experience, shows
why Joseph North's ideal for literary reportage is, on closer investigation,
suggestive of another interpretation. Again, as he noted: "Reportage is three-
dimensional reporting. The writer not only condenses reality, he helps the
reader feel the fact. The finest writers of reportage are artists in the fullest
sense of the term. They do their editorializing through their imagery."[78] The
last sentence about editorializing through imagery reflects the possibility of
still another meaning: that the imagery should unambiguously editorialize
on behalf of ideology. The ends of world revolution justified the rhetoric. The
result, so often, was ideological didacticism and predictability in the interests
of a determinist philosophy.

In such tendentiousness one can detect a variation between literary journalism and literary reportage. As examined elsewhere, it has been suggested
that it is in the nature of literary journalism to engage in what critic Mikhail
Bakhtin described as a "novel" of the "inconclusive present" that resists coming to critical—including political or explicitly ideological—closure.[79] In this
instance the use of "novel" means more than just fiction. It harkens back to
the original meaning of "novel" as something new and contemporary, and
that can be nonfiction.

In literary reportage this may or may not happen. A literary reportage that,
along with literary journalism, does not engage in such a way that Bakhtin
describes is *committed* to the inconclusive present of narra-description. The
inconclusive present derives from the inherent problem of language as a
specular act attempting to mimic a fluid and unfolding phenomenal reality.[80] Such inconclusiveness leaves open interpretive possibilities about our
phenomenal reality. That is because in attempting to account for the world
of phenomena, the open-endedness of such inconclusiveness always provides
a critical space for challenges by different subjectivities to taken-for-granted
assumptions about reality, including ideological prescription. One can detect
this subversive nature in the United States in that version of literary journalism again known as the "New" Journalism of the 1960s and 1970s. It is all but
gospel that the works of such journalists and writers as Truman Capote, Tom
Wolfe, Joan Didion, Norman Mailer, and Hunter S. Thompson challenged
the status quo in their examinations of the American cultural Other.

Ovechkin, Liu, and Solzhenitsyn:
Writers of Mid-Twentieth-Century Reportage

From this point forward, literary reportage continues to reflect such an elasticity. Among the more notable examples of writers of the *ocherk* in the Soviet Union after Stalin's death who had an international influence is Valentin Ovechkin. In the early 1950s Ovechkin published his *ocherki,* or sketches of collective farm life in Russia.[81] Like Tretyakov before him, he wrote about the *kolkhoz,* or collective farm. Ovechkin never lost sight of the socialist dream. By the standards of, perhaps, the American experience, his *ocherki* may appear little different from the reportage of the 1920s and 1930s, because they are still relatively polemical and thus compromised by what Bakhtin called the "distanced image of the absolute past," in which ideology provides closure to the fluidity and interpretive possibilities of the inconclusive present.[82] But in their time Ovechkin's *ocherki* posed a direct challenge to Stalinism and the prevailing literary ideology of "socialist realism." Ovechkin would take greater liberties with the form that approached, from a Western perspective, the fictional. His *ocherki* were based on his experiences as a collective farm manager, but he used fictional names. Yet the *ocherki* were received as journalistic sketches. What we see, then, is the perception that even fictionalization could still be perceived as journalistic. Ovechkin was breaking with the tradition of accounts that dealt with real life reflected in idealized heroes of socialist labor. Instead he chose to write about real-life problems using fictional characters. But the result was an epistemological paradox very much at odds with the prevailing journalistic paradigm in the United States, namely, that real-life problems conveyed as fiction were more credible than the endless stream of real-life heroes idealized beyond belief.[83] Hence we detect still another feature revealing the elasticity of the form.

In 1953 the literary journal *Novy Mir* (New World) published an essay on Ovechkin by the Soviet literary critic Vladimir Pomerantsev. He writes: "Ovechkin speaks of things which previously were not described. Before him, these topics were avoided, treated with silence. Some writers didn't see them at all; others considered these things to be under the jurisdiction of higher authorities and would not undertake to discuss them without their approval. But this writer took the topics and spoke about them so as to aid the higher authorities!"[84] While Ovechkin's sketches may seem ideologically tainted today because they still resonate with propaganda—his purpose too, after all, was to "aid the higher authorities"—they were remarkable in their time because they were willing to challenge the system at all. The challenge, of course, was on behalf of illustrating real-life problems of socialist construction. In other words, they attempted to resist ideological closure by presenting what compromised belief in the success of socialist construction. Indeed, Ovechkin's work, along with Pomerantsev's essay in *Novy Mir,* are considered among the groundbreaking documents for what was called the cultural "thaw" during the Khrushchev period.[85]

Ovechkin's international influence is reflected in the role he played as a mentor to the young Liu Binyan, China's most influential writer of *texie* starting in the 1950s, thus demonstrating once again the cosmopolitan crossfertilization made possible by international communism. Liu Binyan's work eventually proved too subversive for the power structure and resulted in his not being permitted to return to China after he came to the United States in 1988 to teach and write. He spent the rest of his life in exile.[86] As with Ovechkin, Liu Binyan also took greater liberties with the form that approached, from a Western perspective, the fictional. The work that brought him fame in China, "At the Building Site of the Bridges," was based on a real event, used fictional names, and appeared in a journal dedicated to publishing short stories. Yet it was still perceived to be *baogao wenxue* or *texie.*[87]

Undoubtedly the most notable beneficiary of the cultural thaw in the Soviet Union, if for no other reason than that he was a Nobel laureate, was Alexander Solzhenitsyn, whose *Arkhipelag GULAG,* or *The Gulag Archipelago, 1958–1968,* is an example of extended literary reportage on an epic scale, one that Solzhenitsyn characterizes in a subtitle as "An Experiment in Literary Investigation." In the "Author's Note" he insists, regarding the places, people, and events of which he writes, that "it all took place just as described here." But as a literary experiment his has at least as much in common with the reportage of Politkovskaya as with that of Alexeivich in the drafting of mixed rhetorical media. At times Solzhenitsyn's chapters, often first-person accounts of life in the Stalinist slave labor camps, engage largely narra-descriptive modalities. He too took advantage of the critical space between language and the aesthetics of experience to engage in the inherent resistance of Bakhtin's "open-ended present." At other times, however, his is the stance of a polemical historian, engaging in expository analysis. In other words, Solzhenitsyn had learned from his jailers that the ends justify the rhetorical means of production drafted in the interests of his moral enterprise. As he notes cynically of Gorky's *Belomor* in the preface to the first volume of *The Gulag Archipelago,* "material for this book was also provided by *thirty-six* Soviet writers, headed by *Maxim Gorky,* authors of the disgraceful book on the White Sea Canal, which was the first in Russian literature to glorify slave labor."[88]

Such resistance to the ideological platitudes of communism would of course earn him exile from the Soviet Union.

Alexievich and Politkovskaya provided a departure point. But they are also Solzhenitsyn's heirs in the tradition of the cosmopolitan genre of literary reportage because both engaged in examining the cultural Other by working in the tradition of earlier models. Of course, not only are they practitioners of literary reportage as it evolved out of the proletarian European tradition, but also they are derivative of their own native tradition, one that can be traced back at least as far as Turgenev. But Alexievich clearly is a practitioner in the tradition of literary journalism, according to the Wolfean definition. Politkovskaya is instead a sometime practitioner more rooted in the polemical discursive tradition to be found in the European feuilleton, a tradition that is much more rhetorically heterogeneous.

What can be detected in their literary and journalistic roots, then, are two very closely engaged traditions. Literary reportage and literary journalism are much the same when they both emphasize narrative and descriptive modalities and eschew discursive polemic. But while literary journalism engages Bakhtin's inconclusive present, literary reportage historically has either done so or been co-opted by unambiguous ideology (again, what Bakhtin called "the distanced image of the absolute past" in which a response is prescribed instead of a phenomenal inconclusive present left open to interpretation).

Another way to approach the "elasticity" of literary reportage, at least if there is to be some semblance of discrete characterizations of generic forms, is to recognize that while historically "reportage" of European origin may at times have been denominated by political ideology, rhetorically there are really many different literary reportages that can be deduced by modality, and whether there is or is not unambiguous polemical intent (as opposed to subtle and ambiguous intent if one grants that all discourse to some extent reflects ideology). Thus there can be a polemical literary reportage largely discursive in nature, a narra-descriptive literary reportage frozen in the tendentiousness of the distanced image of the absolute past, and a narra-descriptive literary reportage, much like literary journalism, which embraces the inconclusive present of a fluid phenomenal world that grants free interpretive possibilities to the author and reader.

It is to be hoped that such an examination, using as a point of departure two very different journalists from the same cultural milieu, offers promise for further examinations if the comparative study of journalistic forms claiming to reflect the aesthetics of experience is to evolve. Where there was a strong leftist tradition in other countries, there is reason to believe that it influenced national traditions in the ongoing development of a cosmopolitan genre. Some promising examples to explore might include Spain (where Kisch, like many leftist writers, served a tour of duty during the civil war); Portugal (given Rosa Mendes's definition); postwar Germany, as reflected in the work of Günter Wallraff; and Latin America, as reflected in, for example, Gabriel García Márquez's works of literary journalism. Then, of course, there are writers of many other countries still to be identified whose work—some of which is discussed in the following pages—could benefit from such an examination in this emerging area of study.

NOTES

An earlier version of this essay appeared in a slightly different form in the journal *Genre: Forms of Discourse and Culture* 42 (Spring–Summer 2009): 113–34.

1. Lettre Ulysses Award, available at www.lettre-ulysses-award.org; for "narra-descriptive journalism," see John C. Hartsock, "'It Was a Dark and Stormy Night': Newspaper Reporters Rediscover the Art of Narrative Literary Journalism and Their Own Epistemological Heritage," *Prose Studies* 29.2 (August 2007): 257–84.

2. Kevin Kerrane and Ben Yagoda, eds., *The Art of Fact: A Historical Anthology of Literary Journalism* (New York: Simon and Schuster, 1997), 11, 536–48.

3. This is one of the announced goals of the International Association for Literary Journalism Studies (IALJS), founded in 2006 in Nancy, France, available at www.ialjs.org/missions. html; for the "aesthetics of experience," I borrow from and transform the subtitle of Charles A. Laughlin's *Chinese Reportage: The Aesthetics of Historical Experience* (Durham: Duke University Press, 2002).

4. *Webster's Seventh New Collegiate Dictionary,* s.v. "reportage."

5. Tom Wolfe, "New Journalism," in *The New Journalism: With an Anthology,* ed. Tom Wolfe and E. W. Johnson (New York: Harper & Row, 1973), 21–22, 11, and 24. For similar definitions, see Edd Applegate, *Literary Journalism: A Biographical Dictionary of Writers and Editors* (Westport, Conn.: Greenwood Press, 1996), xvi; Gay Talese, *Fame and Obscurity* (New York: Ivy Books, 1993), vii; and Richard Goldstein, *Reporting the Counterculture* (Boston: Unwin Hyman, 1989), xvii.

6. Lettre Ulysses Award, available at www.lettre-ulysses-award.org.

7. Available at www.granta.com/shop/product?usca_p=t&product_id=2823.

8. Rudolph G. Wagner, *Inside a Service Trade: Studies in Contemporary Chinese Prose,* Harvard-Yenching Institute Monograph Series 34 (Cambridge: Council on East Asian Studies, Harvard University, 1992), 376.

9. Peter Monteath, "The Spanish Civil War and the Aesthetics of Reportage," in *Literature and War,* ed. David Bevan (Amsterdam: Rodopi, 1990), 81.

10. Lettre Ulysses Award.

11. Harold B. Segel, *Egon Erwin Kisch, the Raging Reporter: A Bio-Anthology* (West Lafayette: Purdue University Press, 1992), 74.

12. See Laughlin, *Chinese Reportage*, 1.

13. Wagner, *Inside a Service Trade*, 348–49.

14. *Cihai* (Thesaurus), one-volume edition (Shanghai: Shanhai cishu chubanshe, 1979), 679, quoted in Yingjin Zhang, "Narrative, Ideology, Subjectivity: Defining a Subjective Discourse in Chinese Reportage," in *Politics, Ideology, and Literary Discourse in Modern China,* ed. Liu Kang and Xiaobing Kang (Durham: Duke University Press, 1993), 214.

15. Kenneth Katzner, ed., *English–Russian, Russian–English Dictionary* (New York: John Wiley & Sons, 198), 4.

16. Isabel Hilton, "Commentary—A Prize for the Underrated Genre of Literary Reportage," *New Statesman,* October 13, 2003, available at www.newstatesman.com/print/200310130051.

17. John C. Hartsock, "'Lettre' from Berlin," *DoubleTake/Points of Entry* (Spring–Summer 2007): 107–8.

18. Wagner, *Inside a Service Trade*, 360.

19. Laughlin, *Chinese Reportage*, 13, 17–44.

20. Alexander Grigorevich Tseitlin, *Stanovlenie Realisma v Russkoi Literature: Ruskiy Fiziologicheski Ocherk* (The Formation of Realism in Russian Literature: The Russian Physiological Sketch) (Moscow: Izdatlstvo "Nayuka," 1965), 91–94, 159–65, 302–8.

21. Ibid., 1.

22. Ibid., 32.

23. Ibid., 23; Martina Lauster, *Sketches of the Nineteenth Century: European Journalism and Its Physiologies, 1830–50* (Basingstoke: Palgrave Macmillan, 2007), 140–43.

24. Ivan Turgenev, *A Hunter's Sketches,* ed. Ovid Gorchakov (1852; Moscow: Foreign Languages Publishing House, n.d.), 451.

25. John C. Hartsock, *A History of American Literary Journalism: The Emergence of a Modern Narrative Form* (Amherst: University of Massachusetts Press, 2000), 127–28.

26. Turgenev, *A Hunter's Sketches,* 453–55.

27. Leo Tolstoy, *The Sebastopol Sketches,* trans. David McDuff (1855; New York: Penguin, 1986).

28. Fyodor Dostoevsky, *Notes from a Dead House,* trans. L. Navrozov and Y. Guralsky (1862; Moscow: Foreign Languages Publishing House, n.d.).

29. Anton Chekhov, *The Island: A Journey to Sakhalin,* trans. Luba and Michael Terpak (1895; New York: Washington Square Press, 1967).

30. Maxim Gorky, *Through Russia,* trans. C. J. Hogarth (1921; London: J. M. Dent & Sons, 1959), and "How I Learnt to Write," in *On Literature,* trans. Julius Katzer (Moscow: Foreign Languages Publishing House, [1960]), 62–66; Charles A. Moser, ed., *The Cambridge History of Russian Literature* (Cambridge: Cambridge University Press, 1989), 372.

31. Maxim Gorky, "The Ninth of January," in *Selected Short Stories by Maxim Gorky* (New York: Frederick Ungar, 1959), 168–94.

32. Liner notes, Vladimir Arsenyev, *Dersu Uzala,* trans. V. Schneerson (1923; Moscow: Foreign Languages Publishing House, n.d.). *Dersu Uzala* is perhaps best known in the West because of the 1975 Academy Award–winning Soviet film production of the same name by the Japanese director Akira Kurosawa.

33. Gleb Struve, *Russian Literature under Lenin and Stalin: 1917–1953* (Norman: University of Oklahoma Press, 1971), 217.

34. Siegfried Kracauer, *The Salaried Masses: Duty and Distraction in Weimar Germany* (published 1930 as *Die Angellstellten: Aus dem neuesten Deutschland*), trans. Quintin Hoare (London: Verso, 1998), 32. Kracauer probably became better known in the United States as a film critic after his immigration.

35. Danica Kozlová and Jiři Tomáš, *Egon Erwin Kisch: Journalist and Fighter*, trans. John Newton (Prague: International Organization of Journalists, 1985), 18–21; Segel, *Egon Erwin Kisch*, 16–17, 20.

36. Kozlová and Tomáš, *Egon Erwin Kisch*, 20.

37. Paul Harvey and J. E. Heseltine, eds., *The Oxford Companion to French Literature* (Oxford: Clarendon Press, 1969), 272, 632.

38. Segel, *Egon Erwin Kisch*, xi.

39. Marie Majerová, "Als Egonek den Roman Zum Tod Verurteilte," in *Kisch-Kalendar*, ed. Franz Carl Weiskopf ([East] Berlin: Aufbau-Verlag, 1955), 185–86; translation in text by Lydia Fetler Hartsock and John C. Hartsock.

40. John Carey, ed., *The Faber Book of Reportage* (London: Faber and Faber, 1987); idem, *Eyewitness to History* (New York: Avon, 1990).

41. Karl Breul, *New Cassell's German Dictionary*, ed. and rev. Harold T. Betteridge (New York: Funk & Wagnalls, 1958).

42. Frank Berberich, director of the Lettre Ulysses Award, personal interview, Berlin, May 22, 2006.

43. Laughlin, *Chinese Reportage*, 12.

44. Alan Trachtenberg, "Experiments in Another Country: Stephen Crane's City Sketches," *Southern Review* 10 (1974): 273. For more on this, see Hartsock, *A History of American Literary Journalism*, 67–69.

45. Egon Erwin Kisch, *Zaren, Popen, Bolschewiken* (1927; Berlin: Aufbau-Verlag, 1977); *Paradies Amerika* (1929; Berlin: Aufbau-Verlag, 1994); *Changing Asia*, trans. Rita Reil (1932; New York: Alfred A. Knopf, 1935); *Secret China*, trans. Michael Davidson (1933; London: John Lane, 1935); and *Australian Landfall*, trans. John Fisher (1937; London: Secker & Warburg, 1969).

46. Joseph North, *No Men Are Strangers* (New York: International Publishers, 1958), 105.

47. Joseph North, "Reportage," in *American Writers' Congress*, ed. Henry Hart (New York: International, 1935), 121.

48. Xiao Qian, "Shang'ai xinwen gogzkuo, ji Xiao Qian tongzhi dui Zhongguo shehui-kexueyuan xinwen yanjiusheng de yici jianghua" (Beloved Newspaper Work, Comrade Xiao Qian's Talk to Researchers in Journalism at the Chinese Academy of Social Sciences), *Xinwen yanjiu xiliao* 4.74 (1979), quoted in Wagner, *Inside a Service Trade*, 327.

49. See Kisch, *China*; Wagner, *Inside a Service Trade*, 327.

50. "Wuchan jieji wenxue yundong xin de qingshi ji women de renwu" (New Trends in the Proletarian Literary Movement and Our Tasks), *Wenhua douzheng* (Cultural Struggle), quoted in Laughlin, *Chinese Reportage*, 17.

51. Kawaguchi Ko, "Deguo de xinxing wenxue" (A Newly Emerging Literature in Germany), trans. Feng Xuanzhang, *Tuohuangzhe* 1.2 (1930): 732, quoted in Wagner, *Inside a Service Trade*, 348.

52. Yin Junsheng and Yang Rupeng, *Baogao wenxue zong heng tan* (Disquisitions on Reportage Literature) (Chengdu: Sichuan Renmin Press, 1983), 190.

53. "Für Egon Erwin Kisch zum 50. Geburstag," *Internationale Literatur* 4 (1935): 3–30.

54. Wagner, *Inside a Service Trade,* 327.

55. Theodor Balk, "Egon Erwin Kisch and His Reportage: On the 50th Year of a Noted Revolutionary Reporter," *Internationale Literatur* 4 (1935): 67.

56. Kisch, *Changing Asia,* 91–94, 240–58.

57. Segel, *Egon Erwin Kisch,* 32–34.

58. Wagner, *Inside a Service Trade,* 359.

59. William Stott, *Documentary Expression and Thirties America* (New York: Oxford University Press, 1973), 54–55.

60. Struve, *Russian Literature under Lenin and Stalin,* 197.

61. Segel, *Egon Erwin Kisch,* 37.

62. Wolfgang Kasack, *Dictionary of Russian Literature since 1917,* trans. Maria Carlson and Jane T. Hedges (New York: Columbia University Press, 1988), 423–24.

63. [Sergei Tretyakov], *A Chinese Testament: The Autobiography of Tan Shih-hua as Told to S. Tretyakov* (1930; New York: Simon & Schuster, 1934), v.

64. Hartsock, "Lettre," 109.

65. Walter Benjamin, "The Author as Producer," in *Reflections: Essays, Aphorisms, Autobiographical Writings,* trans. Edmund Jephcott, ed. Peter Demetz (New York: Schocken, 1986), 223–24.

66. Walter Benjamin, "On Some Motifs in Baudelaire," in *Illuminations,* ed. Hannah Arendt, trans. Harry Zohn (New York: Schocken, 1969), 159.

67. Hartsock, *A History of American Literary Journalism,* 67–69.

68. Ibid., 263. Harriet Borland, *Soviet Literary Theory and Practice during the First Five-Year Plan* (1950; New York: Greenwood Press, 1969), 62.

69. Maxim Gorky, "O Literature" (1931), in *O Literature,* ed. N. F. Belchikov (Moscow, 1937), 58, quoted in Borland, *Soviet Literary Theory,* 62.

70. Valentin Kataev, *Time, Forward!,* trans. Charles Malamuth (New York: Farrar & Rhinehart, 1933).

71. Quoted in Kasack, *Dictionary of Russian Literature,* 161.

72. Granville Hicks et al., *Proletarian Literature in the United States* (New York: International Publishers, 1935), 62, 213.

73. Maxim Gorky, L. Auerbach, and S. G. Firin, eds., *Belomor,* trans. and ed. Amabel Williams-Ellis (New York: Harrison Smith and Robert Haas, 1935).

74. Ibid., 165.

75. Segel, *Egon Erwin Kisch,* 70–71.

76. Kisch, *Changing Asia,* 186, 258.

77. Segel, *Egon Erwin Kisch,* 38–43.

78. North, "Reportage," 121.

79. Hartsock, *A History of American Literary Journalism,* 49–50; M[ikhail] M. Bakhtin, *The Dialogic Imagination,* trans. Caryl Emerson and Michael Holquist, ed. Michael Holquist (Austin: University of Texas Press, 1981), 39.

80. John C. Hartsock, "'Literary Journalism' as an Epistemological Moving Object within a Larger 'Quantum' Narrative," *Journal of Communication Inquiry* 23 (October 1999): 432–47.

81. Valentin Ovechkin, *Collective Farm Sidelights,* trans. M. V. Romanov (Moscow: Foreign Languages Publishing House, n.d.).

82. Quoted in Cathy N. Davidson, "Ideology and Genre: The Rise of the Novel in America," *Proceedings of the American Antiquarian Society* 96 (1986): 303.

83. Wagner, *Inside a Service Trade,* 249.

84. Vladimir Pomerantsev, "On Sincerity in Literature," *Novy Mir* (December 1953), available at www.sovlit.com/sincerity/.

85. Ibid.

86. Liu Binyan, *A Higher Kind of Loyalty,* trans. Zhu Hong (New York: Pantheon Books), 279–80.

87. Wagner, *Inside a Service Trade,* 147–48.

88. Alexander I. Solzhenitsyn, *The Gulag Archipelago, 1918–1956: An Experiment in Literary Investigation,* trans. Thomas P. Whitney, vols. 1–2 (New York: Harper & Row, 1973), xii.

Chapter 2

Reportage in the U.K.

A Hidden Genre?

JENNY McKAY

W HEN ALEXANDRA FULLER won the world's most prestigious award for literary reportage in 2005, her book was hailed as "a spellbinding literary achievement." Few British readers got to know this, even though Fuller was born in Britain, and her book *Scribbling the Cat: Travels with an African Soldier* (2005), for which the award was made, was published by Penguin, a publishing house that originated in Britain. The reason British readers didn't know was that the award received "next to no mention" in the British press.[1] I found out about it by accident when I was talking to Penguin about books for a new University of Stirling undergraduate course titled "Journalism and Literature." Penguin mentioned Daniel Bergner, saying that his book *Soldiers of Light* (2004) had been shortlisted for an international prize called the Lettre Ulysses Award for literary reportage.[2] I was intrigued both by the fact of its existence and by the fact that I hadn't heard of it before. When I found out more, I realized that for a reader with my tastes and professional interests as a lecturer in journalism, it served the same purpose that the Booker Prize shortlist serves for those whose preference is for reading contemporary fiction in English. Both prizes act as guides to some of the best books currently being published in their genre. One difference is that the contenders for the Lettre Ulysses Award (which was presented annually from 2000 to 2006) were all books of reportage, that is to say, they dealt with real events and the real world; another is that several of these books were published in a language other than English. Indeed one of the benefits of being shortlisted for the prize was that, as a result, funds might become available for translation into other languages.

The organizers of the prize were surprised by the lack of interest on the part of the British press, though it demonstrates the invisibility of reportage in the U.K., a point made by Isabel Hilton, one of the U.K.'s most respected journalists and chair of the award's international, polyglot jury in 2005. "Reportage is a critically neglected form," she says.[3]

International versus British Literary Reportage

There are, though, countries where reportage is valued, and sometimes even feared, for the contribution it can make to public knowledge as well as literary satisfaction. If you happen to be British and doubt this, remember that the award's first winner in 2003 was Anna Politkovskaya, who, it is widely believed, was murdered for her courageous reporting in the former Soviet Union, and Chechnya in particular. A quarter of an hour spent browsing the Lettre Ulysses Award website is an antidote to the sorry mediocrity that is commonly described by those who comment on the British press.

As the renowned Polish journalist Ryszard Kapuściński said in his keynote address at the ceremony for that first Lettre Ulysses Award, "a reporter should be a careful observer, sensitive to seemingly banal details," open to others, and imbued with "respect for another man, his dignity and worth." For Kapuściński, who died in 2007, the art of reportage is the art of noticing, and he spoke about the distinguished history of reportage, the importance of being an eyewitness, about the significance of reportage as a way for cultures to learn about one other, and about the consequent responsibility carried by those who write reportage. He observed that to do their job well, journalists require "passion, curiosity about the world and [about] people, an appetite for information, diligence and devotion"; and if they do it well, they help to promote what he calls "decent knowledge" rather than false stereotypes. He also said that "good reportage is . . . so popular in the modern world."[4]

As I read Kapuściński's words and those of the jury members and keynote speakers from subsequent years, I realized their tone was unfamiliar to me. Yes, there were criticisms of the limited language and stereotypical thought that journalists are guilty of using. But there was also a note of pride that was inspirational, a suggestion that it really matters to humanity that good reportage is written by humane, intelligent, sensitive, curious, persistent reporters. It is reminiscent of the belief of that great twentieth-century American reporter Martha Gellhorn, who said that "honorable reporting should be serious, careful and honest."[5] These words are echoed by John Pilger in his 2004 anthology *Tell Me No Lies: Investigative Journalism and Its Triumphs.*[6] They, and other fine journalists such as Günter Wallraff and Janine di Giovanni, say they are concerned with describing unflinchingly what they see, with holding to account those who hold power, with giving a voice to those who otherwise might not have one.

Kapuściński's speech didn't, however, remind me of the more typical image that we in the U.K. have of journalists and what they write. Kapuściński thought that reportage is popular because "modern people, living in a world conjured up by the media, of illusions and appearance, simulacra and fables, instinctively feel they are being fed untruth and hypocrisy. And so they seek something that has the power of a document, truth and reality, things authentic."[7] This may well be true in other cultures but, in the U.K. at least, the reputation of the press means that its readers are less likely to feel so confident that what they are reading is true.

There is not enough space in this essay to describe in full the unacceptable excesses of British journalists at the lower end of the trade—the folly with which they present stories to their readers, the limited scope of their inquiries, their prurience, their jingoism, their sexism, their obsession with celebrities and television shows, their narrowness of vision. Not all British papers and magazines are like this, but even at the quality end of the market, our newspapers can't be guaranteed to publish serious, challenging reportage. Some of our papers, indeed, have come to resemble little more than shoppers' catalogues on the few pages not taken up with what might be called all-about-me page-fillers, those information-free personal columns written at great speed for great fees. The professional autobiography of one of the U.K.'s best journalists, Andrew Marr, gives a detailed, critical account of this development. Having counted and measured the column inches, he concludes that for those who believe newspapers hold up a mirror to society, "the message of the *Sunday Times* and its competitors is that Britain has gone shopping."[8]

In 2008 Nick Davies, another leading U.K. journalist writing for the *Guardian* newspaper, launched his own attack on the state of British journalism. Like Marr, he laments the extent to which British reporters are manipulated by the public relations and propaganda industries, are so dependent on a small number of press agencies, are so constrained by ever-decreasing levels of staffing and reductions in the amount of time they have to research their stories. In describing this state of affairs he uses the word "churnalism" to distinguish the product from "journalism," the traditional form of reporting at its best that depends on thorough research using primary sources.[9]

Marr is a serious, highly educated, and much-respected political journalist who writes well and broadcasts even better. Yet his own account of his trade is typical of the self-image of journalists in the U.K. They are apt to describe it as being an amateurish, rackety, insecure, badly paid, boorish way of life that is nevertheless great fun; or as Marr sums it up, "on good days, it's heaven."[10] The British even refer to several of their most popular newspapers as "the comics," contributing to the overall view of journalism as rather jokey and lacking in seriousness.

This picture will be familiar to U.K. readers, who are known to hold journalists pretty much in contempt.[11] And it is borne out by reportage champion

Ian Jack, who observes that we depend on journalists for the "proper scrutiny of society" but contrasts this notion with "the strange sad fact . . . that so few people seem willing to call themselves a reporter any more."[12] His view is that "good reporting/reportage means to describe a situation with honesty, exactness and clarity," and so he adopts an almost elegiac tone when he argues that reportage is "something of an English-language specialism" thanks partly to the historical lavishness and competitiveness of the British press and also to the English language itself, "which is such an ally of everyday curiosity with its preference for the concrete over the abstract, the specific over the general, and . . . the prosaic over the poetic."[13]

Literary Reportage and Journalism Studies in the U.K.

The point Kapuściński made about the popularity of reportage is important, and while it may well be true in some if not much of the rest of the world, today in the U.K. reportage is more or less ignored by the literary and journalistic establishments: that it might be regarded as an art, or that it might have some literary worth, is almost unthinkable, not because journalists aren't capable of writing it (although if they want to, they more or less have to teach themselves) but because it has, until recently, lacked any kind of recognition.

For one thing, we English speakers hardly know what to call it.[14] The word "reportage" does exist, as Jack's edited collection, *The Granta Book of Reportage,* shows, but most journalists wouldn't think of using it, and if they did, they probably wouldn't be able to agree about how to pronounce it. They'll get little help from the growing pile of textbooks for the university-level study of journalism in the U.K.: "reportage" is not in the index of most of them. The word doesn't mean quite the same thing as "reporting," although to produce it does require some of the same skills as are needed for plain, workmanlike news reporting. But reportage, as I understand it, demands more of a reporter. Reportage requires more skill and more effort from the writer at the research stage. It requires an awareness of literary qualities and literary strategies as well as an awareness of a story's wider significance. When Tom Wolfe offered in the early 1970s "the New Journalism" as a label for a certain kind of writing (and I would call this a subset of reportage), he argued convincingly that imaginatively written journalism that went beyond the current conventions should be accorded the same (if not more) value as fiction.[15] His ideas weren't universally accepted, and in the U.K., for example, the style of writing he described was dismissed in many newsrooms as being too self-indulgent, too long, too expensive, and too little grounded in reality. This criticism had some justification when it was leveled at the inferior imitators of writers such as Hunter S. Thompson, Truman Capote, or Wolfe himself, imitators who saw the word "I" in Thompson's gonzo journalism and decided it gave them license to drop interviewing and research altogether in favor of describing their own responses to events. Yet there's no doubt Wolfe's anthology *The New Journalism* had some influence, particularly on writers for magazines.

My own interest in reportage began with that anthology edited by Wolfe and E. W. Johnson. Reading it is one of the reasons I became a journalist. When I started out, I joined the best graduate newspaper training scheme for journalists and learned shorthand, law, news values, and how to write an attention-grabbing introduction. I attended mock press conferences complete with gruesome pictures of just-murdered bodies. I reviewed plays and concerts, including a concert in which I myself sang. I attended inquests, interviewed Gypsies and actors and workers on strike. All very much as I had expected. What I hadn't expected, perhaps because I had a degree in English, was that at no time would any of our tutors so much as hint that journalism had any literary value or that for us as beginners it might be instructive to read the best journalism written by others then or in the past. No one ever mentioned Dickens or Defoe or Hazlitt or Gellhorn or Wolfe. Even George Orwell was mentioned rarely, and then only by chief subeditors anxious to ensure that we novices absorbed the advice about writing that Orwell offers in his famous essay "Politics and the English Language" (1946). I soon realized that this was the norm in training in the U.K., and it has not really changed much, even though there have been other significant changes in the way journalists are trained.

One of these is in location. When I was learning the trade, more than half of the recruits to newspapers were still arriving straight from school. Now most have a degree, and some even have a degree in journalism, thanks to the gradual opening up of the doors of the academy over the past thirty years or more to what was, and to some extent still is, regarded as an upstart of a subject. This may seem surprising to those from countries with a different, more intellectual tradition of journalism education, but journalism has had to fight hard for its place in universities in the U.K., and it is perhaps a lingering institutional uncertainty about its worth that makes its position in the academy unstable and somewhat insecure.

When journalism began to creep into universities, even into those with strong academic reputations, it was conceived in an almost entirely functional way. Journalism was seen as a professional practice or craft for which students would be trained. Yet courses were, and are still so often, designed by academics in subjects other than journalism who have no direct knowledge of journalism practice, specialists being hired only after the courses have already been established. The practical subjects are supplemented by more academic or theoretical subjects through which students are encouraged to reflect on journalism practice. "Journalism Studies" is the umbrella for these courses, and they are likely to be taught by specialists in cultural studies, communications, or sociology.

One curiosity here is that sociology is usually directed at journalism as an object of study rather than presented as a methodology that journalism students might learn from. They'll encounter an ethnographic study of foreign correspondents, perhaps, but not be taught how to do such ethnographic work, even though some journalistic writing, such as Åsne Seierstad's international best-selling book *The Bookseller of Kabul* (2004) could certainly be regarded as ethnography.

What university courses in the U.K. don't usually include at either the undergraduate or the postgraduate level is any serious consideration of journalism as a branch of literature. Among the few exceptions was a course taught at the University of Stirling until autumn 2009, one module in a master's course at the University of Lincoln, and the more recent master's in literary journalism at the University of Strathclyde in Glasgow.[16] It's still the case, then, that students of journalism are not routinely introduced to the masters of the craft. They are not encouraged to read widely other than in current newspapers or, occasionally, in magazines. They are not, even in undergraduate degree programs of three or four years, routinely introduced to the historical and literary contexts of the field in which they want to make their careers.

Defining Reportage Literature in the U.K.

I've dwelled on the education of journalists because it is relevant to thinking about why reportage is so invisible in the U.K. Journalism has been in a "closet of denial, invisibility, and contempt" was the observation of journalism historian Laurel Brake,[17] noting that this view has long characterized the relation of literature with journalism both within the academy and outside it. It's striking, too, that authors such as Thackeray, George Eliot, Dickens, and Defoe are more often rated for their fictional than their factual writing.

To take the example of Daniel Defoe, he wrote no fiction (as we would recognize it today) until he was sixty and was probably the most prolific journalist Britain has ever known. Yet for decades, centuries even, his journalism was not accessible outside specialist libraries. His early book-length reportage, an account of the storm that ravaged England in 1703, is occasionally read by English literature students but mostly ignored by journalism departments even though it is of great interest as a specimen of early reportage.[18]

The reasons for this are partly historical and partly social. Among the consequences are that many journalists and most journalism students are ignorant of the rich tradition of journalistic writing. So too are readers, students, and teachers of English because of the distaste, if not downright disgust, with which journalism has been, and largely still is, regarded by the literary establishment. By this I mean not just universities but publishers and also the literary editors of the press. And yet English literature, or at least the English novel, could be said to have had its roots in reportage: the English novel is a genre of fiction that for most of its history has depended on realism for its effect. As such, the novel is in many ways a close cousin of factual reportage as both strive to convince us of the authenticity of the stories they tell.

The state of affairs Brake refers to was intensified in the early days of the formation of the English literature canon. It means that in universities—in just those cultural institutions where you might expect reportage to find critical recognition—you actually find not much recognition at all. This is anomalous if you compare literature with film. Film Studies for obvious reasons developed later than English Studies. Nevertheless, since its earliest days it has recognized the "documentary" as a legitimate art form worthy of study for its aesthetic achievements as well as its capacity to inform its audience about the real world. There has been little comparable attempt in the U.K. to study the history, craft, and art of documentary writing.

Nor is this neglect a characteristic just of the academy, journalistic and literary alike. If you look at the literary pages of the more serious U.K. newspapers and magazines, the ones that might be expected to carry a broad range of book reviews, you will find listings under nonfiction, but most of them will be historical or biographical or political. The journalists' trade magazine, *Press Gazette,*[19] hardly ever carried book reviews, and when it did they were usually either "how to" manuals for young reporters or autobiographies of famous journalists.

There is, of course, a well-established booksellers' category, nonfiction. There's even a prize for it given by the BBC, the Samuel Johnson Award for nonfiction, and twice in its first ten years the award went to books of reportage: Anna Funder's *Stasiland: Stories from Behind the Berlin Wall* in 2004, and Rajiv Chandrasekaran's *Imperial Life in the Emerald City: Inside Iraq's Green Zone* in 2007. But there remains a problem for reportage with defining it as nonfiction. As a category, nonfiction is clearly not synonymous with journalism, nor can it ever be satisfactory to describe a genre, or anything else for that matter, in terms of what it is not. By doing this we imply that we attach much more value to the opposite—to fiction in this case.

This view is borne out by a reading of the reviews of books of journalism too. So often the worth of a piece of documentary reportage is described in terms of its similarity to fiction. Here are examples from reviews quoted on the jackets of books by Janine di Giovanni:

> *The Place at the End of the World* (2006): "A gifted and humane reporter with a novelist's eye for detail," *The Literary Review*
> *Madness Visible: A Memoir of War* (2005): "Her truth is more powerful than fiction," *Irish Times*

Similarly, one reviewer of Funder's *Stasiland* called it "a masterpiece of investigative analysis, written almost like a novel." While it's heartening to read such favorable comments on reportage in the British press, it would be more heartening still if reviewers felt they could depend on their readers' knowledge about reportage through having read enough of it to equip them with a framework of critical reference other than that provided by fiction. This is not a trivial point. It is a use of words that helps to perpetuate the invisibility of a significant and important genre of writing. "Words have consequences," as Steven Poole notes in *Unspeak: The Language of Everyday Deception* (2006), his book about journalistic writing, and so if something has no name, no verbal label, then it can comfortably be ignored.[20]

Here are some further examples of this invisibility. Reportage is not written just for the press, and there seems to have been a gradual increase, even in the U.K., in the number of books of reportage being brought out, whether produced as anthologies of pieces already published in newspapers or magazines, or written as book-length documentaries in the first place. Among the former I would place di Giovanni's *Madness Visible,* Jason Burke's *On the Road to Kandahar: Travels through Conflict in the Islamic World* (2006), and Christina Lamb's book *The Sewing Circles of Herat* (2004). Among the latter—book-length reportage—I would include Seierstad's *Bookseller of Kabul* (translated from Norwegian), Linda Grant's *People on the Street* (2006), James Fergusson's *A Million Bullets: The Real Story of the British Army in Afghanistan* (2008), and Julian Baggini's *Welcome to Everytown: A Journey into the English Mind* (2008).

When books such as these are produced, how do publishers label them? Do they call them reportage? The answer is that they are almost never categorized as journalism or reportage. So readers could be forgiven for not recognizing book-length reportage if publishers don't either. Some are prepared to publish it but continue to categorize it as nonfiction. A trawl through a collection of reportage yields many different labels on the book jackets:

Nick Davies, *Dark Heart* (1997)—current affairs
Tracy Kidder, *Mountains beyond Mountains* (2003)—biography
Jason Burke, *On the Road to Kandahar*—current events/politics
The Penguin Book of Journalism—media studies
Svetlana Alexievich, *Voices from Chernobyl* (1997, 2005)—world history
Daniel Defoe, *The Storm* (1704, 2005)—Penguin literature
The Gay Talese Reader (2003)—journalism/literature
George Orwell, *The Road to Wigan Pier* (1971)—fiction
Anna Funder, *Stasiland* (2004)—nonfiction

More bizarre still is Bernard Hare's *Urban Grimshaw and the Shed Crew* (2006). Its publisher clearly states on the book jacket that it is fiction, but as far as we can tell by reading it, it is not. Reviewers don't think it is fiction either: they say it "grips like a novel" and "it reads like a novel," calling it "the true story of a terrifying joyride through Britain's hell-bound underclass."[21] One exception to this pattern is the third edition of the anthology *The Granta Book of Reportage*. This is, quite correctly, labeled on the jacket as "reportage"; for its first two editions, however, even this book, from the publisher that has done most in the U.K. to promote the publication and the reading of reportage, was labeled "nonfiction" on its jacket.

This uncertainty about categorization is carried over into bookshops and libraries. In the U.K., bookshops rarely devote a section to reportage or even to journalism. "How to" books about journalism appear under media studies or else under writing skills, often in the business or management sections. Any of the kinds of books I have mentioned appear, if at all, only on the library or bookshop shelves that deal with the subject being written about. So you won't find Kidder's *Mountains beyond Mountains* in the University of Stirling's library unless you are browsing in the section for nurses. Similarly, *Murder on Ward Four* (1993), Nick Davies's account of the murders of children committed by the hospital nurse Beverly Allitt, is a superb piece of investigative reportage, but no journalism student will come across it through random browsing in the media section because it's filed under social welfare. You wouldn't think of looking for *The Granta Book of Reportage* on shelves labeled "fiction," but that's where I've seen it in one campus bookshop (not Stirling). You can't go confidently into the U.K.'s major bookstores to browse for a great book of reportage for your train journey. You might come across one by accident, but that's the best you can hope for. In pursuit of Fuller's *Scribbling the Cat,* I was, after much puzzlement on the part of staff, directed to the

African history department. The book wasn't there in any case, even though it had recently won the Lettre Ulysses Award. The point here is that I knew what I was looking for (thanks to the Lettre Ulysses website), but browsing at random is and always should be one of the ways most of us come across new material to read, whether for work or study or pleasure. As long as there is no straightforward category for journalism or reportage for borrowers or buyers of books to browse through, then they are likely to remain in ignorance of the true richness of what has been published.

This was brought home to me several years ago when I designed a course called Journalism and Literature for the University of Strathclyde's English department. It was restricted to department undergraduates then, there being no space to put anything like it into the journalism postgraduate timetable. At that time it was hard to know which books to prescribe other than three key anthologies. Two I've already mentioned: *The Granta Book of Reportage,* edited by Ian Jack, former editor of the *Independent* newspaper, and *The New Journalism,* edited by Tom Wolfe and E. W. Johnson, published in the U.K. in 1975. The third was a collection put together by John Carey, now emeritus professor of English literature at Oxford University and for many years the chief fiction reviewer for the *Sunday Times.* His anthology, *The Faber Book of Reportage,* includes writing from classical times up to the modern day.[22]

These three books haven't been superseded and remain the key anthologies I was able to turn to in 2003 for a course I devised called "Journalism and the Literature of Reality," although there are now a few more collections of writing by individual reporters. *The New Journalism* first appeared in 1973, *The Faber Book of Reportage* in 1987, and *The Granta Book of Reportage* in 1993. They have all stayed in print, and only the last has been revised, although it's curious that the third edition contains only three new pieces and dropped three others to make way for them—curious because Granta was founded for the purpose of publishing a quarterly magazine (in book form) to present a mixture of new reportage and new fiction, but definitely more of the former and much of it of high quality.

One thing these three anthologies have in common is that they carry as their introductions what amount to manifestos making a case for taking the genre seriously. The kinds of writing they promote are not precisely similar, and *The New Journalism* anthology presents a particular kind of reportage published at a specific time. It is instructive that these editors all feel the need to explain what reportage or the New Journalism is and to proselytize about it. The same is true of Pilger's anthology *Tell Me No Lies: Investigative Journalism and Its Triumphs,* where he argues for this kind of journalism to be accorded the status he thinks it deserves but doesn't currently attract. Thanks to these anthologies, it is possible for anyone in the U.K. who is interested in documentary writing to find texts and also to discover the names of writers to follow up.

Literary Reportage and the British Press

So far I've been considering readers and teachers of journalism. But what about the writers? If U.K. journalists want to produce longer, fully researched documentary narratives and have the time to do justice to their "saturation reporting" with the painstakingly and time-consumingly achieved literary quality of what they write, then in Britain at least, they will struggle to get their work published.[23] Few magazine or newspaper editors will contemplate running a piece of more than, say, four thousand words, and even two thousand is considered exceptionally long.[24] Budgets for reporting have been pared to the minimum, and so too must be the time for research and writing unless a reporter is prepared to subsidize the publication.[25]

Editors collude with this situation, believing that readers don't want to read long articles as they don't have the time or the attention span—a point that is perhaps undermined by the burgeoning sales of books and the undoubted and growing success of book festivals in the U.K., the one at Hay-on-Wye in May and the fortnight-long one in Edinburgh in August being the two best-known examples. They would argue, too, that they can't afford to pay for a feature that could take weeks rather than the more typical few hours to research and write, whether by enabling a staffer to devote that much time or by paying a freelancer enough to cover her time.[26] Yet as Marr and countless commentators have pointed out, there is money available, in the national press at least. It's just that it is being spent on astronomically high fees for personal columnists or their admittedly more serious and possibly more interesting to read commentary-column colleagues. What we need, Marr argues,[27] and Davies agrees,[28] are more "real reporters," journalists who are not tied to their desks and computers but who are able to go out into the world, to meet people, to observe, and to put into context what they see.

Davies and Marr are describing a setting where the craft of reportage (however you want to define that) is undervalued. British journalists have nothing comparable to the Nieman Program on Narrative Journalism based at Harvard University (although it suspended its activities in 2009). Nor is it easy to conceive of a gathering of journalists in the U.K. similar to that program's annual conference draw of several hundred delegates devoted to narrative journalism. Even if U.K. writers knew about it and were keen to go, it's unlikely that editors or their publishers would fund the jaunt. Just as entry-level journalism training is accorded low priority from British newspaper editors, so too is mid-career training, at least where writing is concerned.

When I worked for a leading national Sunday newspaper's weekend magazine, I had to pay to attend an advanced features writing course even though my job involved editing features by well-known and respected writers up to and including Graham Greene. The course was organized by the union, not by any publisher. In the U.K. the National Union of Journalists has become a leading provider of training for journalists once they have embarked on careers. Magazines are slightly better at training their staff, although their emphasis tends to be on the technical production or the business aspects of magazine publishing. For this reason, it's disheartening to attend, as I have on several occasions, the annual jamboree for around a thousand magazine publishers and editors in the U.K. organized by the Periodical Publishers Association. There's always plenty of talk about brand extension, cover mounts, sales graphs, about marketing and talent and staff retention, about digital crossover and globalization and content, but almost no mention, ever, of how to achieve, or facilitate, or train people to produce really high-quality, eye-opening reportage.

It will be a hard struggle to change things. In the U.K. we all but ignored the Lettre Ulysses Award and the names of the brave, talented writers from all over the world it sought to bring to our attention. By contrast, our own annual press awards ceremony in London in 2005 degenerated into a brawl.

Yet there is some small cause for optimism. There are increasing numbers of books of reportage being published in the U.K., even if they're not called that, and there are signs of the emergence into the academy of a new subject. "Journalism and Literature" now appears in university syllabi as a module (at Lincoln and Strathclyde at the master's level and, until recently, Stirling at the bachelor's). There are even postgraduate degrees at Imperial College, London, and City University, London. The focus of the former, the M.A. in creative nonfiction writing, is popular science writing. The latter, in the prospectus for its creative writing (nonfiction) M.A., does not mention journalism or reportage, however.

But these are exceptions. In the U.K. we're a long way from according serious recognition to the literary qualities of the best journalism. The trouble is, as Isabel Hilton points out, "the mass media have a very short attention span and the information they dispense is very superficial."[29] They concentrate on headline events and not on the wider context in which those events take place. The limitations of normal journalistic practice troubled Kapuściński too: "The everyday language of information that we use in the media is very poor, stereotypical and formulaic. For this reason, huge areas of reality are then rendered beyond the sphere of description" by ordinary reporting.[30]

Kapuściński's belief in the importance of reportage is echoed, from the literary establishment, by John Carey. He suggests that however enjoyable fiction is, it nevertheless represents "a flight from the real[,] . . . and good reportage is designed to make that flight impossible. It exiles us from fiction into the sharp terrain of truth."[31] He sums up the importance of reportage by saying that it "may change its readers, may educate their sympathies, may extend—in both directions—their ideas about what it is to be a human being, may limit their capacity for the inhuman. . . . Reportage . . . lifts the screen from reality, . . . and since it reaches millions untouched by literature, it has an incalculably greater potential."[32]

On that note, let me place my discussion of reportage into the context of the real world. While there may not be much evidence that man's capacity for inhumanity is restrained by the availability of reportage, its existence does at least limit the capacity for ignorance of that inhumanity. By the same token, good reportage enables readers to share in what Kapuściński calls the "rich, varied, colorful, ineffable reality"[33] of distant cultures customs, and beliefs.

This is what the Lettre Ulysses Award for Literary Reportage was set up to honor and what, in the U.K. at least, we are reluctant to nurture and to celebrate.

NOTES

1. Frank Berberich, Siobhan Dowling, organizers of the Lettre Ulysses Award, e-mail message to the author, May 4, 2005.

2. Bergner's *Soldiers of Light* was awarded third prize at the Lettre Ulysses awards in 2004. The last Lettre Ulysses Award to be given was in 2006. Its website may be consulted at www.lettre-ulysses-award.org.

3. From a 2005 interview about the Lettre Ulysses Award for the Goethe Institute, available at www.goethe.de/prs/int/01/de906768.htm.

4. Ryszard Kapuściński, keynote speech, October 4, 2003, Lettre Ulysses Award, available at www.lettre-ulysses-award.org/index03.html.

5. Quoted in Ian Jack, introduction to *The Granta Book of Reportage*, 3rd ed., ed. Ian Jack (1993; London: Granta Books, 2006), xi.

6. John Pilger, ed., *Tell Me No Lies: Investigative Journalism and Its Triumphs* (London: Cape, 2004), xiii–xxix.

7. Kapuściński, keynote speech.

8. Andrew Marr, *My Trade: A Short History of British Journalism* (London: Macmillan, 2004), 111, 350–75.

9. Nick Davies, *Flat Earth News* (London: Chatto & Windus, 2008), 49–73; Marr, *My Trade,* 384.

10. Marr, *My Trade,* 385.

11. Richard Keeble, *Ethics for Journalists* (Abingdon: Routledge, 2001), 3.

12. Jack, *Granta Book of Reportage,* xiii.

13. Ibid., v.

14. Ibid., vi.

15. Tom Wolfe, "The New Journalism," in *The New Journalism: With an Anthology,* ed. Tom Wolfe and E. W. Johnson (London: Picador, 1975), 22.

16. Yet at the time of writing, even a degree with this title offered only two classes in the literature (and film) of journalism out of the fourteen from which students may choose.

17. Laurel Brake, unpublished conference paper, "Gendered Space and the Press," given as part of the University of Warwick seminars, "Literary Journalism and Literary Scholarship," November 1995 and May 1996.

18. Jenny McKay, "Defoe's *The Storm* as a Model for Contemporary Reporting," in *The Journalistic Imagination: Literary Journalists from Defoe to Capote and Carter,* ed. Richard Keeble and Sharon Wheeler (Abingdon: Routledge 2007), 15–28.

19. *Press Gazette* (formerly *UK Press Gazette*) was the professional weekly periodical for journalists for forty years until 2008, when, as a result of financial difficulties it was transformed into an online site (available at www.pressgazette.co.uk) and a monthly subscription-only magazine.

20. Steven Poole, *Unspeak: The Language of Everyday Deception* (London: Little, Brown, 2006), 238.

21. Reviews quoted in the 2006 Sceptre edition: respectively, Luke Richardson, *Books Quarterly;* Decca Aitkenhead, *New Statesman;* and Christopher Cleave, "Books of the Year," *Sunday Telegraph.*

22. John Carey, ed., *The Faber Book of Reportage* (1987; London: Faber and Faber, 2003).

23. Jenny McKay, *The Magazines Handbook* (Abingdon: Routledge, 2006), 94.

24. Among those that do publish longer journalism are the *London Review of Books,* and the Saturday and Sunday quality newspapers such as the *Guardian, Observer, Telegraph,* and *Sunday Times* and their associated weekend magazines. The left-wing political weekly magazine *New Statesman* announced in autumn 2008 that it intended to publish more reportage and fewer opinion columns.

25. Davies, *Flat Earth News,* 65.

26. These were among the findings from interviews conducted with editors by Gary Meenaghan in 2006 for his undergraduate dissertation at the University of Stirling, titled "So Where Did New Journalism Go? A Comparative Study of the 21st-Century Editions of British and American *Esquire.*"

27. Marr, *My Trade,* 384.

28. Davies, *Flat Earth News,* 60–65.

29. Hilton, Goethe Institute interview.

30. Kapuściński, keynote speech.

31. John Carey, introduction to *Faber Book of Reportage,* xxxvii.

32. Ibid., xxxvii–viii.

33. Kapuściński, keynote speech.

Chapter 3

The Edge of Canadian Literary Journalism

The West Coast's Restless Search for Meaning versus Central Canada's Chronicles of the Rich and Powerful

BILL REYNOLDS

SOME YEARS AGO, American literary journalist John Vaillant, then in his mid-thirties, decided to make magazine feature writing his vocation. Once he had done so, he labored extensively but successfully, experiencing a personal breakthrough in 1999 by having one of his stories published in the *New Yorker.*[1] A couple of years later, the Boston native then moved from Philadelphia to Vancouver because his wife had been accepted into graduate school at the University of British Columbia. This enormous geographic shift—from the East Coast of the United States to the West Coast of Canada—required a proverbial leap of faith. After a life that included many career starts (English graduate from Oberlin College in Ohio, ocean fisherman based in Alaska, post–Soviet Union ESL teacher in the Czech Republic, blues singer–guitarist in Philadelphia),[2] Vaillant wondered exactly how big a leap it was, this migration to the edge of the North American continent and to another country, so far from New York. He wondered, as he applied for landed immigrant status and continued his career as a magazine writer, "Am I writing myself into irrelevance?"[3]

Vaillant need not have been worried. Not long after this upheaval, he sold his second feature to the *New Yorker,* this one about a uniquely golden-colored, old-growth spruce tree thriving in northern British Columbia for hundreds of years before suddenly being chain-sawed by a seemingly deranged forestry worker. But his transitional predicament caused me to wonder what exact role geography has to play in the evolution of literary journalism. In Canada the media center, and magazine writing center, is Toronto. Typically, magazine editors are preoccupied with tales of wealth, status, celebrity, power, and crime. In magazines such as *Toronto Life,* for example, the tone can be smarmy and ironic. The features tend to be profile oriented, which means they are about important people, not ordinary people; about the wealthy, not those in penury; about celebrities, not regulars; in short, about somebody, not nobody.

The idea of editor-driven perfection at these types of magazines, to take an example, would be to assign a well-known gay magazine writer, a winner of many National Magazine Awards for his fine work, to profile a well-known editor in chief of one of Canada's national newspapers.[4] The end result, the risqué projections of a homosexual writer onto a famous, straight editor, may indeed be witty and urbane, but hardly constitutes taking risks with literary journalism. (This is a tactic of the New Journalism, at least as it was practiced at *Esquire* magazine.)[5] But it is exactly this kind of self-satisfaction that passes for sophistication in today's storytelling marketplace.

Another example would be *Maclean's,* one of Canada's oldest magazines, which celebrated its one hundredth anniversary in 2005. A typical cover story in 2006 focused on one of Canada's (and indeed the world's) wealthiest men, Kenneth Thomson, owner of numerous information databases and part owner of the *Globe and Mail,* Canada's most important nationally distributed newspaper (especially to those living in central Canada). Or, more specifically, the cover story focused on his family. More specifically still, his family's perceived weirdness. This is the central Canadian media hothouse in a single snapshot—important family, wealth, power, and gossip. The title says it all: "Canada's Richest Family, the Thomsons, Are Worth $23.8 Billion . . . And They're Just a Little Bit Strange: An Inside Story of Messy Divorce, Private Eyes, a Special Baby, Botox, Nanny Dress Codes, Vindictive Timing and Fine Art."[6] A February 2009 issue of *Maclean's,* in fact, features the ultimate important person/celebrity/world figure, U.S. president Barack Obama. The cover line proudly rolls out the red carpet for the recently elected head of state, who was about to visit Ottawa, the nation's capital, for exactly five hours: "Welcome Mr. President: Everything You Need to Know About Us—On One Page."[7] President Obama is depicted on the cover getting out of his limousine. He is wearing sunglasses. The cover line perhaps inadvertently conjures the question in the reader's mind: everything he needs to know . . . on one page? This seems more like a criticism of Canada than a helpful primer. All of which is to say, Toronto mimics Tom Wolfe's general belief about New Yorkers: that they are obsessed with status and therefore want to read about people more successful than themselves.[8]

By contrast, in Vancouver, situated on the West Coast of Canada, nearly 3,000 miles from Toronto, the intersection of sea, sky, and mountains often creates a different outlook in the minds of editors and writers. What Vaillant found once he got to Vancouver did not quite match his fear of self-consignment to the periphery. He found others who wanted to write stories that placed value on travel, on moving through space, on getting low to the ground with the subject, the topic, or the meeting. He thought this kind of journalistic anthropology might be analogous to a television program called *Be the Creature* he had been watching with his children.[9] The Kratt Brothers' nature program visits animals in their natural habitat. In other words, he thought literary journalists in Vancouver were trying to be the story. Not be *in* the story, but to *be* the story in order to tell the story better, or more thoroughly, reflecting not verisimilitude but reality.[10]

The story in Vancouver is not necessarily about the kinds of topics that pre-occupy the center.[11] Because Vancouver literary journalists are so far removed from the New York and Toronto magazine hubs, they tend to interact with the world more. In fact they seem almost to go out and confront the world. They travel more, they learn languages as best they can, and they try to get at the human condition through history and geography. They read and prepare, yes, but mostly they find that only by being there can they truly understand what is going on.

One writer, Charles Montgomery, traveled to Melanesia. He moved from one island to the next in the archipelago over a six-month period. Under the guise of a travel story, he chased memories of his great-grandfather, a bishop from the Victorian era. He then came home and spent over a year digesting his experiences and writing *The Last Heathen*.[12] Through a kind of specialized travel memoir, he nibbles away at the issue of belief—native beliefs in animated spirits, Christian beliefs based on the teachings of the Bible, and our current belief in the infallibility of technology—and questions our assumption of modern superiority in these matters. Finally, it is an investigation into his great-grandfather's conversion at the end of his life. Montgomery's book was publicly recognized as significant, as he won the 2005 Charles Taylor Prize for Literary Non-fiction.[13]

Another Vancouver writer, James MacKinnon, also exploited a deep personal connection to excellent effect. His uncle, Father Arthur MacKinnon, a Catholic priest who worked at the Scarboro Mission in the Dominican Republic, was murdered—or executed—in 1965. There are those who still believe Father Art was assassinated for his leftist community activism, but the crime was never solved. The younger MacKinnon spent six months in the Dominican Republic, gathering material to write his own combination true-crime mystery, travel memoir, and political commentary. The story had been with his extended family for years—and since he was the writer in the family, they often teased him about writing the book—yet the true motivating factor to begin the investigation and take the story seriously was MacKinnon's noting the similarities between former U.S. president Lyndon B. Johnson's foreign policy in the mid-1960s and George W. Bush's policy of preemption, especially as it pertained to the invasion of Iraq in 2003. Or, as MacKinnon put it, "What are the outward, spiraling repercussions when we go someplace and kill a bunch of people?"[14] Strangely, although MacKinnon's book was about another search for a dead missionary relative in a faraway place, written by yet another male Vancouver writer in his thirties, it won the Charles Taylor Prize for Literary Non-fiction the very next year after Montgomery's.[15] Not without reason, though: one scholar describes it as "an impressive and highly readable combination of memoir, investigative journalism and travelogue."[16]

Still another Vancouver literary journalist, Deborah Campbell, spent approximately six months traveling in Israel and Palestine in 2002. Having been educated at Tel Aviv University a decade earlier, she wanted to return to understand for herself the complexities of the conflict. (She did not trust what she perceived as the zealously pro-Israel media coverage in Vancouver.)[17] Unlike stationed press and broadcast reporters, she went into territories rarely covered by journalists and talked to a wide variety of civilians rather than spokespersons.

Even Vaillant, a former Bostonian, fits the pattern emerging in Vancouver. His excursions took him to northern British Columbia and its temperate rainforest. The Queen Charlotte Islands/Haida Gwaii, 450 miles north of Vancouver, is about as far from Canada as one can get without actually leaving the country.

This recent boom in literary journalistic talent is a classic example of the outsider crashing the citadel. Despite their protestations to the contrary about being outsiders, it is exactly as outsiders that these Vancouver writers have gained their strength. They remain outside the power center, and this has given them precious time to nurture their individual talents and collective spirit. Being on the outside is also what drives their writing. They travel away, and the very excitement of the dislocation fuels the attentive reporting. They cannot afford not to have their wits about them. Being the outsider gives sustenance to their stories, yet leaves them well short of being curdled by the ironic self-satisfaction that turns so much of power-center feature writing in on itself. In this essay I discuss, through a study of four cases, a particular mindset that has taken hold of writers on Canada's West Coast, one that generally does not exist in the more populous, more politically powerful and wealthy East.

There is one caveat to mention before continuing. In some ways, one could easily see this discussion as a straw man argument, since all four have written for Toronto-based general interest publications such as *The Walrus*[18] and *explore* magazine.[19] Nevertheless, while there may be work in the East for these writers, their style is remarkably different. An excellent example of this difference can be found in an anthology of *explore* magazine pieces published in 2006.[20] The Toronto-based journalist Ian Brown, one of Canada's most celebrated feature writers, contributed a piece about seven male friends who embarked on a skiing and mountaineering expedition to an isolated British Columbia ice field in the Rocky Mountains.[21] The feature centers not on the hardship of being placed into rugged surroundings but rather on how to satiate one's suave personal tastes and desires in a demanding environment. In other words, it looks inward rather than outward, a highly amusing yet solipsistic piece about bringing hedonism and creature comforts to the wild. Geography becomes a device, and there is no search for meaning in any greater context. In fact, it is another standard New Journalism–style piece, where instead of the adventurer coming to the metropolis to experience its many pleasures, the adventurers bring their creature comforts with them to the wilderness.

The Outsiders

Here is a brief snapshot of Vancouver's success these days. The *Economist Intelligence Unit,* in its 2005 survey, ranked Vancouver as the best city in the world, out of 127 studied, in terms of livability (factors included personal safety, the availability of goods and services, and strength of infrastructure).[22] The nation's largest newspaper, the *Globe and Mail,* expanded its coverage of the Vancouver and West Coast region in advance of the 2010 Winter Olympics. Vancouver's housing prices have long since eclipsed Toronto's (although the economic recession beginning in 2009 may have affected this distinction). Innumerable condo towers and construction cranes now obstruct the view of the downtown sky. A light rapid transit system has been constructed, although the oldest neighborhood in the core, the Downtown Eastside, despite efforts to clean things up in time for the arrival of the world in February 2010, remains populated with crack and heroin addicts.

Most of this is to the good for the burghers of the city, but for our purposes, from the perspective of literary journalism, perhaps most noteworthy is the formal recognition being achieved by a heretofore little-known group that calls itself the FCC. These initials apparently once stood, briefly, for False Creek Coalition, so named for False Creek in the west end of downtown Vancouver. Then the initials came to signify (again, briefly), the Foreign Correspondents Club, in recognition of the writers' collective desire to travel abroad to experience their stories and bring them home. Now the acronym itself is the name, and signifies nothing except that, by 2010, a group of six (or seven, as Vaillant is an honorary member) like-minded, ambitious, relatively young literary journalists came at the form in a way that is different from much of what was currently happening in Canada. Greg Buium, a Vancouver writer and editor, wrote an article about the FCC for the Canadian Broadcast Corporation's website, thereby introducing the group to a wider, national audience: "The FCC represents something particularly powerful. . . . Their collective voice, no matter how disparate, crosses literature, reportage and cultural curiosity in a way that seems committed to finding its own place in the tradition."[23] In fact their optimism is almost quaint. They believe the story always has a bigger picture. They believe in truth-telling from a subjective point of view; that is, they believe in the postmodern concept of "a truth" rather than "the truth." They believe in expanding the point of view beyond the borders of provincialism to the rest of the world. They see the story as always being about something larger, about existence, about how we live our lives and why.

The six writers, at the time in their mid- to late-thirties—Deborah Campbell, James MacKinnon, Charles Montgomery, Brian Payton, Alisa Smith, and Chris Tenove—began meeting and discussing the books and writers they admired. They started discussing their mutual love of narrative nonfiction as a form of writing. They started to share their technical problems of writing in the form. They started to support one another, to edit one another's work, to challenge one another. They became more ambitious, more serious, more outward looking, and began to develop solidarity as they took on the world. Campbell describes her group as "fiercely independent."[24]

Campbell, whose freelance magazine writing can be found in the pages of *Canadian Art, Modern Painter, Harper's, The Walrus,* the *Guardian,* and the *Utne Reader,* finished her first book in 2002.[25] *This Heated Place* features the writer as narrator, although the "I" is rarely intrusive in the story. Campbell had been educated at Tel Aviv University a decade earlier, but her subsequent research into the Middle East conflict suggested to her that her much-lauded professors had left "huge swaths of information" out of their lectures—including even Nakba Day, the Palestinian people's annual recognition of the "day of the catastrophe," the May 15, 1948, creation of the state of Israel.[26] She wanted to travel throughout Israel and Palestine because she felt she had so many questions that were going unanswered. The resulting work, which attempts to tell the story of what is happening from the point of view of regular citizens on both sides of the divide, and tries to be fair to both sides, was met with some resistance in Canada during her book tour. Interviewers canceled her appearances at the last minute, and the one conclusion she could draw from the experience was that these episodes could have happened only because she chose to look at the conflagration from both sides.[27]

Because Vancouver is isolated from the center of the country—Ottawa, the nation's capital, and Toronto, the nation's largest city, are both situated in Ontario, about five hours apart by automobile or one hour by air travel—these writers feel they must push one another to write to the best of his or her ability. They began with no manifesto. When David Beers—a former editor of *Mother Jones,* a magazine feature writer for *Harper's* and other magazines, the author of the 1996 memoir *Blue Sky Dreams* about growing up in California's Silicon Valley, and founding editor of the Vancouver-based independent on-line news publication *The Tyee*—challenged them to write down their principles, they refused.[28] They did not want to reify their hopes for success in narrative nonfiction and instead challenged one another to grow their talents organically. Beers (whose provenance is San Francisco, but who moved to Vancouver in 1990 because his wife accepted a tenure-track teaching position at the University of British Columbia, and who is now a dual citizen) found that the FCC's dedication to improving craft and subsequent rise to prominence reminded him of earlier movements back home that gathered momentum: the Beats and Lawrence Ferlinghetti's City Lights bookstore; the hippies, Haight-Ashbury, and the Human Be-In; Steward Brand and the *Whole Earth Catalogue* movement; *Wired* magazine; David Talbot and the launch of the Web-only magazine Salon.com; and the vibrant gay literature scene. In other words, for Beers the writers of the FCC went beyond complaining of the status quo and talking about doing something: they created a positive force. Part of this might be attributed to their relative youth. They have few attachments, such as children (except for Vaillant, in his mid-forties), and this lack of obligation allows them the freedom to travel and bring back their stories. Together, they look outward, which is unusual for Vancouver writers. (Terry Glavin, *éminence grise* of the British Columbia literary scene, became so agitated by the FCC's gallivanting around the world in search of stories that he challenged the group to find worthy ones in its own backyard.)[29] They all imbue their writing with personal experience and voice. They all seem to pick up on the greater sense of the mythical that permeates West Coast culture.

Campbell indeed has a personal stake in bringing back what she found out about Israelis and Palestinians, as she spent some of her impressionable, formative years among them and needed to go back with the eyes of a seasoned journalist to get a better sense of what was true, rather than trusting the newspaper and television reports she had been reading and watching. With Montgomery and MacKinnon, the personal involved tracing their roots in a kind of anthropological dig through family history. That family thread—the great-grandfather and the uncle, respectively—gave them what

Beers describes as "the permission to explore," adding that it is the kind of mature and grown-up imagination that is indicative of what is happening on the literary journalism front in Vancouver at the moment.[30]

Influences on the FCC

What influences this group? Whom do they hold in highest regard? The negative answer is, surprisingly, not the "New New Journalism" (more on this later).[31] If there is somebody who has influenced the writers of FCC, it is, according to MacKinnon, Montgomery, and Beers, the Polish journalist Ryszard Kapuściński, whom they call the "grandmaster." MacKinnon had read *The Soccer War* and *The Shadow of the Sun,* loved both, and introduced his comrades in arms to them.[32] A foreign correspondent for the Polish state newspaper in Africa for four decades, Kapuściński told stories in a way that was alien to North American sensibilities. They were personal stories, but there was little of Kapuściński's personality or ego involved. What impressed MacKinnon was that, even though Kapuściński had to be there to get the story, and he was in the story, the story was not in fact about him, but about the country, the place, and the people he was experiencing.

As for another powerful influence, Montgomery mentions the Canadian-based international correspondent Paul William Roberts, who has written extensively on Iraq for *Harper's* (though Montgomery balances this admiration with the realization that Roberts had lately been leaning too far in the direction of embracing conspiracy theories).[33] What Montgomery takes away from Roberts is the profound "sense of urgency" that accompanies the deep reporting, immersion, and research into geopolitical hotspots.[34]

Aside from writers admired, however, there are three other reasons, distinct to Vancouver, why these literary journalists happened to come together with such force at this time. One is that they all met and worked at two Vancouver magazines. Another is the fact that an antiestablishment current runs through West Coast culture. Finally, not to be underestimated is the negative influence the media conglomerate CanWest Global Communications Corporation has had on numerous writers in Vancouver.

One periodical common to the group is *Vancouver* magazine, at least during the period 2003–2006, when it was being edited by Matthew Mallon, a man who was willing to, as the saying goes, let his writers write. To Campbell, it was not so much that the liberal-minded Mallon took chances, but more that he was laissez-faire, and perhaps even malleable, in his approach to assigning stories, which ultimately made *Vancouver* a more interesting vehicle for which to write during his stay there. The other magazine where many

FCC writers met was *Adbusters,* the militantly anti-consumer cultural and political bible, founded by Kalle Lasn in 1989. The most important part of working for these two magazines at that specific time—the first half-decade or so of this century—is the fact that the writers were allowed to follow their own hunches on stories, and develop their writing at their own pace, without having to conform to a kind of focus-group-enhanced, factory-model, magazine-feature-writing template to which so many of Canada's consumer publications now adhere. With both magazines, they did not have to produce magazine writing "that looked like magazine writing," in Campbell's memorable phrase.[35] Nor did they, if it was at all possible to avoid, submit to ideas that were borne out in editorial boardrooms—ideas such as contrived service journalism set-ups, to take one type of beloved story category. Because they were developing their own ideas, they nourished their intensity for the stories. Instead of producing dispassionate pieces—"piecework" might have been a more appropriate term, to use the freelance expression—based on germs of ideas that immediately sounded promising to editors, they were able to dig for angles to stories that initially, when isolated as a "pitch" or query letter, might not have been immediately compelling.

MacKinnon in particular benefited from staying away from mainstream media. During his post-secondary years at the University of Victoria, he co-edited his student newspaper, *The Martlet,* for a year. From there he went directly to *Monday* magazine, a Victoria-based alternative weekly, where even with three hundred–word stories he was encouraged to enhance news articles with narrative elements. After a few years of editing *Monday*—and the inevitable burnout that comes with a small staff churning out a weekly newspaper—he started to freelance edit at *Adbusters* while pitching long-form story ideas to magazines. Thus from university to signing his book contract with the West Coast–based publisher Douglas & McIntyre, he avoided working inside a traditional news environment. By way of contrast, Montgomery dutifully studied journalism at Langara College in Vancouver and then upon graduation found work at one of the two CanWest Global newspapers in the city, the *Vancouver Sun.* There he became quickly stifled, and quit. He tried working in Hong Kong and attempted to mature his writing style, but it was not until later that he found his voice. Montgomery concluded that he needed to jettison everything he had learned in journalism school in order to learn how to write.[36]

At Lasn's *Adbusters* magazine, contributors were not told how to write or what to write, but it was understood that the content should be highly political in nature, and specifically critical of neoliberal global market forces. MacKinnon, already showing a preference for a narrative style that allows "the reader to pick up on things," illustrates this distinction with a memorable image: "*Adbusters* has a certain kind of readership that you don't need to be subtle with. These are not new concepts to most of the readers—you can get right in there and write like you're pounding beers at a university bar, basically."[37] This antiestablishment culture is nothing new in the city that in 1971 brought the world Greenpeace. Individualism is important, but so is community. And nowhere is this more apparent than in the collective contempt in which the FCC holds CanWest Global. The Winnipeg, Manitoba–based media conglomerate's influence on what Vancouverites read and watch is difficult to overstate: as of 2009 the company owned both of the city's daily newspapers, *The Province* and the *Vancouver Sun;* it owned one of two national daily newspapers, the *National Post;* it co-owned the commuter daily *Metro;* it owned twelve community newspapers in the greater Vancouver area; and it owned the Global television network across the country. (At the time, the company was deeply leveraged and mired in the global economic slump; it was in the process of being broken up.) As Campbell sees it: "We all live these days in virtual environments that are created by information. Our perception of life and what matters and what is going on is coming out of media to an unheard-of extent."[38] For her, this means her city is a media vacuum. Unlike, say, members of the media in New York City, among whom the *New York Times* has an extraordinary cachet, these writers do not think they can trust the quality of news written or produced by CanWest. This frees them to get their information from a wider variety of sources and not subscribe to the corporate business agenda of the main media player.

By way of contrast, Toronto's local media are heterogeneously owned. The city has two national newspapers, the *Globe and Mail* and the *National Post;* the largest daily newspaper in the country, the *Toronto Star,* plus the *Toronto Sun,* another local daily; it has two well-established weekly alternative news-papers, *Now* magazine and *Eye Weekly;* and it has the gay biweekly *X-tra* and the gay monthly *fab* magazine. Toronto's many identities would seem to be better served and reinforced by its local media than Vancouver's.

Stifling media control by one corporation may engender a paradoxical sense of freedom to develop more individualistic ideas about what is important in Vancouver, but the euphoria is tempered by these writers' collective acknowledgment that they are relatively new to the field of literary journalism. They believe that they are still learning how to tell stories, which does not necessarily imply being humble in their approach, but rather forewarns them to realize there are many different aspects to a story, and every writer is bringing his or her version of truth to the proceedings.

West versus East: Canada's Media Wars

As mentioned, what animated the work of the FCC at its early stage was a strong desire not to become part of a perceived machine that stamped out identical magazine story structures, cookie-cutter style, for reading consumption. This strong streak of individualism is one reason that brought the FCC writers together; it fueled a collective desire to run away from the story everyone else was doing and instead find their own paths. This approach, of course, involves getting away from the scrum, the roundtable interview, or being sequenced in interview priority by a helpful publicist. They want to bring back to Vancouver stories they feel only they can tell. Campbell calls it doing "social documentary work."[39]

While the writers of the FCC realize that they work on the edge of where things "happen" in magazine journalism, they also freely admit they will never fall prey to the belief that the world ends with their city. Montgomery says he knows they are looking at the world from the outside. At the same time, Campbell says, in terms of her stories, when in Vancouver she feels like she is on the inside. Vancouver is the familiar and poses no risk for her. Part of the thrill of reporting outside Vancouver is that it raises the stakes for these writers. In a foreign environment, everything is challenging. "I have to navigate language, social issues, culture, religion," she explains. "I am constantly dealing with anxieties or worried about getting arrested."[40]

Perhaps it is not so unusual for the FCC writers to travel in order to collect their stories and bring them back, as the tendency to travel generally is so much greater now. Where they may differ is their ability to imagine their stories through travel and then to actualize them. There is always, suggests Montgomery, the usual criticism of travel writers that they do not spend enough time at a place before making pronouncements about it, but he believes there is something to be said for analyzing a destination with clarity before the colloquialisms set in.[41]

How the FCC's theoretical underpinnings play out in the reality of the country's largest media market is another issue. Ask a Vancouver writer to delineate the difference, or set of differences, between Toronto and Vancouver media, and various answers sprout forth.[42] The writers of the FCC believe that Vancouver writers are not territorial but collaborative. Without the significant commercial infrastructure of the central Canadian journalism institutions and the jobs they provide, being competitive is simply not a viable option. Also, appearances are not as important in the West. Whom you know is not as valuable as your latest writing project.

Distance makes a difference. Vancouver is so far removed from the central government in Ottawa and the media center in Toronto that many Vancouverites are simply not engaged with the rest of Canada. To the literary journalist, this means that writers do not feel a necessary connection with the main writing markets in the country. Toronto becomes as important in the Vancouver writer's mind as Seattle or Mexico City. David Beers, editor of *The Tyee,* says the one Canadian myth he has never believed is that Toronto is in fact the media center of anything at all, except perhaps the Toronto-Ottawa power corridor; in other words, there is no good reason for Vancouver writers to subscribe to the Toronto viewpoint because it is a parochial viewpoint anyway.[43] On top of this suspicion is the rejection of West Coast stories and narratives by eastern editors. All the FCC magazine writers have had trouble, at one time or another, persuading Toronto-based editors to care about their Vancouver- and British Columbia–based story ideas. MacKinnon points to Vaillant's story about the chopping down of the one and only golden spruce in the Queen Charlotte Islands as a case in point:

> Here was this amazing story, that is universal and has international appeal, and nobody in Canada picked up on it except for this guy who moved up here from Boston. He was seeing it with fresh eyes and wasn't thinking he was going to sell it to a Toronto publisher. No, he said, I'm going to sell it to a U.S. publisher. Every one of us has had the frustration of trying to explain western stories, stories from our perspective, to eastern editors. You just wonder what's the point. Why not look to the U.S.? You're getting into bigger magazines with a much broader reach and impact.[44]

In Canada there is a long-standing cliché that says Torontonians want to be New Yorkers, and Toronto is sometimes mockingly called the "Little Apple." Toronto does in fact dominate the cultural landscape of the country, but the way in which it dominates differs crucially from the way New York dominates the American cultural landscape. Toronto emphatically does not ingest new ideas from the hinterland into its great maw in the same manner New York does. Beers, who lived and worked in San Francisco for many years and watched the pattern occur over and over, says New York has a long tradition of accepting new ideas from the outlying regions. From populist uprisings such as the California tax revolt and the Reagan revolution to popular culture movements such as the hippies and the Sundance Film Festival, there is a tacit understanding of this relationship. Instead, what Beers says he sees from Toronto is different: "There is simply boredom and contempt toward anything outside of Toronto by Toronto."[45]

Not only are Beers, Campbell, MacKinnon, and Montgomery (and Vaillant) far enough away from the power center that they can develop their art in relative peace and isolation, they are also forced to look and shop their wares elsewhere, as the center's interest in their work goes only so far. It is not an easy decision to make, but they have chosen to live and work in an admittedly beautiful city, not to accept what they consider to be substandard assignments, and to continue to face the adversity of the freelance existence in exchange for the freedom to think and the freedom not to get caught in the grind of the corporate writing world. And that includes moving to Toronto with the ambition of becoming a writer or editor for *Maclean's* magazine, for example—in other words, working for Canada's largest corporate owner of consumer magazines, Rogers Media.

Coda: Contra the New New Journalism

One of the more surprising discoveries I made about West Coast writers is their wariness of Robert S. Boynton's book *The New New Journalism,* and in particular his championing of a specific kind of literary journalism structure: the process story.[46] Of the nineteen long-form magazine practitioners surveyed in Boynton's book, an inordinate number of them cite John McPhee as a major influence, or have been graduates of McPhee's writing seminars at Princeton University. For the literary journalists in Vancouver, this is too limiting. As MacKinnon says: "That stuff has become the 'Old New Journalism' pretty fast, because the form has fallen into a formula. They all do those breakaways where they tell you how the physics of waves works or something like that. John Vaillant's book is of that world, but he did something a little bit different with the mythmaking of the Haida. In John's case he let those breakaways take him to some pretty wild places in cosmology and myth."[47]

The criticism the FCC writers level at process stories is twofold. One, at some point in the narrative, and then for a considerable stretch of text, at least some readers automatically lose interest in the immediate topic at hand, or become bored outright. The reader may already know how the physics of waves works, for example. Or the reader might not be interested in knowing how the physics of waves works, and simply might not care. Then the reader has been lost to the writer because of an unhealthy indulgence in displaying to the reader that he or she has mastered this textbook-like material.

The second problem with the process structure in literary journalism, according to FCC writers, is the formula. To tell the story of a civilization obsessively through, say, the history of salt is a formula that can be repeated ad nauseam. Salt can be replaced by any number of products—ammunition, oranges, phonograph records—to the point where magazines and bookshelves are burdened with the form.

But the main contention raised against process writing is this: What is it for, exactly? McPhee can write tens of thousands of words about oranges, for example, but what does it mean? What greater truth is McPhee trying to capture? Although the passages may be beautifully written, MacKinnon argues that this point is never made clear in process writing.

Montgomery is also concerned that literary journalism might become too limited with the domination of one type of narrative. He absorbed this lesson about his writing early in his career when he defied the teachings of his journalism instructors in order to improve as a writer. They told him, "It is not about you." They commanded, "Thou shall not use 'I' in journalism." Montgomery calls the denial of the personal the "biggest lie" in journalism.[48] In fact, he thinks it is always about him to some degree. He admires writers who squeeze themselves out of their stories, but says the process of eliminating the self necessarily must involve some level of trickery: "This pretending that you are not affected by the stories you tell, it takes away your power to be an honest and engaged storyteller."[49]

When Beers was writing his memoir about growing up in Silicon Valley, it was one of the first pieces in which he had tried to inject his personal voice into the story. At the time, in the mid-1990s, he says the overwhelming success of Mary Karr's book *The Liar's Club* brought the form of the memoir back into the limelight, and he was searching for a new way to tell his story. He noticed that many memoirs insisted on telling the story from a psychological point of view, whereas he was more concerned with the sociological, or even anthropological, point of view. He says:

> I was trying to connect the socioeconomic, political-economic pressures that were coming to bear on this little family trapped in a home. I felt people wanted the writer located in the reporting. They want to know who you are. It's a postmodern idea: What's your class background? What's your formation? What's your value system? There's a difference between a Catholic and a Protestant in the way they're oriented to the world. It doesn't mean you're working off some religious diagram, but rather how was your brain programmed and what things are you filtering? People like narrative, and they like to compare and contrast their narrative with yours. So I kept trying to make the case for this thing I called the sociological memoir, or communal memoir.[50]

Beers developed his own version of the New Journalism, which he called the "personal reported essay." He used the adjective "personal" to signify that the writer is in the story. He used the adjective "reported" to emphasize the fact that the writer must be willing to conduct research and report. And he used the word "essay" to signify that the story being told was an attempt to define some kind of truth; not a grand claim to the "the truth," but "a truth." Following this recipe, Beers thinks, allows the reader to feel as if he or she is participating in "a communal imagination instead of seeing you as a lone actor."[51]

Beers's analysis of what makes this type of journalism work for the reader could easily be applied to the work of the FCC. There is, however, one important caveat, which is to avoid the temptations of the mythmaking impulse. Beers wonders whether Kapuściński did not occasionally fall prey to this syndrome, while MacKinnon believes that Paul William Roberts has succumbed to it as well. Montgomery articulated his personal need to remain wary of the impulse:

> There is an ongoing tension in people who write nonfiction narrative between the impulse to report and the mythmaking impulse, which compels us to tell great stories that will change us and others—stories that reveal the truths of the human soul inside the narrative. The stranger, the more passionate the stories are, the more we want of them. When someone says something outrageous, something you know they don't necessarily believe in, and doesn't represent their general worldview, you're tempted to use it because it sounds great and it works well. Unless it's honestly telling, I try to avoid using that sort of material.[52]

As the writer shifts through his or her material, one of the clearest differences between West and East is the how the story is approached. In Vancouver writing, the search is more important than an overriding theme. In the beginning, the germ of the idea—the nut-graph, or signpost, or theme, or thesis—might be rather mundane; it is only in the search that the really remarkable nuggets start to shine through. This goes back to the true nature of the story. What is the story about? Does the writer actually know what the story is about? In Toronto publications, where stories are almost universally editor-driven, the editors want to know up front who the characters in the drama are going to be. The editors want to know that the reporter will cover the drama from all sides. The editors want to know who the narrator is. All of this must be known at the query letter stage. And the editors will ask for a theme when the writer quite honestly does not yet know the exact nature of the theme. Campbell says she rarely, if ever, knows what the story is immediately. The whole point of doing the research is to find out what the story is. "Otherwise, why would I be there?" she asks. "If there's no search, there's no answer. In writing my book I had to answer a lot of questions for myself. I did not expect what I got. I had an inkling, but that's it."[53]

The tussle for editorial control of the story that FCC writers seem often to find themselves engaged in may sound like just another skirmish in the long war between editors and writers. But they are young, talented, and winning recognition and awards, which perhaps gives them a trifle more clout. Their matter-of-fact admission that they still have a long way to go in terms of becoming masters of the genre is also echoed in their belief that Canada's narrative nonfiction writing is sorely lacking in innovation. They believe that nonfiction writing took chances during the 1960s and 1970s with the New Journalism, but a long-simmering lack of trust in its nonfictional veracity killed the experimentation by the 1980s. The newer form, the New New Journalism, might be scrupulously fact-checked, but it is also sober and restrained. The FCC must fight it out with editors, and yet it is also editors who can save literary journalism in Canada. After all, it was a collection of a few open-minded, frustrated editors in the 1950s and 1960s that led to the arrival of the New Journalism and its wild stylistic flourishes at *Esquire* magazine and the *New York* supplement to the *Herald Tribune* in the first place.

NOTES

1. John Vaillant, "The Ship That Vanished," *New Yorker,* October 11, 1999, 44–54.

2. For more on Vaillant, see my essay "A Metaphor for the World: William Langewiesche, John Vaillant and Looking for the Story in Long-form," *Asia Pacific Media Educator* (Special Issue: *Narrative and Literary Journalism*) 18 (December 2007): 59–71.

3. John Vaillant, personal interview, Vancouver, August 25, 2005.

4. Gerald Hannon, "Keen Eddie," *Toronto Life,* May 2005, 50–57.

5. For more on what I call the "fish out of water" trick in the New Journalism, see my article "Recovering the Peculiar Life and Times of Tom Hedley and of Canadian New Journalism," *Literary Journalism Studies* 1.1 (Spring 2009): 79–104.

6. Anne Kingston and Nicholas Kohler, "Canada's Richest Family, the Thomsons, Are Worth $23.8 Billion . . . And They're Just a Little Bit Strange: An Inside Story of Messy Divorce, Private Eyes, a Special Baby, Botox, Nanny Dress Codes, Vindictive Timing and Fine Art," *Maclean's,* May 8, 2006, 22–32.

7. *Maclean's,* February 23, 2009, 1.

8. Marc Weingarten, *The Gang That Wouldn't Write Straight: Wolfe, Thompson, Didion, and the New Journalism Revolution* (New York: Crown Publishers, 2006), 213. Weingarten recounts a conversation between Tom Wolfe and *New York* magazine publisher George Hirsch in which Wolfe says, "Well, of course, George! It's about status, and status in the number one concern of New Yorkers" (213).

9. Vaillant, personal interview.

10. Ibid.

11. Vancouver, of course, has its own glossy city magazine, *Vancouver,* which under the guidance of former *Toronto Life* senior editor Gary Stephen Ross has indeed provided a typical menu of city fare (service journalism, profiles of local politicians, and so on).

12. Charles Montgomery, *The Last Heathen: Encounters with Ghosts and Ancestors in Melanesia* (Vancouver: Douglas & McIntyre, 2004). Montgomery substantially rewrote portions of the book and then watched his work go through another round of editing before it was published in the United States under the title *The Shark God: Encounters with Ghosts and Ancestors in the South Pacific* (New York: HarperCollins, 2006). Montgomery told me that HarperCollins marketers felt they needed to change the title because they believed the U.S. publishing market might be hostile to the word "heathen."

13. The Charles Taylor Prize for Literary Non-fiction is not an insignificant award in Canada, as the winning author takes home a check for $25,000.

14. James MacKinnon, personal interview, Vancouver, April 5, 2006.

15. Perhaps even stranger, two out of the three jurors were holdovers from the previous year, when Montgomery's book was chosen.

16. Lynne Van Luven, "Twenty Years beyond Definition: How the Practice of Literary Journalism in Canada Has Assumed New Guises," conference paper, Second International Association for Literary Journalism Studies Conference, Sciences Po, Paris, May 18–19, 2007.

17. Deborah Campbell, personal interview, Vancouver, April 5, 2006.

18. *The Walrus,* which was launched in October 2003, is an attempt to bring the quality and ambition of *Harper's,* the *Atlantic,* and the *New Yorker* to Canada. Results have been inconsistent—sometimes excellent, sometimes befuddling—yet it has won more National Magazine Awards (forty-seven Gold as of 2010) than any other Canadian magazine over this period of time.

19. *explore* magazine is a less lavish version—in terms of both its design and the size of its editorial feature well—of the American adventure magazine *Outside.* Its editor James Little, however, is a great believer in literary journalism and has endeavored to include one piece of long-form writing in every issue.

20. James Little, ed., *Way Out There: The Best of explore* (Toronto: Greystone Books, 2006).

21. Ian Brown, "The Boys and the Backcountry," ibid., 277–92.

22. Petti Fong, "Vancouver 'Most Livable' Again," *Globe and Mail,* October 4, 2005.

23. Greg Buium, "Fellow Travellers: Six West Coast Writers Looking to Reinvent Journalism," CBC.ca, available at www.cbc.ca/arts/books/fellowtravellers.html.

24. Campbell, personal interview.

25. Deborah Campbell, *This Heated Place: Encounters in the Promised Land* (Vancouver: Douglas & McIntyre, 2003).

26. Campbell, personal interview.

27. Ibid.

28. David Beers, personal interview with the editor of *The Tyee,* April 6, 2006.

29. Campbell, personal interview.

30. Beers, personal interview.

31. The term was coined by Robert S. Boynton for the anthology he edited, *The New New Journalism* (New York: Vintage Books, 2005). See also Boynton, "Drilling into the Bedrock of Ordinary Experience," *Chronicle of Higher Education,* March 4, 2005, B10–11.

32. Ryszard Kapuściński, *The Shadow of the Sun,* trans. Klara Glowczewska (Toronto: Vin-

tage Canada, 2002), and *The Soccer War,* trans. William R. Brand (Toronto: Vintage Reprint Edition, 1992).

33. See especially Paul William Roberts, "Saddam's Inferno: In Baghdad Things Go from Bad to Worse," *Harper's,* May 1996, 48–58; and "Beyond Baghdad: Lost in the Cradle of Civilization," *Harper's,* July 2003, 68–73.

34. Charles Montgomery, personal interview, Vancouver, April 4, 2006.

35. Campbell, personal interview.

36. Montgomery, personal interview.

37. MacKinnon, personal interview.

38. Campbell, personal interview.

39. Ibid.

40. Ibid.

41. Montgomery, personal interview.

42. The "East" connotes Toronto, or central Canada, or even the Toronto-Ottawa corridor. Westerners often refer to Torontonians as easterners, although this is technically inaccurate, since Toronto is geographically situated in the center of the country. It also has a tendency to upset those living in genuinely "eastern" Canadian urban centers, such as Montreal, Quebec; Halifax, Nova Scotia; Fredericton, New Brunswick; Charlottetown, Prince Edward Island; and St. John's, Newfoundland.

43. Beers, personal interview.

44. MacKinnon, personal interview.

45. Beers, personal interview.

46. Here I am thinking of stories that explain how things work—a regional airport, or Coca-Cola—or how personal computers are built with parts made in several different countries, say, as opposed to the profile or the anatomy of an event.

47. MacKinnon, personal interview.

48. Montgomery, personal interview.

49. Ibid.

50. Beers, personal interview.

51. Ibid.

52. Ibid.

53. Campbell, personal interview.

Chapter 4

The Counter-Coriolis Effect

Contemporary Literary Journalism in a Shrinking World

David Abrahamson

I MUST CONFESS that with this essay, I hope to start an argument, to present more questions than answers, to offer a provocation. If, dear reader, you will permit a moment's digression, it might be helpful if I shared an aside or two suggesting just how modest my goals are.

Early in my career in the academy, one of my mentors made what I thought then—and still believe today—to be a telling observation about scholarship. He said that even though all of the scholarly effort attempts actually to create new knowledge, perhaps as little as 10 percent of what is produced results in something truly valuable: concepts that other scholars might build on, ideas that are incorporated into the canon, knowledge that proves to be of actual value. At the other end of the value scale, he said, there is the vast mass of the scholarly product, perhaps as much as 80 percent of the total output, which—though it may count as an item on a vita or may be part of a tenure or promotion portfolio—is actually of quite modest value. At very best, it will be cited infrequently by later scholars; much more likely, not at all.

And then, he said, there is the remaining 10 percent, below the upper 10 and above the lower 80. The work here will probably not end up in anyone's canon. It will not be celebrated fifty, or even five, years from now. But it does, at a minimum, raise interesting arguments and pose useful questions that may be of service to others, though the actual conclusions themselves may not be of the highest order. With respect to this essay, I can say with some confidence that it will not be regarded as a candidate for the top 10 percent. And if I am lucky, it will not find its place in the lower 80. It is therefore my hope that, fortune willing, it will be allowed to rest comfortably in the middle range. As I have already confessed, I am here to start an argument.

Literary Journalism Goes Global

The title of this essay, with its invention of a presumed "Counter-Coriolis Effect," is an obvious conceit. With all due deference to Monsieur Coriolis, I have unabashedly appropriated the name of a phenomenon in the geophysical world to describe one whose existence I will hypothesize in the world of arts and letters.[1] It is, of course, an imaginary construct, but one I hope might have some heuristic purpose. First, however, a bit of context might be helpful.

Despite the economic turmoil and discontinuities of recent times, it is likely that Thomas L. Friedman, author of *The Lexus and the Olive Tree* and *The World Is Flat,* is correct.[2] For much of the world today, the primary reality for the foreseeable future will continue to be globalization, in all its forms: political, social, cultural, and economic. The world is most certainly shrinking.[3]

If this is true, then the question arises: What, if any, might be the journalistic dimensions of this phenomenon? Is there, in effect, a journalistic aspect to globalization? And if, at least for the sake of argument, one posits that such a journalistic dimension exists, what then would be the role of literary journalism in the consideration of journalism as a whole? Following this axis of inquiry leads one to examine literary journalism in a relatively novel light: one that allows us to consider the genre from what might be termed a deliberately geopolitical perspective.

This attempt may not actually be as strange as it sounds. Literary journalism, after all, most certainly has the potential for profound long-term, even world-historical effects. I doubt there is much disagreement on this point, simply because there are so many apt examples: *Silent Spring* by Rachel Carson and the emergence of a global environmental awareness;[4] John Hersey's *Hiroshima* and the ban-the-bomb movement in the United States, Europe, and elsewhere;[5] and more recently the dispatches by Seymour Hirsch about Abu Ghraib prison in Iraq and the changing tide of public opinion about the American misadventure in that country.[6]

With this in mind, it seems fairly safe to posit that literary journalism can both shape and reflect larger social, cultural, and political currents—at the regional level, at the national level, and perhaps even at the international level. And it is in consideration of these larger currents that one peculiar aspect seems to be evident. Simply for taxonomic purposes, it can arguably be given a name: the Counter-Coriolis Effect.

As we all might possibly remember from our grammar school geography class, the Coriolis Effect, in its simplest possible interpretation, says that geophysical phenomena—ocean currents, global winds, and so on—tend to deflect to the right in the Northern Hemisphere and to the left in the Southern Hemisphere. As a starting point for this discussion, then, let us posit, in literary journalism, the existence of a Counter-Coriolis Effect. The claim is that some evidence can be found for the argument that in the Northern Hemisphere (that is, the North, or the developed world), there is a tendency generally for much literary journalism to represent views from the left side of the political spectrum; the authors' perspectives can often be characterized as progressive, secular, reformist, and critical of existing institutions. In the South (or the developing world), however, a fair amount of literary journalism tends to perceive reality from a rightist point of view. The perspective is often conservative, traditionalist, and self-critical. The resulting question, of course, remains: Is this indeed the case, and if so, why? And finally, could this bear on the possibility that literary journalism in all its forms might contribute to an emerging global conversation?

Literary Journalism and Geopolitics

I freely confess that there are many problems with my thesis. Some of the difficulties arise from what can be called the Micro-to-Macro Fallacy. Projecting inferences drawn from the examination of the particular to reach conclusions about a larger generality almost by definition presents causal problems. Any certainty becomes more than a little elusive. Nevertheless, rather than argue for the absolute truth of my premise, there might instead be value in simply having a conversation, just to see where it leads. As we embark, we might find inspiration in Jay Rosen's *What Are Journalists For?*, which artfully addresses the underlying questions of purpose.[7] Why does journalism exist? Why does it exist in the manner it does? My hope is that our conversation can illuminate some of these issues, as well as perhaps the very purposes of literary journalism.

Let us begin with an examination of the developed world—the North, the industrial West. Allow me to suggest a few names, in addition to those already mentioned, of contemporary literary journalists of some prominence. My list would include Sally Tisdale from *Harper's* Magazine,[8] Frank Rich of the *New York Times*,[9] Ian Frazier from the *New Yorker*,[10] as well as Charlie LeDuff of the *Detroit News*[11] and William Langewiesche of *Vanity Fair*.[12] Also from the *New Yorker*, Katherine Boo certainly qualifies,[13] as does one of my favorites, the brief yet powerful political essays of Hendrik Hertzberg.[14] All these authors write from a progressivist perspective. One of the reasons for this is that, at least in American journalism and the press in the United Kingdom, there has long been a reformist impulse. Indeed, the implicit goal of the profession to some is, in the oft-quoted words of Finley Peter Dunne's Mr. Dooley, to "comfort the afflicted and afflict the comfortable."[15]

On the other side of the coin, in the developing world, the South, there are writers who clearly produce nonfiction work of the highest literary quality, but they have often not been on the left. Authors of great acclaim, masters such as V. S. Naipaul,[16] Derek Walcott,[17] and Mario Vargas Llosa[18] come to mind, all of whom have rarely, if ever, manifested this reformist perspective. If only for purely descriptive purposes, this is the Counter-Coriolis Effect in action.

The interesting questions, of course, lie in the realm of the reasons and rationale behind the phenomenon. In the case of the North, what animates the reformist impulse on the part of journalists? A number of factors must be at play. First, there is a demand for it in the sense that it is desired by their readers—and therefore also by their editors.[19] Second, it is politically and culturally permissible; in the absence of censorship, the writers are allowed the necessary independence. And lastly, there is a certain self-sustaining and self-fulfilling quality to it. If one writes in the hope of trying to right wrongs or to make the world a better place, and if it is possible that what one writes might be acted upon, then the possibility of actual improvement—of, in a word, progress—is, I suspect, the most powerful motivation of all.

In contrast, I suspect that much of the contemporary literary journalism in the South, in the developing world, bears a special burden, a significant portion of which is derived from the ongoing struggle to come to grips with the harsh realities of postcolonialism. Why, in the absence of the former oppressors, does so much human potential still remain unrealized? The result is a genre of literary journalism in the South that is quite self-critical, driven in part by a bleaker view of human nature and of the prospects for progress itself.

And yet, as we are so often told, the world is becoming a smaller place—connected by transportation and, more important, information technology in ways it has never been before. "Hot, flat, and crowded," in the words of Thomas Friedman.[20] To attempt a sociocultural prediction about the twenty-first century that perhaps even a physicist such as Coriolis might appreciate, I am confident that not only will change continue to be a constant, but also the rate of change itself will continue to accelerate. It is possible that one conceivable outcome will be something we can all applaud. The social and economic disparities between North and South will decrease over time, and as a probable byproduct, what I have—admittedly half in jest—called the

Counter-Coriolis Effect will diminish in force. As a result, the place of literary journalism in this shrinking world might grow to be a notably laudable one. And I would argue that it is quite an uplifting prospect to imagine the possibility that there will be an important role for long-form narrative nonfiction in the much-needed and far-reaching global conversation that awaits us all.

NOTES

1. Gaspard-Gustave de Coriolis (1792–1843), a mathematician and physicist, published his most influential work, *Du calcul de l'effet des machines* (Calculation of the Effect of Machines), in 1829. Although he did pioneer the study of kinetic energy in rotating systems, his name was not associated with the now famous geophysical effect until early in the twentieth century.

2. Thomas Friedman is a widely traveled foreign affairs columnist for the *New York Times.* As noted, two of his books explicating his ideas on globalization are *The Lexus and the Olive Tree* (New York: Farrar, Straus & Giroux, 1999) and *The World Is Flat: A Brief History of the Twenty-first Century* (New York: Farrar, Straus & Giroux, 2005).

3. There are, of course, those who dissent from the notion of the inevitability of globalization. Two of the better known are Walden Bello, *Deglobalization: Ideas for a New World Economy* (New York: Zed Books, 2002); and Naomi Klein, *Shock Doctrine: The Rise of Disaster Capitalism* (New York: Henry Holt, 2007).

4. Rachel Carson's *Silent Spring* (Boston: Houghton Mifflin, 1962) is often cited as one of the seminal texts of a new environmentalist awareness which emerged in the mid-twentieth century.

5. *Hiroshima* was originally published as a magazine article, filling much of the August 31, 1946, issue of the *New Yorker.* It appeared shortly thereafter in book form: John Hersey, *Hiroshima* (New York: Alfred A. Knopf, 1946). It is interesting to note that in a survey ranking the one hundred most influential works of twentieth-century American journalism, *Hiroshima* is rated number one, and *Silent Spring* is number two. See www.nyu.edu/classes/stephens/Top%20100%20page.htm.

6. With his exposure of conditions at Abu Ghraib prison in Iraq, Seymour Hersh was reprising his highly influential report on atrocities in Vietnam almost thirty-five years earlier. See both Seymour Hersh, *Chain of Command: The Road from 9/11 to Abu Ghraib* (New York: HarperCollins, 2004), and *My Lai 4: A Report on the Massacre and Its Aftermath* (New York: Random House, 1970).

7. See Jay Rosen, *What Are Journalists For?* (New Haven: Yale University Press, 1999).

8. Sallie Tisdale has an uncanny ability to obscure the line, to wonderful effect, between the personal and the public in her nonfiction work. Two commendable examples are *Talk Dirty to Me: An Intimate Philosophy of Sex* (New York: Doubleday, 1994), and *The Sorcerer's Apprentice: Medical Miracles and Other Disasters* (Washington, D.C.: Beard Books, 2002).

9. Frank Rich, a longtime cultural and political critic at the *New York Times,* was perhaps the most persistently harsh reviewer of the policies of the administration of President George W. Bush. See his book *The Greatest Story Ever Sold: The Decline and Fall of Truth from 9/11 to Katrina* (New York: Penguin, 2006).

10. Ian Frazier's subject terrain is often the less traveled regions of the United States, as well as the less fortunate people who live there. See his *Great Plains* (New York: Farrar, Straus & Giroux, 1989), and *On the Rez* (New York: Farrar, Straus & Giroux, 2000).

11. Charlie LeDuff writes of the travails of the American working class. See his *Us Guys: The True and Twisted Mind of the American Man* (New York: Penguin, 2006), and *Work and Other Sins: Life in New York City and Thereabouts* (New York: Penguin, 2004).

12. William Langewiesche produced the definitive account of New York City's "ground zero." See his *American Ground: Unbuilding the World Trade Center* (New York: North Point Press, 2002).

13. Katherine Boo is a regular contributor to the *New Yorker*. Information on her articles is available at www.newyorker.com/magazine/bios/katherine_boo/search?contributorName=katherine%20boo.

14. A longtime staff writer at the *New Yorker*, Hendrik Hertzberg has often written the lead item focusing on contemporary public affairs in the publication's "Talk of the Town" section. For a collection of these essays, see Hendrik Hertzberg, *Politics: Observations and Arguments, 1966–2004* (New York: Penguin, 2004).

15. Finley Peter Dunne (1867–1936) wrote a nationally syndicated newspaper column using the satirical voice of fictional "Mr. Dooley," an outspoken and somewhat caustic first-generation Irish American bar owner. For more details on the "comfort the afflicted and afflict the comfortable" quote, see www.poynter.org/column.asp?id=1&aid=2852. For an interesting biography of Dunne, see Charles Fanning, *Finley Peter Dunne & Mr. Dooley: The Chicago Years* (Lexington: University of Kentucky Press, 1978).

16. V. S. Naipaul's illiberal and seeringly self-critical voice has been manifest in a number of his works, including *Among the Believers: An Islamic Journey* (New York: Vintage Books, 1981); *India: A Wounded Civilization* (New York: Vintage Books, 1977); and a collection of his nonfiction short stories, *The Return of Eva Peron, with The Killings in Trinidad* (New York: Alfred A. Knopf, 1980).

17. See Derek Walcott, *What the Twilight Says: Essays* (New York: Farrar, Straus & Giroux, 1998).

18. See Mario Vargas Llosa, *A Fish in the Water: A Memoir* (New York: Farrar, Straus & Giroux, 1994).

19. It might be worth noting in passing that one of the very interesting yet underresearched areas in literary journalism studies is the role that "the market" plays as a factor in cultural production. The economic interrelationships between reader, text, publication, editor, and author are certainly ripe for further investigation.

20. The phrase is appropriated from the title of Thomas Friedman's *Hot, Flat, and Crowded: Why We Need a Green Revolution, and How It Can Renew America* (New York: Farrar, Straus & Giroux, 2008).

Chapter 5

The Evolutionary Future of American and International Literary Journalism

NORMAN SIMS

IN 1935 JOSEPH NORTH, who was editor of *The New Masses* in Greenwich Village during the Great Depression, understood how important literary journalism was. He said that literary journalism—or what at the time he called "reportage"—was "three-dimensional" reporting. "The writer not only condenses reality," North said, but also "helps the reader feel the fact. The finest writers of reportage are artists in the fullest sense of the term. They do their editorializing through their imagery."[1]

If North were around to look at the world today, he'd find literary journalism or reportage just as important now as it was then. But I wonder how—and where—it's going to survive. At no time in American history has literary journalism been a primary or dominant form of journalism—not in North's time nor in ours. By the 1920s, standard objective journalism had achieved dominance in American reporting and pushed aside the literary ambitions of writers.

In the history of American literary journalism there have been several turning points where a few select writers moved the craft of literary journalism forward. These moments included such times as:

- the rise of mass circulation urban newspapers in the 1890s
- reporting on World War I
- the traveling of expatriates in Europe after the war
- writing about the Great Depression of the 1930s, or what North called reportage, and the documentary photography of that era
- the New Journalism of the 1960s

And so on. But at no time were those innovators a majority among journalists. Compared to the meat-and-potatoes dinner of standard objective journalism, literary journalism has always been nothing more than a salad or dessert.

I believe we are at another turning point, at least in American literary journalism, which, as many essays in this book attest, will likely affect the practice of literary journalism throughout the world. In fact, some developments in contemporary American literary journalism, both good and bad, may quickly be found at the international level. Innovations spread like viruses in today's world. We can read international journalism daily—something that was never possible before—and we can Google particular authors. Soon there may be automatic translations available. But finding economic support for literary journalism, given the time and labor it takes to produce, will continue to be a problem everywhere. American writers face challenges. This may also be an opportunity for international literary journalists to lead the way.

The Troubles Literary Journalism Faces Today

Several American newspapers have taken "narrative" to heart, including the *Oregonian* and *St. Petersburg Times,* and that's good news for literary journalism. Some have "narrative units" where writers can be assigned for a while. The narrative newsroom may be a way of ensuring that print journalism can survive the Internet age—attracting readers with literature rather than shopping coupons.[2]

This attention at newspapers testifies to the literary power of the form. But unfortunately, even when the movement has real strength at newspapers, literary journalism still faces traditional limits in the amount of *time* a newspaper reporter can spend on a story about ordinary life, the *space* a newspaper can provide for that report, and the *money* provided to support it. Time, space, and money always gave magazines such as the *New Yorker* an advantage over newspapers. But changes are happening at the magazines that once provided an oasis for literary journalism in a desert of objective reporting.

At the *New Yorker,* for instance, the original editors, Harold Ross and William Shawn, had an artistic vision for fact writing. Their magazine was a cathedral built around literary journalism. The staff included literary journalists such as Janet Flanner, Joseph Mitchell, A. J. Liebling, Lillian Ross, John McPhee, Susan Sheehan, Frances Fitzgerald, Calvin Trillin, and more recently Mark Singer, Ian Frazier, Susan Orlean, Nicholas Lemann, and at times Ted Conover, Adrian Nicole LeBlanc, Tracy Kidder, and Jonathan Harr.

Today, some of those old-school writers remain—Singer and Orlean, even McPhee, Ross, and Trillin sometimes—although only rarely does their current work rise to the level of literary journalism. The hot new staff writers at the *New Yorker* are closer to essayists, such as Malcolm Gladwell, author of *The Tipping Point, Blink,* and *Outliers.* The writers with the narrative portfolio, such as Katherine Boo or Larissa MacFarquhar, often treat narrative as a technique to make social policy points rather than as something valuable in itself. They may use narrative structures, but generally only as scenes in a policy discussion.

Writers use the term "reported essay" for something that marries narrative and analysis. Katherine Boo's 2005 *New Yorker* portrait of ordinary people from Louisiana, for instance, was really focused on the policy issues surrounding the hot topic of New Orleans after Hurricane Katrina. Writers tell me that genuine portraits of ordinary people can't get much traction at the *New Yorker* or the *Atlantic* today. The younger writers at the cathedral of the *New Yorker*—meaning those under forty—are more comfortable on the intellectual side, more comfortable editorializing. Those over fifty tend to be more purely literary.

The powerhouse magazines for literary journalism—the *New Yorker, Esquire,* even *Outside* magazine—have gone through cycles as their editors changed. Right now, the world of literary journalism at American magazines seems fragmented. Writers move, as Michael Paterniti did, from *Outside* to *Esquire* to *GQ* (*Gentlemen's Quarterly,* a men's fashion magazine), following migrating editors. Right now, I don't see the magazine equivalent of a cathedral for literary journalism such as the *New Yorker* was from the 1930s to the 1980s and beyond. If there are no cathedrals, some chapels exist, particularly since the *New Yorker, Vanity Fair,* and *GQ* still pay high prices for quality articles by leading writers.

The upward way for literary journalists has always been to write books. It's still true, but even that refuge has changed. Books were once fertile ground where literary journalists with some experience could get a $300,000 advance, as Joe Nocera did, and work for three or four years on a project. But now book advances have fallen to the point—more like $40,000 for an experienced writer—where the money no longer supports a two- or three-year project. Thus the financial risk of a literary journalism book has shifted from the publishers to the writers, and especially so for younger writers. It may nevertheless be easier now to publish a book of literary journalism than a commercial magazine article, if the writer is willing to bear the burden of financial risk.

What Price Literary Journalism?

The challenge today may be more economic than literary.

Somehow, literary journalists have always found a way to publish their work. The form flourishes on new beginnings and at the margins of the marketplace. This may be a moment when journalistic experimentation and literary journalism will find hospitable conditions in new media and in markets outside North America.

Everyone involved in journalism has an eye on the Internet as a transformative medium. The Web is cheap and marginal, as magazines such as *Rolling Stone* and *New York* were in the 1960s. And the Web is global, opening up far larger audiences for literary journalism, especially if works can be translated.

It may come to pass that we will figure out how to read long pieces of literary journalism on the computer screen. Right now, we don't.[3] People typically won't read anything longer than three computer screens on the Web, and it really should be only one screen in length. Short Web-length articles sacrifice complicated structure, characterization, and scenes. Short reports make the time and expense of immersion reporting seem not worth the trouble. Blogs are usually one screen in length, assuming you don't read the commentary that follows, and they may contain voice, attitude, and personality, all possible attributes of literary journalism. But blogs lack the reporting required in literary journalism. In the future—who can predict?—we might find a way to read literary journalism on the Web or on new digital e-books.

Even if that happens, the larger challenge will be finding an economic model for literary journalism on the Internet. In January 2009 David Carr, writing in the *New York Times,* said that we could expect a large-screen reading device with a nine-inch screen; two years earlier, Amazon had teased us with its Kindle, but Apple delivered on the promise by introducing its iPad in early 2010. "It sounds promising for newspapers and magazines," said Carr. "Now all we need is a business model to go with it."[4] It's the age-old Iron Rule of getting published and earning a living:

Information on the Web wants to be free.[5]
But writers want to be paid.

We need only a little spice to make a tasty meal. For literary journalism to survive, however, the financial conditions have to be just right. I fear that some conditions are failing—particularly book advances, and the reliability of magazines as a platform for literary journalism.

Literary Journalism Revindicated

There is also some good news.

The younger writers who think of narrative techniques as old-school tools may find themselves experimenting with voice. A flat narrative voice doesn't work well with ordinary subjects. The technical problems of voice and tone are constant. Never-ending opportunities exist for creative growth. Having mastered the reporting tools, young writers may again consider the literary side of their craft. History is on our side.

When we look back at the American journalism of the past century or more—journalism that remains informative and viable and influential on the world stage—we discover that the leading texts were literary journalism. We find:

- Jack London writing about poverty, tramping, and Alaska
- John Reed writing about wars in Mexico and eastern Europe, and revolution in Russia
- Ernest Hemingway, Reed, and John Dos Passos writing from Europe about World War I and its aftermath
- James Agee, Edmund Wilson, Martha Gellhorn, and George Orwell writing about the Great Depression and war in Europe
- John Hersey on Hiroshima
- Joseph Mitchell, A. J. Liebling, and Lillian Ross creating cultural portraits in the *New Yorker*
- Tom Wolfe, Gay Talese, Truman Capote, Hunter S. Thompson, Michael Herr, and Joan Didion writing experimental narratives during the turbulent 1960s
- Tracy Kidder, Susan Orlean, John McPhee, Jane Kramer, Ted Conover, Michael Paterniti, Frances Fitzgerald, Jonathan Harr, Doug Whynott, Adrian Nicole LeBlanc, and many others who have created portraits of everyday life and of cultural communities in recent years

For me, writing these names is like reading the menu in a restaurant. I can taste the flavors; I can hear their voices in my head.

At the end of the last century, a New York University journalism department project, headed by the historian Mitchell Stevens, constructed a list of the one hundred best works of twentieth-century American journalism.[6] On that list of one hundred texts, at least forty-one were works of literary journalism. All the main forms of journalism—muckraking, objective journalism, and investigative reporting—were represented and helped to create a journalistic portrait of the past hundred years.

But this time literary journalism dominated. John Hersey's *Hiroshima* was the top item on the list, which also included John Reed's *Ten Days That Shook the World,* James Agee and Walker Evans's *Let Us Now Praise Famous Men,* W. E. B. Du Bois's *Souls of Black Folk,* and Lillian Ross's *Reporting.* Tom Wolfe, Norman Mailer, Truman Capote, Michael Herr, Hunter S. Thompson, and Joan Didion were on the list, as were Ernest Hemingway, J. Anthony Lukas,

John McPhee, Joseph Mitchell, Jane Kramer, Martha Gellhorn, and A. J. Liebling. On this list of the twentieth century's best, literary journalism was the main course rather than a side dish.

Toward an International Literary Journalism

International literary journalism has gained audiences even in countries that do not have a Western press system or a democratic government. In its ability to portray characters with real emotions and the drama of everyday life, literary journalism has a natural advantage that almost ensures its survival even in harsh conditions.

Historically, literary journalism has provided the intimacy, subtlety, and artistry we need to understand the times in which we live. The ordinary characters, the immersion reporting, the craft and artistry in the writing, the recognition of complicated problems in representing reality—all these give literary journalism a lasting quality when the interest in momentary details has passed.

Literary journalism will always be there, I hope, despite the challenges it faces. The quest for the future may be in discovering *where* it will appear.

NOTES

This essay was originally presented in different form as the keynote address at the Second International Association for Literary Journalism Studies Conference, Sciences Po, Paris, May 18–19, 2007.

1. Joseph North, "Reportage," in *American Writer's Congress,* ed. Henry Hart (New York: International, 1935), 121. On the term "reportage," see also chapter 1 in this volume, John C. Hartsock, "Literary Reportage: The 'Other' Literary Journalism."

2. On literary journalism at newspapers, see John C. Hartsock, "'It Was a Dark and Stormy Night': Newspaper Reporters Rediscover the Art of Narrative Literary Journalism and Their Own Epistemological Heritage," *Prose Studies* 29.2 (August 2007): 257–84. See also Paul Many, "Literary Journalism: Newspapers' Last, Best Hope," *Connecticut Review* 18.1 (Spring 1996): 59–69.

3. The iPad, Kindle, Sony Reader, and other similar devices have been touted as revolutionary new approaches to reading, and they are attracting a mass following. The literary journalist Tracy Kidder told me he believes that the book printed on paper has a long future. There may be generational differences, but so far, many people find reading long texts on their computer screens unappealing. E-book readers such as the iPad or Kindle have a better interface, and they also carry the advantage of paying the writer for the book.

4. David Carr, "Let's Invent an iTunes for News," *New York Times* online, January 11, 2009, available at www.nytimes.com/2009/01/12/business/media/12carr.html .

5. "Information wants to be free" is a phrase that perhaps originated with the writer Stewart Brand.

6. The "Top 100 Works of Journalism in the United States in the 20th Century" was compiled at New York University and selected by a panel consisting of Madeleine Blais, Alan Brinkley, David Brinkley, Lydia Chavez, Karen Durbin, Clay Felker, Jeff Greenfield, Pete Hamill, Nancy Maynard, Mary McGrory, Eric Newton, Dorothy Rabinowitz, Gene Roberts, Morley Safer, David Shaw, George Will, and Ben Yagoda; and by the New York University Journalism faculty, including David Dent, Todd Gitlin, Lamar Graham, Brooke Kroeger, Susie Linfield, Michael Ludlum, Robert Manoff, Anne Matthews, Pamela Newkirk, Michael Norman, Richard Petrow, Mary Quigley, Marcia Rock, Jay Rosen, Stephen Solomon, Mitchell Stephens, Carol Sternhell, Jane Stone, and Ellen Willis. The list can be found at www.nyu.edu/classes/stephens/Top%20100%20page.htm.

Part II
Journalistic Traditions

Chapter 6

Dutch Literary Journalism

From Pamphlet to Newspaper (ca. 1600–1900)

CLAZINA DINGEMANSE AND RUTGER DE GRAAF

WHEN EXPLORING the field of literary journalism, one undoubtedly encounters Tom Wolfe's volume *The New Journalism*. In one section called "Is the New Journalism Really New?" Wolfe discusses several possible early examples of literary journalism. He focuses primarily on eighteenth-, nineteenth-, and twentieth-century novelists, concluding that while some could definitely be considered "not half-bad candidates," literary journalism in general did not come into its own until the twentieth century.[1]

Our intent here is to reexamine Wolfe's question of early examples of proto-literary journalism by taking a closer look at the popular pamphlet press. The intermingling of literary techniques, fiction, reality, and news was a familiar characteristic of early modern pamphleteering in western Europe. Because of its long history as a varied news medium, the pamphlet is sometimes considered to be the "predecessor of the features, editorials, serials, personal columns, human interest stories, and news reports of our newspapers and magazines."[2]

In this essay we examine the literary techniques that were used in pamphlets from the late sixteenth to the nineteenth century, focusing specifically on the traces of literary pamphleteering in the nineteenth-century newspaper. We argue that, during a time of journalistic experimentation, routines and journalistic genres were "borrowed" from this century-old predecessor to be used in the newspaper. This process of reinventing journalistic practices has been called remediation.[3] Because new media tend to take over typical characteristics of older media, the older media must adapt in order to survive. If they risk losing some of their old characteristics in the process, they gain new ones as well, catering to different audience needs to find a niche in which to exist.

To discuss the changing European media landscape, we focus on the Netherlands for two main reasons. First, Dutch pamphlet production has been well documented. Second, historical studies show that the growth of Dutch pamphleteering and the inception of newspapers were symptomatic of wider changes taking place in the written media of other western European countries, notably France, Germany, and Britain. Therefore an examination of the development of and literary techniques in Dutch pamphlets in particular may very well shed light on the historical evolution of European literary journalism in general.

The Pamphlet: A Varied Platform for News and Opinion

Pamphleteering started in the sixteenth century during the religious conflicts that were spreading across Europe. The early German Reformers understood the potential of the printing press and used it to reach and address a broad and varied audience. The printed propaganda of the German Reformation soon reached far and wide and began influencing the growth of the popular pamphlet press elsewhere in Europe. The pamphlet established itself as part of the literary scene by the end of the sixteenth century. These booklets were noticed by contemporary observers and were considered a literary novelty.[4]

In the seventeenth century, pamphleteering grew to a remarkable scale: the pamphlet became the primary mass medium for communicating news and opinion throughout western Europe. As one Dutch pamphleteer said in 1650, "I don't know what I am more surprised about: the quantity and abundance [of pamphlets], or the differences of opinion in the same amount."[5] Pamphlets did not replace other, often quicker sources of disseminating news, such as oral communication and handwritten letters. But within days after a newsworthy event, pamphlets provided a mass public with detailed information and commentary. Especially in times of crisis, such as during a war, domestic conflicts, or political upheavals, hundreds of pamphlets "rained down on the country."[6]

In the periods 1614–1617 and 1648–1652 in France, for example, floods of printed propaganda challenged the royal government.[7] Because of their youth, Kings Louis XIII and Louis XIV respectively could not govern the country themselves, which resulted in a destabilized monarchy and political unrest. An English example is the beginning of the Civil Wars of the period 1642–1651. Especially in 1641–42 there was a massive pamphlet production, wherein the Royalists, supporting King Charles I, and the Parliamentarians, supporting the Long Parliament, opposed their political voices.

Peak Years in Dutch Pamphlet Production

As in France and England, newsworthy events and periods of crisis in the Netherlands corresponded with a peak in pamphlet production, as shown in

Figure I. One such crisis was the Eighty Years' War (1568–1648), in which the Dutch revolted against their Spanish overlords.[8] For example, the 1618–19 peak in pamphlet production (point *a* in figure I) occurred during the Twelve-Year Truce (1609–1621), when religious and political conflicts escalated, ultimately leading to the trial and execution of one of the most influential leaders of the country. Pamphlets flooded the cities, markets, and taverns; they were sold on the streets, in bookshops, and even in faraway villages by traveling peddlers. Those who could not read themselves attended public readings or listened to the singing in the streets and in taverns, for quite a few pamphlets were in rhyme and were meant to be sung.

The peace negotiations with Spain around 1648, as well as the dynastic ambitions of stadtholder William II, who in 1650 wanted to gain absolute power over the province of Holland and its wealthy capital, Amsterdam, caused a second spike in pamphlet production (point *b* in figure I). The attack failed, however, as his troops lost their way on the moors during bad weather the night before the attack. A messenger traveling from Hamburg discovered them and arrived before them in Amsterdam to warn the city, thus spoiling the surprise attack. This news was published in many pamphlets and led to a great debate about the question of who was to be in charge of the country.

The major seventeenth-century crisis for the Dutch Republic, however, was the so-called Year of Disaster (1672), when the country was attacked on

FIGURE 6.1: Dutch pamphlet production, 1600–1853, based on the Knuttel catalogue of pamphlets from the Dutch Royal Library in The Hague.

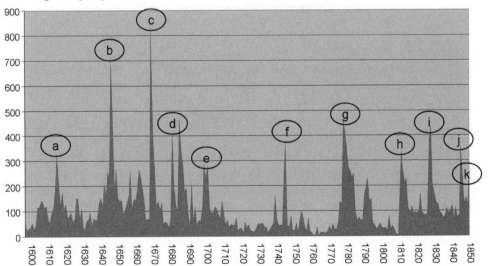

FIGURE 6.2: Dutch pamphlet from 1672, in which recent events are discussed in a conversation between two burghers on a barge from the cities of Rotterdam and The Hague. Knuttel 10472, title page. Courtesy of the Dutch Royal Library, The Hague.

three fronts at once: by France from the south, England from the west, and Münster and Cologne from the east. The war caused chaos in the unprepared republic. Consequently, pamphlet production was never before or after as large and varied as in this year (point *c* in figure 1): hundreds of pamphlets appeared to air opinions and to communicate the latest news on the battles at sea and on land (see figure 2). The war and domestic troubles led to a political murder and a shift in power, as the two most important leaders of the country, the brothers Johan and Cornelis de Witt, became scapegoats for the disastrous situation. Rumors and a spiteful pamphlet campaign had influenced the public for months, setting the stage for the eventual lynching of the De Witt brothers by a furious crowd.

Another significant peak in pamphlet production occurred in 1688. After the deaths of the De Witt brothers, stadtholder William III of Orange-Nassau governed the country. His primary task was to defend the republic against France. In 1688 he made the bold decision to go to war against the English king, James II, his cousin and father-in-law, in order to replace him as monarch and thus gain England as an ally for the republic. He succeeded and became King William III of England. His invasion and accession to the throne, known as the Glorious Revolution, brought about a new watershed in pamphlet production (point *d* in figure 1), in England as much as in the Netherlands.

Throughout the eighteenth and nineteenth centuries, periods of war and political unrest repeatedly coincided with increased pamphlet production: international tensions and the death of King William (point *e* in figure 1); a French attack and a debate about the stadtholdership (point *f* in figure 1); the Fourth Anglo-Dutch War and Batavian strife (point *g* in figure 1); the defeat of Napoleon (point *h* in figure 1); the Ten-Day War against Belgium (point *i* in figure 1); a new constitution (point *j* in figure 1); and the so-called April Movement (point *k* in figure 1).

Characteristics of a Literary Chameleon

Pamphlet production encompassed a wide variety of publications. Topics varied from political, economic, military, and religious issues to festivities, burials, and local news. The little books were written as letters, dialogues, poems, songs, biographies, treatises, plays, last wills and testaments, speeches, programs, announcements, legends, lists, prophecies, and all kinds of stories, from factual reports to accounts of dreams.

The pamphlet campaign against the De Witt brothers in 1672 and their eventual lynching led to a wide variety of pamphlets: for example, *Sententie, Van den Hove van Hollandt, jegens Mr. Cornelis de Witt* (Sentence of the Court of Holland, against Mr. Cornelis de Witt); *Missive uyt 's Graven-hage, Op den twintighsten Augusti 1672* (Letter from The Hague, on the Twentieth of August 1672); *Afbeelding, en waarachtig Verhaal, Hoedanig de Heeren, Mr. Johan de Witt, benevens zijn Broeder, Mr. Cornelis de Witt, zijn om 't leven gebracht* (Picture and True Story, of How the Gentlemen, Mr. Johan de Witt, and his Brother, Mr. Cornelis de Witt, Were Brought to Death); *Vriende-Praetjen over het Eeuwig Edict* (Chat between Friends on the Eternal Edict); *Brillen voor Alderhande Gesichten* (Spectacles for All Kinds of Views); "Echo"; *Catalogus*

Van Boecken Inde Byblioteque Van Mr. Jan de Witt (List of Books in Mr. Jan de Witt's Library); *Politycque Prognosticatie* (Political Prognostication); *Genees-middelen voor Hollants-Qualen* (Cures for Holland's Diseases); *De Spreeckende Geesten van Jan en Cornelis de Witt* (The Speaking Ghosts of Jan and Cornelis de Witt); *Graf-Schrift, Van Johan de Witt* ("Epitaph on Johan de Witt"); and *'t Leven en Bedrijf van Mr. Jan van Oldenbarnevelt, Over-eengebraght met dat van Mr. Jan de Witt . . . Als volgels van eenderley veeren* (The Life and Work of Mr. Jan van Oldenbarnevelt, in Comparison with That of Jan de Witt . . . as Birds of a Feather).[9]

These pamphlets might be satirical or serious, lively or sober, written in prose or in rhyme. The great variety of genres was in fact an important selling point for the pamphlet and contributed significantly to its success as a popular mass medium. As such, the pamphlet was extremely varied as a news medium, "a literary chameleon," as Sandra Clark has put it.[10] It had to be, because a pamphlet served a variety of goals: to inform, persuade, mobilize, instruct, emote, criticize, and amuse.

Given such a multiform medium, one question comes to mind: What exactly is a pamphlet? George Orwell provided an apt response: "To ask 'What is a pamphlet?' is rather like asking 'What is a dog?' We all know a dog when we see one, or at least we think we do, but it is not easy to give a clear verbal definition, nor even to distinguish at sight between a dog and some kindred creature such as a wolf or a jackal."[11] In short, while pamphlets are easy to recognize, they are hard to define. Most pamphlet researchers favor a definition that encompasses all the abovementioned purposes. In their opinion, a pamphlet is a printed, non-periodical message that covers a current topic.[12]

Pamphlets were mostly printed in larger cities and distributed all over the country by booksellers and peddlers (see figure 3).[13] In public places like coffeehouses and taverns, the pamphlets would lie on tables to be read and discussed. Between friends and family, there was a culture of exchanging and copying pamphlets. Thus the impact of a pamphlet extended beyond the initial buyer. The more controversial and clandestine publications were distributed with caution; during the night they were posted on public buildings or left on doorsteps to be discovered in the morning.

For printers, publishers, booksellers, and peddlers, pamphlets were a profitable business. The production of pamphlets was relatively cheap, and because of their immediate relevance, they promised to sell readily. Presentation was equally essential for marketing the product. Printers tried to attract readers with sensational titles and a variety of genres.[14] For all these reasons, pamphlets were popular among many readers from the upper, middle, and even lower classes. Pamphlets were often published without the name of the author

FIGURE 6.3: A peddler trying to sell his pamphlets to two peasants who are interested in the news he brings. Knuttel 3080, detail. Courtesy of the Dutch Royal Library, The Hague.

and printer, or they were published under a false name. Authors included not only famous writers and political or religious leaders but also schoolteachers, merchants, clergymen, booksellers, printers, and preachers.

It was very hard for governments to gain control over pamphleteering because of its incidental nature (one never knew when and where a pamphlet would be published), its anonymous character, and its quick distribution. Censorship was always late in coming and thus very ineffective. Governments were often forced to use the same strategy and publish their own pamphlets, to inform and inoculate the public against the hit-and-run criticism of the antiestablishment press, or if all else failed, to prohibit pamphlets or to strike back in case of a public attack.

Pamphlets: Proto-Literary Journalism?

Notwithstanding this elusive character of pamphlets, we have divided them roughly into three groups to discuss the literary devices that were used to present news and opinions: (1) news pamphlets with a descriptive structure aimed at informing; (2) pamphlets presenting learned arguments with a rhetorical structure and an emphasis on persuasion; and (3) inventive pamphlets with an entertaining presentation.[15] A quantitative study of early-nineteenth-century pamphlets in two typical Dutch cities shows that the inventive pamphlets constitute the largest group (41 percent), the learned arguments the second largest (35 percent), and the news pamphlets the smallest (24 percent). Of course, these percentages are not indicative of the total pamphlet production over three centuries, but they may offer an indication of the relative predominance of each group.[16]

Reporting Facts and Embellishments

Typical genres of the first group, descriptive news pamphlets, include announcements of news, true stories, newsletters, descriptions, reports, journals, and the like. The pamphlets describe recent events in detail—for example, military actions, the accession of a king or high government official, developments in overseas trade, (inter)national changes in power, local festivities, and burials. Sensational news is also a common trait. Murders and executions, the birth of a deformed baby, a giant whale washed ashore, a comet in the sky, and other strange human or natural phenomena are widely discussed. Even though the authors of the descriptive pamphlets are not reporters in the modern sense of the word, they often present their stories as eyewitness accounts with a flair for detail. The pamphlets are relatively realistic and factual, although truth is sometimes exaggerated and embellished.

For example, the pamphlet *Amsterdams Journael* (1650) describes from day to day and from scene to scene what happened during the five-day siege of Amsterdam by stadtholder William II in 1650. As mentioned earlier, bad weather, and the encounter with a messenger traveling from Hamburg to Amsterdam who reported the gathering of the troops, foiled the surprise attack. A lot of the information in this pamphlet is based on hearsay reports from eyewitnesses, as is evident in this observation: "There were also two large ships floating and coming into town over the Amstel River up to the Long Bridge, loaded (as people say) with more than two hundred soldiers."[17] The reporting in news pamphlets is frequently supported by other literary genres, such as poems, songs, lists, or letters. In the *Amsterdam Journael,* the day-to-day descriptions of the assault on Amsterdam are intermingled with prophecies, historical descriptions and parallels, anecdotes, citations from letters, and even a list of other pamphlets concerning the conflict. Official documents, such as letters from William II to several Dutch towns and provinces, are included to prove the report's reliability. The scene-by-scene descriptions, however, come closest to present-day literary journalism.

The authors of descriptive pamphlets use a number of literary devices to make these descriptions of scenes more appealing. First, we find the stylistic device of *amplificatio:* involving the reader by magnifying certain elements in the story. The goal is often to play on people's emotions. In fact, *amplificatio* is an essential technique in almost any pamphlet. Second, and as part of *amplificatio,* we have the technique of vivid description (*evidentia*), through which an event is described as if it were unfolding before the reader's eyes.

The *Amsterdam Journael,* for example, glorifies the city of Amsterdam and its burghers: "It was astonishing to see how a city, used to rest and peace, was able to take up arms in an instant so courageously"; and "While the people were filled with fear, the drums were beaten, [and the] enlisting soldiers . . . were immediately accepted in large numbers."[18] The author then sums up all the measures that were taken to defend the city. In particular, one burgomaster receives favorable mention, Cornelis Bikker, lord of Swieten, who was able to keep order in the city. Reports such as this one are often accompanied by an illustrative engraving or woodcut. The *Amsterdam Journael* even contains a map that indicates the position of Amsterdam, surrounded by William II's troops.

Rhetorical Tricks and Arguments

Learned arguments, the second group of pamphlets, are not literary journalism as such, but the pamphlets' rhetorical and literary styles do merit quick discussion here. Pamphlets of the learned argument type are aimed at stating an opinion; reporting, if present at all, is subject to persuasion. Frequently used genres in this group include treatises, speeches, sermons, comments, revelations, defenses, objections, and prophecies. The main goal of these texts is to persuade the reader to a certain point of view on current events and urge him to act accordingly. The texts are mostly in prose, and the subject can be almost anything, but the main concerns are the military, the economy, politics, and religion.

In the early modern period, the classical art of rhetoric was considered an essential element of all literature. Especially in persuasive pamphlets, authors used rhetorical means to convince and involve their readers, and frequently those authors were well-known literary figures who were politically engaged. Characteristic of their learned arguments is the use of classical rhetorical structures and techniques, in which rational arguments exist alongside false reasoning. Emotional appeals (*pathos*) are equally dominant. Standard argumentation to elicit indignation or pity is frequently used as well. Accordingly, the style often seeks to persuade the reader through the use of *exclamatio* (exclamation), *interrogatio* (rhetorical queries), *repetitio* or *geminatio* (repetition), *anaphora* (phrasal repetition), the imperative, and direct address. Pamphlets that are aimed at discrediting people frequently contain *ad hominem* arguments. These and other rhetorical and literary devices are all classic elements of persuasive pamphleteering.

Inventive Literary Techniques

The largest and final group of pamphlets takes a more ludic approach to the news and is perhaps the closest ancestor of the three to what we consider today to be literary journalism. The combination of entertainment and information makes the news more sellable and any persuasive message more effective. This group consists of literary genres like dialogues, poems, songs, stories, last wills and testaments, tragedies, comedies, and legends. Often they have a metaphorical, playful, or mocking title; are written in prose or in rhyme or in a combination of the two; and combine fact and fiction.

One example of this type of pamphlet is *Trits van Verstanden* (Trio of Minds), a conversation among three peddlers about current events in the republic that starts in rhyme but soon changes to prose. The dialogue is interrupted by poems, prophecies, and other texts the peddlers want to sell. The three sellers play with the question: Which view of the events is true? Throughout the seventeenth century, this metaphorical type of pamphlet, playing with this theme of the correct view of events, was quite popular. Usually the author or the main character(s) of these dialogues, stories, letters, or arguments recommends and sells spectacles, eye salves, telescopes, and pamphlets to clarify the reader's (and customer's) sight.[19]

The line between fiction and reality is often very thin and indistinct in these inventive and witty pamphlets. Some of the texts are fictitious but realistic, while others are more fantastic, referring to a world of fables, legends, and myths. Fantastic or not, in the end they all discuss a "real" news topic. To discuss all of the different genres and literary techniques of pamphlets is beyond the scope of this essay. Therefore we have chosen to pay close attention to the two most popular literary genres: poetry and dialogue.

Perhaps the most popular device in pamphlets is poetry. Pamphlets are written as songs, ballads, various types of poems (for example, sonnets or echo poems), and rhyming dialogues. Poetry is also often combined with prose: lines of verse from famous writers support the argument within a prose text, or brief poems introduce or repeat the message at the beginning or end of a pamphlet. The use of rhyme has various advantages: it is often easier to read and to memorize, and it is entertaining. For the author it is a chance to use all kinds of wordplay and to show off his literary capabilities. Poetry is not used just for entertainment, however; many poems and songs have an informative, persuasive, or polemical goal as well.[20]

Around August 30, 1672, about ten days after the murder of the De Witt brothers, a venomous polemical poem titled *Hollants Venezoen* (Holland's Venison) was published. It defended the De Witt brothers' deeds and portrayed stadtholder William III and his supporters as money-grubbing power mongers:

> *The vile misers, forgetting oath and honor,*
> *Dare, for dirty pleasures (O terrible disgrace!),*
> *To put the keys of our land in the hands*
> *Of an imperious prince: The care entrusted to him,*
> *Is now too woefully forgotten because of the gold.*[21]

According to the pamphlet, not only William III but also the English king, Charles II, could not be trusted. The Dutch government did not tolerate this kind of affront and tried to arrest the presumed publishers, but nothing in the end was proved.

An example of a pamphlet that interweaves poetry into a dream story is *Wonderlijcke Staatkundige Droomen en Gesichten* (Astonishing Political Dreams and Visions).[22] This pamphlet is a short story, written in the first person, in which a man falls asleep and narrates his dreams to his readers. In his dreams he has visions in which he encounters several people who speak with him about the current situation in Holland. The narrative parts are in prose, while the speeches are presented in rhyme. When the man wakes up, he continues the story, going to an inn, where he overhears a conversation between two farmers, which is also reproduced in rhyme.

Dream stories were a rather popular type of pamphlet in the seventeenth century, written in the first or third person, in prose or sometimes combined with rhyme. The main character has all kinds of experiences and engages in conversations with several people. The stories can be staged in a realistic or a more fantastic, mythical world. These texts read like short stories and may be seen as forerunners of the novel.

Similar to dream stories though more realistic, dialogue pamphlets also resemble short stories. While the dominant mode is prose, now and then the dialogues are combined with poetry—for instance, in the many comical dialogues in which peasants defame government officials in the city by gossiping about their misconduct—or with drama. Set against an everyday backdrop (a market, pub, barge, street, doorstep, room, or the like), they feature all kinds of recognizable people, from merchants, innkeepers, and soldiers to bargemen, peasants, and persons from various towns, provinces, and countries who meet and enter into conversation about current affairs. These dialogues are presented as direct speech, such as in this example of three peasants conversing about apparently trivial matters of personal appearance:

> JAEP SOET: Good morning, neighbor Klaes, why are you looking so confused? Didn't you get any sleep, or have you been drunk?
>
> KLAES SWAER-HOOFT: What do you ask? That I was drunk? You should know better; have you ever seen me drunk?
>
> JAN GOET-HART: Don't be mad, neighbor Klaes, that neighbor Jan asks you that; I am also surprised that you look so funny. We didn't expect that from you, so one of these things has to be true: either drunkenness or unrest has kept you from sleeping. Or shall I get you a mirror so you can see for yourself?[23]

Neighbor Klaes finally admits that he looks strange and reveals the reasons for his sorrows: the war and the soldiers are putting him in debt, taking away his home, wife, and land. As the men go on discussing the state of affairs in the country, we discover that the dialogue has brought the discourse down to a more narrative level without sacrificing the political commentary.

Although the events discussed in the dialogue are very real, the speakers themselves are fictional and serve a rhetorical purpose. They are mostly stereotyped according to the rhetorical principle of *decorum,* or appropriateness.

Thus their role in the dialogue fits their type. Main speakers in such dialogues are often reliable and reasonable; they are knowledgeable and just and deliver the primary viewpoint. In a 1608 dialogue between a nobleman, a burgher, a peasant, and a bargeman, the nobleman is the main speaker. At first, everyone vents his opinion, but soon the nobleman begins to dominate the discussion. His high position, his knowledge of state affairs, and his venerable age make him a man of experience and lend him an aura of authority. The burgher is his main opponent. Eventually the nobleman succeeds in convincing him of his point of view. The other, minor speakers do not have many arguments and are usually ignorant, comical, or rude. The bargeman in the 1608 dialogue, for instance, has very little to say, and when he does talk, he is crude and uses invective.

Other characteristics such as the profession of a speaker, the use of dialect, or the physical appearance of a character can support or undermine the authority of the speaker in the dialogue. For example, peasants tend to be simple, sailors rude, someone with a trembling voice uncertain of his views, and a person with a red nose drunk. The physical appearance of neighbor Klaes Swaer-hooft in the quoted dialogue characterizes him as a confused person, which he appears to be in word and deed throughout the remainder of the dialogue.

The literary device of *writing to the moment,* which would become popular in early novels, is already present in these dialogue pamphlets. The goal of using this technique is to present a past event as if it were happening before the reader's eyes. The event could be the dialogue itself, for example, as when the author tells his readers that he was a silent witness to a conversation and then narrates it in direct speech. But it could also be an event that is reported by one of the speakers in the dialogue. For example, a messenger in the 1672 pamphlet *Leger-Praetje* (Army Chat) informs the other interlocutors about the murder of the De Witt brothers. He recounts their awful deaths with descriptions so vivid that he relives his own emotional experiences and even enraptures his spellbound friends as if the events were happening right then: "But here the burghers of The Hague have despised the law, and made themselves judges, and have, as cruel executioners, at once executed [the De Witt brothers], and that while they were people of their own religion; and they didn't just kill them, but they have maltreated them after their deaths so horribly."[24] A clear description of the bodies being torn apart and sold to the highest bidder follows.

The distinctions among the three categories (news pamphlets, learned argument, and inventive pamphlets) are of course not as strict as presented here. Many pamphlets have characteristics of all three groups. The pamphlet

Den Oprechten Hollandsen Bootsgesel (*The Sincere Holland Ship's Mate,* 1666), for example, is another dialogue that reads like a short story, containing news and argument. It begins with a short description and dialogue in a realistic setting:

> *Three persons sitting in a barge, sailing from Dordrecht to Rotterdam, one being a merchant from Amsterdam, talking to the ship's mate.* Well, friend, as I can tell by your clothing you seem to be a ship's mate or bargeman, and from your appearance that you are ill or injured. Have you been in the fleet and in the latest sea battle? . . . Are you coming from Zeeland?
>
> SHIP'S MATE: Yes, sir. I come from Zeeland. . . . I am a ship's mate . . . and I have been in the latest sea battle where I was wounded by a splinter that bounced into my arm, but it is not that bad, so I hope to be cured soon and to go with the fleet out to sea again to see if we can revenge the haughty and murderous English . . . to force them to reason and peace.[25]

The two discuss the war against England and the situation of the Dutch fleet, in particular the position of one of the admirals. An inhabitant of the town of Delft participates as well. When the barge arrives, the three go to a tavern, where the host gives them a hearty welcome and informs them about the latest news, which causes a new argument.

In short, pamphlets like this one represent a very diverse medium in which a wide variety of literary devices were used to present news and opinion. Pamphlets are by no means the equivalent of literary journalism today, but they can be considered examples of proto-literary journalism. Several questions at this point remain: Did the pamphlet survive the rise of the newspaper? What happened to its playful and multiform elements? Were they taken over by the new medium, the newspaper, in accordance with the theory of remediation?

The Rise of the Mass Newspaper in the Netherlands: A "New" Journalism

Although the newspaper had been in existence since the seventeenth century, it had never been a true medium for the masses. Because of heavy taxes and government control, it had failed to reach a wide audience in most European countries. The transformation of the newspaper started as a slow trend toward commercialization and popularization only in the late eighteenth century. More and more countries abandoned the taxes and laws that held the newspaper back, opening up new avenues for journalistic change. In the second half of the nineteenth century, the gradual popularization of the newspaper intensified under the influence of commercial press barons and powerful editors.

These innovative newspapermen drastically changed journalistic practices and ideals, revolutionizing the industry by introducing novel elements in the paper and by appealing to a new and broader public. The resulting burst of journalistic renewal has been dubbed "new" journalism in recent years.[26] New topics, new genres, and new journalistic ideals transformed the paper into a true medium for the masses.

The American brand of "new" journalism was inspired mostly by the commercial approach of newspaper publishers William Randolph Hearst and Joseph Pulitzer. Editors focused mainly on reaching a mass audience by making the news more attractive with an engaging writing style, new genres such as the interview, and reportage. Also, certain grand journalistic ideals became more intertwined with the profession than before. Among these ideals, objectivity and neutrality of the press were the most prevalent. Although it was American in origin, most European countries developed their own unique brand of this "new" journalism.[27]

In Europe the ideal of objectivity was never as widespread as in the United States. Although there were papers that advocated political neutrality, many newspapers became involved with a political party or ideology, serving not so much as an objective news platform but more as a political signpost, telling readers what to think of current events and putting the news into a larger ideological perspective. In most European countries the main aspect of "new" journalism was the introduction of an attractive writing style and novel genres for presenting the news. Journalists experimented with the techniques used in literary realism and naturalism. Moreover, novelists explored the world of journalism, often contributing to newspapers themselves, thus stimulating the give-and-take between news and literature.[28]

The situation in the Netherlands is ideal for studying the introduction of literary elements in the newspaper press during the nineteenth century. The main reason is that the Dutch newspaper business did not change as gradually as in most other countries. The Dutch government long held some very strict ideas about the handling of the press. Although the law itself was quite liberal, there were many loopholes that gave government officials the opportunity to prosecute members of the press. This did not change until 1848 with a new constitution explicitly stating the freedom of the press. Also, until 1869 a series of heavy taxes were levied on newspapers, making them so expensive that it was not particularly profitable to own or work at a newspaper.

When these taxes were finally abolished, the Dutch newspaper business changed almost overnight. Newspaper owners were finally able to profit from the increasing education, wealth, and leisure time of the Dutch public. Because the price could now be lowered, the newspaper came within the grasp of middle- and lower-income households. Also, women and children were targeted by publishers as potential readers. The result was a huge increase in newspaper circulation. Many new papers were founded, and papers grew larger and circulated more frequently. Instantly there was a huge demand for journalists to fill the expanding pages.

To attract and keep these new groups of readers, editors and journalists encouraged experiments with new and interesting ways of presenting the news.[29] It is therefore not surprising that some journalists looked to the pamphlet for inspiration.

Remediation of Pamphlet Genres in the Newspaper

The difference between the old and new newspaper becomes immediately clear when we look at the genres that were used to present the news. In the first half of the nineteenth century, the main genres in Dutch newspapers were news articles, government announcements, and service messages (lists and programs). Relatively new to the Dutch newspaper was the opinion piece. This genre came into use during the 1830s, when editors began commenting on government policy in open letters and featured articles. Increasingly, letters by readers were published as well, usually strengthening the viewpoints of the editor in chief.[30]

Rhetorical argumentative devices were also being introduced in the paper. Many of these were well known from their use in pamphlets. And indeed, if we trace back the first opinion pieces in the paper, they show great similarities to the argumentative genres of the pamphlet discussed earlier in this essay. One of the main opposition papers in the 1830s, *De Noord-Brabander,* was in fact founded by a group of Catholics who had frequently published pamphlets and were looking for a way to get their message across at more regular intervals. They appointed a fellow pamphleteer, Hein de Wijs, as the paper's first editor in chief. Some of the earliest opinion pieces in this paper were actually verbatim copies of pamphlets that were circulating at the time.

De Noord-Brabander is one of a few examples we can use to establish a direct remediation of pamphlet genres in the newspaper. In most Dutch newspapers, however, we can only note the many similarities between the old genres of the pamphlet and these new genres of the newspaper. Perhaps the introduction of pamphlet-like elements is best illustrated through a discussion of two literary genres that became prominent after 1869: reportage and the feuilleton.[31]

Although these were relatively late additions to newspaper journalism, both relied on century-old techniques used in pamphleteering. When reportage was first introduced, there were mainly two types. The first consisted of literal reports on public meetings, celebrations, and the like which were told chronologically and contained much direct dialogue. More often than not, however, they were quite boring and lengthy.[32]

The second type of reportage was much more literary in the sense that it read like a short story. In these publications we find many elements of the old pamphleteering style. Engaging writing, flowery language, metaphor, amplification, vivid description, direct dialogue, and all sorts of literary devices made the news more appealing, alive, and real.[33] Some journalists embraced the new journalistic ideals, going undercover for months, posing as sailors, workers, or traveling musicians to get their stories right.[34]

Reporter M. J. Brusse, for instance, wrote for the newspaper *Nieuwe Rotterdamsche Courant* a series of articles about the disenfranchised of Dutch society. He disguised himself as a drifter and traveled with "beggars and poachers," sharing their food and way of life. In one reportage he describes a rude awakening in a flea-infested barn where he spent the night with another vagabond named Toon:

> "Are ye awake, buddy?" Toon cried out to me. . . .
>
> "Are ye itch'n, brother?"—Toon asked again. "Me neighbor here, he says that it was worse in the summer. . . . Me, I just keep pounding the little buggers."[35]

Brusse, like many reporters experimenting with immersion in his day, used literary techniques to capture the moment and to give a precise portrayal of his characters. Devices such as dialogue, vivid descriptions, dialect, and quaint accents served to make the descriptions come alive for the reader.

Sometimes realism took a back seat to romanticized descriptions and embellishments. This depiction of a quiet walk on a nice day, for instance, sought more to capture the subjective impression of the event rather than the facts of the event itself: "The dawn was delightful and whispered promises of spring. A cool wind brought the scent of flowers and oak trees. Our traveler, comforted by cheerful thoughts, made haste. He was humming a pastoral tune and petting his dog. The animal could not choose; first it was standing still under its master's hand, then it was hopping and running, giving vent to its joy simply by its restlessness."[36]

Still another form of reportage was the "portrait," which contained a detailed description of the physical appearance of a person (or sometimes a

town) to illustrate character: a great pointy moustache indicated an extrava-
gant personality, while a hunched back was a sign of a broken will.[37] In short,
journalists had significant freedom within the genre because it was as yet
undefined. But with the increasing standardization of newspaper practices,
this freedom slowly diminished. Reportage became a real genre, with generally accepted rules and specialized practitioners. The same can be observed for
another "new" genre, the feuilleton.

Today, the term "feuilleton" indicates an installment of a serialized story.
In most European countries, however, the nineteenth-century feuilleton was
more than that. There were few or no rules concerning the feuilleton, so journalists were free to invent or reinvent the genre. The feuilleton therefore consisted of a variety of (sub)genres, such as news poems, songs, dream stories,
plays, and symbolic tales. What these genres had in common was that they
discussed the news in a lighthearted and inventive way. The Dutch newspaper
De Vlinder, for instance, started every day's edition with a fictive dialogue on
the front page in which current topics were discussed by two clown figures,
Pier and Pol. On April 30, 1898, they discussed a large fire in a factory that
made ice skates:

> PIER: "Fire! Fire! Fire!" I saw a boy running toward the fire alarm and I called
> after him, "Where?"
>
> "The ice skating factory is on fire."
>
> Well, you'll understand, my dear Pol, that in no time the whole town had
> gathered to watch.
>
> POL: I believe you. But did the firemen come as well, and how did it all end? I
> wonder because you seem in such a rush, so unnerved today.[38]

Pier and Pol continue to discuss the fire, posing questions about the owner's
insurance and wondering if there would be enough ice skates to make it
through the winter. These fictional characters serve as a lighthearted way to
discuss news and sometimes to provide harsh criticism that would otherwise
have been unfit for print. This mixture of fiction and fact was typical for most
genres belonging to the feuilleton.

Although the many subgenres of the feuilleton were new to the newspaper, they were in fact quite common in pamphlets. There was at this time
still an active pamphlet press throughout most of Europe; newspapers and
pamphlets coincided. There are many examples of newspapermen producing
pamphlets when it suited them. It is therefore not surprising that journalists experimented with popular pamphlet genres in the newspaper when they
wanted to appeal to a wider audience.[39]

Although dialogues, news poems, songs, symbolic tales, and other pamphlet genres appeared in Dutch newspapers after 1869, they grew less common toward the end of the century. After an initial experimental period, genre conventions became more rigid. Journalists lost their freedom to experiment, and as a result the feuilleton sacrificed much of its multifaceted nature. The "new" twentieth-century feuilleton was indeed only the serialized story that we have come to know today.

The End of the Literary Pamphlet

With the rise of the newspaper came the end of the pamphlet as the primary medium for news and opinion in Europe. While the pamphlet was still being produced in great quantities, it lost much of its playfulness and literary character.[40] The more inventive and entertaining genres that had been predominant for centuries slowly ceded terrain. Although poems and songs still appeared at the end of the nineteenth century, genres such as dialogue, the news story, the dream story, and the fake will and testament were no longer used. After 1870, the use of argumentative genres also decreased in popularity. The role of the pamphlet as a platform for debate and opinion had been transferred to the newspaper.

Most late-nineteenth-century pamphlets were manifestos, programs, reports, lists, and instructions. In short, the more descriptive genres became the most dominant pamphlet format, thus supplanting the entertaining and argumentative pamphlet genres. The style of the pamphlets changed as well, and they lost whatever literary cachet they had once had: the use of flowery language, vivid description, and playful embellishment disappeared almost completely. The pamphlet had been transformed from an open and diverse news platform into a uniform propaganda tool for political parties, institutions, and corporations.

It is by no means the intent of this essay to suggest that all literary journalism started with the pamphlet, but we have attempted to show that the tradition of mixing news and literature goes back as far as the sixteenth century. The early modern pamphlet was in many ways a multiform platform on which different ideas and news topics were presented in a myriad of genres. Various literary techniques were employed to get a certain message across. By contrast, the newspaper at that time used only three journalistic genres: news articles, announcements, and service messages. At the end of the eighteenth century, this slowly began to change, a process that intensified in the second half of the nineteenth century. New journalistic genres were introduced into the developing newspaper, and the "new" newspaper supplanted the pamphlet as the main platform for news, debate, and literary journalism.

Did the pamphlet tradition add to the diversification of journalistic genres in the nineteenth-century press? It seems a probable supposition. The pamphlet was still used throughout the nineteenth century and coexisted with the newspaper. Many journalists and politicians used both newspapers and pamphlets as their means of communication. This could explain how elements of pamphleteering were introduced into the paper, and it would certainly explain the similarities between pamphleteering genres and "new" genres in the papers. In some cases this remediation hypothesis can be proved conclusively, but in most cases we can only note the striking resemblances.

In line with the remediation theory, the pamphlet adapted and survived. The production of pamphlets in the Netherlands continued in almost the same numbers as before. But some traditional genres, most noteworthy the more inventive and literary forms such as dialogues, dream stories, and the like, disappeared, while the informational genres gained in prominence. The pamphlet became a relatively uniform, monothematic propaganda tool for political parties and organizations. The long run of the literary pamphlet had ended. But some of its genres and characteristics lived on in the newspaper.

NOTES

1. Tom Wolfe and E. W. Johnson, eds., *The New Journalism: With an Anthology* (New York: Harper & Row, 1973), 41–46, 49–50.

2. Sandra Clark, *The Elizabethan Pamphleteers: Popular Moralistic Pamphlets, 1580–1640* (London: Athlone Press, 1983), 38–39. See also Jeffrey K. Sawyer, *Printed Poison: Pamphlet Propaganda, Faction Politics, and the Public Sphere in Early Seventeenth-Century France* (Berkeley: University of California Press, 1990), 7.

3. For more on remediation theory, see Jay David Bolter and Richard Grusin, *Remediation: Understanding New Media* (Cambridge: MIT Press, 2000); L. B. Becker and K. Schönbach, *Audience Reactions to Media Diversification: Coping with Plenty* (Hillsdale, N.J.: LEA, 1989); Carolyn Marvin, *When Old Technologies Were New: Thinking about Electric Communication in the Late Nineteenth Century* (New York: Oxford University Press, 1988); and Marshall MacLuhan, *Understanding Media: The Extensions of Man* (New York: McGraw-Hill, 1964).

4. Clark, *Elizabethan Pamphleteers,* 17. See also Joad Raymond, *Pamphlets and Pamphleteering in Early Modern Britain* (Cambridge: Cambridge University Press, 2003), 11–15; Miriam Usher Chrisman, *Conflicting Visions of Reform: German Lay Propaganda Pamphlets, 1519–1530* (Atlantic Highlands, N.J.: Humanities Press, 1996), 3; and Craig E. Harline, *Pamphlets, Printing and Political Culture in the Early Dutch Republic* (Dordrecht: Martinus Nijhoff, 1987), 3–5.

5. *Amsterdam Journael* (1650), Dutch Royal Library, The Hague, Knuttel catalogue number 6706, 26. All translations from Dutch, unless otherwise noted, are our own.

6. Gert Jan Johannes, *De barometer van de Smaak: tijdschriften in Nederland, 1770–1830* (The Barometer of Taste: Magazines in the Netherlands 1770–1830) (The Hague: Sdu Uitgevers, 1995), 171.

7. Sawyer, *Printed Poison*, 1–2. Hubert Carrier published several books on the pamphlets of the "Fronde" (1648–1652); see, for example, *Les muses guerrières: Les Mazarinades et la vie littéraire au milieu du XVIIe siècle; courants, genres, culture populaire et savante à l'époque de la Fronde* (Paris: Klincksieck, 1996), and *La presse de la Fronde (1648–1653): Les Mazarinades, la conquête de l'opinion* (Geneva: Librairie Droz, 1989).

8. For more on the history of the Dutch Republic, see Jonathan Israel, *The Dutch Republic: Its Rise, Greatness and Fall, 1477–1806* (Oxford: Clarendon Press, 1998).

9. Dutch Royal Library, The Hague, pamphlets from the Knuttel catalogue, numbers 10188, 10192, 10196, 10333, 10327, 10356, 10343, 10363, 10376, 10404, 10398, and 10432.

10. Clark, *Elizabethan Pamphleteers*, 18.

11. George Orwell, introduction to *British Pamphleteers*, vol. 1, ed. George Orwell and Reginald Reynolds (London: Allan Wingate, 1948), 7.

12. For an overview of the discussion about the definition of the Dutch pamphlet, see Marijke Meijer Drees, "Pamfletten: een inleiding" (Pamphlets: An Introduction), and Piet Verkruijsse, "'Gedruckt te seghwaer, op de pars der Lijdtsaemheyt': Boekwetenschap en pamfletliteratuur" ("Printed in Seghwaer ['Truth-telling'], on the Press of Patience": The Science of Book and Pamphlet Literature), in *Het lange leven van het pamflet: Boekhistorische, iconografische, literaire en politieke aspecten van pamfletten 1600–1900* (The Pamphlet's Long Life: Publishing, Iconographical, Literary, and Political Aspects of Pamphlets, 1600–1900), ed. José de Kruif, Marijke Meijer Drees, and Jeroen Salman (Hilversum: Verloren, 2006), 9–28 and 31–43 respectively. See also Joost Vrieler, *Het poëtisch accent: Drie literaire genres in zeventiende-eeuwse Nederlandse pamfletten* (The Poetic Accent: Three Literary Genres in Seventeenth-century Dutch Pamflets) (Hilversum: Verloren, 2007), 13–18.

13. For more on peddlers, see Jeroen Salman, "Peddling in the Past: Dutch Itinerant Bookselling in European Perspective," *Publishing History* 53 (2003): 5–19.

14. Carrier, *Les muses guerrières*, 17, 195–492; Clark, *Elizabethan Pamphleteers*, 121–22, 257; Harline, *Pamphlets, Printing and Political Culture*, 53; Raymond, *Pamphlets and Pamphleteering in Early Modern Britain*, 214–24, 350–55; Sawyer, *Printed Poison*, 11; Chrisman, *Conflicting Visions of Reform*, 8–11.

15. For more on literary techniques and rhetorical devices in Dutch pamphlets, see Vrieler, *Het poëtisch accent;* Drees, "Pamfletten: een inleiding"; and Clazina Dingemanse, *Rap van tong, scherp van pen: Literaire discussiecultuur in Nederlandse praatjespamfletten (circa 1600–1750)* (Glib Tongues, Sharp Pens: Literary Discussion Culture in Dutch Pamphlets [circa 1600–1750]) (Hilversum: Verloren, 2008). For literary techniques in English pamphlets, see Clark, *Elizabethan Pamphleteers;* in French pamphlets, Carrier, *Les muses guerrières;* and in German pamphlets, Johannes Schwitalla, *Deutsche Flugschriften 1460–1525* (Tübingen: Niemeyer, 1983). For an Italian influence on Dutch pamphlets, see Clazina Dingemanse and Marijke Meijer Drees, "Pasquino in Early Modern Dutch Pamphlet Literature (ca. 1500–1750)," in *Ex marmore: Pasquini, Pasquinisti, Pasquinate nell' Europa moderna*, ed. Chrysa Damianaki, Paolo Procaccioli, and Angelo Romano (Manziana: Vecchiarelli Editore, 2006), 477–98.

16. Rutger de Graaf, "Voor ieder wat wils: Journalistieke genres in Bossche kranten en pamfletten 1813–1899" (Something for Everyone: Journalistic Genres in Newspapers and Pamphlets from the City of Den Bosch, 1813–1899), *Tijdschrift voor tijdschriftstudies* 23 (2008): 4–20.

17. *Amsterdam Journael* (1650), Dutch Royal Library, The Hague, Knuttel catalogue number 6704, 17.

18. Ibid., 18, 19.

19. For more on this type of pamphlet, see Marijke Meijer Drees, "Goed voor de ogen: Brilmetaforiek in vroegmoderne pamfletten" (Good for the Eyes: Spectacle Metaphors in Early Modern Pamphlets), in *Het lange leven van het pamflet,* 129–42.

20. On poetry in Dutch pamphlets, see Vrieler, *Het poëtisch accent.*

21. *Hollants Venezoen* (1672), Dutch Royal Library, The Hague, Knuttel catalogue number 10606, 3.

22. *Wonderlijcke Staatkundige Droomen en Gesichten* (1672), Dutch Royal Library, The Hague, Knuttel catalogue number 10494.

23. *Leger-Praetje* (1672), Dutch Royal Library, The Hague, Knuttel catalogue number 10603, 3.

24. Ibid., 15.

25. *Den Oprechten Hollandsen Bootsgesel* (1666), Dutch Royal Library, The Hague, Knuttel catalogue number 9331, 3.

26. For a brief but excellent discussion of this "new journalism," see Mitchell Stephens, *A History of News,* 3rd ed. (New York: Oxford University Press, 2007), 194–97.

27. Dutch "new" journalism is covered extensively in Huub Wijfjes, *Journalistiek in Nederland, 1850–2000: Beroep, cultuur en organisatie* (Journalism in the Netherlands, 1850–2000: Profession, Culture, and Organization) (Amsterdam: Boom, 2004), 30–33. New journalism in several other countries is discussed in Svennik Høyer and Horst Pöttker, *Diffusion of the News Paradigm, 1850–2000* (Göteborg: Nordicom, 2005).

28. For the Dutch situation, see Wijfjes, *Journalistiek in Nederland, 1850–2000,* 62–65.

29. See, for instance, ibid., 30, 48–52; Remieg Aerts, "Het algemeen-culturele tijdschrift in het negentiende-eeuwse medialandschap" (The General-Cultural Magazine in the Nineteenth-Century Media Landscape), *Tijdschrift voor tijdschriftstudies* 11 (2002): 42; Marcel Broersma, *Beschaafde vooruitgang: De wereld van de Leeuwarder Courant, 1752–2002* (Civilized Progress: The World of the *Leeuwarden Courant,* 1752–2002) (Leeuwarden: Friese Pers Boekerij, 2002), 261; Joan Hemels, *De Nederlandse pers voor en na de afschaffing van het Dagbladzegel in 1869* (The Dutch Press Before and After the Abolition of the Newspaper Stamp in 1869) (Assen: Van Gorcum, 1969) 22; and Maarten Schneider and Joan Hemels, *De Nederlandse Krant 1618–1978: Van "Nieuwstydinghe" tot dagblad* (The Dutch Newspaper, 1618–1978: From "Nieuwstydinghe" to the Daily), 4th ed. (Baarn: Wereldvenster, 1979), 11, 97, 157.

30. We discuss only the news section of the paper, thus excluding the advertisements. For the development of advertisements in Dutch newspapers, see G. H. van Heusden, *Een eeuw adverteerkunde: De sociaal-economische en psychologische ontwikkeling van het adverteren in Nederlandse kranten* (A Century of Advertising Science: Socioeconomic and Psychological Development of Advertising in Dutch Newspapers) (Assen: Van Gorcum, 1962).

31. This diversification of news genres continued in the twentieth century with the introduction of the interview. See Wijfjes, *Journalistiek in Nederland, 1850–2000,* 31–32; Hemels, *De Nederlandse pers,* 22; and Schneider and Hemels, *De Nederlandse Krant 1618–1978,* 97, 157.

32. Broersma, *Beschaafde vooruitgang,* 172–76.

33. Wijfjes, *Journalistiek in Nederland, 1850–2000,* 54–60.

34. Ibid., 58–60.

35. His articles were later published in M. J. Brusse, *Landlooperij: zwerftocht van een dagblad-*

schrijver onder stroopers en schooiers (Vagrancy: The Wanderings of a Journalist among Poachers and Bums) (Rotterdam: W. L. & J. Brusse, 1906), 407–9.

36. *Provinciale Noordbrabantsche en 's Hertogenbossche Courant,* January 13, 1890.

37. Wijfjes, *Journalistiek in Nederland, 1850–2000,* 58; Korrie Korevaart, *Ziften en zemelknoopen: Literaire kritiek in de Nederlandse dag-, nieuws- en weekbladen 1814–1848* (Sifting and Straw-Splittering: Literary Criticism in the Dutch Daily, News, and Weekly Magazines, 1814–1848) (Hilversum: Verloren, 2001), 163–70; Nico Cramer, *Parlement en pers in verhouding tot de overheid* (Parliament and the Press in Relation to the Public) (Leiden: Stenfert Kroese, 1958), 80–81.

38. *De Vlinder,* April 30, 1898 (newspaper collection, Groningen Archives).

39. The presumption that the feuilleton attracted new groups of readers is voiced in a nineteenth-century Dutch book on journalism, Rimmer van der Meulen, *De Courant,* vol. 2, *Samenstelling en beheer van groote en kleine nieuwsbladen* (The Composition and Management of Large- and Small-Scale Newspapers) (Leiden: A. W. Sijthoff, 1885), 32–34.

40. Orwell, introduction to *British Pamphleteers,* 14–16. For an overview of the number of pamphlets produced in European cities, see de Graaf, "Voor ieder wat wils."

Chapter 7

Literary Journalism's Magnetic Pull

*Britain's "New" Journalism and the Portuguese
at the Fin-de-Siècle*

ISABEL SOARES

IN REFERRING TO, studying, or reading about literary journalism, the tendency is to consider it an Anglophone phenomenon if for no other reason than the fact that a proto-literary journalism emerged in the nineteenth century on both sides of the Atlantic: the "new" journalism ascribed to W. T. Stead, Henry Mayhew, and Andrew Mearns in Britain, and to Jack London and Jacob Riis in the United States.[1] Moreover, names such as Tom Wolfe, Norman Mailer, and Truman Capote have become so synonymous with the form's evolution in the twentieth century that the bond between the English language and literary journalism seems impenetrable.

Literary journalism, however, is a widespread journalistic form whose pioneering practitioners can also be found outside the linguistic boundaries of the English language.[2] In fact, Portuguese, today's sixth-ranked world language in terms of speaking community, also proved a fertile ground for early experiments in literary journalism. Some of the most prominent Portuguese journalists of the late nineteenth century aimed at breaking away from a more conventional journalism and became activists for a freer, more personal way of reporting. Very difficult to catalog and define, even by themselves, these journalists were recipients of transnational influences imported from France and, most notably, Britain. Also writing at precisely the same time that the *Pall Mall Gazette* was popularizing its "new" journalism and shocking audiences along the way, they became the form's pioneer practitioners in Portugal. As such, they should be counted among the generation of "new" journalists in Britain for having helped found the genre we identify today as literary journalism.

In this light it comes as no surprise that fin-de-siècle Portuguese journalism has drawn much attention from the academic community. The consensus among academics is that the Portuguese press, particularly during the closing decades of the nineteenth century, went through tremendous changes that ranged from the astounding increase in the number of periodicals in circulation to the varied topics being covered by journalists: political debates, sports events, international affairs, and so on. Notwithstanding the increasing number of studies devoted to the analysis of the Portuguese press in the nineteenth century, be it by single authors or newspapers, or regarding specific periods or topics, little has been written about the founding of a Portuguese literary journalism at the fin-de-siècle.[3] Yet of special importance to this climate of change in the Portuguese press were the literary experiments of four journalists—Eça de Queirós, Ramalho Ortigão, Oliveira Martins, and Batalha Reis—whose articles were so popular, provocative, and new at the time that they still resonate among Portuguese readers of journalism and literature today, just as they did throughout the twentieth century.

The Portuguese Press at the Fin-de-Siècle: Transnational Influences and Change

Regarded as a small rectangular piece of land in the westernmost part of Europe, trapped between the immensity of the ocean and the huge Spanish landmass, Portugal has always endured a somewhat marginal status within continental Europe. Not only is it traditionally perceived abroad as a nation on the remote fringes of the Atlantic coast, but also it is acrimoniously described by Portuguese nationals as lagging behind all other major European powers. And never was the perception of an economically frail, culturally stagnant, and politically ineffective country more acute than in the last decades of the nineteenth century, when a self-conscious and active intelligentsia took both the literary realms and the press by storm, bitterly denouncing the failings of the nation, directly accusing the monarchy and Parliament of responsibility for what they considered to be the imminent demise of the country. Paradoxically, the truth is that, with the exception of the centuries of the great maritime discoveries and conquests, when Portugal ruled the first overseas empire of modern times, never had the nation thrived as much as at the fin-de-siècle. There were massive investments in the modernization of industry and in the construction of the much-needed infrastructure—railway networks, roads, and viaducts—that would enhance the economic development of the country. Illiteracy levels started to decrease as education was given priority on the political agenda. Financially, the foreign debt, a chronic concern of all governments, was finally brought under control as a result not simply of fiscal measures but mostly of the country's ambitious modernization policies and consequential economic boom. At the political level, a constitutional monarchy ruled through Parliament, where successive governments alternated between the two leading parties, the more liberal Partido Progressista and the conservative Partido Regenerador. And significantly, these were times of peace following the Napoleonic invasions and the civil wars that had ravaged and divided the country earlier in the century.

Concomitantly, this was the heyday of the Portuguese press. Hundreds of national, local, daily, and weekly periodicals flourished, not only in the greater urban centers of Lisbon and Porto but also in smaller provincial towns. In fact, by the end of the century the press enjoyed a far greater degree of freedom of expression than it would in the middle decades of the twentieth century, when censorship was reinstated during the totalitarian Estado Novo regime, which was in power from 1933 to 1974. Furthermore, it benefited from the speed of communications provided by the new telegraph lines and from the revenue obtained from advertising. There were politicized newspapers, literary magazines, and specialized periodicals in such varied fields as agronomy and music, and the satirical press attained enormous popularity. Broadsheets invariably published the day's parliamentary debates and news related to the royal family; there was also a *fait divers* section; and a section called *folhetim*—a clear import from the French feuilleton[4]—typically devoted to the serialization of short stories and chapters of novels that would subsequently appear in book form.

Portuguese journalists Eça de Queirós, Ramalho Ortigão, Oliveira Martins, and Batalha Reis all wrote articles during this period of relative affluence, greater freedom of speech, economic and social changes, and industrial progress. But surprising as it may seem, Portugal was interpreted by these four writers and their fellow intellectual elites as a nation in decay, corrupted by the ineptitude of its politicians and by the apathy of its journalists, who wrote nothing more than gossip or clinically transcribed the parliamentary debates of the day. As opinionated journalists, they were the first, and the most fearless, to criticize the press, which they thought had done a poor job of informing and, given the high concentration of stories devoted to gossip and scandal, educating the public. Queirós, also the best-selling novelist of the period and a renowned author in his own right, went so far as to fill his novels with caricatures of sloppy journalists who do not bother to check sources and whose articles are either a dense mass of words difficult to decipher or a venomous personal attack.[5] Simultaneously, and in an attempt to free literature from what they considered to be the noxious influence of romanticism, they advocated a realistic aesthetics such as that championed by the French masters Émile Zola, Gustave Flaubert, and Victor Hugo, only later to be disenchanted by its limitations. Against this backdrop, a new journalistic form, whose models were found abroad, was coming to light in Portugal.

Seduced first by the satirical French periodical *Les Guêpes,* founded by *Le Figaro* editor Jean-Baptiste Alphonse Karr, these four authors would later succumb to the novelty of W. T. Stead's style, and the *Pall Mall Gazette* quickly became their target of emulation, a straightforward example of the transnational influence the foreign press exerted on late-nineteenth-century Portuguese journalism. Importing and adapting the French model of *Les Guêpes* to a Portuguese audience, for instance, Ortigão and Queirós pioneered an experiment with a new kind of journalism at home. In June 1871 they released the first issue of a revolutionary and controversial periodical titled *As Farpas* ("Barbs"), the front page of which featured a picture of the devil Asmodeus, the Prince of Hell known for his sarcasm, a clear indication of the editorial objectives of the newspaper.

For the following two years, both authors engaged in a crusade against the inertia of factual journalism that, as they explicitly admitted in the inaugural issue, taught the public nothing. On the contrary, through abundant doses of irony and humor, *As Farpas* aimed at pointing out what could be termed the national "progress of decadence."[6] When Queirós embraced a diplomatic career and left Portugal for the Spanish Antilles, where he was to become consul in Havana, Ortigão carried on their mission single-handedly for the next eleven years. The purpose of *As Farpas* was clear from the outset. As editors, journalists, and reporters, Ortigão and Queirós wanted to stir the stagnant pool of Portuguese journalism. If nothing else in the periodical was innovative, the style adopted by these journalists would in itself be enough to break away from the canon of conventional Portuguese reporting. The articles in *As Farpas,* like all journalistic articles, accomplished the function of informing the public of the latest newsworthy events. Yet they addressed the reader directly, were not meant to be impartial, and resorted to humor and irony in order to reveal openly what was wrong in the political, social, and economic systems of fin-de-siècle Portugal.

As the authors bluntly state in the periodical's inaugural issue, which sold out immediately after publication: "Readers of good sense—who curiously open the first page of this booklet, know . . .—that it was written for you . . . ! And the idea of giving you each month, for as long as you wish, one hundred ironic, happy, caustic, fair pages was born the day we could find out, through the confusing mist of facts, part of the outline of the profile of our time."[7] With a single blow, Ortigão and Queirós had gained a legion of faithful readers and a cohort of detractors. The periodical's literary imprint, irrefutably supplied by Queirós, who was pursuing a successful parallel career as a novelist, paved the way for a new form of journalistic writing in Portugal. Nevertheless, what is most relevant about these very first, and elaborate, statements of this new periodical is that the authors openly sought the readers' complicity and therefore addressed their public directly.

Similarly, these journalists struggled to make sense of a rapidly changing world, that "confusing mist of facts" for which there was no easy interpretation. They also wanted to avoid the mass production and distribution of the news. With the invention of the telegraph and the new transatlantic ships came the power to shorten distances and to speed up communication. And further developments in the printing industry allowed for faster production and wider distribution of papers that disseminated this news. All of this fueled the repetition of news stories in endless periodicals, which led to a saturation of objective reporting in the press. Consequently, what "new" journalists wanted, and these Portuguese writers in particular, was to break with the constraints of conventional journalism.

Of course, As Farpas cannot be considered straightforward literary journalism, as it poses a series of problems to academics no matter what angle it is viewed from; but the periodical did open the door to further journalistic experiments in Portugal. Those critics who fail to locate As Farpas comfortably within a journalistic tradition nonetheless unanimously defend the notion that it represents a turning point in Portuguese journalism. And quite a new and different one at that, given the periodical's admixture of narrative with political and economic analysis and a somewhat satirical interpretation of what was wrong within the country. The journalists proposed to tell the news a way that aroused the public conscience and thus intervened at the social level.[8] More than a decade before Matthew Arnold complained about the impertinent "new" journalism of W. T. Stead—a label that soon, and most likely to his own bewilderment, came to define a revolutionary way of presenting news that would mark the late Victorian press—two journalists from a small country had already felt the urge to give a new stamp to Portuguese journalism by critically addressing controversial issues and neglecting the objective stance of news reporting.[9] The first steps had been taken. Never again would the Portuguese press experience such dynamism as in the last three decades of the nineteenth century, when, in the wake of the success the articles of Queirós and Ortigão found with the public, a new generation of journalists—sharing the same disillusionment with conventional factual journalism as their counterparts writing in English on both sides of the Atlantic—started to experiment with and adopt a whole "new" way of writing journalism.

Breaking the Constraints of Raw Factuality:
Queirós and Ortigão as "New" Journalists

After becoming disenchanted with his consular position in Havana, where for two years he had to bear the heat and dust, and the lack of an intellectual elite with whom he could discuss literature and politics, Queirós was transferred to Newcastle-upon-Tyne in England.[10] The change of climate and the return to his beloved Europe marked a period of intense literary and journalistic production. Therefore, apart from his having to draft the unavoidable bureaucratic documents dealing with coal transactions, his activities as consul in Newcastle left him plenty of free time to devote to writing, both his first best-selling novels and his articles on England and the English. Queirós thus became a novelist and a press correspondent to Portugal. Leading a life of intellectual solitude—in his private letters to Ramalho he confessed that after a year of exile among the Britons, the only person with whom he could seriously talk about feelings and general ideas was his physician—Queirós encountered the real world outside the consulate only through the daily charts of the price of coal and, most important, the British press.[11] Queirós was in fact a compulsive and eclectic reader; he would read virtually every paper from *The Times* to the *Pall Mall Gazette* to *Vanity Fair.* He read local, daily, and weekly papers, as well as monthly magazines and literary supplements. And he was in awe of the British press, which he would continue to praise until his untimely death in 1900. Here in Newcastle, and later at the consulate in Bristol, Queirós, an inveterate Francophile, now came to admire Charles Dickens and was deeply influenced by British journalism.

When Queirós started collaborating with the Portuguese newspaper *A Actualidade* in 1877 with a series titled "Cartas de Inglaterra e Crónicas de Londres" ("Chronicles from London" or "Eça's English Letters"), little did he know that his articles would make a tremendous impression, not only on his longtime friend and former French teacher Ortigão but also on other contemporary Portuguese journalists, who would try to imitate his style and his new way of writing journalism. In "Chronicles from London," a more mature Queirós emerges. His stories cover numerous international conflicts in which Britain found itself, from the annexation of the Transvaal to the Eastern Question concerning Turkey and Russia, where Britain's vested interests included the protection of the strategic Suez route to India.[12] But "Chronicles from London" also describes British society at length. Queirós mentions the latest concerts, plays, and book releases, or explains the miners' strikes in the county of Northumberland. He also comments on various scandals that shook the foundations of Victorian respectability: the publication of Charles Knowlton's *Fruits of Philosophy* (basically a guide to birth control aimed at the working class), several adultery and divorce cases among members of the aristocracy, or the most recent incidents involving the Prince of Wales. In fact, Queirós took his role of press correspondent very seriously; but the way he delivered the news was absolutely unorthodox for a Portuguese journalist at that time. The irony and corrosive humor of *As Farpas* were still there, more refined than ever, and he again addressed his readers directly. But this time he added dialogues, created entire scenes, and narrated telling episodes of events he had observed. And as a story unfolded, Queirós gave his personal opinion and his own interpretation of the facts that he was narrating to the public back in Portugal. He did not fabricate the news; everything he stated was true and based on real events. It is his interpretation of those facts, colored at times by a pinch of sensationalism, that clearly sets "Chronicles from London" apart from the basic factuality of conventional Portuguese journalism.

Reading, for example, the developments involving the Eastern Question, just as Queirós wrote them, is almost like reading a novel. In each article of his so-called chronicles, the journalist composed new chapters that captivated the readers' attention and anticipated future events. When war finally erupted between Russia and Turkey, he reported:

> Here, naturally the great concern is the future attitude of England; and it is not easy to understand, through the many discussions in the papers, and through the confusing debates in Parliament, which is the true will of the country: I believe that, just like the [Foreign] Ministry, the country wants to intervene. Obviously the ministry declares . . . its neutrality: but . . . it is a conditional neutrality.
>
> . . . As soon as the Russians . . . march across Constantinople—England must say, "Hold it there."
>
> . . . It is India that would be threatened, either directly or indirectly by the route leading there. . . . On top of this, if one adds that Russia is the natural enemy of England; that England wants to show her strength, and her influence . . .—one will be able to detect the popularity of the idea of intervention. Besides this, the press . . . is clearly asking for a war: and *Punch* was right the other day . . . in inciting the enormous British Lion to make it rise up and roar.[13]

No doubt Queirós is reporting on a serious question facing Britain. He mentions the public commotion regarding the possibility of war, he lets his readers know about the intricacies of the issue, and he talks about the official position of the British government. But he also weighs in on the topic of the war, predicting the attitudes that Britain might take and enlightening readers as to the real motives behind the need, or the desire, for British intervention in a conflict in the Near East. In article after article the plot becomes more complex; and when the British Foreign Ministry recognizes the important strategic role that Greece may play in opposing Russian expansionism, it is not without irony and, again, a touch of sensationalism that Queirós declares in his article of March 28, 1878, "Lord Derby, and with him all England, has just made an immense discovery: Lord Derby has discovered Greece" (*CI* 329). Clearly the journalist is trying to amuse the reader, while simultaneously voicing his own antipathy toward the way Britain was meddling in the conflict between Russia and the Ottoman Empire—something unthinkable (and unprintable), for instance, in the factual reports of war correspondents.

Similarly, and also important when it comes to defining Queirós as a literary journalist, he maintains an intimate dialogue with his readers. As war drags on in the Near East, with no definite end on the horizon, he finds a way to clarify further his position on the uselessness of armed warfare, and on this conflict in particular, by stating: "The monotony of war . . . makes for the unhappiness of press correspondents: even I have been postponing this article for a few days in the hope that either the Russians or the Turks, in Asia or in the Danube, would charitably offer me some touching episode or decisive feat. But nothing!" (*CI* 214). Here the journalist's own persona is exposed to the reader. His opinions, his writing process, his apprehension of the facts, his ironic commentary on a complex reality, and his unveiling of the person behind the reporting combine to help bridge the divide between provider and receiver of the printed news.

By the time Eça de Queirós ended his collaboration with *A Actualidade* in 1878, he was so popular and so influential as a journalist in Portugal that in 1880 a Brazilian newspaper invited him to write similar signed dispatches for its pages. Thus emerged "Cartas de Inglaterra" (Letters from England), a series that not only secured Queirós's reputation among Brazilian readers but also allowed a Portuguese "new" journalism to cross the Atlantic. His correspondence for the *Gazeta de Notícias* in Rio de Janeiro would, in fact, be prolific, lasting until September 1897.

In the meantime, back home, Ramalho Ortigão, whose priority was to maintain *As Farpas*'s usual standards of controversy, decided to take a trip to England and visit his dear friend Queirós. In 1887 the repercussions of Stead's anti-prostitution campaign, "The Maiden Tribute of Modern Babylon," serialized in 1885, were still being felt, and Ortigão was so fascinated by Stead's journalism—or, better, the newly proclaimed "new" journalism—that he decided to have a try at it himself. On his return home, he wrote *John Bull: o Processo Gordon Cumming, Lord Salisbury e Correlativos Desgostos* (John Bull:

A Witness' Account on Some Aspects of English Life and Civilization), which mixes numerous references to Stead and to the "Maiden Tribute" together with Dickensian descriptions of London's East End slums, as well as with his own personal account and interpretation of a paradoxical country where great affluence walked alongside abject poverty. In line with Queirós, Ortigão enjoyed inventing scenes and liked having the freedom to get in some sensationalist lines.

Even more than his predecessor, however, Ortigão became a character in his accounts. He lets his readers overhear conversations he had with people he met on the streets. He describes his daily activities as a tourist in London, and he even recalls a visit he made to his beloved compatriot Queirós, at the time residing in Clifton. Everything he sees in England becomes a reason for writing, as when he describes the famous British fog to a Portuguese public not familiar with this peculiar weather condition:

> In one of the days I spent in London, and having finished some paperwork at about eleven a.m., I started to shave at a mirror hanging from the window frame. Through the windowpane . . . I could see a beautiful day outside. . . . Suddenly, as I was already drying the shaving razor, I realized the sky had changed its wonderful pearl white . . . into a thick ochre yellow. . . . After five minutes everything was black, pitch black, and I had to light two candles to finish dressing.
> It was the fog.
> Not a slight little fog for the rheumatism of foreigners . . . but a true and authentic *London fog.*[14]

Noticeable in *John Bull* is the way travelogue and journalistic reporting overlap, a phenomenon that helps situate Ortigão within a "new" journalistic tradition wherein, as critics have suggested, the boundaries between travel literature and literary journalism became blurred.[15]

Furthermore, drawn to the *Pall Mall Gazette*'s articles and fascinated with "the new power of the interview in the influence and destiny of contemporary journalism" (*JB* 45), this Portuguese traveler and journalist explicitly reveals his intentions to follow in Stead's steps, declaring in *John Bull:* "The London scandals, recently brought to public light by the terrible inquiry of the *Pall Mall Gazette,* have brought my attention to the study of prostitution in English society; and it is to this question that I intend to devote some brief pages, adding to the revelations of the *Pall Mall* the modest fruits of my own observation in the great capital of the United Kingdom" (*JB* 41). From his words it is possible to conclude that Ortigão was a reporter willing to verify the accuracy of Stead's findings regarding the prostitution and immorality allegedly pervading British society, which were given ample media coverage in the wake of the "Maiden Tribute" affair. He assumes the position of the conscientious journalist who wants to research the subject of his reporting in depth and thereby acquire firsthand knowledge of it.

In addition to covering the scandals revealed in the pages of the *Pall Mall Gazette,* Ortigão also concentrates on other subjects—such as the poverty of the working class, the religious practices of the English, and their education system—in an attempt to better depict the society of the nation he is visiting. As a travel writer, he visits museums and art exhibitions, restaurants and pubs, theaters and great department stores, documenting all of his experiences for readers in Portugal; as a journalist, he adds objective data in the form of charts, percentages, and statistics that he has taken from press articles and official reports in order to show his commitment to reporting the truth, its subjective interpretation notwithstanding.

But since "Maiden Tribute" is at the heart of Ortigão's journalistic interests, *John Bull* would not be complete unless the author was able to prove, or reject, the revelations put forward by Stead's crusade against prostitution. Unfolding a scene in which he is the lead character, Ortigão confesses that the facts stated in the articles in the *Pall Mall Gazette* bear the stamp of authenticity:

> Coming down from Regent Street . . . after having dined at the Royal . . . I had the opportunity to observe the fundamental phenomenon focused on in detail by the *Pall Mall Gazette.*
>
> It was nine in the evening. . . . Beyond St. James's [Park] . . . three ladies *fell over* me . . . like ravens over a dead carcass. I had to shove them and involuntarily hit one of them. I apologized and gave her a florin. The other two then told me they would not mind being shoved for a penny. I gave them half a shilling. (*JB* 107–8)

Ortigão goes on to tell of similar encounters and describes the unspeakable things he witnessed in Hyde Park which confirmed for him that London was, after all, a corrupt and morally decaying "modern Babylon": whole families sleeping at night on park benches, illicit sex being bought and sold in the open, right under the eyes of the police, and hordes of drunken people, for whom solace was to be found only at the bottom of a bottle of gin, dragging with them their miserable existence of poverty. His opinions coincide with Stead's, but he validates them with observations and research drawn from his own immersion reporting and delivers them in a personal manner characteristic of a "new" journalist. He is there at night in Hyde Park, for example, witnessing the social horrors that transform London into a capital of duplicity, just as he is there when the prostitutes attempt to lure him.

If *John Bull* cannot entirely be compared to Jack London's *People of the Abyss* (1903), in which the respected American journalist becomes an East End street vagrant, Ortigão is nonetheless a reporter in close contact with the reality of life in east London, its otherness. And since literary journalism "stands as a humanistic approach to culture as compared to the scientific, abstract, or indirect approach taken by much standard journalism"[16] in lending a voice to the socially disenfranchised, Ortigão can be considered both a precursor of modern literary journalists and a Portuguese equivalent to the British "new" journalists because of his contribution to making visible the sufferings of the underprivileged classes in Victorian London.

In the Wake of Queirós and Ortigão: Batalha Reis and Oliveira Martins

Similarly impressed with Stead's journalistic revolution, and following their friends Queirós and Ortigão to England, Batalha Reis and Oliveira Martins were also seduced by the "new" journalism of the fin-de-siècle. In 1884 Reis was appointed consul in Newcastle (precisely where Queirós had been posted some years before) and, four years later, would also be invited by a Portuguese periodical to become a press correspondent in England. Consequently he published a series of seventeen articles throughout 1888 titled "Revista Inglesa: Crónicas" (English Review), and between 1893 and 1896, while he worked as a consul in London, he also contributed twenty-seven more articles, again called "English Review," to the Brazilian journal *Gazeta de Notícias.* During this time, Oliveira Martins resigned from his position as Portuguese minister of finance after four exasperating months and sought refuge in England in 1892. In the autumn of that year Martins published a series of articles about his trip called "A Inglaterra de Hoje: Cartas de um Viajante" (The England of Today: Letters from a Traveler), which would be published in book form the following spring under the same title and quickly translated into English as part of a collection with the revealing title *How Others See Us.*

If Eça de Queirós introduced a new journalistic form in Portugal and Ramalho Ortigão closely followed in Stead's steps, by the time Reis and Martins were writing their accounts of England, "new" journalism was indeed flourishing: Charles Booth had brought to light his monumental inquiry *Life and Labour of the People in London,* which he published from 1886 to 1903; Andrew Mearns had published *The Bitter Cry of Outcast London* (1883); and *Horrible London* (1889), the collection of articles by George Sims, had just been released in book form. Booth, Mearns, Sims, and so many other writers had obviously been influenced by Stead, but they were also drawn to the study of London's East End underworld, first presented by an earlier pioneer of "new" journalism, Henry Mayhew. Mayhew's numerous articles on the topic of London's seedy underbelly had appeared in the pages of the *Morning Chronicle* to such public acclaim that they were subsequently revised and republished under the title *London Labour and the London Poor* (1850–1852).

As writers, Reis and Martins did not want to be left out of this fin-de-siècle fascination with the underworld of poverty and crime that blackened London, the heart of the largest and most prosperous empire ever. Simultaneously, as journalists—both of them had a long career behind them as editors, founders, and collaborators on several magazines and newspapers—they wanted to explore sensational topics and experiment with the varied techniques of "new" journalism for themselves and adapt them to a Portuguese context. Therefore, just like Stead, Mayhew, and Booth before them, Reis and Martins went to the East End with the clear intention of writing about their own experiences there.

Martins even hired a detective to guide him through the dimly lit alleys of the East End labyrinth, where he had the opportunity to enter overcrowded and squalid houses that he compared to the dens of wild animals. In doing so, he appropriated the vocabulary so dear to the "new" journalists, who were interested in capturing as closely as possible in words the miseries endured by the lower classes. In fact his description of those houses closely resembles the images captured by Mearns and others. As Martins saw it, on entering one of the dens:

> It was a room that was about double the size of the iron bedstead placed in one corner. An oil lamp . . . lit the room coldly, if we can call the place where we were a room. On the bed . . . drinking filthy liquids, covered in nameless rags, was a bald man, drunk with gin. His breath, mixed with the smell of oil and with . . . rottenness, formed an air impossible to breathe. A woman standing at the bedside told the detective:
> "He hasn't had work at the docks for fifteen days."
> And I do not know what kind of womanly name I should give this creature, old before her days, with a swollen belly, . . . wearing on her bare shoulders a shawl green with dirt and an even dirtier skirt. . . . She had the air of an imbecile.
> "She drinks too"—the policeman told us, gravely.[17]

As we can see here, Martins is not just a reporter; he is more a literary journalist who describes a whole scene, its setting, its details, its smell, and its color. He even passes judgment, particularly when describing the woman as "an imbecile" or when using an adverb to refer to the way the policeman informed him of the woman's fondness for drinking. As such, he makes his readers aware of his presence and of his personal interpretation of what lay before his eyes.

Martins also visited gin palaces and opium dens, and on writing about his journeying into the East End, he introduced his Portuguese readers to an impressive account of the hopelessness in which the so-called submerged classes lived. Bolder than Martins, Reis even ventured into the dangerous East End during the horrible weeks in which Jack the Ripper became notorious for his crimes. Reis went to the Whitechapel district at night when another ghastly crime was imminent. In the articles he published in the aftermath of his dangerous incursions into Whitechapel, Reis transcribes the letters that the unknown murderer sent to the police. He also describes the crimes in great detail, characterizes the victims, and informs his readers about all the fear and commotion produced in Britain by the crimes. Recalling his immersion in the East End, Reis gives a clear picture of the neighborhoods and their inhabitants and includes whole scenes and dialogues in which he took part, such as an encounter with a woman of the streets:

> To one of those women . . . with whom I found myself . . . for a moment on the corner of a street, I asked:
> "Would you like to come with me?"
> "Sure"—she answered, taking my arm.
> "What if I were the Whitechapel murderer?"
> The woman faced me, smiled, and shrugging her shoulders told me:
> "Do you think it is better to starve?"
> And when I hastily went away, that woman started insulting me from a distance because I had not taken her with me.[18]

Here Reis is simultaneously the reporter gathering news firsthand and the "new" journalist revealing his emotional responses to that news, just as the British "new" journalists and his three compatriots had done. Like Queirós, Ortigão, and Martins, he too had embarked on a trip to England and had fallen prey to the seduction of "new" journalism.

As a transnational phenomenon, proto-literary journalism pervaded the Portuguese press of the fin-de-siècle in the same way it had the Anglophone press. Eça de Queirós, taking advantage of a diplomatic career, was one of the first Portuguese journalists to experiment with this new form of reporting. In England he observed closely, and with great interest, the journalistic changes that led to this late-century "new" journalism. Having already written articles of an opinionated nature with Ortigão for *As Farpas,* he embraced the freedom afforded him by that "new" journalism he was reading in the British press and wrote his articles on England in a similar style, thus transporting "new" journalism to a Portuguese-speaking audience.

After Queirós, Ramalho Ortigão also undertook a trip to England that greatly influenced his already controversial journalistic writing. Astounded by the popularity of Stead's style and shocked by the revelations put forward in the "Maiden Tribute," Ortigão endeavored to validate Stead's findings and translate them for his public back home. His contribution to Portugal's body of journalistic belles-lettres, *John Bull,* is further proof of the transnational nature of literary journalism.

Finally, following the lead of Queirós and Ortigão—and, notably, long before Jack London wrote his own heart-wrenching and best-selling account of the East End's downtrodden, *The People of the Abyss,* widely acclaimed as a monumental tribute to "new" journalism—Batalha Reis and Oliveira Martins offered to Portuguese and Brazilian readers similar disturbing images of urban social decay. The "new" journalistic techniques they used to capture these images combined the experimental writings of Queirós and Ortigão in *As Farpas* with the investigative journalism of Henry Mayhew earlier in the century. Simply put, at the fin-de-siècle, innovative Portuguese journalists were unable to resist "new" journalism's magnetic pull.

More striking, however, is the fact that through the "new" journalism of a Mayhew, a Stead, a Booth, or a *Pall Mall Gazette,* all four Portuguese writers were able to discover an England that was as much a nation in decay as was the motherland they had so criticized. "New" journalism helped them to dissect this strange Other across the channel and, consequently, renew their pride at home. In examining the Other, they could finally see the "I."

Queirós, Ortigão, Reis, and Martins were pioneers in the sense that they tried to bring an element of change to Portuguese fin-de-siècle journalism. Being influenced by changes already taking place in France and in Britain, and being themselves disenchanted by the journalism of gossip they found in their national press, they were very much seduced by the allure of British "new" journalism and thus became its first practitioners within a Portuguese context. They thus demonstrate that when discussing the emergence of this literary-journalistic form, we should not disregard its transnational roots.

NOTES

1. To avoid confusion with Tom Wolfe's term "New Journalism," I refer to this fin-de-siècle journalistic style throughout this essay as "new" journalism.

2. This should not be confounded with the expression "linguistic imperialism" coined by Robert Phillipson in his influential if not controversial *Linguistic Imperialism* (1992), regarding the prolific debate surrounding the hegemonic influence of the English language.

3. Only recently has Portuguese literary journalism of the late nineteenth century been subject to close scrutiny. See Isabel Soares, "O Império do Outro: Eça de Queirós, Ramalho Ortigão, Batalha Reis, Oliveira Martins e a Inglaterra Vitoriana" (Ph.D. diss., Universidade Nova de Lisboa, 2007).

4. In English, feuilleton came to mean "serial." Originally "feuilleton" referred to the bottom part of a newspaper page, where subjects not directly related to the main content of the periodical were published. These included theater and literary critiques, philosophical articles, and short stories. See Ernesto Rodrigues, *Mágico Folhetim: Literatura e Jornalismo em Portugal* (Lisbon: Editorial Notícias, 1998), 201–3.

5. In Queirós's *Os Maias* (The Maias), for instance, the image of the disreputable Lisboan journalist is epitomized by the character Palma, the editor of *The Devil's Horn*, a newspaper that specializes in scandal. Physically repugnant, fat, and sticky with perspiration, Palma is the incarnation of the immoral journalist peddling false and defamatory news for money.

6. Eça de Queirós and Ramalho Ortigão, *As Farpas: Crónica Mensal da Política, das Letras e dos Costumes* (Cascais: Principia, 2004), 17. All translations from Portuguese, unless otherwise noted, are my own.

7. Ibid., 16.

8. See Annabela Rita, *Eça de Queirós Cronista* (Lisbon: Edições Cosmos, 1998), 104.

9. In 1887 the essayist, literary critic, and poet Matthew Arnold contemptuously defined Stead's work as "new journalism" for "its appeals to mass taste and its often cavalier treatment of fact." See Kevin Kerrane, "From *If Christ Came to Chicago:* W. T. Stead," in *The Art of Fact: A Historical Anthology of Literary Journalism,* ed. Kevin Kerrane and Ben Yagoda (New York: Simon and Schuster, 1997), 49.

10. From his personal correspondence it is possible to verify that Queirós did not enjoy being posted in the Spanish Antilles, as Cuba was known at the time. He found the weather unbearable, and above all as a cosmopolite, he missed the intellectual comforts that Havana, which he described as a very provincial town, could not provide. Writing to Ortigão in 1873, Queirós complained about what he felt to be an experience of exile while being posted in Havana: "I am far from Europe, and you know how profoundly European we are, you and I. This [place] here—either because of its Spanish rudeness or because of its curious American character of the United States, is very different from what I need. I need politics, critique, literary corruption . . . ; here, I am stuck in a hotel, and when I argue, it is about exchange rates—and when I think, it is about *coolies*." Eça de Queirós, *Correspondência* (Lisbon: Imprensa Nacional-Casa da Moeda, 1983), 71. "Coolies" were Chinese workers from Macao (at the time an overseas Portuguese province) who came to Cuba to work on the sugar cane plantations.

11. See "Letter to Ramalho, 1 February 1875," ibid., 145.

12. Because of Turkey's strategic importance in the route to India, Britain maintained close diplomatic and economic relations with the Ottoman Empire, protecting it from traditional rivals such as Russia. See Bernard Porter, *The Lion's Share: A Short History of British Imperialism, 1850–1995* (Harlow, Essex: Longman, 1996), 89–90.

13. Eça de Queirós, *Cartas de Inglaterra e Crónicas de Londres* (Lisbon: Livros do Brasil, 2001), 206–8. Subsequent references appear parenthetically in the text, abbreviated *CI*.

14. Ramalho Ortigão, *John Bull: o Processo Gordon Cumming, Lord Salisbury e Correlativos Desgostos* (Lisbon: Livraria Clássica Editora, 1943), 127–30. Subsequent references appear parenthetically in the text, abbreviated *JB*.

15. See John C. Hartsock, *A History of American Literary Journalism: The Emergence of a Modern Narrative Form* (Amherst: University of Massachusetts Press, 2000), 13. For a more recent study, see Isabel Soares, "*South:* Where Travel Meets Literary Journalism," *Literary Journalism Studies* 1.1 (Spring 2009): 17–30.

16. Norman Sims, *True Stories: A Century of Literary Journalism* (Evanston: Northwestern University Press, 2007), 12.

17. Oliveira Martins, *A Inglaterra de Hoje: Cartas de um Viajante* (1893; Lisbon: Guimarães Editores, 1951), 224.

18. Batalha Reis, *Revista Inglesa: Crónicas* (Lisbon: Publicações D. Quixote/Biblioteca Nacional, 1988), 106.

Chapter 8

Literary Journalism in Spain

Past, Present (and Future?)

Sonia Parratt

A CASUAL LOOK at Spanish newspapers and magazines today is enough to give a general impression of how important literary journalism is to the print media in that country. To be sure, literary and journalistic activities have shared a long and complex history, although many years had to pass before that relationship was considered as an object of analysis. In Spain in particular, the situation is not much different. Although the origins of that journalism versus literature debate there can be traced back more than a century and a half, how the relationship between journalism and literature began in Spain and why it developed the way it did over time remain essentially unexamined in the secondary literature. This essay aims to correct that oversight.

Evolution of the Relationship between Literature and Journalism in Spain

Journalist José Acosta Montoro claims 1845 to be the year when literary journalism was first publicly acknowledged in Spain. When Joaquín Rodríguez Pacheco delivered his induction speech into the Real Academia Española, he defended the literary rights of journalism as an "independent genre."[1] Later, during the second half of the nineteenth century, references to journalism began circulating in Spanish textbooks on literature, which spoke about the existence of diverse trends for the classification of journalism. Ramon Salaverría describes these trends as having represented people who

1. considered journalism a literary genre closely linked to political life;
2. defined journalism as a didactic literary manifestation; and
3. declared themselves incapable of placing journalism in any known literary or oratorical genre.[2]

The conclusion Salaverría drew from this debate is that the first monographic textbooks about journalism were published as a result of the fact that the rules of writing for newspaper reporters in the nineteenth century were outlined by literature teachers. From a scholastic point of view, then, the main topics on news writing in Spain had their beginning in academic literature books.

From a practitioner's perspective, however, a review of history shows that in the early stages of its development in Spain, journalism was for the most part considered only as literature. This was the case because straight news, the bulk of the information that dailies provide nowadays, occupied only a small portion of space in the newspapers. Most of a paper's content was devoted to the publication of essays, poems, and popular writings. This, of course, was not unique to Spain.

British scholar Jean K. Chalaby describes how the early Anglo-American press and the French press both contained examples of literary journalism in their pages but differed on what "literary" actually meant. In the Anglo-American context, the press soon grew independent of literature because literary writers were incapable of imposing their values and rules on journalists. At the end of the nineteenth century, the few novelists and poets who did publish work in newspapers were literary reviewers who very rarely departed from this kind of writing. In fact, one significant British novelist tempted by a journalistic career was Charles Dickens, who became the publisher of the *Daily News* in 1846 but left this job three weeks later.[3]

In France, however, literary figures and celebrities were traditionally very close to journalism and occupied important positions in the press until after 1870. Although being a successful journalist was not enough to provide social recognition, journalism was seen by many young people as a first step toward a political career. The presence of the literary elite in the French press also explains the importance that literary values had for French journalists. Proof of this lies in the fact that admittance into the Académie française was considered to be the greatest honor for a French journalist, and the few who were chosen always signed their articles with mention of the French Academy.[4]

For these reasons, the distinctions in France between a journalist and a literary figure in the nineteenth century were essentially unidirectional; that is, a poet or a novelist could be a journalist, but a journalist was rarely thought of as an author of more noble literary genres. Perhaps because of this, the *Dictionnaire des professions* (1842) did not even list journalism as a profession. One's literary status alone, Jane Chapman explains, was sufficient "to call oneself a journalist in order to collaborate in the publication of a newspaper; indeed, there was no clear separation between journalism and other forms of literature."[5] That the many contributors to the Parisian daily *La Presse* in the nineteenth century were also well-known novelists (like Balzac), or poets (Lamartine), or both (Victor Hugo) only illustrates the fact that the French drew more of a distinction between an author and a journalist than they did between literature and journalism.

Unlike in the Anglo-American press, factual stories were not separated from commentaries in French newspapers, and writings deemed too journalistic were criticized by the established writers, who denounced the *américaniza-tion* of French journalism and fought to maintain its more literary bias. The journalistic writings that did get published were used as social criticism and dealt with topics such as the conditions of life of the working class, poverty, prostitution, and crime.[6] A clear example of this was journalist and author George Sand's attempt in the 1840s to reach the masses by using newspapers to support republicanism, expose the exploitation of workers, and defend women's rights.[7]

Anglo-American journalism and French journalism were visibly different, but they had in common the fact that they both had a great influence on other countries, including Spain. Still, Spanish journalism had its own peculiarities. There the word "literature" was synonymous with culture and included all sorts of human knowledge, such as medicine and philosophy. Writings on these fields used to be placed in the literary section of newspapers.[8]

The press also had a lot to do with awakening public interest in fictive narratives. Besides informing readers about works by various authors, some newspapers began to include fragments or summaries of novels and stories. Some examples are the short story "¡Adiós Codera!," written by Leopoldo Alas Clarín and published in 1892 in the daily *El Liberal,* and the novel *Mariquita y Antonio,* written by Juan Valera and published in installments during 1861 in *El Contemporáneo.* The rise of journalism and the birth of the modern novel were contemporaneous in Spain, which could certainly account for the fin-de-siècle debate just described on the relation between journalism and literature. As Enrique Chao Espina suggests about the modern Spanish novel, it "is not a literary work; it is journalism applied to the feelings, the passions, the intrigues of life. . . . 'Novelists are not literary writers, they are journalists,' said writer Nicomedes Pastor Díaz."[9]

In a way similar to what had happened in France, certain Spanish writ-ers, especially poets, aspired to political appointments.[10] Such was the case with writer Mariano José de Larra and poet José Espronceda,[11] who were both members of Parliament in 1836 and 1842, respectively, or writer Ángel de Saa-vedra, who was mayor of Madrid in 1843 and ambassador to Paris in 1859. The way to obtain such a position often consisted of joining the editorial staff of a socially prestigious newspaper, where contacts and the support of a politician could open political doors for a writer or, as in the case of a poet, enable him to have his work published.

The form of journalism that was predominant during the nineteenth century in Spain was certainly more literary than informative, but that is not to say that all the writers who worked for newspapers were considered journalists in the French sense of the word. The difference between a writer and a journalist was that the journalist was assigned to do mainly news reporting. Therefore, although Spanish newspapers did publish writings that were not literary but purely informative,[12] they were placed in specific sections of the newspaper in order to differentiate them from the more literary pieces.

At the end of the nineteenth century, various literary movements such as romanticism and realism emerged in Spain, but the diffusion of journalistic literature through books was still scarce. A cultivated group of writer-journalists arose in newspapers, most of whom belonged to the so-called Generation of '98, the Spanish literary renaissance that restored to Spanish letters a prestige that had been lost for centuries. This was an active group of novelists, poets, essayists, and philosophers who were concerned about the moral, political, and social crises that Spain experienced following its defeat in the Spanish-American War. Miguel de Unamuno, Azorín (José Martínez Ruiz), and Pío Baroja, among others, wanted to change society, and journalism was the best way for them to express themselves and to reach the masses. They published most of their work in dailies and literary periodicals, which shows that journalistic and literary activities in Spain remained in parallel.

In the twentieth century, the press still occupied a privileged place in introducing literary movements in Spain. During the first third of the century, newspapers became the main vehicles for cultural diffusion, and it was said that most intellectual works became known through them. Many admit that the press had usurped the place of books as media for cultural dissemination. In 1904, for example, Miguel de Unamuno complained that his novels were hardly known, whereas his press articles helped him to achieve national recognition. At that time, though, Spanish journalism began to pale in comparison to the Anglo-Saxon or Germanic press in terms of objective reporting; as I have already said, the Spanish press was more literary and ideological, and therefore less objective. But it counted on great intellectuals and writers. Newspapers like *El Resumen, El Globo,* or *El País* numbered among their contributors the most outstanding figures of the Generation of '98.[13]

Some years after this renaissance, things changed with Miguel Primo de Rivera's dictatorship, which lasted from 1923 to 1930. Primo de Rivera maintained that the government's censorship was excellent for newspapers because the exclusion of political topics forced journalists to look for higher, more spiritual subjects to write about. The major newspapers were rivals in getting the most prestigious writers, philosophers, essayists, and novelists to contribute to their pages. *El Sol* of Madrid, for example, attracted José Ortega y Gasset, Gregorio Marañón, and other well-known literary figures, thus fulfilling the government's idea of offering the readers literary, politically neutered writings.[14]

During these years, Spanish writers approached their journalistic activities as both a quick way to make a living and a means of communicating with the public.[15] Their efforts elevated journalism in Spain to what was then considered a higher standard, one that strove for accuracy and privileged scientific rigor in a way similar to that of today's press, although periodicals of that time still differed widely in terms of content and format. And it was certainly these writers who created a genuine journalistic style that represented the union between journalism and literature.[16] Two of the best examples are Unamuno and Ortega y Gasset, both of whom were respected as much for their literary production as for their work as journalists. Their contributions to newspapers such as *El País, El Sol,* and *El Imparcial* were real journalistic writings (articles, news analysis, and features) on current affairs that met the highest literary standards.

A few years later, after the Spanish civil war had come to an end in 1936, a group of writers who were not strictly professionals of journalism chose magazines and newspapers as media for their literary expression. Newspapers offered them a better financial return than books, as well as fame and immediate success as writers. This was so because in the early days of Franco's dictatorship, Spain's economy was badly damaged and publishing opportunities were scarce. This was also the case with César González-Ruano or, in earlier times, Josep Pla. González-Ruano, who worked as a correspondent in Paris and in Rome, published his autobiography in installments in the daily *El Alcázar.* Pla connected with political and cultural elites by reporting on Parliament, and he also published articles periodically for the weekly *Destino.*

A new phase began at the end of the 1950s and the beginning of the 1960s, represented by a generation that defined themselves as writer-journalists. Francisco Umbral was one of them. He published his first books under the protection of Nobel Prize winner Camilo José Cela, and he won many prestigious literary awards. At the same time, he became well-known for his acerbic columns in outstanding periodicals, such as the dailies *El País* and *El Mundo,* and the magazine *Interviú,* as well as for his ability to capture the hidden side of current events through his news articles, some of which were published in anthologies. Manuel Vázquez Montalbán also belonged to this generation. Winner of the Premio Nacional de las Letras Españolas, Spain's most coveted literary prize, Montalbán also worked for *El País* and *Interviú,* demonstrating a clear influence of the literary language in his interviews, news articles, and reportage.[17] In 1963 he published an essay that is considered to be one of the best studies on journalism in Spain "Informe sobre la Información" (Report about Information).

With the eruption of American New Journalism in the 1960s and 1970s, the bonds between journalism and literature in Spain grew even tighter. This is evidenced by various Spanish journalists who imported certain literary techniques into their journalistic writings (internal monologue, realistic descriptions, proximity to the protagonists, vivid dialogues, and so on), and who adopted a greater narrative presence in their daily chronicles and reportages at the time when they began competing with the immediacy and the impact of audiovisual media.[18] Spanish writers worked as journalists, and Spanish journalists entered the literary field by writing long-form reportages and publishing them as books. Rosa Montero's *Crónica del desamor* (*A Chronicle of Disaffection,* 1979) is commonly referred to as the first example of long-form reportage in Spain.[19] In it, Montero offers a bitter portrait of Spain's post-dictatorial hardships through the everyday life stories of the country's disillusioned young. The transition shows Elena, one of the book's main characters, that democracy is not achieved by political parties' or trade unions' street protests:

> Some guys from the trade unions pushed through the crowd until they managed to place their banners at the front: "Let's stop the speculation in land," and "Decent homes at decent prices." Their acronyms could be read under their slogans. . . . Elena grew hoarse arguing with them: "No acronyms, get away from the front of the crowd," but they, unperturbed, . . . let themselves be photographed with the same delectation as movie stars. . . , and those newspaper photos would show the damn acronyms.[20]

Another good example of the new type of long-form journalism is the "novel" *Galíndez* (1991) by Manuel Vázquez Montalbán, which is actually a book-length reportage about the disappearance of a Spanish politician during the dictatorship in the Dominican Republic.

Before the first Spanish translation of Tom Wolfe and E. W. Johnson's volume *The New Journalism* appeared in 1976, the authors just mentioned had already shown through their reportage innovative tendencies that broke with the models of traditional press reporting and even shared some formal characteristics with the phenomenon that was taking the United States by storm. This is why some Spanish writer-journalists like Maruja Torres and Julio César Iglesias, and academic researchers like Lluís Albert Chillón, believe that the acclaim bestowed on some of America's New Journalists for their innovative character has been overestimated. It is also unclear if the social causes that researchers say precipitated the New Journalism in the United States (that is, the hippie movement, counterculture, and antigovernment protests of the 1960s) really apply to the Spanish case.[21] Most Spanish scholars agree that New Journalism in Spain was represented by a generation of journalists who thought that the complexity and the changes in society had to be explained (and not only reported) to their readers, and this could be done properly only through high-quality, unconventional news writing.[22]

By the time the impact of New Journalism in Spain had waned two decades later, most of these journalists' contributions to the print media were appearing in more literary publications, such as Sunday supplements and conventional magazines. But today their influence is once again apparent in the pages of most Spanish dailies, in both features and news reports, in an effort to attract readers through what is known as *redacción periodística literaria* (literary news writing). And what is more, Spanish novelists have begun experimenting with journalistic techniques to reinvigorate literary formulas.

The Boom in Literary News Writing in Spain

As the twentieth century progressed, literary activity in the press became more pronounced in many countries. Suggestions for breaking with the traditional informative models emerged in the last decades of the century and inclined toward more narrative forms. One of the most significant proposals came from the North American scholar R. Thomas Berner, whose opposition to all traditional topics of news writing promoted a journalistic style called "literary news writing." He defended this concept as a way of showing reality exactly as it is because, as he has said, it represents in writing the marriage of thorough documentation and literary techniques.[23] Neale Copple summarizes the "added value" of literary news writing thus: "There it is again—information. Facts, information, more facts. Yet alone they do not make a story. A list of facts is not a story. Although a list of facts may satisfy the journalistic precept that we get all the facts, the list alone makes no sense. The difference between a list of facts and a story is style. . . . Style is the way you use words to express those facts. . . . Style is the way you turn those facts into a complete, satisfying story."[24]

Spanish researcher Lluís Albert Chillón has established three levels of journalistic products based on the greater or lesser presence of literary news writing in journalistic texts. Although it is questionable that we can speak strictly about the presence of only three levels, Chillón's proposal is very useful in terms of expressing the extent to which "literary news writing" is reflected in the Spanish press today.

The first level consists of *periodismo informativo de creación* (creative informative journalism). This is the style mentioned earlier, based on the fusion of a purely informative language with a more literary and aesthetic one. It is accepted as long as the expressive freedom does not cloud or displace the article's informative purposes. As Portuguese researcher Ernesto Rodrígues notes, "A writer is fully obliged to respect the truth and professional ethics, and yet, with no compromise to his literary creation, he can afford to dream, play with ideas, and let his imagination fly freely."[25] It is necessary to make one essential point clear: *creation* here does not mean *invention*. A creative news story is no less objective for all of its literary techniques. This way of writing is as valid as objective journalism. In fact, it can even bring a stronger sense of reality to readers than the typical events-oriented style of journalism. These are some of the characteristics that define works of creative informative journalism in Spain:

- they are mainly informative texts;
- they are narrative, descriptive, and argumentative simultaneously, and they do not follow the rigid structures of conventional journalism;
- they break with the formal point of view of classical Spanish journalistic genres (e.g., the news report, chronicle, reportage, and opinion article);
- they avoid stereotypical language, and their innovative ways of writing include literary techniques such as diverse narrative points of view, transcriptions of dialogues in their entirety, or global portraits of characters; and
- they avoid subjectivity, but they are not essentially objective either, because their readers count on the certainty of being informed by a person they can recognize and who has a personal style that is not overshadowed by the newspaper he or she works for.[26]

Creative informative journalism is mostly characterized by its use of expressive literary techniques that traditionally distinguished conventional informative reporting from the so-called interpretive genres in the Spanish press, such as reportages or chronicles. Today it has extended its influence to the reporting of straight news, such as the decisions of Parliament, in which the personal style makes the reader feel as if he or she was actually present at the political debates.

Chillón's second level is *narrativa creativa no ficticia* (nonfiction creative narrative), what various authors have previously referred to as long-form, in-depth interpretive stories, called the *grandes reportajes* in Spain. It may be more appropriate to call it "creative journalistic nonfiction narrative," since there is no reference to journalism in the term suggested by Chillón. Today's creative journalistic nonfiction narrative is what Spaniards refer to when they talk strictly about literary journalism. It was inherited from the neo-journalistic wave of the 1970s and has since enjoyed much currency, but this form of news writing today is still often hindered by factors such as the lack of time, money, or talent needed to write exemplary reportage. This is why only the major newspapers like *El País* or *El Mundo* can afford to publish this sort of reportage today. When they do, it is mainly in their weekend supplements, *El País Semanal* and *El Magazine,* which have achieved wide prestige among readers.

The third and final level that Chillón cites is called "'noveled' reportage," a term he coined in his 1990 doctoral dissertation, "El reportatge novel.lat: tècniques novel.lístiques de composició i estil en el reportatge escrit contemporani" ("Noveled" Reportage: Novelistic Techniques of Style and Composition in Contemporary Reportage). In this work he defines "noveled" reportage as a journalistic and literary product characterized by the symbiosis of two genres historically, morphologically, and functionally differentiated: on the one hand reportage, and on the other the fictional novel.[27] As for the reasons behind its boom in the Spanish press during the last decades, he writes: "It is understood as an unequivocal symptom of the changes that the mass print media is going through. As it has lost the monopoly of news reporting to audiovisual media and the new information technologies, the press (dailies and magazines) has been showing technical, productive, aesthetic, thematic, and stylistic transformations for some time."[28]

"Noveled" reportages are hybrid modalities that fuse the techniques of representation and of composition typical of nineteenth-century novels with the testimonial attitudes and procedures of documentation that characterize reportage. They also incorporate technical narratives from the cinema and television documentary, such as juxtapositions or compositions based on successive scenes.[29] Their extreme proximity to literature and the fact that they are sometimes published as novels make them representative of the highest level of literary news writing in Spain.

These three levels proposed by Chillón have helped scholars of the Spanish press to discern how "literary news writing" has materialized in Spanish journalism in recent years, and where the trend, greatly increasing in frequency among Spanish newspapers and magazines, is likely headed.

The "Reportagization" of News

Parallel to (and in a certain way as a consequence of) the increase of "literary news writing" in Spain, another trend has been reflected in the Spanish press related to literary journalism. In 1980 a team of North American researchers known as the Missouri Group published a handbook titled *News Reporting and Writing.* In it they announced the decline of the news report as understood in the classical sense (that is, as a straight story about a current and unexpected event likely to interest the public) in favor of texts linked less to breaking news and more to the reader's everyday life.[30] In other words, the decline of hard news stories has given rise to the soft news story and to "creation news,"[31] which are pieces of straight news written with reportage techniques. This can be defined as the "reportagization" of news, and it can be found in two essential journalistic sites in Spain: in interpretive reportage and in headline news.

The first and most significant way in which it has become visible in Spain is through the vast increase of reportage published in Spanish dailies such as *El País, El Mundo, La Vanguardia,* and *La Voz de Galicia,* to name a few. This spate of "reportagization" stories includes not only conventional reportage about current events that are not strictly breaking news reported objectively, but also (if not more so) the increasing number of interpretive reportages that provide in-depth coverage of recently published news items.[32]

A variety of the latter is biographical reportage, or stories about the people touched by certain events that have already been covered in the news. These types of stories do not need to be front-page news because they do not have a genuine impact on the events that directly or indirectly caused them; but they usually draw the reader's attention because they are related to news that had a great impact. Such is the case of *El Mundo,* which, soon after the March 11, 2004, terrorist attack in Madrid, published one reportage a day on each of the victims of the train bombings and the psychological, social, and economic impacts of their death on their families.

Other examples of interpretive "reportagization" are circumstantial reportages, or stories that help readers understand better the circumstances surrounding an event that has already been reported, or that provide additional information not initially reported because of the pressure of deadlines. These stories are seen frequently when an event occurs unexpectedly and just prior to a newspaper's closing time. One example is the case of the *El País* reports on the plane crash at Madrid's Barajas airport that killed 154 people in August 2008, all of which were based on extensive reportage of the accident.

One final form of interpretive "reportagization" of the news can be seen in topical reportages, or stories indirectly related to current affairs of general interest or with a great impact on society that analyze an event's consequences for the citizens in their everyday life. Examples of these types of topical reportage were the pieces published in all Spanish dailies following the introduction of the euro in Spain.

As for the second way in which "reportagization" appears in Spanish newspapers, we have the proliferation of what is known as "reportaged news." For many years, there was the custom of associating reportage with the soft news that appears in the Sunday papers or in certain sections of the dailies. At present it is often unclear where the distinction lies between a reportage and many of the news articles that are published in the Spanish press because traditional news reporting has been adopting the techniques of reportage more and more. This phenomenon has given rise to "reportaged news," or reporting about breaking headline news in a more interpretive and creative way rather than in the more traditional informative style.

Thus there are essentially two options in Spain today for reporting straight news: to provide the facts as they occurred, following traditional news writing guidelines, or to present those facts in a different manner that still informs readers accurately but that also makes the story livelier.[33] In the opinion of *New York Times* journalist Rick Bragg, it is precisely this second approach that differentiates reading news superficially from reading the whole story with human interest.[34] The increase of "reportaged news" stories in Spanish newspapers today can be traced directly to the need to keep the public's interest—and patronage.

Finally, the boom that "reportagization" is experiencing in Spain affects not only the contents of the press but also the pages of other publishing sectors. Spanish readers have seen a proliferation of "reportage-novels" or "reportage-books," arising from the adoption of journalistic techniques by novelists. Colombian author Francisco de Paula Muñoz's *El crimen de Aguacatal* (*The Crime of Aguacatal,* 1873), probably the first reportage-novel written in Spanish, is described as "a narration that tells a whole, coherent, and factual story."[35] Since then, the evolution of journalism in Spain has witnessed a growing number and variety of reportage-novels that are similar in style to those written by the Americans Gay Talese, Norman Mailer, Truman Capote, and Tom Wolfe. Some well-known examples are *Mariposas sobre la tumba* (*Butterflies on the Tomb,* 2006) by Pedro Avilés, based on real events in Ireland and on the Spanish Mediterranean coast; *Territorio comanche* (1994) by Arturo Pérez–Reverte, about the war in Bosnia; and Manuel Rivas's compilation of reportages titled *El periodismo es un cuento* (*Journalism Is a Story,* 1998).

Despite the fact that these reportage-novels have been catalogued as literature (since it is not their main objective to be informative), they show that the influence of reportage has transcended the press and has reached long-form narratives that combine commercial success and literary writing—to say nothing of their doses of suspense and their psychological penetration into the thoughts and behavior of their characters.[36]

I have conducted research on the evolution of literary journalism in the Galician press from 1960 to 2000 (Galicia is one of the seventeen autonomous Spanish communities) and have found an increase both in the number and in the variety of reportage topics in newspapers. This confirms that neither competition from other media nor trends toward a more visual design in newspapers is preventing Spanish reporters from practicing literary journalism; if anything, it shows that short and long stories are not incompatible in the same newspaper. On the contrary, data obtained from the study have proved that this type of writing is extending its influence to other genres as well, resulting in the "reportagization" of news. This means that in Spain, even breaking news stories are being written in a more creative style, are more featurized, and employ a more complex structure that before was present only in long-form journalism.

In short, if the tendency shown in my research continues, it can be anticipated that literary journalism will eventually increase its presence in Spanish newspapers. This will potentially help the press reach readers of the twenty-first century, offering them attractive stories with profound insight into current affairs not found in other media such as television. Journalist and writer Manuel Rivas best summarizes this current and future trend of viewing reportage as the paradigm of literary journalism in Spain: "It doesn't make sense to buy a newspaper to read about what the audiovisual media have already told us; the advantage of print media is that it can go beyond these other media by cultivating words. . . . Definitely, I think that reportage is the future, and not only that; it is the word that best summarizes the aim of print media."[37]

The relationship between journalism and literature in Spain can be summed up thus: Ever since the dawn of the modern press, journalism and literature were not considered to be mutually exclusive and, if anything, have been frequently linked, with many writers earning their living writing for newspapers, and many journalists devoting themselves to literary endeavors. Nowadays a peculiar phenomenon is taking place in Spain. After the gradual separation of the two disciplines in the post–New Journalism era, Spanish novelists are now experimenting with journalistic techniques to reinvigorate literary formulas, just as the Spanish press has begun using literary techniques known in Spain as *redacción periodística literaria* to boost dwindling readership. Literary journalism seems poised to achieve both aims.

NOTES

1. José Acosta, *Periodismo y literatura,* vol. 1 (Madrid: Guadarrama, 1973), 82. All translations from Spanish and Portuguese, unless otherwise noted, are my own.

2. Ramón Salaverría, "La noticia en los manuales de Periodismo: evolución del concepto y de las normas redaccionales" (News in Journalism Manuals: The Evolution of Its Concept and Editorial Standards) (Ph.D. diss., Universidad de Navarra, 1998), 52.

3. Jean K. Chalaby, "Journalism as an Anglo-American Invention," *European Journal of Communication* 11.3 (1996): 303–26.

4. Sonia F. Parratt, "Periodismo y literatura: una contribución a la delimitación de la frontera" (Journalism and Literature: Delimitating the Border between Genres), *Estudios sobre el Mensaje Periodístico* 12 (2006): 275–84.

5. Jane Chapman, "The Personal Is the Political: George Sand's Contribution to Popular Journalism," in *The Journalistic Imagination,* ed. Richard Keeble and Sharon Wheeler (New York: Routledge, 2007), 45.

6. Sonia F. Parratt, *Introducción al reportaje: antecedentes, actualidad y perspectivas* (An Introduction to the Feature: Past, Present, and Perspectives) (Santiago de Compostela: Universidade de Santiago de Compostela, 2003), 60–61.

7. Chapman, "The Personal Is the Political," 44–57.

8. María del Pilar Palomo, ed., *Movimientos literarios y periodismo en España* (Literary Movements and Journalism in Spain) (Madrid: Síntesis, 1997), 45.

9. Enrique Chao, *Pastor Díaz dentro del romanticismo* (Pastor Díaz during the Romantic Period) (Madrid: CSIC, 1949), 40.

10. Jorge Urrutia, *La verdad convenida* (The Accepted Truth) (Madrid: Biblioteca Nueva, 1997), 65.

11. Maximiliano Fernández, *Larra, en las elecciones de 1836: Cómplices y adversarios* (Larra during the 1836 Elections: Accomplice and Adversaries) (Segovia: Fundación Instituto Castellano y Leonés de la Lengua, 2009), 120.

12. María Cruz Seoane, *Historia del periodismo en España,* vol. 2, *El siglo XIX* (The History of Journalism in Spain, vol. 2, The Nineteenth Century) (Madrid: Alianza, 1983), 65.

13. Palomo, *Movimientos literarios y periodismo en España,* 286–87.

14. Felipe Torroba, *La información y el periodismo* (Information and Journalism) (Buenos Aires: Eudeba, 1968), 42.

15. María Cruz Seoane adds to the economic motivations the wish to make a name for oneself, the need to leave the smaller world of the book and to reach a wider reading public, and, in many cases, to do effective cultural and/or political work by disseminating one's ideas through newspapers. See María Cruz Seoane, "La literatura en el periódico y el periódico en la literatura," in *Periodismo y literatura* (Journalism and Literature), ed. Annelies van Noortwijk and Anke van Haastrecht (Amsterdam: Rodopi, 1997), 17–25.

16. Félix Rebollo, *Periodismo y movimientos literarios contemporáneos españoles 1900–1939* (Journalism and Contemporary Spanish Literary Movements, 1900–1939) (Madrid: Huerga y Fierro, 1997), 14.

17. Reportage in Spanish journalism is defined as a text published in a newspaper which usually reports on facts that are current but not necessarily news, and which contains more depth, explanation, and analysis than plain news reports. Its author is freer to use structural, expressive, and other literary resources, and he generally signs his writing and accompanies it with photographs or infographs.

18. The first public news broadcast in Spain took place at the end of 1956, but Spanish television did not enjoy any real success until two decades later because of technical difficulties produced by the country's mountainous landscape, as well as censorship rules that Franco enforced until his death in 1975.

19. Palomo, *Movimientos literarios y periodismo en España*, 482.

20. Rosa Montero, *Crónica del desamor* (A Chronicle of Disaffection) (Madrid: Debate, 1979), 50.

21. Parratt, *Introducción al reportaje*, 54.

22. Lluís Albert Chillón, *Literatura y periodismo: una tradición de relaciones promiscuas* (Literature and Journalism: A Tradition of Promiscuous Relationships) (Valencia: Universitat de València, 1999), 359.

23. R. Thomas Berner, "Literary Newswriting: The Death of an Oxymoron," *Journalism Monographs* 99 (1986): 2.

24. Neale Copple, *Depth Reporting: An Approach to Journalism* (Englewood Cliffs, N.J.: Prentice-Hall, 1964), 79.

25. Ernesto Rodrígues, *Mágico Folhetim: Literatura e Jornalismo em Portugal* (The Magic *Folhetim:* Literature and Journalism in Portugal) (Lisbon: Editorial Notícias, 1998), 77.

26. Sebastiá Bernal and Lluís Albert Chillón, *Periodismo informativo de creación* (Constructing Informative Journalism) (Barcelona: Mitre, 1985), 85–88.

27. Lluís Albert Chillón, "El reportatge novel.lat: tècniques novel.lístiques de composició i estil en el reportatge escrit contemporani" (Ph.D. diss., Universitat Autònoma de Barcelona, 1990), 52.

28. Ibid., 737.

29. Ibid., 127–28.

30. Salaverría, "La noticia en los manuales de Periodismo," 190.

31. Mar de Fontcuberta, *Estructura de la noticia periodística* (Structuring News Stories) (Barcelona: ATE, 1980), 169.

32. Parratt, *Introducción al reportaje*, 107–10.

33. Mark Kramer, "Narrative Journalism Comes of Age," *Nieman Reports* (Fall 2000): 5–8.

34. Rick Bragg, "Weaving Storytelling into Breaking News," *Nieman Reports* (Fall 2000): 29–30.

35. Juan José Hoyos, "Pioneros del reportaje en Colombia" (Reportage-Writing Pioneers in Colombia), *Folios* 2 (1997): 14–32.

36. Gay Talese, "Orígenes de un escritor de no ficción" (Origins of a Nonfiction Writer), trans. Maryluz Vallejo and Juan José Hoyos, *Folios* 3 (1998): 3–20.

37. Xosé López, *A reportaxe de prensa en Galicia* (Reportage Writing in the Galician Press) (Santiago de Compostela: Universidade de Santiago de Compostela, 1998), 52.

Chapter 9

Social Movements and Chinese Literary Reportage

Peiqin Chen

Chinese literary reportage, or *baogao wenxue,* is a genre that combines journalism and literature, in which the journalism should be truthful and the literature artful. How truthful or how artful remains a contentious subject within the Chinese academy, though scholars do agree that literary reportage should meet the basic requirements of journalism—truthfulness, timeliness, and freshness—and be written with passion and literary skill similar to that of novelists. Furthermore, Chinese literary reportage, as stated in the authoritative Chinese dictionary published in 1988, must serve a political end. Leading Chinese critics believe that sharp criticism of society is the soul of literary reportage, and without this edge of social criticism, any work of literary reportage becomes meaningless.[1] Because of this, literary reportage has also been defined as "a literary report to expose social evils," and as "a dangerous genre."[2] Therefore, if writers of literary reportage were to stand up and comment directly on society in their works, they would have to do so with aplomb and with conviction about exposing and correcting its ills.[3]

The history of Chinese literary reportage, despite its relative brevity, is a testament to the efforts writers have undertaken to fulfill these two contracts with their readers. I say "relative brevity" because Chinese literary reportage is a modern phenomenon in a country with a rich and expansive history. In ancient China there did exist prose accounts of significant historical events, but the close relationship between literary reportage and the modern news media distinguishes it from the factual prose of that earlier age. From this, scholars generally acknowledge that modern newspapers have given rise to Chinese literary reportage. Likewise in ancient China there were writings that combined history and literature, such as biographies and memoirs. Again, though, neither had the necessary news value that literary reportage possesses. For these reasons, scholars date the birth of Chinese literary reportage to the end of nineteenth century, when modern industry began to reshape China and various newspapers recorded those changes.

From its emergence at the end of nineteenth century to today, Chinese literary reportage has thus served as an important tool for social advocacy, effectively portraying cultural revolutions and political conflicts more dramatically than Chinese novelists ever could. For this reason, several Chinese novelists turned to literary reportage during the Second Sino-Japanese War in the 1930s, when China was invaded by the Imperial Japanese Army.[4] Some 80 to 90 percent of the nation's distinguished novelists, poets, and essayists used literary reportage as a means to capture the soul of the nation, making it the mainstream in Chinese literature.[5] Tracing such a history reveals that the genre boomed when Chinese society was most in transition.

This essay thus examines Chinese literary reportage as a response to the nation's major social and political upheavals, dividing its development into five phases: its emergence from the 1850s to the 1920s in relation to the 1898 Reform Movement in China; its first boom in the 1930s and 1940s, when China began its anti-Japanese campaign during the Second Sino-Japanese War; its function as a tool for political action from the 1950s to the 1970s, after the new China was founded in 1949; its second boom in the 1980s, accompanying China's market-oriented reforms, which began in 1978; and its mutations after the 1990s, when the market economy exerted its greatest influence on people's ideas and lives, and when conservatism had become the dominant force in the country. Once literary reportage turned to serving the explosive growth of Chinese commerce, however, the genre soon went into decline.

Early Chinese Reformers and the Emergence of the Genre

During the Qing dynasty (1644–1911), foreign countries frequently invaded China. The Late Qing dynasty in particular, which was extremely corrupt, was unable to protect the country from these hordes, and the survival of the whole nation was put in jeopardy. At this time a group of Chinese intellectuals founded newspapers to advocate Western ideas and to promote social reforms that would challenge the corruption and restore the nation to its golden age. These intellectuals, called Reformists in Chinese history, influenced Emperor Guangxu and initiated a constitutional reform in 1898. The reform was crushed one hundred days later by Empress Dowager Cixi, who held the real power over the nation in her hands. Emperor Guangxu, though still an emperor in name, was put under house arrest, and all the other Reformists either were killed or fled to other countries.

Liang Qichao was one of the most influential of these Reformists.[6] He sought exile in Japan in October 1898, and in November that same year he founded a newspaper there, *Qing Yi Bao* (Public Opinion). This newspaper, issued biweekly, published in its third issue in December a detailed account of the 1898 reform written by Liang himself. Titled *Wuxu Zhengbian Ji* (An Account of the 1898 Reform Movement), it is considered the first representative work of Chinese literary reportage, and because of this, Liang is also considered the founder of Chinese literary reportage.[7] As a witness to and an important participant in the reform, Liang supplied original material for this work of about 100,000 Chinese characters, which included the proposal Emperor Guangxu received from the Reformists, the papers outlining Guangxu's reform, and reports on how foreign newspapers had covered the event. Liang vividly portrayed different figures in the reform and sharply and openly criticized the political system of the time.

While depicting Tan Sitong, one of the leading Reformists who refused to leave China and chose instead to martyr himself for the cause, Liang quotes him as saying: "No other country has had successful reforms without bloodshed. In China, I have never heard that anyone died for reform. Now I want to be the first one to die for reform."[8] Besides Tan, six leading Reformists were also killed. Liang stood up to the corrupt government and commented: "There was no trial before the six heroes were put to death. In today's world, even the most savage country does not have this kind of system."[9]

After Liang, reporters and writers continued to publish works of literary reportage. Some are travel accounts, narrating and commenting on experiences in Europe; some are accounts of social unrest, such as student movements or worker uprisings. The true rise of literary reportage, however, came only in the 1930s after the Second Sino-Japanese War broke out.

The Second Sino-Japanese War and the Rise of Chinese Literary Reportage

In the 1930s and 1940s China again underwent great social turmoil. The Imperial Japanese Army began occupying the country at a surprisingly fast pace, with the northeast falling completely into Japanese hands. The entire nation was called to defend its independence and its sovereignty. Literary reportage at this time became an effective tool for reporters and writers to rally citizens to that call for immediate action against the Japanese invasion and the corrupt Guomindang government. Literary reportage during this time was thus closely aligned with, and even developed alongside of, what has since been called the Second Sino-Japanese War (1937–1945).[10]

A significant amount of literary reportage was published and read during this time, especially by young people, as they were quite eager to learn more about the ongoing war—not just the facts but also the details of the war and the life of the soldiers fighting at the front. As the famous Chinese literary critic Yi Qun observed, "Writings of literary reportage occupied the largest portion of all literary periodicals (about 70 to 80 percent), while readers anticipated new works of literary reportage with great enthusiasm."[11] Literary journalism not only flourished in the 1930s and 1940s but also became mainstream, characterized by original theoretical articles as well as discussions on the theories and works of literary reportage from other countries, such as Russia, the United States, and various nations of Europe.

The first use of the Chinese term for literary reportage, *baogao wenxue,* translated from the German word *reportage,* was in an article in 1930 introducing Egon Erwin Kisch (1885–1948). Kisch was Czech reporter who visited China in 1932 and from his experiences and observations wrote *Secret China* (1933), a collection of literary reportage on the situation of China at the time. Kisch's designation of literary reportage as "a dangerous genre" is still used in China today to describe its critical nature of.[12] In addition to Kisch, critics of Chinese literary reportage in the 1930s also wrote about works of American writers, such as Upton Sinclair's novel *The Jungle* (1906). Foreign literary journalists, such as Edgar Snow, actually came to China and wrote reportages during the 1930s, thus cementing the transnational bonds that link Chinese literary reportage with the rest of the journalistic world. Even today, Snow's *Red Star over China* (1937) is considered a model of literary reportage by the Chinese.

Works and collections of literary reportage by Chinese writers were published continuously and exerted a great influence on the direction the country was to take during the war. *Shanghai Shibian Yu Baogao Wenxue* (Literary Reportage and the January 28 Incident in Shanghai), published in April 1932, was the first collection in China to use the term "literary reportage" in its title.[13] Edited by A'Ying, a renowned Chinese writer, the book contains a selection of twenty-nine newspaper articles about the war. It records how Chinese soldiers and ordinary people fought against the Imperial Japanese Army when Japan attacked Shanghai on January 28, 1932.

In spite of all of this, the most influential event in the history of Chinese literary reportage in the 1930s was a project sponsored by the Chinese Literature Society and initiated by the famous Chinese writer Mao Dun. Mao Dun chose a date, May 21, 1936, asked readers to record the events of their lives on that day, and then compiled a book titled *Zhongguo De Yi Ri* (*One Day in China*) based on the stories people sent in. In his call for pieces of literary reportage, Mao stressed that the goal of the book was twofold: to record "events and phenomena, large or small, which occurred within the twenty-four hours of May 21 in the territory of China, whether at sea, on land, or in the air," and to carve out "a slice of life in China."[14] Within a short time after the request appeared in the newspaper, the editorial board had received more than three thousand pieces of writing. Mao and his editorial board finally selected 490 of them and published the book that September.[15]

In addition to collections of literary reportage such as Mao Dun's, other renowned Chinese writers also contributed to the flourishing of literary reportage at this time. Works such as Xia Yan's "Bao Shen Gong" (Slave Workers, 1936), Song Zhide's "1936 Nian Chun Zai Taiyuan" (Spring 1936 in Taiyuan, 1936), and Xiao Qian's "Liu Min Tu" (Sketches of Migrants, 1936) targeted the corrupt Guomindang government and exposed the bitter life of ordinary people under the regime, For their efforts, each received praise from the nation's leading literary critics.

Another subject—descriptions of Mao Zedong, the leader of the Chinese Communist Party (CCP), and his battles against the Japanese invasion—aroused great interest. Popular at the time were profiles of the leader, such as Yang Shuo's "Mao Zedong Texie" (Mao Zedong Profile, 1939) and Huang Gang's *Wo Kanjian Le Balujun* (Route 3 as I Saw It, 1940). Each contributed significantly to the positive image of the Communist Party leaders at the time. The trend of depicting the lives of party members during the Second Sino-Japanese War would later develop into political encomiums that focused only on, and at times even exaggerated, the triumphs of party programs following the new republic's founding in 1949.

Political Movements and Chinese Literary Reportage after 1949

Chinese society entered into an entirely new era after October 1, 1949, when the People's Republic of China was founded. The CCP and the government exerted great influence on literary production, and literature soon became politicized, functioning as a mouthpiece for government policy. Writers of literary reportage willingly fabricated certain details of events to satisfy the demands of the political authorities. For most writers, owing to their sincere belief in communism, they idealized everything they wrote. Others lied to please the authorities for personal or political gain—or both.

If Chinese literary reportage in the 1930s and 1940s was devoted mainly to social criticism, from the 1950s to the 1970s it consisted entirely of these political encomiums. In the 1950s, for example, the Chinese masses were mobilized to speed the nation's economic growth and industrialization in what has been called the Great Leap Forward movement. Though conceptually rational, the program was implemented overzealously. During this period, works of literary reportage were filled with high praise, and the events being reported were not simply untrue but defied common sense. Xu Chi, a well-known writer who in the late 1970s became famous for "Ge De Ba He Cai Xiang" (The Goldbach Conjectures, 1978), a work about Chinese scientist Chen Jingrun, contributed a report typical of this 1950s trend. In his "Gang He Liangshi" (Steel and Grain, 1958), Xu writes:

> A flag flies at one side of the [farm] field, on which is written, "Reach newest record in the nation, Compete for number one in the world." Please look, how proud we are!
>
> When I first visited this rice field, I was told that the highest yield was 60,000 *jin* [30,000 kg] per *mu* [0.0667 hectares]. But this patch before me could produce 120,000 [60,000 kg] per *mu*. This figure, however, is not at all rare, or even new, as Chinese farmers are working to produce a higher yield.[16]

The figures provided here are surely fabricated. A farmer with any common sense would immediately doubt their veracity. Even with today's technology, let alone in the 1950s, the highest figure for rice production that Chinese scientists could ever hope to produce is less than 1,000 kilograms per *mu*. The figure was probably invented not by Xu Chi but by the farmers themselves. Xu simply wrote it down and treated it as fact.

In the 1950s some writers did try to write about the problems that existed in China. Works such as Liu Binyan's "Zai Qiaoliang Gongdi Shang" (On the Bridge Construction Site, 1956) and "Benbao Neibu Xiaoxi" (Inside the News, 1956) and Li Qin's "Ma Duan De Duoluo" (The Fall of Ma Duan, 1956) focused on the corruption of some leaders of the CCP. These writers, however, were severely criticized for their muckraking. Even Mao Dun, who edited *One Day in China,* castigated them for having "focused on the dark side of life and thought it was true," adding, "they actually distorted the reality, and questioned our social system."[17]

China's Liberal Movement in the 1980s and the Second Reportage Boom

The political atmosphere in China changed drastically at the end of the 1970s. With the end of the Maoist period, a new era was ushered in. A national debate among the intellectuals about the standard of truth in 1978 helped clear the way to freer thinking. The discussion actually initiated a new age of enlightenment to accompany those of the 1898 Reform Movement and the May Fourth Movement of 1919, which advocated science and democracy.[18] Under their auspices came a new era of prosperity for Chinese literary reportage.

Not only did the amount of literary reportage quickly increase, but also it began to assert national influence. As one Chinese critic commented, "Chinese literary reportage is booming and has established itself as an important genre in literature."[19] Just as in the 1930s, there was a surge in the production of literary reportage. In 1988, for example, 108 literary periodicals joined together to start a movement called Zhonghuo Chao (China Tide), calling for the submission of works of literary reportage. During that year these periodicals published more than a thousand pieces of literary reportage. The vast amount of works produced and the popularity they enjoyed also triggered the study of the genre. In 1988 practitioners gathered six times in China to discuss literary reportage.[20] The work of foreign writers was introduced as well, which advanced the gains in transnational synergy experienced at the beginning of the twentieth century. During this decade the literary journalism of Tom Wolfe, Norman Mailer, Truman Capote, and Gay Talese was being translated into Chinese for the first time.

Reportage that explored social problems in this period gained in popularity. These works, called *wenti baogao wenxue* (social problem literary reportage), are considered the summit of the genre in China since 1949.[21] They often focus on certain social phenomena or problems of the 1980s, ranging widely from corruption, transportation, family planning, marriage, education, and environment to the "brain drain." Liu Binyan's "Ren Yao Zhi Jian" (People or Monsters?, 1979), for instance, was the first work of literary reportage to focus on social problems after 1978. By tracing the history of a notorious woman found guilty of corruption, Liu explored the political system which nourished that corruption.

Other writers, such as Su Xiaokang and Han Yi, also produced important works of reportage that covered different social problems of the time. Su Xiaokang's *Yin Yang Da Liebian* (The Cracking of "Yin" and "Yang"), published in 1986, explores the divorce trend of the 1980s, which, partly owing to the newly implemented marriage law of 1980, indicated that Chinese society was liberating itself from the feudal bondage that once controlled its mores. In the 1980s arranged marriage was still being practiced in many places in China, and Su examined the problems inherent to modern Chinese marriage, especially the situation of women, by narrating in detail several divorce cases. For Su, the divorce trend was a symbol of the development of Chinese society, which gave people more freedom to pursue individual notions of love and happiness. Han Yi's *Zhongguo De "Xiao Huangdi"* (China's "Little King"), by contrast, explored in 1986 the issue of the "spoiled" only child. Ever since China began implementing its one-child policy in the late 1970s, questions concerning the family's and that child's sociological and psychological health had been raised. And since the traditional view in China holds that a family which does not have a son to carry on its line is ultimately shamed, those with an only son treated him like royalty. Having consulted a considerable number of family cases in the course of researching the book, the author presents her deep concerns about these spoiled (male) children.

In the 1980s there was another category of literary reportage that was unique to the history of the genre in China—*lishi baogao wenxue* (historical literary reportage). Despite its name, not all historical events were considered subjects for this kind of investigative reportage, but only events that had "news value." Because of their particular political environments, the true accounts of certain significant historical events that took place from the 1950s to the 1970s could not have been published at the time they occurred. Hence these events became "frozen news." In the 1980s, during the new political thaw, writers could finally record what had actually happened and provide fresh insight into past events, such as the Tangshan earthquake of 1976.

The immediate media coverage of the earthquake had been very limited. But after 1978 the relatively free political atmosphere permitted the uncovering of overlooked or withheld details surrounding the natural catastrophe. For instance, when the earthquake hit in 1976, reporter Qian Gang was sent to Tangshan to cover the event, but he was not allowed by his news agency to write about what he saw, as all the news stories at that time were to have a positive spin. He did so only ten years later when, in 1986, he went back to Tangshan to interview the survivors and finally published his findings in *Tangshan Da Dizhen* (*The Great China Earthquake*, 1986). By providing the facts of the disaster—that is, different people's accounts of the quake and its aftermath, as well as the reports from various newspapers at the time—Qian convincingly captured the situation in the city following the catastrophe and exposed how the government of the day, which declined all offers of international aid, had reacted irresponsibly. Qian interviewed General Chi Haotian, the vice chief director of the rescue operation, who, as one of the leaders at the headquarters providing aid to Tangshan, later expressed regret for his government's decision:

> The leader of the central government at the time came to the badly stricken area and told us that foreigners wanted to come to China and give us help. But the great People's Republic of China didn't want anyone to interfere in our affairs. We did not need anyone to help us. When we heard these words at that time, we were very excited. We applauded, were moved to tears. . . . Many years later we came to understand what a foolish thing we did. Natural disasters are disasters for all human beings. Every year we provide much aid to other countries suffering natural disasters.[22]

Two other revisionist examples of historical literary reportage involve the notorious "Hu Fen's Antirevolutionary Gang" of 1955 and the Chinese Red Guard of 1966. Tracing the former well-known case in his *Wentan Beige* (Elegy of the Literary Circles, 1988), Li Hui narrates how the writer and renowned literary critic Hu Fen and his followers were thrown into prison just because they held bourgeois views of literature. Twenty-one hundred people were labeled members of the "Antirevolutionary Gang," and ultimately ninety-two people were arrested and thrown into prison. The wrong was redressed in 1978, and Hu was set free after spending more than twenty years in prison. Similarly, *Lishi Chensi Lu- Jinggangshan Hongweibing Da Chuanlian Er Shi Zhounian Ji* (Meditation on History: To the Twentieth Anniversary of the Red Guards, 1987) tells the stories of the Red Guards at the beginning of the Cultural Revolution. Its two authors, Hu Ping and Zhang Shenyou, who were both Red Guards themselves, recount how in 1966 Red Guards from all over China climbed Jinggang Mountain to pay homage to Mao Zedong. Jinggang Mountain was where Mao had successfully implemented the guerrilla warfare that finally led the CCP to military victory. In their account, Hu and Zhang narrate how the revolutionary passion of those young Red Guards motivated them to overcome all difficulties—at the cost of their lives in some cases—to accomplish this feat.

Revisionist histories such as these are valuable contributions to the canon of Chinese literary reportage, not only because they recover precious information that has been securely guarded all these years but also because they engage closely with the politics of their immediate times. *The Great China Earthquake,* like the other so-called historical literary reportages that reveal facts once suppressed during the Cultural Revolution, contributed to the second boom of literary reportage in the 1980s. As some Chinese literary critics claim, Chinese literary reportage actually became mainstream in the 1930s and again in the 1980s because it was the genre that best served to describe a society in rapid flux, a time when real events were so exciting that no novel or news story could do them justice.[23] But once the market economy was in full swing during the 1990s, literary reportage catered to new needs. Seduced by graft and payola, numerous writers of literary reportage flattered those entrepreneurs who got rich overnight by taking advantage of the country's new economic policies. The genre, as a consequence, quickly went in decline.

Turning "Sweet": Chinese Literary Reportage in the Market Economy

In the 1990s China's market economy began greatly influencing people's ideas and lives. Individualism and materialism became the dominant modus vivendi. During this time, the cultural radicalism of the 1980s was replaced by a cultural conservatism. Most people were carried away by the commercial tide and grew more concerned with their own interests than with those of the nation and its people.

Since the early 1900s, all movements in China have been political. After the market reforms of the 1990s, however, any movement inherently became economic in nature. During this decade all organizations and individuals were encouraged to make money, often by whatever means necessary. Steered by a planned economy for many years, the country's economic system was very much in disorder. At times, professors and scientists earned less than those who sold cakes on the streets. As the government could not give enough financial support to academic institutions, schools were encouraged to gener-ate extra money on their own. This opened the door to widespread corrup-tion. Schools made money by offering part-time courses, while newspapers and magazines took money from companies in exchange for publishing advertising copy as news stories.

Literary reportage at this time also changed for the worse. As Peisong Fan, a renowned critic of Chinese literary journalism, has pointed out, China's literary reportage in the 1990s was going "sweet," meaning that writers had pens for hire and would write for anyone who had money to offer.[24] Very few of these works of literary reportage were critical in nature; on the con-trary, most of them were often "mass produced" in a market economy, either praising "successful entrepreneurs" or sensationalizing the news with stories of crime, blood, and sex. Those who were described in these reportages as heroes often turned out later to be criminals who were cheating the public out of its money. Furthermore, a considerable number of works after 1990 were written simply as reports, not as literary reportage. As the critic Bingyin Li has noted, many were just collections of raw materials, without even the most basic respect for literary values or journalistic ethics. As a result, these works were dull and failed to move the reader at all.[25] The reputation of the genre went into decline.

Although most reportage writers after 1990 produced works of poor qual-ity, there were a few who wrote stories that targeted social problems brought about by the freewheeling market economy. In narrating their stories, they returned to ordinary people as their subjects. These stories were often very similar in nature, involving people of the same class or generation. Works such as Wu Jianmin's *Zhongguo Gaokao Baogao* (A Report of China's College Examination, 2000), for example, which revealed the problems linked with enrolling in a Chinese university, and Wu Haiming's *Zhongguo Xinwen Jingshi Lu* (The Corruption of the Chinese Media, 1995), which exposed how journalists sought out clients for whom they happily provided slanted copy for a fee, belong to this group of quality reportage. Different from reportage of the 1980s, these two works did reveal societal problems after 1990, but they did not use the real names of people involved or employ immersion reporting skills to probe what lay behind the story.

There were a few literary reportage writers who did scour a story's underbelly, but they often found their efforts rewarded with lawsuits. Lu Yaogang provides a good example. As a reporter who worked for the newspaper *Zhongguo Qingnian Bao* (China Youth), Lu made his name writing literary reportages such as "Yi Renmin De Mingyi" (In the Name of the People, 1993) and *Da Guo Gua Min* (Big Country, Small People, 1998). In the latter, Lu narrates how he and his newspaper got into trouble when he wrote a story that tried to help a female victim of domestic violence. This woman, living in a small village in Shanxi in the midwest of China, was often beaten cruelly by her husband. When she asked for a divorce, her husband poured sulfuric acid all over her body. Seeking redress, she turned to the courts to sue her husband, but in spite of her eight-year effort, her husband was acquitted. The story was published in *China Youth* on August 8, 1996. Lu Yaogang and his newspaper were then sued for libel by the woman's husband and other people involved in the crime. During this time, Lu started writing *Big Country, Small People,* describing how these people, with their network of power and money, successfully manipulated the law and escaped punishment despite having committed a terrible crime. Explaining why he wrote the story as reportage, Lu said: "In a situation like this, novels are just so pale. I have to say it. I must say it and speak out directly. So I turned to a sword: literary reportage."[26]

Lu was one of the very few journalists writing after 1990 who still used literary reportage as a weapon in the tradition of the Chinese literary reportage writers of the 1930s and the 1980s. Too many journalists today have used literary reportage to flatter their "customers," and the genre has lost some of its luster, its readers, and even its soul. Magazines are no longer as eager to publish works of literary reportage as they once were in the 1980s. At present only three journals, *Baogao Wenxue* (Literary Reportage), *Beijing Wenxue* (Beijing Literature), and *Zhongguo Zuojia: Jishi* (Chinese Writers: Nonfiction), still publish works of literary reportage regularly.

But there are some pieces of literary reportage that have won both commercial success and critical acclaim. *Tianshi Zai Zuo Zhan* (The Angel Is Fighting, 2006), written by Zhu Xiaojun, a professor who teaches writing at a university in Zhejiang province, became popular immediately after it was published in the sixth issue of *Beijing Literature*. In it, Zhu Xiaojun records how a female doctor named Chen Xiaolan fought corruption single-handedly at the hospital where she worked. More than ten newspapers, including some with a large circulation, such as *Beijing Qingnian Bao* (Beijing Youth) and *Nanfang Zhoumo* (Southern Weekend), published the story in serial form, and a TV and film production company also bought the film rights to the work. The piece, which won first prize in the Fourth Luxun Literary Award of 2006, a renowned national literary honor, offers hope for the future of Chinese literary reportage. The Lunxun Literary Award board said of this work: "*The Angel Is Fighting* shows the full strength of literary reportage. The writer not only chose an important subject that concerns the lives of people, but also showed great courage to explore it in depth."[27]

Besides long-form narrative works such as *The Angel Is Fighting*, shorter works of literary reportage seem to be growing in popularity and drawing much attention from readers as well as critics. Certain newspapers, such as the high-circulation national weekly newspaper *Southern Weekend*, often run in-depth stories that display features of literary reportage. These works also offer hope for the future of literary reportage in China. Some literary reportage critics have even claimed that these in-depth literary reports in newspapers are actually better than those appearing in journals.

Having emerged as a genre at various times when society was in great flux, Chinese literary reportage, armed with its double-edge sword of "truth" and "aesthetics," has repeatedly served as an important weapon in the struggle to expose social ills. As one critic has pointed out, however, the history of Chinese literary reportage has developed a kind of "tragic complex."[28] Despite the numerous works of literary reportage that have appeared in China over the last century, most that are remembered today and considered worthy of the appellation "literary reportage" are tragic stories presenting tragic heroes in tragic situations.

Indeed, tragic heroes repeatedly fill the pages of China's literary reportage: from the representative work about the failure of China's 1898 Reform Movement to Xia Yan's 1936 masterpiece "Slave Workers," in which the writer vividly depicts how a teenage Chinese girl nicknamed Stick (because she was so thin) led her miserable life in a foreign-owned factory; and, again, from

Qiang Gang's *The Great China Earthquake* in 1986 to Zhu Xiaojun's *The Angel Is Fighting* in 2006. The genre grew more and more tragic because the times did as well, and society needed to be shown those who survived the drastic changes confronting or altering traditional Chinese life.

Yet as a genre born alongside modern Chinese journalism, and categorized as a literary genre, literary reportage has remained throughout the last century a consistent yardstick by which to measure the societal changes China has had to endure. And while it is difficult to predict how the genre will develop in the age of the Internet, given its potential for literary charm and its power to enact social change, it is certain that literary reportage will still hold an important position in China in the new century.

NOTES

1. Peisong Fan, "Lun Jiushi Niandai Baogao Wenxue De Pipan Tuiwei" (The Weakening of Social Criticism in the Literary Reportage of the Nineties), *Dangdai Zuojia Pinglun* (Contemporary Writers Review) 2 (2002): 131. All translations from Chinese, including book and article titles and publishers' names, unless otherwise noted, are my own.

2. Zhifang Jia, trans., *Yi Zhong Weixian De Wenxue Yangshi* (A Dangerous Genre) (Shanghai: Nitu Press, 1953), 7.

3. Zinan Zhu, ed., *Zhongguo Wenxue Cidian* (A Dictionary of Chinese Genres) (Changsha: Hunan Education Press, 1988), 107.

4. Bingyin Li, "Baogao Wenxue De Xianshi Xingzou Zitai" (The Reality of the Development of Chinese Literary Reportage), *Wenyi Zhengming* (Literature Debate) 8 (2008): 46.

5. Yi Qun, "Kangzhan Yi Lai De Baogao Wenxue" (Chinese Reportage since the Second Sino-Japanese War), in *Baogao Wenxue Yanjiu Ziliao Xuanbian* (Selected Materials for Literary Reportage Research), ed. Ronggan Wang (Jinan: Shantong People's Press, 1983), 683.

6. Since the Chinese put their surnames first, Liang is Liang Qichao's surname. Throughout this essay, when historical figures or writers are mentioned, all names appear according to Chinese usage. But in the endnotes, I have inverted the names of various Chinese scholars to harmonize with Western customs.

7. Chunning Zhang, *Zhongguo Baogao Wenxue Shi Gao* (A History of Chinese Literary Reportage) (Beijing: Qunzhong Press, 1993), 21–22.

8. Qichao Liang, *Wuxu Zhengbian Ji* (An Account of the 1898 Reform Movement) (Beijing: Zhonghua Book Company, 1954), 109.

9. Ibid., 92–93.

10. Yi Qun, "Kangzhan Yi Lai De Baogao Wenxue," 683.

11. Ibid., 682.

12. Xiaoyuan Ding, "Wenhua Shengtai Yu Bai Nian Zhongguo Baogao Wenxue Liu Bian" (The Evolution of Cultural Ecology and the Development of Chinese Reportage in the Twentieth Century) (Ph.D. diss., Suzhou University, 2001), 55.

13. Jinbo Chen and Yongqiang Ma, *Baogao Wenxue Tan Lun* (A Study of Literary Reportage) (Lanzhou: University of Lanzhou Press, 1997), 80.

14. Mao Dun, "Guan Yu Bianji De Guocheng" (On Editorial Process), in *Zhongguo De Yi Ri* (One Day in China), ed. Mao Dun (Shanghai: Shanghai Bookstore, 1936), 4.

15. Ibid., 1.

16. Xu Chi, "Gang Yu Liangshi" (Steel and Grain), *Renmin Wenxue* (People's Literature), October 1958, 25–26.

17. Mao Dun, "Guanyu Suowei Xie Zhenshi" (On the So-Called Writing about Reality), *Renmin Wenxue* (People's Literature), September 1958, 20.

18. Xiaoyuan Ding, "Wenhua Shengtai Yu Bai Nian Zhongguo Baogao Wenxue Liu Bian," 101.

19. Guangnian Zhang, "Baogao Wenxue Sui Gan Lu" (Some Thoughts about Chinese Literary Reportage), *Wenyi Bao* (Literature News) 12 (1982): 10.

20. Xiaoyuan Ding, "Wenhua Shengtai Yu Bai Nian Zhongguo Baogao Wenxue Liu Bian," 115.

21. Hui Wang, "Yishi Xingtai Yu Bai Nian Zhongguo Baogao Wenxue" (Ideology and One-Hundred-Year-Old Chinese Literary Reportage), *Shehui Kexue Ji Kan* (Social Science Journal) 2 (2004): 147.

22. Gang Qian, *Tangshan Da Dizhen* (The Great China Earthquake) (Beijing: Contemporary China Press, 2005), 145.

23. Boyi Hu, "Baogao Wenxue Yu Xiandai Wenxue De Guanxi" (The Relationship between Literary Reportage and Contemporary Literature), *Wenyi Zhengming* (Literature Debate) 8 (2008): 51.

24. Peisong Fan, "Lun Jiushi Niandai Baogao Wenxue De Pipan Tuiwei," 130.

25. Bingyin Li, "Baogao Wenxue Lun" (On Literary Reportage), *Zhongguo Zuojia* (Chinese Writers) 4 (2006): 219.

26. Yaogang Lu, "Wo You Hua Yao Shuo" (I Have to Say), *Zhonghua Wenxue Xuan Kan* (Chinese Literature) 3 (1994): 112.

27. Hui Wang and Xiaoyuan Ding, "2007 Nian Baogao Wenxue De Nianjing Xieyi" (A Review of Literary Reportage in 2007), *Zhongguo Xiandai, Dangdai Wenxue Yanjiu* (Research on Modern and Contemporary Chinese Literature) 5 (2008): 13.

28. Tianzhen Wei, "Lun Zhongguo Baogao Wenxue De Beiju Qingjie" (On the Tragic Complex of Chinese Literary Reportage), in *Zhongguo Xin Shiqi Wenxue Yanjiu Ziliao Hui Bian* (Studies of Literary Reportage in the New Period), ed. Xueyong Zhao (Jinan: Shangtong Press, 2006): 161–69.

Chapter 10

A Century of Nonfiction Solitude

A Survey of Brazilian Literary Journalism

Edvaldo Pereira Lima

From the very late 1800s to the very early 2000s, literary journalism has played out an errant but meaningful history in Brazil. While it has never been mainstream in the Brazilian news media, literary journalism has proved its staying power through the writings of two exceptional individuals, Euclides da Cunha and João do Rio. The unforgettable, albeit brief, golden age of the genre in the 1960s and 1970s—thanks to a daily newspaper, *Jornal da Tarde,* and to a monthly news magazine, *Realidade*—has left a legacy that even now sparks the dreams of veteran and young Brazilian writers alike.

Today the dream has modestly extended its reach, has multiplied its forms of manifestation, and has been given an additional boost from the academic community. Though the trade is still a solitary business, voices clamoring from the four corners of the nation are increasingly being heard and met with like responses.

Euclides da Cunha: Grandfather of Brazilian Literary Journalism

In the early hot summer days of August 1897, civil engineer, former military officer, and writer Euclides da Cunha joined an army expedition into the northeastern hinterlands of Brazil against a group of peasants who, back in the capital city of Rio de Janeiro, were seen as rebels opposing the country's inevitable march toward progress. This enormous country had moved out of a monarchy and into a republican regime just a few years previously. Power had been seized in 1889 by a military coup d'état commanded by army marshal Teodoro da Fonseca. Emperor Dom Pedro II was forced to leave the country, which he did peacefully, heading overseas to his ancestors' homeland, Portugal. Fonseca was backed by a republican movement heavily influenced by the positivist theories of the French philosopher Auguste Comte. Comte's ideology was so influential that the flag of the new republic, unfurled four days after Fonseca seized power, bore the new state motto, "Ordem e Progresso" (Order and Progress), inspired by Comte's saying "L'amour pour principe et l'ordre pour base; le progress pour but" (Love as a principle, order as the foundation, and progress as the goal).

The prevailing sense was that Brazil lagged behind other, more modern nations precisely because of its outmoded monarchy. What the country needed was an agile, flexible, future-oriented political regime that would modernize Brazil's economy, insert the country into the growing internationalization trend of the day, and unify the massive nation into a comprehensive cultural and social body politic.

When he was thirty-three years old, Cunha left Brazil's beautiful coastline to follow the army into the dry hinterlands. The third president of Brazil, Prudente de Morais, represented the rising forces of local capitalism that were associated with international banking interests, mainly British. Morais was supported by the increasingly influential social class of coffee growers who saw an opportunity to improve their country's fortunes by providing leading European nations with the "green gold" of its coffee plantations. Exports would inject the funds needed to finally modernize the "sleeping giant" of South America.

This dogma, however, was unexpectedly challenged by a group of rebels who refused political centralization and seemed to uphold the old monarchic values. Anyway, that was how the story was being told in the corridors of power in Rio de Janeiro. The newborn republic, still gaining strength, threatened the odd messianic movement of leader Antonio Conselheiro, who established a settlement in the extremely poor region of Canudos, in the northeastern state of Bahia, apparently seeking economic autonomy and political independence.

Conselheiro seemed to be moved much more by mystical inspiration than by political ideologies. As thousands of peasants and their families joined his settlement, the Rio politicos decided that the movement had to be quashed immediately for fear that it would ignite a nationwide revolt. First the police, then the army, were sent in to neutralize the settlers. An unexpectedly fierce reaction by Conselheiro and his people, however, stirred an even fiercer federal government response, resulting in a civil war that by 1893 would be the largest and bloodiest conflagration in Brazil's history. Between fifteen thousand and thirty thousand people were killed during the conflict, depending on the source consulted.

Cunha marched with the army toward Canudos as a war correspondent for a daily that would grow to become one of the two most influential newspapers in Brazil, *O Estado de S. Paulo.* Eight other major newspapers sent correspondents to cover the final and most dramatic stage of the war. Three expeditions had already been defeated, so this time the army sent in a force of six thousand men, who seized and occupied the village of Canudos for three months before completely destroying it. No prisoners—men, women, or children—were taken.

None of the other war correspondents chose the same road of radical innovation in covering the conflict that Cunha did. Bringing to the field his cultural background in positivism and social Darwinism, on the one hand, and naturalism—as applied to both science and literature—on the other, he composed war dispatches that avoided the shallow, fact-oriented approach of his competitors and instead put the dramatic situation into a personal perspective. He linked the Canudos War to events of a similar nature in other parts of the world. He also attempted to understand the psychological profile of the *sertanejos*—the backland peasants who so enthusiastically followed Conselheiro and his messianic promise—placing a great amount of emphasis on the geographical environment and its effect on human temperament and mood.

Cunha did not limit his role to just telling a story in linear terms. He wanted above all to understand the underlying currents that shaped the Canudos War. While his competitors stayed with the military's expedition party, Cunha conducted research on his own, taking notes, observing, talking to locals, and exploring the environment, trying to make sense of this tragic encounter of mutually misunderstood worlds in the backlands of his nation. Avoiding the discourse of both the military establishment and the highly emotional supporters of the republic, Cunha delivered a realistic narrative, reporting on the environment, portraying real-life characters, and weaving together historical, political, and social circumstances.

Brazil did not know it then, but readers of Cunha's dispatches in *O Estado de S. Paulo* were encountering the nation's first pieces of journalistic nonfiction that would later be identified as literary journalism, making Cunha the "grandfather of Brazilian literary journalism." He would confirm this honor a few years later with *Os Sertões* (*Rebellion in the Backlands,* 1902), a seminal nonfiction book that furthered his coverage of the Canudos War.[1] *Rebellion in the Backlands* had such an impact on Brazilian literature as a whole that it would change the nation's belles lettres forever. Like Émile Zola's work *Le roman experimental* (*The Experimental Novel,* 1880) in France, *Rebellion in the Backlands* introduced Brazil, then heavily steeped in literary romanticism, to the era of naturalism.

Written in three parts, *Rebellion in the Backlands* opened the nation's eyes to its poverty, racism, prejudice, and cruelty, transcending the rather naïve view of life that one found in the writings of José de Alencar and other romantic writers before him. The first part, "A Terra" (The Land), is a portrait of the thorny desert lands of the northeast and the setting of the war, conveying the idea that the *sertanejos'* predisposition to endure extremely harsh conditions was due mostly to the geographical landscape. The second, "O Homem" (Man), portrays the region's people, its phenotype, and shows how the backland peasants differ sharply from Brazilians living on the coast. The last part is a report on the war itself, "A Luta" (The Struggle), a piece of literary reportage from the premodern era.

Half a century after its original publication in Portuguese, *Rebellion in the Backlands* found international praise. As essayist, critic, and *New York Review of Books* cofounder Elizabeth Hardwick wrote in *Bartleby in Manhattan,*

> Euclides da Cunha went on the campaigns [against Conselheiro] as a journalist and what he returned with and published in 1902 is still unsurpassed in Latin American literature. Cunha is a talent as grand, spacious, entangled with knowledge, curiosity, and bafflement as the country itself. . . . On every page there is a heart of idea, speculation, dramatic observation that tells of a creative mission undertaken, the identity of the nation, and also the creation of a pure and eloquent prose style.[2]

By way of illustrating Hardwick's claim, I offer two extended excerpts from *Rebellion in the Backlands,* this first one from the section titled "The Land":

> One time at the end of September, fleeing the monotony of a listless cannonading and the dull, heavy reverberations of rounds of fire at intervals, we were wandering about the environs of Canudos, when, upon descending a slope, we came upon an irregular amphitheater, with a number of hills disposed in a circle around a single valley. Small shrubs, verdant icozeiros growing in clusters, interspersed with brilliant-flowering palmatórias, gave this place the exact appearance of some abandoned garden. To one side a single tree, a tall quixabeira, towered above the sparse vegetation.
>
> The western sun was casting its long shadows over the plain, and in the shadow—arms flung out and face upturned to the heavens—a soldier was taking his ease. He had been taking his ease there—for three whole months.
>
> He had died in the assault of July 18. The trampled gunstock, the sword belt and cap tossed to one side, and the uniform in shreds told that he had succumbed in a hand-to-hand struggle with a powerful adversary. He had fallen, certainly, doubled over backward, as the result of a violent blow on his forehead, which was marked by a dark scar. And when they had come to bury

the dead, days afterward, he had gone unnoticed. For this reason he had not shared the common trench of less than three- quarters of a yard in depth into which the comrades fallen in battle had been placed in a last reunion. The fate which had brought him so far from his abandoned fireside had made him at least one last concession: it had saved him from the mournful and repugnant promiscuity of a trench burial and had left him here as he was, three months ago—arms thrown wide and face turned heavenward—beneath the ardent suns, the bright moons, and the gleaming stars.

His body was intact. It had dried out a little, that was all; had undergone a mummification which had preserved the outlines of his physiognomy to such an extent as to give the precise illusion of a tired fighter taking a peaceful nap in the shade of that benevolent tree. Not even a worm—most vulgar of the tragic solvents of matter—had defiled his tissues. He had returned to life's melting-pot without any unseemly decomposition, through an imperceptible draining-off process. In brief, here was an apparatus that revealed, absolutely and in the most suggestive manner, the extreme aridity of the atmosphere.[3]

What sort of human being does this environment produce? In "Man," Cunha takes a look at the *sertanejos* who joined Conselheiro's messianic movement and who, in time, would turn into soldiers of an army of desperados fighting to the death for the survival of their world, which no one in the palaces of power in Rio de Janeiro seemed to understand:

It is impossible to imagine a more inelegant, ungainly horseman: no carriage, legs glued to the belly of his mount, hunched forward and swaying to the gait of the unshod, mistreated backland ponies, which are sturdy animals and remarkably swift. In this gloomy, indolent posture the lazy cowboy will ride along, over the plains, behind his slow-paced herd, almost transforming his "nag" into the lulling hammock in which he spends two-thirds of his existence. But let some giddy steer up ahead stray into the tangled scrub of the caatinga, or let one of the herd at a distance become entrammeled in the foliage, and he is at once a different being and, digging his broad-roweled spurs into the flanks of his mount, he is off like a dart and plunges at top speed into the labyrinth of jurema thickets.

Let us watch him at his barbarous *steeple chase.*

Nothing can stop him in his onward rush. Gullies, stone heaps, brush piles, thorny thickets, or riverbanks—nothing can halt his pursuit of the straying steer, for *wherever the cow goes, there the cowboy and his horse go too.* Glued to this horse's back, with his knees dug into its flanks until horse and rider appear to be one, he gives the bizarre impression of a crude sort of centaur: emerging unexpectedly into a clearing, plunging into the tall weeds, leaping ditches and swamps, taking the small hills in his stride, crashing swiftly through the prickly briar patches, and galloping at full speed over the expanse of tablelands.

His robust constitution shows itself at such a moment to best advantage. It is as if the sturdy rider were lending vigor to the frail pony, sustaining it by his improvised reins of caroá fiber, suspending it by his spurs, hurling it onward—springing quickly into the stirrjups, legs drawn up, knees well forward and close to the horse's side—"hot on the trail" of the wayward steer; now bending agilely to avoid a bough that threatens to brush him from the saddle; now leaping off quickly like an acrobat, clinging to his horse's mane, to avert collision with a stump sighted at the last moment; then back in the saddle again at a bound—and all the time galloping, galloping, through all obstacles, balancing in his right hand, without ever losing it once, never once dropping it in the liana thickets, the long, iron-pointed, leather-headed goad which in itself, in any other hands, would constitute a serious obstacle to progress.

But once the fracas is over and the unruly steer restored to the herd, the cowboy once more lolls back in the saddle, once more an inert and unprepossessing individual, swaying to his pony's slow gait, with all the disheartening appearance of a languishing invalid.[4]

If Cunha's place in the Latin American canon has been assured, there is a case to be made for his induction into the pantheon of international literary journalism as well. His immersion reporting and commitment to telling the stories of people not in any social or political position to tell it themselves certainly place him in a position of honor equivalent to that of two other contemporary nonfiction pioneers in North America, John Reed and Jack London. Just as Cunha had ventured out of Rio de Janeiro for his war dispatches, Reed left the comforts of New York City to cover Pancho Villa's revolution for *Metropolitan Magazine* and the *New York World,* also turning his reportage into a book, *Insurgent Mexico* (1914). Later he would cover the Bolshevik Revolution for *The Masses* and write his masterpiece, *Ten Days That Shook the World* (1919). Similarly, Jack London wrote his chef d'oeuvre, *The People of the Abyss* (1903), on the socially disenfranchised masses of east London. Daring young pioneer reporters all of them, artists of immersion, writers who took life as an adventure, the three met their deaths at a relative young age and in dramatic circumstances: Reed died in Moscow at age thirty-two, a victim of spotted typhus; London died under controversial circumstances at his ranch in California at the age of forty; and Cunha was killed in a duel by his wife's lover, a young army lieutenant, in Rio de Janeiro when he was forty-three. Their tragic deaths lend weight to the theory that literary journalists are ultimately the main protagonists of their stories.

João do Rio and Early-Twentieth-Century Urban Nonfiction Literature

Nothing like a movement or a school of narrative nonfiction developed in Brazil in the wake of Cunha's achievements, despite the impact his work had on the nation's letters. It remained for a long time a single, isolated case of literary pioneering. Nevertheless, another outstanding writer of independent initiative would contribute to the emergence of the art in the opening decades of the twentieth century. This time it would not take place in the distant, dusty backlands plagued by famine and drought but right in the urban heart of Brazil.

Brazil's rulers decided it was time to upgrade the capital city of Rio de Janeiro and modernize its cultural and social infrastructures in terms of what science and the industrial revolutions had brought to the leading European nations. French architects and urban planners were brought in from Paris to reconstruct the urban face of "A Cidade Maravilhosa," or "The Marvelous City." French musicians, painters, singers, and actors came to town as guests of various cultural programs and initiatives aimed at establishing a cultural renaissance equal to the one taking place in "The City of Light." Soon after the Lumière brothers displayed their cinematographic invention in Paris, cinemas began popping up all over Rio de Janeiro. The automobile too became the great technological marvel, and wealthy *cariocas*—the name bestowed on locals—quickly mobilized to import the curious contraption. Even the press abandoned its romantic past for an affair with the industrial revolution.

Between 1900 and 1920 Rio de Janeiro changed dramatically. João do Rio—the pseudonym of João Paulo Alberto Coelho Barreto—caught the spirit of the time and became for Rio, as Honoré de Balzac had been for Paris, its great chronicler.[5] Unlike his French counterpart, who preferred fiction, João do Rio was mostly a nonfiction writer, the prototype of what would be known later in the press community as a reporter. There was no such profession in the Brazilian press when João do Rio obtained his first full-time job at the daily *Gazeta de Notícias* in 1903. Up until then, famous journalists were actually members of the intellectual elite who wrote part-time for newspapers, mainly articles and social commentary with a typical Brazilian flavor which would give birth to a local genre not known elsewhere, the *crônica* (situated between journalism and literature, but differing from the time-oriented *chronicle,* a term derived from Greek roots). They wrote their *crônicas* to make money, to gain national exposure, and to find loyal readers for their fiction, which is where their interests really lay.

João do Rio seized the opportunity to work full-time as a paid journalist and became a pioneer of Brazilian reportage written on a regular basis. To locate subjects for his stories, he did what many today call immersion: he went into the street, took notes, interviewed people, and reported their views on the changing social picture of Rio de Janeiro. In January and February 1904, for instance, *Gazeta de Notícias* published his series titled "As Religiões do Rio" (The Religions of Rio de Janeiro), which captured the attention of the public and brought him immediate fame. He may have been the first intellectual to have paid attention to religious syncretism, a very Brazilian social phenomenon in which African mysticism is blended with Catholicism.

João do Rio's approach was gracefully received by *carioca* readers who, for the first time, found in their newspapers urban narrative nonfiction based on firsthand observations and direct inquiries among the city's people. The series was also published in book form as *As Religiões do Rio* and became a national best-seller (taking into account the country's widespread illiteracy), with some eight thousand copies sold in six years. Despite the book's tremendous success, some readers did not accept it as factual, believing it instead to have been the product of a writer's vivid imagination. They had no previous comparable reference to relate his work to outside of fiction. Members of the cultural elite, however, immediately considered the series to be a truly powerful piece of anthropological and sociological analysis, produced long before social scientists would examine this particular aspect of Brazilian society.

The encouraging response of the public may have injected an extra dose of enthusiasm, as Rio kept on producing narrative reports based on interviews, inquiries, and direct field observations. Working for the *Gazeta de Notícias* until 1913, and for other media outlets from then on, Rio wrote a number of other nonfiction pieces that were turned into books, all of which helped consolidate the peculiar narrative approach to the city he so much identified with. *O Momento Literário* (*The Literary Moment*, 1905) was the result of an extensive inquiry into the changing literary scene; three years later *A Alma Encantadora das Ruas* (*The Enchanted Soul of the Streets*, 1908) emerged as a social portrait of street life; the following year *O Cinematógrafo* (*The Cinematographer*, 1909) tackled the social frisson caused by the arrival of the first cinemas in town. Two further meditations on daily life appeared, and then in 1919 a couple of others were published in Portugal. That same year his last nonfiction book was published, *Na Conferência da Paz*, his coverage of the Paris Peace Conference which followed the end of World War I.

An excerpt from his *Alma Encantadora das Ruas* testifies to his pioneering work as a writer who finds real life pulsing and begging to be told in it own surroundings. He walks about Rio de Janeiro, depicting a broad social portrait of street vendors, harbor workers, dancers, police officers, prostitutes, juvenile beggars, and thieves:

> In four days we interviewed ninety-six kids, foreigners, blacks, mulattos, an unsteady and painful society. Among them, little ones who support their families and precocious thieves by the quay who go their way through punches and jostles.
>
> The first we found is Felix, a black orphan who lives in a family's house near Do Costa Street. As things are difficult, he goes out with a bag to steal and beg. He was jailed before for having taken several samples at a store, but a policeman, who is in love with one of the girls at the store, released him.
>
> —What are you up to, today?
>
> —Today I have to steal cheese. Madame said I can't go back home without cheese today.
>
> Armando, a ten-year old boy, says he is Italian, just in case. He stops at Largo da Sé and says, in a rather naïve way, that his family has not cooked for three years. He is the one who gets everything, including money. José Vizuvi, also Italian, is the son of the well-known beggar Vizuvi. He leaves Alcântara Street, where he lives, at five in the morning, looking for bread that bakers usually put on the windowsill or next to the doors of the houses. When the window is high, he uses a goad-like stick. His father taught him how to steal. Dudu de Oliveira spends the day at the market and at the central districts of town. His mother, pretending to be blind, begs at Largo do Machado. He carries suspicious messages and makes himself available to do ignoble things.[6]

Like Euclides da Cunha before him, João do Rio was ahead of his time as a reporter. Consequently, no one followed in his footsteps. Nor did the primitive media industry of his day exploit the obvious market opportunities opened up by the enthusiastic response of readers to his literary reportages. Unfortunately, it would take Brazil more than twenty years to witness other (rather modest) instances of nonfiction production, which would prepare the soil for a more fruitful harvest in the future.

Writers of Mid-Twentieth-Century Brazilian Literature of Reality

In the 1940s and 1950s, Brazil produced some early versions of literary reportage, but they were more the result of the intuitive initiatives of individual writers than an orchestrated movement. These writers displayed characteristics universally accepted today as signs of artistic expression—such as immersion and voice—and were spokespersons for a literary social realism in Brazil similar to that in the United States at the time. Above all, they possessed that typical Brazilian tendency for writers to take a position in their stories, interpreting facts and social situations from within a peculiar, judgmental point of view.

Joel Silveira, for instance, was a young reporter working for the top news conglomerate of his day, the Diarios Associados chain of dailies, newsmagazines, and radio broadcasting stations, when he was commissioned to cover World War II. Following the Brazilian armed forces' actions in Italy in the winter of 1944, Silveira stayed at the war front for ten months. During this time he wrote narrative journalism that blended factual information and lyricism, portraying scenes of a nation lacerated by conflict. He presented real-life characters—top-level officers, lowly rank-and-file soldiers, and other war correspondents—and revealed his perilous job of checking information and data under fire. When he returned to Rio de Janeiro in 1945, Silveira put together the best of his dispatches in a nonfiction book, *O Inverno da Guerra* (The Winter of the War), once again attempting to plant literary journalism definitively on Brazilian soil. A decade earlier Silveira had already tried his hand at the trade, writing a story on the aristocratic lives of the social elite in São Paulo, a city that was quickly moving beyond its modest past to become the powerhouse of Brazil.[7]

Silveira's pieces differ from the narrative style chiefly associated with literary journalism today, however. He frequently blended reporting with irony, offering opinion commentary (especially when he was covering politics) that was widely accepted by readers. His stories portrayed political figures and revealed the backstage stories of their power struggles with a sense of both malice and good humor. If his war dispatches catapulted Silveira to fame, these pieces maintained his celebrity status. He would go on to write several more books in a long career (he died in 2007 at the age of eighty-eight), including nonfiction, novels, and short stories. Silveira showed that by following the steps of Euclides da Cunha and João do Rio before them, reporters could take up the challenge of going out into the world and returning with real-life stories as exciting as novels.

Throughout the 1940s and 1950s three other journalists contributed to the re introduction of reportage in the Brazilian media. Edmar Morel wrote a series of stories for the daily *Última Hora* that focused on political issues, criticizing the federal government, or unveiling social problems in a mode similar to today's investigative journalism. David Nasser became the most influential Brazilian reporter of the 1950s, writing for the top weekly newsmagazine of that era, *O Cruzeiro*. Both Morel and Nasser would compile their pieces into nonfiction books. Neither, however, produced literary journalism on a par with that of Cunha or Rio, and Nasser in particular was later found to be unreliable, having invented facts and data in several cases. Still, both employed adjectives in abundance and mixed opinion with narrative facts, reinforcing the idea that literary craftsmanship could be useful in covering news.

Like them, playwright, novelist, biographer, and journalist Antonio Callado wrote a series at the daily *Correio da Manhã* (and later at the daily *Jornal do Brasil*) which was heavily influenced by the social criticism forged in literary realism. A left-wing political activist, Callado was imprisoned by the military regime in the early 1960s. At his first newspaper, *Correio da Manhã,* where he became an editor, he took a stand against the introduction of the technique of writing a lead for every story. He railed against the factual reductionist trend that was rampant in the Brazilian press of the 1950s. Like Silveira's, his style was literary but blended comment, judgment, and opinion with narrative. His series were also turned into nonfiction books. *Os Industriais da Seca* (*Industrialists of the Drought,* 1960) presents the dramatic situation of people facing drought in the northeast, while *Vietnã do Norte: Esqueleto na Lagoa Verde* (*North Vietnam: Skeleton in the Green Lagoon,* 1969) depicts North Vietnam during the war there in the 1960s. Both are today considered classic examples of the spirit of reportage taking root in Brazil.[8]

At *O Cruzeiro* other reporters occasionally produced stories that brought into play at least a few elements of today's literary journalism. In 1956 Mario de Moraes and Ubiratan de Lemos won Brazil's top journalism award, the Prêmio Esso de Jornalismo (inspired by the Pulitzer Prize in the United States), for their immersion reporting. Disguised, they rode on one of the many passenger-laden trucks that served as improvised buses, taking northeastern migrants to Rio de Janeiro over dusty, dangerous roads. In their case the trip took eleven days in a truck carrying 102 men and women. Trucks transported a large portion of the estimated 11 million rural migrants of the 1950s, the largest inner-migration flow in Brazil up to that time. Moraes and Lemos went beyond displaying facts and data, however. They also described scenes, structured a story around their trip, and put the migration issue in context: migrants, they pointed out, fled the northeast not just because of the drought; poverty, the lack of opportunities for work, poor living conditions, and a hostile environment also drove the men, women, and children to move to the city. Moraes himself caught typhus while conducting his fieldwork; he was still recovering from the disease when he heard on the radio that he and Lemos had won the Esso award.[9]

To be sure, Cunha and Rio were writers very much ahead of their time, writers who planted the seeds of a Brazilian culture of literary reportage that unfortunately did not bear immediate fruit. While a few nonfiction writers in the 1950s had contributed significantly to the emergence of the modern reporter in the Brazilian press, they nevertheless represent isolated cases of the advancement of the genre in Brazil. The 1960s, however, would witness two spectacular cases of a modern style of Brazilian literary journalism, transnationally influenced to a certain extent by the American countercultural revolution and the introduction of the New Journalism.

The roots were planted some years earlier, between 1955 and 1960, during the presidency of Juscelino Kubitschek de Oliveira, who brought Brazil its first full period of widespread democracy. With that democratic freedom came advances in various segments of popular culture. In music, the bossa nova was born, becoming a style that would achieve international recognition. In the movie industry, the Cinema Novo movement found respect abroad. In the field of drama, new playwrights and directors proved there was such a thing as a Brazilian theater with its own language, artistic agenda, and genuine themes.

Similarly, achievements in international sports placed Brazil at the center of the global stage. Its national men's soccer team won the World Cup for the first time in Sweden in 1958, beginning a victorious tradition still unmatched today. (Brazil is the only five-time world soccer champion, and its team remains the sport's gold standard.) Top-ranking victories in other sports, such as tennis, boxing, and basketball, helped enhance the collective national self-esteem.

Kubitschek definitively set the wheels of the nation's destiny in motion toward achieving universal industrialization, urbanization, and mass culture. Daringly enough, he moved the capital from Rio de Janeiro to Brasília, 621 miles away in the geographical heart of the country, a capital city built from scratch in five years. Once Rio de Janeiro lost its status as the nation's political capital, its rival in national importance and prestige 266 miles to the south, São Paulo, began asserting itself as the country's business capital. It is not coincidental, then, that São Paulo would also serve as the base for two historical instances that represented a shift in power in the field of mass media, with São Paulo becoming the most important news media market in the nation.

In 1964 Brazil took a step backward in democratic status, however. The armed forces took and began ruling the country. Despite this, the legacy of the exciting late 1950s still lingered in Brazilian hearts and minds. A new social class of young professionals rose to leadership in the corporate world, while many more people earned degrees in higher education. As Brazil's metropolises expanded in population, the favorable conditions for an ambitious kind of journalism were put in place.

Two years later the traditional *O Estado de S. Paulo* mass media group—the same daily that had sent Euclides da Cunha to the civil war front of Canudos a century before—launched a new daily, the *Jornal da Tarde,* one that would explore coverage of the news in a fashion never before seen in a Brazilian newspaper. Resembling somewhat the Clay Felker–edited *New York* supplement to the *Herald Tribune,* but delivering a much more flexible and creative art design and layout, the daily would raise the narrative format of literary journalism to a new standard. Tell a story well; dig deep where facts are found; place human beings on the news pages, not just as sources of information but rather as real-life characters; and give major stories a quality narrative style: these were the distinguishing characteristics of this fresh, agile younger sibling of *O Estado de S. Paulo.* While *O Estado* hit the newsstands in the wee hours of the morning, the *Jornal da Tarde* came out later in the day. Instead of delivering headline news and hard facts, it provided in-depth behind-the-scenes coverage of the hows, the whys, and the possible consequences of the facts reported earlier in the day. On weekends it would carry stories written to provide context, understanding, and symbolic immersion of readers in the exciting atmosphere of the 1960s. It was a daily paper that delivered Sunday magazine–style stories.

A young generation of writers, identified in the newspapers' organizational parlance as "special" reporters, would achieve fame for outstanding journalistic performances that combined factual precision, a sharp eye for spotting and capturing on paper real-life characters, and a literary voice and style. In comparison to what the previous generation had achieved in the 1950s in Rio de Janeiro, Marcos Faerman, Fernando Portela, Demócrito Moura, Percival de Souza, and others raised the bar in newspaper literary journalism quality. A glimpse at a story by Faerman, "O Sertão" (The Backlands), reveals to some extent the sophisticated skills that a generation of daring reporters were applying to their nonfiction pieces: "Bent over Margarida's balcony, João thinks on life. Everything went into some doctor's hand when his wife got sick. 'I was ready to die before,' he thinks, 'today I can't. We can die only when we have something in life. Things that we leave for somebody we like. What am I going to leave for my children? When one is just like I am now, one can't ask death to pass his way. My God, this drought is the mother of '32.'"[10] Their texts replaced their predecessors' opinions, adjectives, judgments, and commentaries with more in-depth information, description of scenes, and immersion reporting, such as that found in this story. A certain degree of narrative naïveté identifiable in some of the 1950s stories had given way to a more mature, cautious, and complex reporting style.

Realidade and Brazil's Golden Age of Literary Journalism

Despite its central position in the history of literary journalism, the *Jornal da Tarde's* influence remained rather modest because of its geographically limited circulation and because of its editorial priority, the city of São Paulo. Another 1966 initiative, however (again out of São Paulo), would achieve wider national prestige and impact. That year the mass media conglomerate Abril, which had broken into the business a decade earlier by publishing local versions of Disney's Donald Duck cartoons, launched its first general news magazine, *Realidade*.

The first issue came out in April. Its circulation, 251,250, was a huge figure at the time. To the surprise of everyone involved in the process, it sold out in three days. The cover, portraying soccer star Pelé—the World Cup was to take place later that year in England, and Brazil hoped to become champion for the third time, an unprecedented achievement up to then—was reprinted on a full page in the French magazine *Paris Match*. A monthly publication, *Realidade* continued its unprecedented sales in subsequent issues: the second issue sold 281,517 copies, the third an unbelievable 354,030 copies, and by the eleventh issue it has surpassed 500,000 copies, a new record.

Realidade quickly replaced *O Cruzeiro* as the favorite general news magazine in Brazil. The latter seemed naïve, outdated, and tendentious in comparison with the exciting new publication out of São Paulo, which reached all regions of the country. Its pages depicted a country unknown to most of its inhabitants, as well as the exciting international social and political tensions of an era of agitation and change around the world. The magazine helped Brazilians discover their country's many faces, bringing to its editorial pages profiles of high-wattage political, sports, and show business celebrities alongside stories of everyday people—fishermen, salt mine workers, homeless children in big cities, prostitutes—going about their lives from the northern tropical rain forests of the Amazon to the southern cattle ranches bordering Uruguay and Argentina. It gave its readers a behind-the-scenes look at Brazilian television soap operas—and would grow to become not just a top exporter of this mass media product worldwide but also a great innovator in the transformation of the form and its language. It struggled with stories of death at emergency hospitals and paved the way for future sports champions. It gave voices to midwives, soccer fans, scientists, cardiologists, and pool sharks. It touched on third-rail social issues, such as single mothers who preferred to remain unmarried and Catholic priests who wanted to get married. And it delivered major stories on young people who broke from the norms and revolutionized the arts, the workplace, and the family.

It also provided an eye on the outside world. Brazilian writers were sent to cover the Vietnam War, to penetrate North American ghettos, to discover the real China behind its walls, to show what was happening in the neighboring but ignored countries of Bolivia and French Guiana. When Brazilian eyes were not available, the magazine sent the famous Italian literary journalist Oriana Fallaci to profile actress Julie Christie in Europe, boxing star Muhammad Ali in the United States, and actress and social militant Melina Mercouri in Greece.

In short, the magazine's reporters were not just reporters. They went beyond, and they went deep. They stayed weeks, sometimes a month or more, to get a story, living with real people, exploring their environments, and trying to understand their situations. They conducted research, studied people, and tried to be as precise as possible when covering their stories. They produced special serials—sometimes devoting a whole edition to a single subject—which resulted in excellent sociological readings of an evolving country and its people. All of this immersion reporting was then framed in a compelling narrative style.

The reporters were also authors. They wrote stories with grace, talent, style, and innovation. Some of them gave minute attention to the descriptions of places and people, while others shifted points of view in the same story to provide a multi-angle perspective for its readers. All of them traveled to where their real-life characters lived; many tried to live as they did, eat what they ate, work as they worked, all in an attempt to depict a fuller picture of life as they saw it. In each issue, readers discovered a kaleidoscope of contemporary life as shown through the many colorful, dramatic aspects woven throughout its pages into a carefully built work of literary nonfiction. Many were young professionals, eager to make a name in the trade, bringing their enthusiasm and love to their narratives—names like José Hamilton Ribeiro, Narciso Kalili, Fernando Mercadante, Roberto Freire, Mylton Severiano da Silva, Hamilton Almeida, José Carlos Marão, Carlos Azevedo, Paulo Patarra, Luigi Mamprin, Jorge Butsuem, and Lana Novikowa. Some were fiction writers, such as short story writer João Antônio or playwright Jorge Andrade, who accepted the challenge of writing nonfiction. Their kind of journalism had never been seen in Brazil before in such volume, consistency, and regularity.

As Roberto Freire, for example, narrated in his *Realidade* profile "Este Homem é Um Palhaço. Este Palhaço é Um Homem" (This Man Is a Clown. This Clown Is a Man):

> Buses stop at the door of the João Caetano Theater in São Paulo. Children in uniforms come down by the dozens, and queue up. There's a gleam of impatience in their eyes. The orphanage teachers have some trouble in making

them walk in order into the theater. There's a tranquil expectation, however, while they wait for the show to start.

Three elderly men wearing thick jackets—it is a chilly, dark, and sad afternoon—jump out of a car and quickly walk to the actors' entrance at the back of the theater. They are relatives of one another. They are all Seyssel family members. The eldest, Waldemar, by the way he speaks, his elegance and posture, his polished manners, looks like a diplomat. They walk up the steps to the dressing room. Half an hour later, three of the most famous and beloved clowns in Brazil appear on stage: *Arrelia, Pimentinha,* and *Henrique.*

The children applaud, laugh, and scream. Then together, as in a chorus, they repeat with Arrelia and Pimentinha the traditional salute among these clowns:

—How do you do, how do you do, how do you do; how do you do, do, do, do?

—Very well!

—Well, then, very well, very well, very well. Very well, well, well, well, well!

Always participating, clapping, laughing, the children—at the end of the show—respond to the clowns' hand waves. There's more this afternoon, however: they go down to the audience, row by row, child by child, handshakes, kisses, affection. A child kisses Arrelia's turned-up wax nose tip.

No child leaves without a funny gesture of love and, in the midst of that happiness, up pops the warmth of that very tender and timeless true friendship between children and their idol forever: the clown.[11]

The scene continues:

Waldemar Seyssel leaves the theater and gets into his car. Before the driver pulls off, one of the orphanage's directors brings a boy to the window:

—Thank you, Mr. Waldemar. The boy wants to thank you on behalf of his little friends.

Waldemar Seyssell looks at the child and can hardly hold in his emotions. A tear starts to roll down from his eye. He timidly shakes the boy's hand. The boy can't say a word. The car leaves. After a long silence, Waldemar turns to Henrique:

—See? Waldemar doesn't deal easily with children. If he were like Arrelia at that moment, he would somersault on the sidewalk and would laugh together with that kid. No need for thank you, and no one would suffer for needing help and for wanting to help.

Although they live in the same person, Waldemar Seyssell and Arrelia are two entirely different men.[12]

How did all of this come about at *Realidade*? Encouraged to produce top-quality narrative journalism without a fixed editorial agenda, the *Realidade* writers achieved their marks of authorship and style independent of any mandates handed down by the magazine's editors. They did, however, find initial support in Roberto Civita, heir to the Abril conglomerate and editor in chief at *Realidade*, who had just returned from his graduate studies in the United States and was familiar with the New Journalism revolution in North America. Some brought to their stories their expertise from previous fictional writings, while others read novels and short stories for inspiration. As the magazine advanced into the late 1960s and early 1970s, some of the staff became transnationally influenced by the works of Gay Talese, Tom Wolfe, Truman Capote, and other authors of the New Journalism. Mylton Severiano da Silva even said in a 2001 Web interview that one of his inspirations was John Reed.[13]

While most of the stories were the work of individuals, on certain occasions the staff proved it could produce high-caliber literary journalism as an orchestrated team. In October 1971 the magazine put out a special 320-page mega-edition on the huge Amazon region, the result of five months of immersion-based research, written and edited by a team of sixteen reporters under the leadership of writer Raimundo Rodrigues Pereira and editor Audálio Dantas. To produce their masterpiece of literary journalism, the team traveled as many as 1,200 hours by boat, flew more than 115,000 miles by airplane, and walked or plunged into countless rivers alien to most of their readers.

The successful and glamorous story of *Realidade*, unmatched in the history of the Brazilian press, did not last long. Just over two years into production, it was hit badly by the military regime's move to establish control over the media in December 1968 through a draconian censorship law. Censors were sent to the newsrooms, and newspapers and magazines received daily a list of issues they were to ignore, names of public celebrities they had better never mention; entire editions were blocked from sale on the streets if they contained a forbidden story.

Freedom of expression and democracy are instrumental to literary journalism's prosperity. How can you practice immersion reporting and write scenes of everyday life if you feel you are being monitored, if you are not allowed to tell readers the stories you want to tell? How can you do so when writers are being arrested, tortured, and killed? Once these external factors were in place, internal strife began eroding the enthusiasm and drive that the *Realidade* team had built from the beginning. Abril later decided against supporting *Realidade* and instead invested most of its resources in a new product, a hard news weekly magazine fashioned after America's *Time*. Conflicts between members of the original editorial staff and a change of editorial leadership beginning in December 1968 also drained the magazine of its enthusiasm and creativity.

It still put out anthology editions, such as the special edition on the Amazon mentioned earlier and one on Brazilian cities a year later in 1972. These two masterpieces of Brazilian literary journalism were the magazine's swan songs, however, for it soon went into decline and was finally phased out completely by 1976.

As for the *Jornal da Tarde,* it was also badly hit by censorship. Over time it lost its momentum when most of its upper-echelon editorial staff was dismissed. The *Jornal da Tarde* is still in circulation today, but its editorial persona is entirely unrecognizable. Save for the newspaper's title, nothing that had made it one of Brazil's premium sources of literary journalism remains.[14]

Contemporary Literary Journalism in Brazil

Once *Realidade* and the *Jornal da Tarde* faded in the 1970s, literary journalism ended its first major cycle of activity in Brazil, and the genre slowly slipped from the nation's memory. Literary journalism had never again achieved celebrated status in the business of nonfiction literature, and it seldom went mainstream in such eloquent ways as it had done in *Realidade* and the *Jornal da Tarde.* The era of iron-hand dictatorship and fierce censorship had asphyxiated Brazilian literary journalism and nearly cast it into oblivion forever.

By the early 1980s, though, a new generation of journalists had taken on positions as editors and editorial directors in major newsrooms. They had no cultural links with the narrative school of literary journalism, and in fact most of them did not even know such a thing existed. The iconic newspaper of the day, *Folha de S. Paulo,* rose to become Brazil's top-selling nationwide daily by practicing an objectively written, hard fact, reductionist news reporting that came straight from the pages of its 1984 in-house style book. The model to follow was *U.S.A. Today,* with its infographic novelties and neutered stories. No room for long-form narrative; no space for authorial voice. Simultaneously, the most influential newsmagazine of the time was *Veja,* an offspring of the same Abril conglomerate that had launched *Realidade* before. As readers followed the pages of *Veja,* they felt as if the whole magazine had been written by a single writer, so insipid and homogeneous were its stories from the business pages to politics, from sports to entertainment. Literary journalists of the 1960s and 1970s generations were thus put out of business, replaced by younger, ambitious mavericks of the press. They soon retired or found jobs outside the newsroom. A few remained, working in the mainstream media environment and adjusting themselves as well as possible to their new circumstances.

The spirit of literary journalism did not die entirely, however. On rare occasions it was resuscitated in nonfiction book form. Nothing fancy, no high level of craftsmanship, but at least some of literary journalism's exuberance was once again perceptible in a Brazil that had recovered its democratic bearings in 1985. Nonfiction books were produced by authors eager to recount what they had been forbidden to unveil in the dark ages of the military regime. Investigative journalism rose to fame, but hard facts, not literary journalism, were its conduit. Narrative journalism had always been a solitary, isolated business throughout most of the history of the press in Brazil, but perhaps it never reached such a degree of solitude as in those dark years from the late 1970s to the mid-1980s.

Then, throughout the 1990s, the spirit of literary journalism found a new home in the academic world at the School of Mass Communications of the Universidade de São Paulo.[15] Concurrent with these advances in the academic environment, narrative journalism spontaneously returned to life in Brazil through the initiative of writers who expanded the production of reportage books, particularly biographies with a literary journalism flavor. Readers have found this approach to biographies much more enjoyable than the prior academic models, and some titles have even reached best-seller status.

Brazil has also recently seen the return of literary journalism to mainstream Brazilian media. Eliane Brum, a reporter at the weekly news magazine *Época,* has surprised the public by publishing stories that deal with such sensitive issues as how hospitals deal with terminal patients or what residents face living in a major slum on the outskirts of São Paulo (today one of the five largest metropolises on the planet). Brum's stories are usually several pages long and dedicated to the lives of ordinary people. She has published three nonfiction books—usually anthologies of her newspaper or magazine work—and has been given more than thirty awards.[16]

Making this picture even more complete is the publication of three new mainstream newsmagazines that dabble in literary journalistic techniques: *Brasileiros, piauí,* and *Rolling Stone Brasil.*[17] And a major publishing house, Companhia das Letras, has launched a collection of classic nonfiction books, offering Brazilian readers for the first time titles by authors such as Joseph Mitchell, Lillian Ross, and John Hersey. Many aspiring young writers are finding in these books confirmation that what they are reading today in Brazil's newspapers and magazines has a long and rich international history. Despite these advances, literary journalism is hardly the genre of choice in the mainstream media today, where it is still mostly a path off the beaten track stubbornly traveled by solitary writers who have fought the good fight against unsympathetic editors and fact-loving publishers.

A Promising Portal into the Future

What most Brazilian men and women in powerful media positions today do not acknowledge is that daily newspapers are losing readers. Many readers are unhappy with the media's shallow coverage of the complexities of our time. They deplore the fact that too much attention is being devoted to the dark side of modern society, and even then in only an unimaginative hard news style. They can find, and have found already, their real-time news elsewhere on websites and blogs, where space does not limit the in-depth approach these readers desire. Sometimes the stories there are even delivered in a reasonably good narrative style akin to literary journalism.

If Brazilian readers cannot find a story to read the way they want, and if there is no reportage book on the theme of their choice, they have one other media alternative available to them that does exploit many literary journalistic techniques: the film documentary. In a major metropolis like São Paulo, almost every week Brazilians encounter a new documentary that does what the newspapers are failing to do, that is, capturing, in the tradition of immersion reporting, the multicultural and multifaceted Brazil of today for Brazilians. These documentaries, recounting the lives of people from motorcycle delivery boys in major cities to soccer boys dreaming of climbing out of poverty, approach their stories with grace, creativity, and sophistication. Other topics have included how old people await death in the country's backlands or the way that the phonetic musicality of the Portuguese language has provided nourishment for poets, composers, and lyricists alike.[18]

Everybody but the newspaper moguls seems to recognize the obvious: there is no future for daily print journalism if it does not introduce literary journalism—or anything inspired by the narrative school of thought—into its pages. Even if this does not happen, literary journalism will still go on evolving in Brazil through the endeavors of mad dreamers who have kept the faith of this thousand-year-old truth: deep down, everybody loves a story told well, even in the nonfiction world of today.

The good news is that the voice of the literary journalist is no longer alone in Brazil. The voices echo, finding resonance in a modest but increasing number of peers and readers across the land. And if the writers' talents do not find expression in the regular media outlets as we understand them today, out of necessity and creativity they will find ingenious new ways of making their stories heard—all because literary journalism is truly more than a trade or a dated fashion. It is a spirit that renews and reshapes itself through the ages, landing gracefully each era in the center of a new society, pleasing its people with true stories that entertain, educate, and make one reflect. The challenge now is for literary journalism to adjust to the global media demands of today and to the dramatic rise of a planetary civilization.

Indeed, are we all, as navigators of this magnificent narrative ship, ready for the voyage?

NOTES

1. First published in 1902, *Os Sertões* was finally translated into English in 1944 by Samuel Putnam, and then reissued by the University of Chicago Press in 1957 as *Rebellion in the Backlands.*

2. Elizabeth Hardwick, *Bartleby in Manhattan and Other Essays* (New York: Random House, 1983), 251.

3. Euclides da Cunha, *Rebellion in the Backlands,* trans. Samuel Putnam (1902; Chicago: University of Chicago Press, 1957), 23–24.

4. Ibid., 90–91.

5. It is worth noting that the literary realism movement practiced in France by Gustave Flaubert, Honoré de Balzac, Guy de Maupassant, and others in the nineteenth century may have not only influenced early versions of literary reportage in Brazil but also played a major role later in rearing a generation of Brazil's best fiction writers in the 1930s—Jorge Amado, Rachel de Queirós, Graciliano Ramos, and Érico Veríssimo—who would go on to produce high-quality fiction for the next three decades at least. Unlike in the United States, where writers who were influenced by this movement—John Dos Passos and Ernest Hemingway, for example—produced both fiction and narrative nonfiction books, in Brazil only one writer, Veríssimo, wrote narratives that resemble literary reportage. All of his reportages are travelogues, however. Two trips to the United States, one to Mexico, and one to Israel were turned into four nonfiction books: *Gato Preto em Campo de Neve* (*Black Cat on Snowy Field,* 1941), *A Volta do Gato Preto* (*The Return of the Black Cat,* 1946), *México* (1957), and *Israel em Abril* (*Israel in April,* 1969), respectively.

6. João do Rio, *A Alma Encantadora das Ruas* (1908; Rio de Janeiro: Crisálida, 2007), 76. All translations from Portuguese, unless otherwise noted, are my own.

7. See Joel Silveira, *A Milésima Segunda Noite da Avenida Paulista* (São Paulo: Companhia das Letras, 2003). This story was first published in the weekly *Diretrizes* in 1938, where Silveira had worked before moving to the Diários Associados group.

8. See Antonio Callado, *Os Industriais da Seca* (Rio de Janeiro: Civilização Brasileira, 1964), and *Vietnã do Norte: Esqueleto na Lagoa Verde* (Rio de Janeiro: Paz e Terra, 1977).

9. For more on this first-ever Esso award, see Ana Beatriz Magno, "A Agonia da Reportagem" (The Agony of Reportage) (M.A. thesis, University of Brasília, 2006).

10. Marcos Faerman, "O Sertão," *Jornal da Tarde,* January 16, 1976: n.p.

11. Roberto Freire, "Este Homem é Um Palhaço. Este Palhaço é Um Homem," *Realidade,* October 1966, 110.

12. Ibid.

13. Mylton Severiano da Silva, interview, available at prof.reporter.sites.uol.com.br /myltainho.htm.

14. For an overview of the history of literary journalism in Brazil, from Euclides da Cunha to *Realidade* and the early-twenty-first-century contemporary scene, focusing mainly on issues of narrative and reporting technique, see my *Páginas Ampliadas: O Livro-Reportagem como Extensão do Jornalismo* (Amplified Pages: The Reportage Book as an Extension of Journalism and Literature), 4th ed. (São Paulo/Barueri: Manole, 2009). Chap. 3 on Cunha, Rio, and *Realidade* and chap. 5 on the contemporary literary journalism scene in Brazil are highly recommended.

15. As professors in the Department of Journalism there, Cremilda Medina and I were determined to keep literary journalism alive, Medina emphasizing that journalism should redevelop other ways of covering the news than the hard-nosed model that has prevailed in newsrooms, and I stressing literary journalism as a panacea for Brazil's newsroom ills. Then in 2003 Celso Falaschi, Rodrigo Stucchi, Sergio Vilas Boas, and I established the first Brazilian website fully dedicated to literary journalism, *TextoVivo—Narrativas* da Vida Real (www.textovivo.com.br), which has since become an online literary journalism magazine. Working together in 2005, we designed and launched the first graduate program fully dedicated to literary journalism in Brazil, and later established the Brazilian Academy of Literary Journalism (www.abjl.org.br). Two years later we organized the first conference on literary journalism in Brazil and invited international speakers Mark Kramer, Paulo Moura, and Anne Hull. Guests from abroad joined local speakers Eliane Brum, Caco Barcellos, Ricardo Kotscho, Helio Campos Mello, and Marcelo Rech. For more on this, see *Páginas Ampliadas*, 315–50, 413–23, and 437–48.

16. See Eliane Brum, *O Olho da Rua: Uma Repórter em Busca da Literature da Vida Real* (Eye on the Street: A Reporter in Search of Real Life Literature) (São Paulo: Globo, 2008).

17. See their respective websites: www.revistabrasileiros.com.br, www.revistapiaui.com.br, and www.rollingstone.com.br.

18. The similarities between the two forms of expression are evinced by the fact that João Moreira Salles, founder and publisher of *piauí*, is also an accomplished documentarist. His professional mentors, he said, were not moviemakers or documentarists but rather literary journalists such as Joseph Mitchell and Lillian Ross.

Chapter 11

Literary Journalism in Twentieth-Century Finland

MARIA LASSILA-MERISALO

LITERARY JOURNALISM is practically an unknown term in Finland. That does not mean the form does not exist there, however. On the contrary, literary reportage emerged in Finnish newspapers around the same time that journalism itself started becoming a full-time profession in the country, that is, at the dawn of the twentieth century. The problem instead is one of semantics and of recognition. This essay aims to recover the tradition of literary journalism in Finland by highlighting certain points relevant to the development of Finnish journalism throughout the twentieth century.[1]

To begin with, there are a couple of reasons why literary journalism as a specific genre has been historically neglected in Finland. One explanation can undoubtedly be found in the academy. Journalism education in general was built on positivist scientific beliefs and the ideal of objective reporting, and print journalism in particular has concentrated on newspapers and, more specifically, on hard news. Professional standards have required journalism students to perfect the inverted pyramid model.[2] As a result, creative or emotive-style journalism, be it reportage, personality stories, or features, has been marginalized to a few select courses in university programs scattered throughout Finland. Moreover, as in the United States, literary journalism in Finland has been excluded from the curricula of library sciences.[3] Even the first professorship in magazine journalism (which in Finland is virtually understood as non-news journalism) was not established until the beginning of 2007. Through all of this, Finnish literary journalists have had to educate themselves, and, consequently, a common culture of literary journalism has not developed there.

Another explanation for the troubles facing a literary journalistic tradition in Finland can be found in the field of fiction. It has been said that the defining characteristic of Finnish reading culture is a desire for the truth. Because of this, the realistic novel traditionally has reigned. A book has to tell its readers about reality, things as they really are: "If the story is fictitious, at least the details have to be accurate and the events have to be potentially possible."[4] Finnish readers also use (popular) literature distinctively as a source of knowledge. Many of the most successful novels in Finland can be thought of as factual narratives: "They attempt to stay with the facts, and they are based on researched data, in so far as fiction can be. Narratives are believed to reflect the past as it was. Hence Finnish literature sometimes competes with history, and correspondingly with sociology when the stories are situated in the present time."[5] It could therefore be suggested that the distinctive role of "factual fiction" in Finnish literature has led to a situation in which there is less demand for "fictional fact."

Despite these two significant obstacles, literary journalism has made an appearance in Finnish media, though one long in coming at first. I begin tracing its journey here with the emergence of reportage at the start of the twentieth century, and then turn to the heroes, antiheroes, and storytellers of the 1950s and 1960s. Finally, I examine urban culture in Finland in the 1980s, which spawned a plethora of small magazines and an interest in the gonzo journalism of Hunter S. Thompson. From an American perspective, given its strong traditions in both the practice and the study of literary journalism, Finland is indeed on the periphery. As the many examples discussed here will show, Finnish literary journalists of the second half of the century were greatly influenced by transnational sources, specifically America's New Journalists. From a European perspective, however, Finland is perhaps more in line with journalistic trends that began looking to American New Journalism only when it was felt that objective journalism had begun to lose its bearings at home.

Finnish Reportage: Where It All Began

The Finnish press originally developed through new variations of earlier printed matter such as broadside ballads, books, and newsletters.[6] In the nineteenth century, the line between the magazine and the newspaper—as well as the book—was very thin.[7] What brought them together were travel stories.[8]

The first Finnish reportage—and consequently the country's first piece of literary journalism—is considered to be a series called "Resebeskrifning öfwer Finland af en Stockholmsbo" (A Description of a Journey in Finland by a Citizen of Stockholm),[9] which was published in eighteen parts during 1800–1801. It was a travel story, covering a trip that had been made six years earlier. Described as "an impressive reportage before the age of reportage," it contained descriptions of characters and places, first-person narratives, and keen observations,[10] much of which can be seen in this extract:

An even more unusual feature of modern freethinking was pointed out to me by the bell ringer himself, with the look of a fellow who is still a bit afraid of ghosts himself, but points at his friend on a stub in the dark corner, and says: you probably view that as a ghost, but it is just a stub. "See, my master," the bell ringer said, "how our church lies? We have north there." I now noticed that the church was not situated in an east and west direction, like orthodoxy hitherto had demanded, but in a north and south one. The light-minded building contractor had namely put less weight on the old traditions than on the nature of the spot: and had rather dared to place the altar in the west (it lies in a corner), and turn the church around.[11]

Despite this text's resemblance to literary journalism, it would take a century before the age of Finnish reportage seriously began. Reports appeared in Finnish newspapers during the nineteenth century, but at the end of the century, reporters started to use more subjective observations and experiences in their writing.

Early Finnish reportage was typically very light and entertaining and did not meet with much appreciation.[12] It often dealt with new technological inventions. For example, the first icebreaker came to Finland in 1890, and the first electrical streetcar was introduced in Helsinki in 1900. Both events were described in a playful, light style,[13] although the social implications behind the technology are distinguishable as well: the new inventions were presented in an amusing way so that people would not be intimidated by the strange new devices, which did not even function properly at first.[14] Both the icebreaker and the streetcar were also given some of the characteristics of living organisms: the icebreaker was compared to a strong, unidentifiable creature with a will of its own—as if it were not steered and controlled by man at all, and the streetcar was described in the following words: "Yesterday that miracle started moving between Töölö and Hietalahti—for now only temporarily or on trial. I mean the electric streetcar, which rushes on without a horse pulling it, with no steam striving, on its backside a tail of iron in the air, and through that it propels power."[15]

One of the first truly serious examples of reportage, however, was written by the famous Finnish poet and journalist Eino Leino, and it dealt with the end of the Great Strike in Finland in 1905. The story ran on the front page, a sign of new appreciation, since prior reportages had been modestly placed well inside the newspaper.[16] The story began on a very bombastic and emotional note:

Good news travels throughout the country. Millions of minds excited to the extreme hear it and bless it. It is easier to breathe everywhere because: The Great Strike has ended! Legality has been reached!

Heads clear, reason runs the show again and the hurricane settles. An ocean of people still roils in the surge, and the bottom mud which has risen onto the waves clouds the clarity. A little while more, and everything will be calm again.[17]

Reportage had become an established genre by the 1920s, when the two biggest Finnish newspapers, *Helsingin Sanomat* and *Uusi Suomi,* began publishing weekly supplements. They contained numerous reportages from Finland as well as from abroad.[18] Ture Ara, for example, provided Finns with a taste of Italy:

A self-registering thermometer in Milan showed 36 degrees in the shade. The brain seemed to be close to the melting point. The last sensible thought said: run! So: one quickly gathered one's belongings and ran to the train. And in less than two hours a bluish surface glittered through the sun's haze, and the train stopped in Desenzano for a minute. The same furious speed to the ship. A warm but clean and fresh wind strikes. While sitting on the deck, the hullabaloo of the big city evaporates from the brain, and to my joyful surprise I notice that I am safe and sitting on a ship cruising Lago di Garda.[19]

The impersonal narrator is being used for literary effect, showing how the narrator has lost his identity in the big city and discovers it again on the ship, which allows him to return to the first person. Temporal elements are also used to emphasize the difference: the scene in Milan is narrated in the past tense, whereas from the train journey on, the story is written in the present.

Although reportage had become a familiar genre to the Finnish, the quality of the stories still varied greatly. In 1930, for example, journalist J. F. Ruotsalainen displayed a great deal of confidence in his readers' English skills when he wrote about a dogsled race in North America. He reported the shouts of the mushers in English ("mush, mush on—you malamutes! hurry! hurry!") instead of translating them into Finnish. This seems to have been a rather elitist decision, given Finnish culture at that time; most readers were likely left guessing the meaning of the lines.

The 1950s and 1960s: The Time of Storytellers

World War II affected Finnish media as indeed it affected the whole nation. Magazines played an important role in providing people with information, as well as entertaining them in those dark times.[20] The 1950s and 1960s could be defined as the golden era of storytellers in the Finnish media. A good starting point might be 1952, when two remarkable occasions took place: the Helsinki Olympics and the crowning of a Finnish girl, Armi Kuusela, in the first-ever Miss Universe contest. An effective use of the material these occasions provided explains the huge growth of the magazine *Viikkosanomat,* for example, in the 1950s.[21] *Viikkosanomat* later became, as I have described elsewhere, home to the greatest number of narrative literary stories in Finnish journalism.[22] But before that, there were the *Apu* reporters Matti Jämsä, who became the most famous reporter in Finland because of the daring stunts he conducted, and Veikko Ennala.

Jämsä was hired by *Apu* magazine in 1952. He was a polite twenty-two-year-old narcissistic dandy, who started smoking only because he thought that the style of his tweed jacket demanded it.[23] From the beginning, Jämsä's stories stood out from the others in the magazine—and those in other magazines as well—because of their panache and the unconventional presence of the narrator.

Jämsä became notorious for his daredevil stunts, which began when he tested the alertness of the salespeople in a department store by stealing a carpet and a bicycle, among other things. Jämsä and two female reporters, who went by the nicknames Jami and Ippa, developed ever more action-packed story ideas. Jami and Ippa were mostly used as frightened background characters who added excitement to the story. In "Laskuvarjohyppy neljästä kilometristä mereen" (A Parachute Jump into the Sea from Four Kilometers Up), for example, which was published in three parts in 1953, there were three narrators: Jämsä, who reported the events from his own heroic point of view; Ippa, who joined Jämsä in the plane; and Jami, who followed the events from a boat. The three narrators wrote more or less simultaneous observations of what they saw happening. The first extract gives Jämsä's thoughts when they are all heading out to sea:

> I glance out the door. I can see a small cluster of buildings, I can see stone buildings and smokestacks. . . . I can see the bridge, too, I can see my home.
>
> I can feel something rising in my throat. I look the other way and notice that my reporter colleague Ippa, who has joined me in the plane, is smiling encouragingly.[24]

In the next extract the narrator is Ippa, who describes the same moment but from a different point of view:

> Matti was sitting next to the door in his heavy, uncomfortable equipment, his face glistening with grease. He didn't look nervous, not really even excited, but he was severe. I tried to smile encouragingly. I don't know if I succeeded, but I did get a smile in return.
>
> "I'm not afraid, not at all," Matti said, as if he was surprising himself, "but this all feels so unreal."

Unreal? I thought this felt way too real, real in an unpleasant and nerve-wracking way.

"I'm not afraid either," I lied. "I'm positive that everything will be just fine."

Matti tried to look as if he believed me. And I tried to look as if I believed myself. (*MJt* 56)

The narrators' observations of one another help create the piece's anxious mood.

The story continues with detailed narration from the points of view of each of the three narrators. Because the reader is always one step ahead of the narrators, his or her interest is sustained effectively. The narrators express fear and excitement in numerous ways:

And the sun is going down, down. Why won't he jump already? We're scared. —Matti dear, jump already. Soon we won't be able to see the plane, not to mention you as you jump. . . .

And in a fraction of a second it hits me that it's our Matti who's falling there now. The insane Matti who wouldn't listen to us in time. My heart convulses with fear. (*MJt* 59, 63)

The most exciting moments take place when Ippa in the plane feels relieved as she hears the pilot say that Jämsä will definitely have been lifted out of the sea by now. At the same time, Jami is in a state of panic in the boat, trying to find Jämsä in the dark water, while Jämsä feels himself becoming stiff, swallowing water, and drifting farther out to sea. The story reads like a thriller, and it can be seen as a turning point in his career.[25]

Matti Jämsä continued writing less dangerous reportages as well, but stunts that risked his health and even his life became his trademark, and such stories were what readers expected of him. He boosted his heroic reputation by reminiscing about his earlier adventures and giving detailed information about the planning and the background of upcoming ones. In the story "Uhkayritys" (A Hazardous Venture), written in autumn 1954, he notes:

After I had pulled off the stunt in Rovaniemi and performed as a beauty contestant, I once again reached a dead end. Where could I find the next improbable story? Readers demanded them. They would no longer settle for regular reportage. I had to come up with something sensational, special. "What on earth can we expect next time?" "What special [stunt] do you have in mind this time?" people would ask. "When are we getting another good story?" the editor in chief asked. I wondered and wondered. Night after night. Everything that I could think of to do had already been done. "Soon you'll have nothing left to do but take your own life," some of my friends said. Oh, I think that they're probably right. (*MJt* 156)

The topic of this story eventually turned out to be an attempt to break the record for diving in frogman's gear, which he did. He dove to a depth of two hundred feet—and was sent to a tuberculosis sanatorium for four months to recover.

From 1956 onwards, Jämsä wrote his stories with reporter Veikko Ennala, who came to work at *Apu* magazine. Ennala started describing Jämsä's stunts, and as a skillful writer, he was able to raise Jämsä's reputation even higher.[26] Short newsreel films of Jämsä's stunts started to be shown in cinemas, and Jämsä's reputation even reached the United States. In May 1958 *Time* magazine published a story about Jämsä called "Fearless Finn."[27]

By the time that profile was published in *Time*, however, Jämsä's career was already in decline. The star reporter had become an alcoholic and could no longer come up with innovative story ideas. Also, *Apu* underwent a period of transition, attempting to transform itself from a popular rag into a quality magazine. There was no room for Jämsä and his stunts in the new configuration.[28] Jämsä wrote a lot of stories that were of such poor quality that they could not be published, and he could only write at all if he himself was the center of the story. Nevertheless, he continued to enjoy the respect of his colleagues, since they all agreed that he had devoted his whole life to the magazine. As compensation, he drew a lifelong salary from the magazine, until his death in 1988 at the age of fifty-eight.[29]

Jämsä's greatest influences on Finnish journalism were twofold: first, putting the reporter's own experience at the center of the story; and second, using dramatic techniques in magazine stories, where they had not been used before. Jämsä's remarkable success can be explained by the nature of the times in which he lived: his career began when Finland was searching for new ideals. Jämsä was an apolitical hero—or antihero—of the younger generation, someone very different from the idols whom "official Finland" had promoted thus far.[30] Veikko Ennala explained Jämsä's special quality by pointing out how reporters before him had settled for interviewing their subjects and asking them how things felt, whereas Jämsä had experienced things himself. Ennala also noted the many taboos a reporter like Jämsä had to face prior to the 1950s: one could not write about the church, prison administration, or the justice system; one could not refer to sex, and characters of questionable morality could only be used didactically, to send a message about proper social conduct.[31] Ennala himself, however, became an even more remarkable writer when it came to breaking taboos and influencing Finnish society.

It has been claimed that Veikko Ennala wrote gonzo journalism before it even existed in the United States.[32] The man who made this claim, editor Harri Haanpää of WSOY publishing house, based his opinion on, among other things, the fact that Ennala experimented with morphine even before Hunter S. Thompson himself became familiar with mescaline. In 1952, the year of the Helsinki Olympics, for example, Ennala wrote a story titled "Hashish ja kokaiini saapuneet Helsinkiin" (Hash and Cocaine Have Arrived in Helsinki). In the story he observes the drug trafficking in Helsinki and decides to take a closer look at the phenomenon:

> On the morning of May 29, after the man had arrived at his regular place, I made a daring attempt. Feigning a vague state of pain, I stopped in front of him and growled:
> – Morf?
> The man cast a glance at me. Then his face made an expression that described some kind of condescending understanding. And a hoarse voice hissed back:
> – It's twenty a line today.
> Without waiting for an answer, he turned around and continued his slow time-killing good-for-nothing walk to Albert Street. I joined his company.
> It was only in an even grubbier toilet of a grubby lunchroom, whose key had to be picked up from the cash desk, when I realized I had entered into a questionable adventure. But bravely I bared my left arm. (*L* 337)

Ennala also wrote about alcohol and its effects on society. In 1955 he wrote a piece in which he is taken into police custody for public drunkenness. The story, told with much irony, details the process of becoming intoxicated, as in the following extract, in which he meets two bums:

> I am at the shore of Hakaniemi again. And soon I am fraternizing with two vagrants who are both drunk as skunks. I am suddenly filled with love for my fellow men. I have to offer them both a drink. What, a drink? Two drinks is what they're having, these great fellas. One of them is a former sailor. Oh yes, how I have always loved sailors. There's something grand and noble in sailing distant seas, far away from home, and thus honorably serving one's native country.
> The sailor explains the story of his life. He has faced thirst and hunger and poverty. He's an apprentice, an old apprentice, and he knows everything about sailing. Every detail. Such a good, excellent, and fair man. And honest. Never took a penny from anyone without asking, that's who he is.
> And that's that. A man that honest definitely deserves a drink. We all drink up and hug one another. Plup-plup-plup. Then I give them both a hundred marks so that they can go to a shelter. I am touched by my own generosity.
> Saarinen has already taken a photo of the scene. He's giving me some kinds of signs now. What's he gesturing there? Does he think that I am drunk myself? Yeah, right! I can drink five bottles of wine at once and that won't do anything to me. That's how I am. (*L* 371)

As the extract shows, the story describes vividly the conflict between reality and a distorted consciousness—an idea widely exploited later in Thompson's gonzo journalism. Ennala's use of onomatopoetic language in the story (the "plup-plup-plup" as he empties the bottle) was a new feature in Finnish journalism as well.

Ennala also wrote about the effects of LSD. In 1968, the year Tom Wolfe's *Electric Kool-Aid Acid Test* was published, Ennala wrote a two-piece story titled "Taivas ja helvetti sokeripalassa—LSD" (Heaven and Hell in a Lump of Sugar—LSD). In it, Ennala, a reporter, and the editor in chief, Jorma Virtanen, look on as the magazine's artist, Jyrki Paavola, takes a dose of LSD (Ennala had wanted to experiment with the LSD himself, but a doctor advised him not to because of his history of mental problems and self-destructiveness):

> Jorma Virtanen asks him [Paavola] what is wrong. Can't we see, he responds. We can't see anything. Can't we see his leg, how it has atrophied. He shows his leg. It's a normal leg, just like any healthy leg, there hasn't been anything special about it before and there isn't now. Except in his own eyes. In his eyes it has atrophied and twisted to the left. And the more his leg atrophies and twists to the left, the more it makes him laugh. He's about to choke. And soon, goddamnit, the baby buggy will fall, too.
> – The baby buggy?
> Yes, the baby buggy. He's in a baby buggy. Can't we see? Probably not, because we're one-eyed. Have we actually ever had two eyes? he asks between the hiccups. Oh, what a joyful day. He is in a baby buggy with an atrophied leg and we are his babysitters, we one-eyed men. Cyclopes. (*L* 357)

Ennala's motive for writing stories about illegal drugs was in the end educational. In the LSD story, he claimed that sharing useful and accurate information would be a more effective tool in fighting the drug problem than intimidating people or denying the problem in the first place. The morphine story even ends with a repulsive description of a group of four drug addicts: blood and sweat and dried up veins rejecting the syringe. And in the end, Ennala stumbles out and vomits in the gutter.

Despite these journalistic pieces about the Finnish drug culture, the most significant topic that Ennala addressed in his writing was sex. In doing so, he broke a great many taboos in Finnish society. When he wrote for *Hymy* (Smile)—a sensational magazine that in 1974 caused an amendment to be passed to the law protecting a person's privacy, the so-called "Lex Hymy"—his stories challenged society to reconsider its moral imperatives against public discussions of what it considered to be strictly private matters.

In 1967, for instance, he interviewed Annikki Ant-Wuorinen, who was willing to share her thoughts about women's sexual needs. At the beginning of the story, Ennala writes: "Is this interview a case history of a woman who suffers from nymphomania or a characterization of a woman who is a completely uninhibited, honest, and healthy child of nature, the editors cannot say."[33] The interview itself was presented in question-and-answer form. Ennala asks the woman critical but rather detailed questions, which she answers in full. Furious readers attacked the editors of *Hymy* for having published the story in the first place, but Ennala was not dissuaded. On the contrary, he "was loose and had decided to stick his hand into the pants of the proud society."[34] Ennala next wrote a story about masturbation and declared that the practice was a virtue rather than a vice. Letters again came pouring into the magazine. Many readers were livid, but many were relieved as well; nevertheless, a large part of the readership belonged to "the generation of sexual restraint," and sexual topics, especially women's sexual autonomy and masturbation, were to them too sensitive to put into print.[35] The liberalizing of sexual attitudes and behaviors only started in Finland in the 1970s,[36] so Ennala can be seen as a pioneer of sorts.

Ennala, who wrote four books, hundreds of short stories, and thousands of magazine pieces, certainly transcended the limits of convention and good taste every so often. He drew many of his sensational stories from personal experience; he was himself familiar with alcoholism and attempted suicide several times. It was even claimed that Ennala's writing about his marriage was a contributing factor in his wife's suicide.[37] Because of this, he was considered by many of his contemporaries, journalists in particular, to be a yellow journalist. Sakari Virkkunen, the managing editor of *Suomen Kuvalehti*, even listed Ennala among the top one hundred Finnish opinion makers in 1970, calling him a "true trashcan journalist," and adding that "as long as men like Ennala keep writing, there is no hope of the social estimation of magazine journalists getting any higher."[38]

Magazine journalists such as Matti Jämsä and Veikko Ennala were indeed ill-reputed in Finnish society. In fact they were often referred to as "burned-out graduates."[39] A few journalists working for "quality magazines" in particular wanted to draw a clear distinction between themselves and those working at sensational magazines. Ennala's writings were often described as *sosiaaliporno* (social porn), a term that refers to his scandalous descriptions of society's pariahs.[40] At the same time, though, the majority of journalists harbored a quiet admiration for Ennala's work. As biographer Osmo Lahdenperä notes, "many reporters confess, after a glass of beer, their desire to write as freely as Ennala. But that would cost them their jobs."[41]

Recently Ennala's reputation has changed in Finland for the better. In his preface to Ennala's posthumously published *Lasteni isä on veljeni ja muita lehtikirjoituksia* (*The Father of My Children Is My Brother and Other Magazine Stories,* 2007), Tommi Liimatta describes him as "a stylist to whom the reading value of the story meant everything, and who included more subtleties in a little report about the Viitasaari mud fair than the topic deserves."[42] Liimatta is quick to point out that, as early as World War II, Ennala used the same literary techniques that Tom Wolfe years later would present as his criteria for the New Journalism,[43] including scene-by-scene construction, dialogue in full, third-person point of view, and the recording of everyday gestures, habits, and so on.[44] Liimatta adds that Ennala depicted a time of great social changes, again including the same phenomena that Wolfe depicted: the gap between generations, the counterculture, sexual tolerance, and the death of God.[45]

Viikkosanomat and Further Experiments in Finnish Literary Journalism

From the point of view of narrative literary journalism, even more important stories than those of Jämsä or Ennala were published in a less sensational magazine, the illustrated weekly *Viikkosanomat,* which doubled its circulation from 1952 to 1954. The magazine rose quickly to a previously unknown eminence in Finnish media: a fast read, international in scope, and multifaceted. It is often defined as a photo magazine, but it was also a venue for literary journalists.

Many fictional techniques were used in the magazine's pieces, and the text became more professional, balanced, and coherent over time. The style was free and permissive. In 1952, for example, there were many stories written in local dialects—something that has never been common in Finnish media, not even today. Dialogue was used, descriptions were vivid, and first-person narrators were unmistakably present in the stories.

Simopekka Nortamo, later editor in chief at *Helsingin Sanomat,* the largest newspaper in the Nordic countries, was one of the most remarkable contributors to Finnish literary journalism and to feature writing in a broader sense of the term. He emphasized the value of non-news material and was an important factor in the founding of both the Saturday and Sunday feature pages, as well as the monthly supplement of *Helsingin Sanomat,* all of which published a great deal of narrative literary journalism over time. Nortamo also continued writing reportage even when he became editor in chief.

An example of Nortamo's style, a piece about the unemployed that ran in *Viikkosanomat* in 1957, shows how he, as the narrator, situates himself in the moment he depicts:

The name, age and occupation of the laborer have already been written down on a sheet of paper by the secretary to the manager and board of the Lappeen-ranta employment agency. The man opposite her doesn't really know whether to sit down or stand up when he is being asked questions—he chooses a position in between, right on the edge of the chair. He doesn't bow to the masters or get nervous at the official tone of the bureau. His nervousness arises from deeper and bigger things; it's a question of everyday bread.

– What is the person's[46] address?

During the past twenty-five years the secretary, Räty, has developed her own way of speaking around this table; the third person both implies a suitable distance and shades into politeness, while the impersonal expression comes naturally to the spoken Finnish language.

– I don't remember what the address is, but it's at the guesthouse where I am staying.

– How is the person there, does the person not live in the neighborhood?

– No, I don't. I come from Tampere.

– How come the person came here to search for a job? Didn't the person know that there's not enough work even for the local people here? This is one of the hardest regions.

– Well, I didn't figure that out. Had to try somewhere.

– Does the person know how to bake buns?

– No, I don't think I do. Why?

– We've got only one vacancy and it is for a baker-confectioner. That's all we've got. And the person can't register as unemployed here since the person doesn't live here. The person should apply for benefits in the hometown.[47]

The narrator has an authoritative hold on the story and its subjects,[48] which results in its strong literary impression, and the scrupulously recorded dialogue adds to the documentary power of the text.

Another remarkable writer in the golden era of *Viikkosanomat* was Juha Tanttu. As editor in chief, Nortamo implied in Tanttu's obituary for *Helsingin Sanomat* that the importance of form in his work was often underestimated: "Unlike many of his colleagues, Tanttu always remembered that content is not all that matters in a story. Form is important as well—offering the reader a pleasurable reading experience."[49] Tanttu was indeed conscious of form. The following example is from a five-part story called "Kirjeitä Amerikasta" (Letters from America), which he wrote in 1964 for *Suomen Kuvalehti*. The beginning of the story, quoted here, is in a way delayed, as if one beginning had been written on a sheet of paper, then crumpled up and thrown into the trash. And then again. And still this apparently wasteful use of paper takes the reader deeper and deeper into the world that is being depicted, its details, and its mood:

Dear Reader,

How should one begin a letter like this? There are so many ways. Well, one can always try and start from the beginning:

The wheels of the Air France Boeing 707B thumping onto the runway at Kennedy Airport . . . no, that's cliché.

How about "Back to New York"–style:

The face of the city is the same. The mist in the openings to the subway. The smell of cheap hamburgers. The damp air winds around your neck like a soft, wet blanket. The nervous hoots of the cars. The glaring neon lights, the dark whisky bars. The bare pistol butts and the long billy clubs of the expressionless policemen. "Radiation shelter" signs in the gateways. The depressed Negroes sweeping the streets. And at every moment the feeling of endless solitude—here no one asks, no one wonders. The forest of signs, guides, billboards outside the town. Don't drive here! Keep left! Watch out for merging traffic! Watch out—a gas station! And suddenly in big letters, like a command in a science fiction novel: XPWY! Don't worry, it means expressway—the Americans simplify and shorten. The expressway runs through the ugliest and widest cemetery in the world. On either side of the cemetery are two dirty factory buildings, the Spare Parts Storehouse and the Can Factory.

Was that OK for a beginning? No? Of course we can start with the people.[50]

The narrator makes self-referential remarks to himself as the narrator of the story—here the writer of a letter—and also creates an imaginary dialogue with the reader, whom he positions as the reader of the actual letter. The factual nature of journalistic storytelling becomes manifest here: a story is always preceded by a number of choices the writer has made. The story thus becomes "meta-factual"[51] or "meta-nonfiction,"[52] telling the story of its own creation.

Another writer from *Viikkosanomat* deserves mentioning here: Sakari Määttänen, who started working at the magazine in 1962. The following year he received a World Press Institute scholarship and worked at *Newsweek* for a year. After returning to Finland for a short time, he went back to the United States and lived there until 1973. He was a very sociable person and became acquainted with many famous reporters, including Norman Mailer. This transnational influence of American journalism led him to write colorful stories for the Finnish press. He gathered admirers around him and became a kind of star reporter, a role that has been rare in Finland.[53]

Määttänen, however, is a problematic figure in the history of Finnish literary journalism because he stretched the boundaries of factual narration. The frame of his stories was often an actual event, but the narrator, for instance, reported characters' thought processes in a manner that justified the reader's suspicion of the story's authenticity.[54] As Markku Lehtimäki states:

What distinguishes nonfiction from fiction . . . is that nonfiction should include its sources and references and stress how these mental images and inner thoughts have come to the knowledge of the author, whereas in fiction the author is free to invent any thought or vision his or her imaginary character may have. Hence it is one of the requirements of nonfiction that the thoughts of another person are available to the reporter mainly through narrative acts such as interviews, possibly letters, diaries, testimonies, and so on.[55]

The following extract is taken from a story that describes a young girl's night out. Määttänen, apparently referring to himself in the third person (à la Norman Mailer) as "an elderly loiterer," penetrates the thoughts of the main character, regardless of the fact that in the story the narrator and the main character never meet or exchange words; the narrator only implies that he witnessed the events firsthand:

Knock! Knock! Knock! Twist! Iiiiih! The half-day-old black patent leather and high-heeled shoes of the Young Miss Early Spring twist in the stairway. Inexperience. Agony. She soon forgets her pain.

And again the empty staircase repeats the clatter of the new shoes. Knock, knock, knock. Knockknockknockknock.

The Young Miss hops merrily to the street. She kicks a couple of stones the sun has melted during the day. Turns the corner.

The feet that earlier today skipped wildly in the schoolyard are now hurrying determinedly toward the Expo Hall. . . .

The shoes clatter lightly, joyfully. The sound predicts the beginning of a sprouting love. Those are probably the last clear thoughts in the Young Miss's head. Then she sighs in her happiness, because she has heard that one must sigh if one is happy.[56]

These reports are undoubtedly based on interviews, but the sources are not supplied in the text.

Määttänen's texts also needed a lot of editing. Grammar, syntax, and spelling did not mean much to him, and his stories kept editors busy, as Nortamo notes in Määttänen's obituary for *Helsingin Sanomat*.[57] Colleagues from *Helsingin Sanomat* also remember that there were frequent doubts about the authenticity of his stories. One or two were alleged to be plagiarism, but the suspicions were dealt with behind closed doors, and no documents from the inquiries remain. In the end, Määttänen did not enjoy great respect at *Helsingin Sanomat*.[58] Nevertheless, it is clear that he popularized the genre of literary journalism in Finland and inspired the many writers who followed in his footsteps.

The 1980s: *Kuukausiliite* and Freedom of Expression

Urban culture came to Finland rather late but also rather quickly, in comparison to other western European societies.[59] At the beginning of the 1980s Finland shifted from a controlled economy to a free market one, which meant moving from large bureaucratic systems and a strong belief in the positivistic science of collectivity to an emphasis on the individual and market competition.[60] Soon there was an upswing in the economy. At the same time, the first generation to follow the depopulation of the countryside was coming of age.

Great changes took place in the Finnish media as well. The monopoly of the Finnish Broadcasting Company was broken, and the first local commercial radio stations obtained their licenses in 1985. Cable and satellite television came to Finland, and a new national commercial TV channel began broadcasting. In magazines, information technology made it possible to start up new titles at moderate expense, and the flourishing subcultures that followed the narrow-minded 1970s led to the founding of many new publications. Punk culture in particular gave rise to dozens of small magazines, which became havens for aspiring literary journalists in Finland.[61]

Gonzo journalism also officially arrived in Finland at this time. The Finnish philosopher Esa Saarinen, working out of the University of Texas, collaborated with a Finnish artist friend on publishing their correspondence in book form. In 1981 Saarinen wrote an enthusiastic letter in which he talked about his latest discovery—gonzo journalism:

> From the philosophical point of view the standing of gonzo is crystal clear: a gonzo journalist is always himself a part of reality. The book vaporizes the positivistic separation of subject and object and mixes the observer and the observed into one inseparable web. . . .
>
> Gonzo journalism . . . high-beat guitar riff, direct beat from the central nervous system, where fiction and realistic journalism are one and the same boiling fireball, where the whole weighs more than its individual parts, where truth is a quality of the whole, not of individual sentences, where traditional realistic reporting is abandoned as being formal, dreary, and misleading, where the screaming insanity of reality beams straight out from the text. All the rules have been broken, for in gonzo journalism the focus is not what reality looks like but what it really is.[62]

Selections from the Hunter S. Thompson collection *The Great Shark Hunt* were translated into Finnish and published in 1982.[63] Word started to spread, and gonzo as well as New Journalism began inspiring Finnish writers in, for instance, the monthly supplement of *Helsingin Sanomat,* which began circulation in 1983.

The most famous reporter in the early days at *Kuukausiliite* was Esa Kero. One of his first stories, titled "Bangkok," appeared in *Kuukausiliite* in 1985.[64] The story is a very unembellished and unashamed description of Kero's journey to Bangkok and his encounters with prostitutes there. Writing about one's own experience with prostitution was hardly a commonplace feature of Finnish journalism, much less in a respected newspaper such as the *Helsingin Sanomat*. In general, there is little prostitution in Finland,[65] and Bangkok would have been considered an exotic destination for Finns in the 1980s. As a result, Kero's story includes several elements that would have been unfamiliar to its readers. This extract shows how Kero used first-person narration, combining literary expression with prosaic details of his journey:

> A little beggar boy is sitting on the burning hot street, as tiny as a guenon, sitting with a plastic mug, not sitting, lying as if dead. I go past him. People. Beautiful well-dressed people everywhere. Three hours go by and I return along the same Sura Wong Street. The boy is lying in the same position. Dead? Not any more dead than I am.
>
> I eat well. In an Indian restaurant this time. The owner is very friendly. I tip him 30 bahtis.
>
> To the little boy I didn't give anything.
>
> Still the little boy doesn't show up with his empty can in my air-conditioned hotel room dream. We've already gone so far, seeing and experiencing. What good is all this seeing and experiencing? Should we have cultivated the stony fields, sat on the stairs of Turvala and wondered at the arrival of the swallows? Who knows the same swallows that sit on the power lines in the center of Bangkok, I'd say millions of them, side by side, endlessly. . . .
>
> Or then you can do it as on that first night in Bangkok. Our Thai friend Virabat, whose kindness and care are beyond words, asked if we would be interested in getting a massage. Well, surely a good spa would do us good after a long flight.
>
> So he and his cute girlfriend Leki took us to a big building. And only when we saw twenty Thai girls waiting for customers behind a huge glass window did we realize what this was all about.
>
> Virabat negotiated a price for us and we went in. This was already becoming comical. There was just one minute left until the closing of the massage parlor, and they claimed that there were only three proper masseuses available. Well, I was sober and left with the least attractive one, if I may say so.
>
> Up in the elevator. Inside the private washing room. Clothes off and into the tub. Even took the glasses off my head, bastard. Then she washed me like a little child, though extra thoroughly in some parts. Pojong! That was expected.
>
> I wanted to laugh—I laughed out loud and wiped water from my eyes. Here I was, sitting in a tub in my birthday suit and the soap commercials

were running on the TV next to me. Then on the rubber mattress for a massage—the girl performed the massage with her body, with a slide technique.

Rinse and off to a round bed for a dry massage. Not much more happened even though anything would have been possible. That girl, who adjusted the TV every now and then while massaging me, didn't really turn me on. And why shouldn't I tell all: I came on the mattress already.[66]

The level of intimacy in the story is remarkable by Finnish journalistic standards. Instead of trying to give the impression of being a stud, Kero offers an honest report about what happened, even if it was not very flattering. He was also able to take a critical look at himself as a Western tourist without being hypocritical.

Sex was not all Kero wrote about. One typical feature of his writing was his way of taking different roles in his stories. In February 1986 he wrote a story about a town named Rautavaara, where every fifth person was unemployed. The whole story was actually just a proposal for a story, written in the second person, in which one reporter gives advice to another reporter on how to write the piece. On another occasion he was Comrade Kero, who introduced Muscovite street fashion to tourists. In another instance he went along with a group of Finnish senior citizens to a health spa in Romania. In March 1989 he even went to talk to Jesus and asked him why he had not returned to earth yet, even though there was so much pain and suffering.

As far as the borderline between fact and fiction is concerned, Kero too is a challenging case. He has written stories in which he has stated at the beginning that the article is partially fabricated. It is fair to ask whether such stories can be considered journalism, let alone literary journalism. The reader may have an enjoyable reading experience, but faith in the story's factuality is threatened. As Eric Heyne has stated, "a fictional text has neither factual status nor factual adequacy; a nonfiction text has factual status, but readers would have to resolve individually or by debate the question of its factual adequacy."[67] What if a nonfiction text calls its own factual status into question? What conclusion does the reader then come to with regard to its accuracy? What is nevertheless clear is that Kero's style was original and inimitable, and probably the most significant aspect of his stories was his ability to make seemingly small and unimportant details stand out.

This same effect can be seen in the work of his colleague Ilkka Malmberg, who started working at *Kuukausiliite* in the mid-1980s. Along with Kero, Malmberg is probably the best-known journalist at *Kuukausiliite,* and whereas Kero no longer works as a journalist, Malmberg's career there continues at this writing. As was the custom in the 1980s, his stories also concentrated on the individual experiences of the reporter. Over time, the information density in his stories became extraordinary; as one of his colleagues puts it, "when Malmberg writes a meter of text, he has gathered a hundred meters of information for it."[68]

For example, in 2007 Malmberg wrote about his journey to the United States on a freighter. Along with the story of his own trip, he tells about two other passengers, as well as members of the crew. He shifts from the present time to writing about the Finnish immigrants of the nineteenth century and then to the ships *Titanic* and *City of Benares:*

> "Maybe Bush has resigned in the meantime," Brian dreamed when we were wondering about what was happening in the world, something we knew nothing about. We were in a complete news blackout. With a good radio one could have listened to, say, the shortwave transmission that the Finnish Broadcasting Company directs to the North Atlantic.
>
> Ramona said that during the presidential election in the USA she was working in Mozambique. Their school was so far-flung that they did not know about the winner for days. Then there came a driver who knew.
>
> But a cable had been run from Ireland to Newfoundland already in 1858. It felt incomprehensible. Aleksis Kivi was writing *The Seven Brothers* then.[69] The cable, however, worked for only three weeks before it became saturated and was ruined. The whole slog had been for nothing.
>
> A permanent cable was laid in 1866. So the immigrants who arrived in New York were able to telegraph that they had reached their destination.[70]

Detailed reporting has been an important feature of Malmberg's distinctive style, which creates an interconnection between Finnish nonfiction and realistic fiction. Best-selling Finnish novelists have said that the exhaustive collecting and checking of enormous amounts of detailed information is part of their work process, and still a reader will not hesitate to let the writer know if she has placed the chimney incorrectly on the roof of the Carelian sauna.[71]

Two other magazines that began publishing in the 1980s, clearly arising from the awakening urban culture in Finland, are *Image* and *City*. *Image* started as an avant-garde culture album, and the free paper *City* was born of the remains of two other short-lived magazines. In both *Image* and *City,* New Journalism has been an obvious source of inspiration. The onomatopoetic touch in this passage from a story in *City*, for example, clearly bears the influence of Tom Wolfe:

> Vvvrouummm . . . a light aircraft Cessna is wheeling above the city. It could very well be the Lord Mayor, Raimo Ilaskivi, who's chilling out again.
>
> Vvvrrauuumm . . . no, the Lord Mayor is at work after all. He's circling above the harbor area and planning in his mind how to change it into subdivisions.

"The bird's-eye view gives you a heck of a sight. You don't get everything just by looking at pieces of paper," he says.

Vvvrrrruuumm . . . he has brought along with him some foreign visitors. He motions with his hand above his dominion and tells them: "That's my city."[72]

The extract is an enlightening example of the yuppie culture and the economic boom in Helsinki during the 1980s, and *City* magazine attempted to describe this new lifestyle in a trendy way. It was shallow, elitist, and arrogant. It often wrote about fashionable subcultures and minorities—cultural changes that were taking place in Finnish society—and the magazine used the same tools in its attempt to capture the essence of the new "world" much as the New Journalists felt they had done in America two decades earlier.[73]

In 1988 *City* began circulating twice a month. The recession was closing in, though, and at the beginning of the 1990s it finally struck Finland. *City* survived the economic downturn, but high-flown speeches about Tom Wolfe were no longer heard in the editorial office.[74] Literary journalism in *Image*, by contrast, really took off in the 1990s. One of the most influential journalists in those days was managing editor Panu Räty, who had earlier worked at *City*. For example, he wrote a story about Samuel, a twenty-two-year-old man who burned down an erotic restaurant in Helsinki because it was a sinful place. Räty reconstructed the events of the day of the fire this way:

A car door slams farther away, some passer-by, but Samuel does not care. He hits the hole again to make it bigger. He has thought this through so many times beforehand that he moves quickly but surely as an industrial robot.

Lets the hammer fall from his hand. Opens the cap, lifts the canister in his arms. Pours half of the gasoline on the restaurant floor. Then pushes the whole can inside.

Thou preparest a table before me
in the presence of mine enemies.[75]

The short, truncated sentences give the narrative a cinematic dimension, as if they were stage directions in a screenplay. And the recurrent citing of Psalm 23, which is interpolated into the text a couple of verses at a time at the end of significant passages, provides an interior monologue of sorts that attempts to justify Samuel's illicit act from his point of view.

Although it can be concluded that Räty does not share Samuel's values, the narrator uses free indirect discourse to blur the border between his own thoughts and those of Samuel, which helps to create a literary effect in the text.[76] The story also reflects the changes taking place in Finnish society. Three decades earlier, a person who spoke openly about his or her active sexual behavior, and a journalist who reported it candidly, were considered scandalous. Now, a young man who disapproves of premarital sex and immorality is the exception, and the fire he set to "correct" it is entirely newsworthy in itself.

Something Old, Something New

Some ten years ago, when I became aware of literary journalism, I started looking for evidence of it in Finland. At first I concluded that it was practically nonexistent there. Since then I have delved further into the nation's past and have uncovered more and more instances of what I argue here are examples of Finnish literary journalism, or at least journalistic texts that bear the imprint of the writer's literary aesthetics. There has simply not been enough common understanding, theory, or shared opinion among the practitioners, scholars, or readers of Finnish journalism to have accepted that a brand of literary journalism has existed or exists still in Finland.

As I have tried to demonstrate in this essay, Finnish literary journalism does indeed exist, although it may at times differ in voice and style from other nations' reportage literature. And yet the lively reportages in *Viikkosanomat* and *Kuukausiliite* do contain various characteristics of what we have come to accept as literary journalism, be it America's New Journalism (and its offshoot, gonzo journalism), or Europe's socially conscious reportage. Recently, journalism in Finland has become more factual and viewpoints more preprogrammed, leaving little room for coincidence and exploration, two trademarks of earlier Finnish literary journalism. Today, news stories are so packed with information and magazines so narrowly reader-targeted that narrative literary journalism is rarely to be found anymore.[77]

This has led me to the conclusion that Finnish literary journalism's future might be not with magazines but instead with the newspapers' Sunday pages and supplements. Newspapers have wider and more heterogeneous audiences, and an interest in narrative journalism in Finnish newspapers has been noted of late. Narrative stories are thus being presented as a potential asset for newspapers, since they cannot compete in speed with online journalism or blogs. The recent economic crisis, however, has cut resources in Finnish media, too, and since the whole media scene is in a state of massive change, the future of Finnish literary journalism remains an interesting chapter yet to be written.

NOTES

1. I understand literary journalism to be a subspecies of literary nonfiction; I direct my observations in this essay to journalistic products such as magazine and newspaper stories mainly written by professional journalists. The term "literary" suggests that the texts borrow techniques that are generally associated with the realistic novel and short story. See John C. Hartsock, *A History of American Literary Journalism: The Emergence of a Modern Narrative Form* (Amherst: University of Massachusetts Press, 2000), 11.

2. Heikki Luostarinen, "Moneksi muuntuva journalismi" (Journalism Comes in Many Forms), in *Median varjossa,* ed. Touko Perko, Raimo Salokangas, and Heikki Luostarinen (Jyväskylä: Mediainstituutti, 2002), 23. All translations from Finnish, unless otherwise noted, are my own.

3. Hartsock, *A History of American Literary Journalism,* 7.

4. Kimmo Jokinen, "Lukijalle ei saa valehdella: Totuudellisuuden vaatimus yhdistää suomalaista lukemiskulttuuria" (One Must Not Lie to the Reader: The Requirement for the Truth Unites the Finnish Reading Culture), in *Kirjallisuuden kentillä: Kirjoituksia kirjallisuuden sosiologiasta ja reseptiosta,* Acta Universitatis Tamperensis, series A, vol. 270, ed. Markku Ihonen (Tampere: University of Tampere Press, 1989), 55.

5. Kimmo Jokinen, "Suomalaisen lukemisen maisemaihanteet" (The Ideal Landscapes of Finnish Readers) (Ph.D. diss., University of Jyväskylä, 1997), 43.

6. Päiviö Tommila, "Suomen sanomalehdistön alkuvaiheet" (The Early Stages of Finnish Newspapers), in *Suomen lehdistön historia,* vol. 1, *Sanomalehdistön vaiheet vuoteen 1905* (Helsinki: Finnish Newspapers Association, 1988), 28–34.

7. Ari Uino, "Aikakauslehdistön vakiintumisen kausi 1830–1880" (The Period of the Established Magazine Press, 1830–1880), in *Suomen lehdistön historia,* vol. 10, *Aikakauslehdistön kehityslinjat* (Helsinki: Finnish Periodical Publishers' Association, 1992), 41.

8. See Maria Lassila-Merisalo, "Faktan ja fiktion rajamailla: Kaunokirjallisen journalismin poetiikka suomalaisissa aikakauslehdissä" (On the Borderline of Fact and Fiction: The Poetics of Literary Journalism in Finnish Magazines) (Ph.D. diss., University of Jyväskylä, 2009), 127.

9. The story was written in Swedish. At that time Finland was a part of Sweden, and Swedish was the official language. Finnish became an official language in Finland in 1863.

10. Jyrki Pietilä, "Kirjoitus, juttu, tekstielementti: Suomalainen sanomalehtijournalismi juttutyyppien kehityksen valossa printtimedian vuosina 1771–2000" (Written Item, Story, Text Element: Finnish Print Journalism in Light of the Development of Journalistic Genres from 1771 to 2000) (Ph.D. diss., University of Jyväskylä, 2008), 338.

11. Frans Mikael Franzén, "Erään tukholmalaisen matkakuvaus Suomesta (1800–01)" (A Description of a Journey in Finland by a Citizen of Stockholm, 1800–1801), in *Suomen kansalliskirjallisuus,* vol. 6, *Suomennoksia kansanrunoudesta sekä eri kirjailijain tuotteista 1600-luvulta noin vuoteen 1809,* trans. Joel Lehtonen, ed. Emil Nestor Setälä, Viljo Tarkiainen, and Vihtori Laurila (Helsinki: Otava, 1931), 293.

12. Pirkko Leino-Kaukiainen, "Kasvava sanomalehdistö sensuurin kahleissa 1890–1905" (The Growing News Press in the Shackles of Censorship, 1890–1905), in *Suomen lehdistön historia,* 1:608.

13. Alli Rytkönen, *Päivälehden historia,* vol. 2, *Päivälehden ulkonaiset puitteet ja kirjalliset profiilit* (*The History of Päivälehti,* vol. 2, *The Visual Frames and Literal Profiles of Päivälehti*) (Helsinki: Sanoma, 1946), 134.

14. Esa Sirkkunen, "Sähköraitiotievaunussa: Matkoja tekstistä kontekstiin (ja takaisin)" (On the Electric Streetcar: Travels from Text to Context and Back), *Tiedotustutkimus* 3 (1998): 65.

15. Timoteus, "Sähköraitiotievaunussa," *Päivälehti*, September 5, 1900, 3, available at digi. kansalliskirjasto.fi/index.html?language=en.

16. Leino-Kaukiainen, "Kasvava sanomalehdistö sensuurin kahleissa 1890–1905," 608.

17. Eino Leino, "Vapausliike" (The Freedom Movement), *Helsingin Sanomat*, November 7, 1905, 4.

18. Raimo Salokangas, "Puoluepolitiikka ja uutisjournalismi muuttuvilla lehtimarkkinoilla" (Party Politics and News Journalism in a Changing Newspaper Market), in *Suomen lehdistön historia*, vol. 2, *Sanomalehdistö suurlakosta talvisotaan* (Helsinki: Finnish Newspapers Association, 1987), 385.

19. Ture Ara, "Riva Sul Garda," *Helsingin Sanomat viikkoliite*, October 14, 1928, 3.

20. Pirkko Leino-Kaukiainen, "Aikakauslehdistön itsenäistymisvuodet 1918–1955" (The Years the Magazine Press Became Independent, 1918–1955), in *Suomen lehdistön historia*, 10:257.

21. Pirkko Leino-Kaukiainen, "Yleislehtien kuohuvat vuodet" (The Restless Years of the General Magazines), in *Suomen lehdistön historia*, vol. 8, *Yleisaikakauslehdet* (Helsinki: Finnish Periodical Publishers' Association, 1991), 153.

22. Lassila-Merisalo, "Faktan ja fiktion rajamailla," 144.

23. Juha Numminen, *Tarina A-lehtitalosta* (The Story of the Magazine House A-lehdet) (Helsinki: A-lehdet, 2003), 32–34.

24. Matti Jämsä, *Matti Jämsän tempaukset* (The Stunts of Matti Jämsä) (Jyväskylä: Gummerus, 1960), 55. Subsequent references to this work appear parenthetically in the text, abbreviated *MJt*.

25. Numminen, *Tarina A-lehtitalosta*, 39.

26. Ibid., 40.

27. Available at www.time.com/time/magazine/article/0,9171,863423,00.html.

28. Numminen, *Tarina A-lehtitalosta*, 65.

29. Markku Rautonen, *Apu: Sanan voimalla 1933–1983* (*Apu: By the Force of the Word, 1933–1983*) (Helsinki: A-lehdet, 1983), 69; Numminen, *Tarina A-lehtitalosta*, 68.

30. Rautonen, *Apu*, 54.

31. Veikko Ennala, *Lasteni isä on veljeni ja muita lehtikirjoituksia* (The Father of My Children Is My Brother and Other Magazine Stories), ed. Tommi Liimatta (Helsinki: WSOY, 2007), 527. Subsequent references to this work appear parenthetically in the text, abbreviated *L*.

32. Harri Haanpää, "Miksi Veikko Ennala?," September 5, 2007, available at www.wsoy. fi/index.jsp?c=/news&id=884&catId=1.

33. Veikko Ennala, "Helsinkiläisrouva sanoo: 'En voi elää ilman miehiä'" (A Madam from Helsinki Says: 'I Cannot Live Without Men'"), *Hymy* 12 (1967): 55.

34. Osmo Lahdenperä, *Neron heikkoudet: Veikko Ennalan elämä* (The Weaknesses of a Genius: The Life of Veikko Ennala) (Helsinki: Lehtimiehet, 1978), 174.

35. Elina Haavio-Mannila, Osmo Kontula, and Anna Rotkirch, *Sexual Lifestyles in the Twentieth Century: A Research Study* (New York: Palgrave, 2002), 6.

36. Ibid., 7.

37. Lahdenperä, *Neron heikkoudet*, 215–17.

38. Sakari Virkkunen, "Vuoden 1969 sata suomalaista vaikuttajaa" (A Hundred Opinion-Makers in Finland in 1969), *Suomen Kuvalehti* 1 (1970): 25.

39. Leino-Kaukiainen, "Aikakauslehdistön itsenäistymisvuodet 1918–1955," 264.

40. Lahdenperä, *Neron heikkoudet,* 179.

41. Ibid., 181.

42. Tommi Liimatta, preface to Ennala, *Lasteni isä on veljeni ja muita lehtikirjoituksia,* 25.

43. Ibid., 16.

44. Tom Wolfe, "The New Journalism," in *The New Journalism: With an Anthology,* ed. Tom Wolfe and E. W. Johnson (London: Picador, 1973), 46–47.

45. Liimatta, preface, 17.

46. Translator's note: In Finnish, the word for "it"—*se*—is used. Since one cannot use "it" in this context in the English language, I have translated this as "the person" in the dialogue. It has the same implications here, I think, as the Finnish *se.*

47. Simopekka Nortamo, "Työttömät," *Viikkosanomat* 5 (1957): 7.

48. Maria Lassila-Merisalo, "Friend or Foe? The Narrator's Attitude towards the Main Character in Personality Stories," in *Real Stories, Imagined Realities: Fictionality and Non-fictionality in Literary Constructs and Historical Contexts,* ed. Markku Lehtimäki, Simo Leisti, and Marja Rytkönen (Tampere: University of Tampere, 2007), 97–127.

49. Simopekka Nortamo, "Toimittaja Juha Tanttu. Pehmeän journalismin mestari" (Reporter Juha Tanttu: Master of Soft Journalism), *Helsingin Sanomat,* July 26, 1998.

50. Juha Tanttu, "Kirjeitä Amerikasta 1.—Mikä on viimeisin elefanttivitsi?—New Yorkin maailmannäyttely?—Juu. Ja republikaanien puoluekokous" (Letters from America 1.—What's the Latest Elephant Joke?—The New York World's Fair?—Yeah. And the Republican Party Convention), *Suomen Kuvalehti* 30 (1964): 9.

51. Mas'ud Zavarzadeh, *The Mythopoetic Reality* (Urbana: University of Illinois Press, 1976), 123.

52. Daniel W. Lehman, *Matter of Fact: Reading Nonfiction over the Edge* (Columbus: Ohio State University Press, 1997), 179.

53. Lassila-Merisalo, "Faktan ja fiktion rajamailla," 149.

54. Dorrit Cohn, *The Distinction of Fiction* (Baltimore: Johns Hopkins University Press, 1999), 24; Markku Lehtimäki, "The Poetics of Norman Mailer's Nonfiction: Self-Reflexivity, Literary Form, and the Rhetoric of Narrative" (Ph.D. diss., University of Tampere, 2005), 37.

55. Lehtimäki, "The Poetics of Norman Mailer's Nonfiction," 37.

56. Sakari Määttänen, "Kun nuoret ovat nuoria Expo-hallissa" (When the Young Are Being Young at Expo Hall), *Viikkosanomat* 15 (1963): 19–23.

57. Simopekka Nortamo, "Toimittaja Sakari Määttänen: Lahjakas kirjoittaja, lannistumaton journalisti" (Reporter Sakari Määttänen: A Talented Writer, an Indomitable Journalist), *Helsingin Sanomat,* January 24, 1992.

58. Lassila-Merisalo, "Faktan ja fiktion rajamailla," 150.

59. Sampo Ruoppila and Timo Cantell, "Ravintolat ja Helsingin elävöityminen" (Restaurants and the Enlivening of Helsinki), in *URBS: Kirja Helsingin kaupunkikulttuurista* (Helsinki: Edita, 2000), 51.

60. Pertti Alasuutari, *Toinen tasavalta: Suomi 1946–1994* (Tampere: Vastapaino, 1996), 104–15.

61. Veikko Kallio, "Katsaus aikakauslehdistön kehitykseen vuoden 1955 jälkeen" (A Survey of the Development of the Magazine Press after 1955), in *Suomen lehdistön historia,* 10:298.

62. M. A. Numminen and Esa Saarinen, *Terässinfonia* (Steel Symphony) (Espoo: Weilin & Göös, 1981), 363.

63. According to publisher Timo Kanerva, the reason for the partial translation was technical; the whole book would have become too large to be bound as one volume, and the small

publisher could not afford to make it a hardcover book. Thompson and his agent approved of the decision and of the selection of stories; some of the older pieces were left out, as well as articles that addressed American politics and were not of much interest in Finland. Timo Kanerva, telephone interview, March 17, 2009.

64. A complete translation of this article into English recently appeared in the Spring 2010 issue of *Literary Journalism Studies*. I supplied a scholarly gloss on the piece.

65. Haavio-Mannila, Kontula, and Rotkirch, *Sexual Lifestyles in the Twentieth Century*, xiv.

66. Esa Kero, "Bangkok," *Helsingin Sanomien Kuukausiliite* 4 (1985): 46.

67. Eric Heyne, "Toward a Theory of Literary Nonfiction," *Modern Fiction Studies* 33.3 (1987): 480.

68. Lassila-Merisalo, "Faktan ja fiktion rajamailla," 162.

69. Aleksis Kivi is Finland's national writer, and *The Seven Brothers* is the first important novel written in Finnish.

70. Ilkka Malmberg, "Rapakon taa," *Helsingin Sanomien Kuukausiliite* 1 (2007): 60.

71. Jokinen, "Suomalaisen lukemisen maisemaihanteet," 44.

72. Eeropekka Rislakki, "That's My City," *City* 2 (1986): 12.

73. See, for example, John Hollowell, *Fact & Fiction: The New Journalism and the Nonfiction Novel* (Chapel Hill: University of North Carolina Press, 1977), ix.

74. Antti Isokangas, Kaappo Karvala, and Markus von Reiche, *City on sinun: Kuinka uusi kaupunkikulttuuri tuli Helsinkiin* (The City is Yours: How a New Urban Culture Came to Helsinki) (Helsinki: Tammi, 2000), 103.

75. Panu Räty, "Samuelin tuli," *Image* 4 (1997): 44.

76. Phyllis Frus, *The Politics and Poetics of Journalistic Narrative: The Timely and the Timeless* (Cambridge: Cambridge University Press, 1994), 51.

77. Lassila-Merisalo, "Faktan ja fiktion rajamailla," 196.

Part III
Transnational Influences

Chapter 12

Riding the Rails with Robin Hyde

Literary Journalism in 1930s New Zealand

Nikki Hessell

Readers of the june 1936 issue of the *New Zealand Railways Magazine* were greeted with an exhortation from the Government Tourist Bureau to "Know Your Own Country." Accompanied by pictures of Mitre Peak and Mount Egmont, the bureau's promotional material asked New Zealanders to see travel and tourism as their patriotic duty: "This country of ours is a land of which we can be justifiably proud, for in no other country in the world is there concentrated such a wealth of scenic splendour."[1] One series of articles included in the magazine at this time particularly complemented this message. It was composed by Iris Wilkinson, the novelist and poet better known in New Zealand literary studies by her pen name, "Robin Hyde."

Since large-scale settlement of New Zealand by Europeans had begun in the mid-nineteenth century, the new colony had produced its own novelists, poets, and historians, many of whom searched for an indigenous voice that could accurately reflect the experience of a people who paradoxically still saw themselves as British despite living thousands of miles away.[2] White (or "Pākehā") New Zealand authors like Hyde (who nonetheless found inspiration in the literary journalism of Upton Sinclair and George Orwell) thus had a difficult relationship with the journalistic traditions and transnational influences that this volume seeks to address, often struggling to find an effective balance between joining the international literary conversation and generating an authentically local style.

The 1930s were a seminal period for the development of the New Zealand literary canon. Many of New Zealand's emerging cultural heavyweights began to question the traditional reticence and deference to Britain that had characterized the nation's history. As the centenary year of 1940 approached, public discourse focused on the question of New Zealand's cultural identity. Iconic publications such as the poet Allen Curnow's collection *Not in Narrow Seas* (1939), the novelist John Mulgan's *Man Alone* (1939), and Frank Sargeson's short story "The Making of a New Zealander" (1940) are now widely accepted as key examples of this phenomenon. But what of writing in other, more marginal genres? Stuart Murray provided a forceful reminder in *Never a Soul at Home: New Zealand Literary Nationalism and the 1930s* that, despite the richness of the material available, the 1930s have not received enough detailed critical attention.[3] Yet very little notice has been given in recent scholarship to the way in which genres such as literary journalism might have contributed to the nationalist debate or to the way in which New Zealand authors drew on both the established historical conventions of and international developments in literary journalism to make it their own.

This lacuna is unfortunate because, in addition to marking a watershed in New Zealand letters, the 1930s were also a crucial period in the history of literary journalism generally and of the travelogue in particular. As Bernard Schweizer has argued, the decade leading up to World War II saw a burst of activity among intellectuals who "pioneered a new tradition by employing travel writing self-consciously as a platform for voicing radical political ideas."[4] Schweizer's work traces how English intellectuals brought the dominant cultural concerns of the era to bear on their consideration of other countries and their inhabitants, which inevitably led to reconsiderations of the political and social dynamics of Britain. Traveling to the colonies helped to sharpen their understanding of their own society.

Writers in and of the colonies were part of this same global movement but faced a more intriguing literary challenge: to travel *within* their own nation's borders in order to discover, document, and critique its characteristics. This challenge involved engaging with the history of British travel journalism about one's own country and reclaiming control of the narratives that such writing had generated. New Zealand had been the subject of numerous works of travel reportage throughout the nineteenth century. As Lydia Wevers has pointed out, much of this writing assumed that New Zealand, like the other British colonies, was simply an extension of the imperial center, an "other England" or part of "greater Britain."[5] As a consequence, there were very few original perspectives contained in these texts, since "most of the travel writing about New Zealand from the late 1870s was already overdetermined by the reiteration of travel routes, genre conventions, and the expectations of a metropolitan reading public about what there is to see in the world and what to think about it."[6] An opportunity existed for a colonial writer to rework these narratives to suit a different audience and a different set of cultural and political goals.

Robin Hyde was peculiarly well placed to take up this opportunity. She was an immensely prolific author who was able to turn her hand to a wide array of genres. Novels, memoirs, poems, biographies of curious New Zealand figures both historical and contemporary, and an enormous body of newspaper and magazine journalism all flowed from her pen during her short career, which began with a newspaper internship at the age of seventeen and ended with her suicide in London, when she was only thirty-three, in August 1939.[7] Her oeuvre was principally concerned with two key areas: experimenting with genres and addressing questions of identity. While these concerns manifested themselves throughout her body of work, they are perhaps particularly evident in her journalism. As Gill Boddy and Jacqueline Matthews have pointed out, Hyde's journalistic writings were devoted to the need to "find our own song" by mixing Māori and Pākehā New Zealand identities to create a truly indigenous culture.[8]

Hyde thus represents an important intersection between several strands of literary and journalistic history, both nationally and internationally. This essay aims to show how her railway essays bring the journalistic tradition of travel writing about her homeland and the transnational influence of developments in travel journalism to bear on the cultural debates of 1930s New Zealand. Like her literary counterparts in Britain, Hyde was subverting and reforming the travelogue to meet a particular cultural and political need. Unlike them, she did not need to go abroad to find uncharted territory in which to conduct this experiment in literary journalism. In a country with such a fragile sense of its place in the world politically, culturally and artistically speaking, there were opportunities to consider national identity without clearing Customs.

Hyde's Railway Essays and the Conventions of Travel Journalism

The *New Zealand Railways Magazine* appeared from May 1926 to June 1940. It was originally designed as reading material for railway employees and their families but expanded in 1933 to become a general interest publication.[9] Hyde wrote for the magazine during the period when it reached its peak circulation of around 26,000 copies.[10] Twenty of her essays appeared between April 1935 and September 1937. The first twelve (published in April, May, June, and August 1935, and then monthly from January to August 1936) were presented as a series under the title "On the Road to Anywhere." This title was dropped for the final eight essays, published monthly from February to September 1937. The series covered a comprehensive list of New Zealand's major cities and tourist attractions, from Wellington to Northland, the central North Island (including Rotorua, Tauranga, Waitomo, Tongariro, and Wanganui), the South Island (including the Marlborough Sounds, Nelson, Christchurch, Arthur's Pass, Central Otago, and Dunedin), and Stewart Island. The articles were frequently accompanied by photographs or cartoons relating to her experiences, although these were not supplied by Hyde herself.

Hyde's railway essays can be read as conventional, almost commercial travelogues, designed to market destinations to readers and to dwell on the most positive aspects of the visitor's experience. The initial essays had in fact begun life as promotional pieces for the Tourist and Publicity Section of the Ministry of Industries and Commerce, which Hyde approached in November 1933. The brief given to her by the manager of the section was for pieces of a "bright descriptive nature" that would cover "some of the outstanding features likely to attract visitors."[11] While these pieces were rewritten for the *New Zealand Railways Magazine* series, they retained some of the gloss of public relations material, and the itinerary I have outlined was a fairly standard tourist route.

But Hyde's series ultimately went far beyond this conventional formula in terms of both composition and execution. The impression created by the articles was of a roving reporter on a mission to visit the best and most scenic parts of the country, and the series read as the chronicle of a continuous (if somewhat circuitous) trip around New Zealand. In fact her itinerary was considerably more fragmented than it seemed. After her initial contact with the Ministry of Industries and Commerce, Hyde traveled to Northland to gather material. She also undertook a long journey around the South Island in late 1936 which was reflected in several essays.[12]

Other pieces, however, were derived from memories of past visits to places like Waitomo and Wanganui.[13] Such economies were understandable; Hyde was under considerable financial strain at the time, and although the magazine paid for her contributions, it does not appear to have paid any of her expenses. She was also in poor physical and psychological health during this period, and had voluntarily admitted herself to Grey Lodge, a treatment center at Auckland Mental Hospital.[14] But this approach to composition also demonstrates her intention to move beyond both reportage and tourist propaganda to construct her essays instead as literary meditations on ideas that she considered to be important for her readers. As a result, the articles manifest consistent underlying concerns regardless of the place or the experiences she describes. A narrative of nationalism, arising out of Hyde's strong sense of New Zealand's place in the world, is what emerges most forcefully. The literary journalist, not the picturesque location, ultimately determines the shape and themes of the series.

Hyde also undermined the formula for the New Zealand travelogue by adopting some of the politicization that characterized transnational trends in travel journalism. As well as encouraging New Zealanders to visit this or that location, her articles consistently asked readers to examine their attitude toward their country and its qualities. Hyde achieved this blend of the conventional and the subversive by exploiting the opportunities that the travelogue genre provided. The traditional narrative of traveling in New Zealand drew constant parallels between the colony and the imperial center. The landscape and the people of New Zealand were unfailingly compared with British or European examples in order to suggest "interchangeable geographies and cultures."¹⁵ Where such comparisons were difficult to sustain, such as in the case of Māori New Zealanders, these narratives perpetuated the idea that the colony would eventually shed the characteristics that made it distinct from Britain: Māori would die out or become entirely assimilated; flora, fauna, and land use would reflect British examples and practices; and the aspirations and identity of New Zealand people would be in line with those of imperial subjects the world over. Hyde's railway journalism, by contrast, made New Zealand the center of the universe.

Creating National Identity through Literary Journalism

Hyde consistently inverted the conventions of the New Zealand travelogue throughout the railway essays in order to focus on national, rather than imperial, identity. Far from presenting her travelogue in the standard nineteenth-century form of "a giant inventory of colonial possessions," Hyde stressed both the singularity and the autonomy of New Zealand's various tourist destinations.¹⁶ She traced the ways in which her homeland might actually be superior to Europe by European standards, arguing that New Zealand could have its own cultural institutions that celebrated the colony's unique history and advocating recognition of those aspects of the nation that were at least as special as anything to be found in Europe. Visiting the decrepit office of Bishop George Selwyn in Kerikeri, for example, Hyde pressed for some formal memorial of New Zealand's settler past:

> But surely it will not be long before New Zealanders, recognising in "these old shades" the builders of their land, in the tranquility of the cobwebbed room the cradle from which something of greatness and dignity emerged, commemorate the early missionaries in the best possible way. Why is not this upper chamber of meditation, now given over to the spider and to the keeping of a few stores, entered only by a steep and twisted old staircase, converted into a museum where every possible relic of its old occupants might be kept?¹⁷

In a more creative vein, she urged New Zealanders to reconfigure the way they saw themselves and to move beyond traditional areas of cultural pride, such as sporting prowess, in favor of the indigenous qualities of the land-scape. As she archly remarked in relation to the famous glowworm caves at Waitomo, "New Zealanders are sometimes said to have an inferiority complex, which is as may be . . . not about their football, or their racing, any-how . . . but it is certainly true that they don't, so far, seem to have grasped the fact that they really possess Waitomo, and that every other country in the world would give its eyebrows for the privilege."[18] The tendency to value anything international (especially anything European) over the homegrown variety is gently mocked in these articles; in commenting on the quality of the onions on D'Urville Island, Hyde noted: "The red-skinned stacks and strings of them make one imagine 'Italy!' But really there's no need to brood on foreign lands afar. I should think that for sheer beauty, this part of New Zealand would be incomparable the world over."[19] This sort of comparison was entrenched in the history of travel narratives of New Zealand, with Europe held up as the pinnacle of achievement.[20] Hyde frequently found otherwise, arguing that her homeland could hold its own when judged against European norms.

This approach to considering national identity was in itself a fairly radical overturning of the traditional New Zealand travelogue. More radically still, however, Hyde often set aside the usual criteria for measuring nationhood and national worth that were derived from Europe in favor of new standards that privileged and celebrated areas in which New Zealand was typically presented as lacking. Her articles defend and promote the very qualities that tended to contribute to the New Zealand inferiority complex: a feeling of newness and unsophistication in a world in which nationhood was measured by tradition and cosmopolitan style. In her visit to Christchurch, the most English of the major New Zealand cities, Hyde was blunt about her sense of disappointment:

> I suppose every city in the world has its little disadvantages. With Christ-church, City of the Canterbury Plains, the trouble is not, as some have sup-posed, too many bicycles, but too much decorum. The very same English gentility which was responsible for its grey Gothic arches, its avenues lined with fatherly chestnut and other trees, has done something repressive to its spirit of adventure. It is a city of charming people who, to my mind, rather lack the élan of young New Zealand. There is too much sitting about in the twilight listening to muted music. Of course, this is in some sense a relief—Christchurch, like Andrew Marvell's garden, is "a green thought in a green shade"—but the quietude and the contemplation are not the things I like best in a New Zealand which is too young and frisky to have developed much genuine poise as yet.[21]

The city of Dunedin brought out a similar feeling in Hyde:

> I could understand why one Dunedinite liked the stone quarries better than anything else in the city. The hard, new rattle of stone, leaping clean and blue from dents pickaxed out in the hills, had about it a sort of promise for the future. Something hadn't stopped happening, it was still in progress, or about to happen differently, with a rattle and clatter of falling stones. I think the young are more impatient for their youth under the shadow of old trees and old houses than in other surroundings; and I think, too, that they are right. They have their own miracles to produce, their own city to pattern.[22]

These comments about national history and the newness of the settler colony were principally concerned with Pākehā identity. But Hyde was also alert to some of the issues of Māori identity, and in particular the challenges posed by colonization and policies of assimilation. Her encounters with Māori people in the railway essays stress the uniqueness of their contribution to New Zealand life and the misguided nature of the stereotypes that prevailed in the 1930s. In a typically sardonic remark she noted, "The Maori mind does not, and in my opinion will not, function along accepted lines."[23] The comment perfectly captures the patronizing tone of many contemporary attitudes toward Māori, but Hyde's journalism turns the sentiment on its head by frequently endorsing the alternative worldview produced by "the Māori mind."

This attribute is particularly obvious in her writings on Wanganui, a town rich in precolonial history with a large Māori population, and a town with which Hyde was familiar from her stint as "lady editor" at the *Wanganui Chronicle* in 1929–30. After explaining the importance of Māori storytelling in explicating the place-names and geographical features of the region, Hyde tells her readers: "When approaching Wanganui, my strong advice both to New Zealander and tourist is to remember that here, just under the surface, is Maori world—Maori talk, Maori custom, Maori charm. You won't get the best out of Wanganui if you eliminate the Maori from your quest" (MPK 35). The unfairness of the portrayal of Māori in national discourses struck Hyde profoundly; commenting on the very steep farms worked by Māori farmers around Wanganui, she wrote, "I always remember the Maori river farmers when listening to the wise discourse on the impracticability, or the unwillingness to labour, of the Maori race" (MPK 39). These remarks are in stark contrast to the conventional presentation of Māori in travel narratives about New Zealand, where they were uniformly stereotyped as lazy, drunken, and greedy.[24] While Hyde acknowledged that "to talk about the Maori without sentimentalising him is a difficult business," she was resolute about the centrality of Māoridom to New Zealand's identity.[25]

Hyde was particularly struck by the connection she perceived between Māori people and the land. Visiting the kauri forests of Northland, she wrote that "only the Maoris know the real ins and outs of the great forest."[26] This kind of truly indigenous knowledge of the country was the model for her concept of a fully realized national identity. She lamented that most Pākehā New Zealanders had not experienced the natural environment of places like Waipoua, predicting that "some day New Zealanders will understand what Waipoua really is. But until you have seen peach-coloured manuka blossoms, saluted Tane Mahuta, and devoured tawhara fresh from the tree, you know only part of what New Zealand can offer you."[27] The natural landscape offered some uniquely New Zealand experiences that Māori already had access to and that Pākehā could choose to enjoy too. Out of the knowledge of these experiences, a shared and forward-looking national culture could be formed.

Hyde's often vivid descriptions of New Zealand's natural beauty thus did not simply present the attractive portrait of a location or scene that readers of a travelogue might expect; they also drew attention to the country's unique qualities and connected them to a correspondingly unique national identity. This technique can be seen in the way she describes the sensory stimulation experienced by the traveler. When visiting the Central Otago region, for example, she declared: "What I like about New Zealand (apart from the several things I love about it), is its power of quick-change artistry. It is like a book of small, brilliantly coloured and varied pages."[28] She concurred with Alan Mulgan that the North and South Islands smelled different and catalogued an argument about distinctive New Zealand flavors, noting: "I have known some who swore by toheroa as the flavour characteristically New Zealand; others who could not be weaned from mutton-bird, more again who made oblation to the memory of Stewart Island rock oysters or of Picton bloater. But my vote is ever with the golden-brown wild honey."[29]

This confident tone was a deliberate contrast to the register of the "usually reserved New Zealander."[30] Throughout the essays Hyde stayed true to this confidence, insisting on the special and distinctive qualities of her homeland. Traveling to Rotorua she noted: "I have taken the train journey through the Waikato after months and months of a Sydney world which was baked to a crisp. Outside the windows flashed the douce green pastures, dotted with daisy-like lambs. A green world, a white world, and very frisky cirrus clouds entirely in sympathy. Then I knew I was back in my own land."[31] Once settled in Rotorua, she was deeply impressed by Whakarewarewa, a park comprising geysers and mudpools and featuring performances by Māori artists, writing, "I felt that I was seeing a part of the world, my world, which belonged so especially to New Zealand."[32] Her focus on quintessential New Zealand experiences is important in the context of an era in which the country looked to Britain for self-definition and often struggled to pinpoint the characteristics that made New Zealand special. Hyde's essays not only aim to define these characteristics but also assume that the existence of such characteristics is a given. They display a level of confidence in the national identity that is almost revolutionary for the time.

This confidence was complemented by a sense of scorn at the distortions of New Zealand identity that had been perpetuated by the existing travel literature. In an attack on the novelist Charles Reade, Hyde sneered that "Reade was fathoms deep in scientific error when he described the Antipodes as a place where the birds have no song, and the flowers no scent. Charles had never heard a tui tinkle in the depths of the big kauri trees: nor had he made one of the party, when the service car, emerging from the last swart shadow of Waipoua's giants, plunges into a grey-blue evening whose sudden, sleepy fragrance makes one's nose twitch in appreciation."[33] The misrepresentation of the country's natural history had also led, in Hyde's opinion, to a narrow and inaccurate view of the country's characteristics and achievements. Writing from Stewart Island, Hyde noted: "It's not every Saturday night you can go to the southernmost picture theatre in the entire world, and, wrapped up in a borrowed fur coat, hear a most impressive rendering of the late King's Jubilee speech to his Empire. . . . New Zealand, of course, was represented by sheep. Why the deuce can't they give us ambergris or mollymawks for a change? After all, we *can* achieve other things besides frozen mutton."[34]

The hopeful note of this last sentence points to the fragile optimism that characterized Hyde's attitude not only to New Zealand's national identity but also to its cultural life. She firmly believed in the potential for a distinctive local identity that would translate into an identifiable artistic style, but she knew that this potential was largely untapped. The railway essays provided an obvious forum for her to link this wider concern with New Zealanders' neglect of their own places of natural beauty. Travelogues as a genre of course provoke meditations on sights and sounds, particularly of the picturesque variety, but Hyde extended this motif into her discussions of the nascent indigenous literary canon, or rather to the problem of developing such a canon. As Hyde lamented, a lack of engagement with the uniqueness of the country's natural phenomena had stunted the literary output: "Were these trees of fragrance on the Continent, in the Isles of Greece, or even stationed in the Kipling country, poets would plaster them with sonnets. As things are, they go through life unsung, frequently even unsniffed."[35] This lack applied to both bucolic and urban settings; Hyde called the small, desolate town of Reefton "the ghost-town about which somebody should have written the great New

Zealand novel, but hasn't."[36] She remained optimistic about the future of a New Zealand literature fueled and sustained by this natural setting, however, pointing out during her trip across the Canterbury Plains that "the real poet of that grand South country has not arisen yet," and prophesying that "some day the New Zealand parallel to Olive Schreiner's 'Story of a South African Farm' [sic] will be written here."[37]

The prophetic tone signals the significance of Hyde's travel journalism and its unconventional style. Although the genre of the travelogue lent itself to describing the present, Hyde was constantly aware that there was "something in progress" in her homeland. Ruminating on the locations she visited, she also looked ahead to the kind of New Zealand that might emerge from the uncertainties of her own era. At times Hyde's sense of the future of her homeland can seem eerily prescient; her words of praise for the sands at Ninety Mile Beach, for example, "sands that are whiter, shapelier, lonelier than anything filmed at Hollywood," foreshadow the extraordinary exposure that New Zealand would receive in the wake of the *Lord of the Rings* films and, more aptly in this case, Jane Campion's film *The Piano*.[38] Likewise her violent response to a tourist from the United States who recommended commercial development of the southern lakes—"I would rather see the entire American nation, man, woman and child, subside a thousand feet into You-know-where, than see a hair of Lake Wakatipu's head perturbed"—echoes twenty-first-century unease about foreign (especially American) ownership of iconic land.[39] Such comments are indicative of the dual importance of Hyde's literary journalism in the 1930s: it both reflects and calls into being some quintessentially New Zealand concerns, using the land as a starting point for reimagining the nation and its people.

The series ends with Hyde attempting to get to Spirits Bay in the far north. It is an appropriate place to close her tour of the country; Spirits Bay is the spot at which, as she explains to her readers, Māori believe souls depart for the afterlife (F-OP 43). While admiring Ninety Mile Beach, Hyde produces one of her characteristic observations, at once briskly realist and hauntingly metaphorical, as she declares that on the shore "there wasn't anything real except a few blurred faces, Maori and white" (F-OP 45). This half-formed presence, visible but shaky, intimately tied to the landscape and only slowly emerging into clear sight, is a subtle image of the national identity Hyde perceived.

The *Railways* Essays as Literary Journalism

Hyde joins a long list of New Zealand artists in the early decades of the twentieth century who viewed the land itself as the major source for a distinct national culture. What is special about Hyde's contribution to this debate, however, is that she is writing in a genre that specifically requires her to report on the landscape, natural beauty, and inhabitants of the places she visits, not simply to draw on them metaphorically. She exploits some of the formal features of the travelogue to generate her message about New Zealand identity; readers get the expected taste of local color and descriptive writing with an extra dose of cultural debate.

Hyde thus represents a very important example of the way in which traditions in literary journalism played out in a country like New Zealand in the early decades of the twentieth century. As Ben Yagoda has persuasively argued, the definition of what constitutes literary journalism must go beyond "laudable nonfiction" and demonstrate true journalistic qualities.[40] In particular, Yagoda singles out the need for "active fact-gathering—not just working from memory or sensory observation but doing what reporters call reporting."[41] For this reason, Yagoda regards the travelogue as problematic in the canon of literary journalism. Hyde's railway essays can nevertheless be considered examples of the genre of literary journalism because they are written in a hybrid form that manages to comply with and contravene Yagoda's criteria simultaneously. Much of what Hyde produced was based on memory and sensory observation, but she also undertook train travel and collected material specifically for the project. She did not adopt the technique, common in the 1930s, of passing off entirely invented travel as if it were real.[42] Moreover, by choosing a publication outlet that was specifically journalistic, rather than literary, she aligned her writing with the world of narrative reportage rather than imaginative literature. In other words, she brought together the literary and the journalistic in a rather unconventional way, modifying her technique to suit the circumstances. What resulted was a surprisingly coherent body of work that carried off the illusion of first-hand reportage and perhaps falls naturally into the borderland between narrative literary journalism and the travelogue that John C. Hartsock has described.[43]

Hyde's railways essays also qualify as literary journalism because they were highly topical. The years in which she wrote and published her railway journalism produced some of the first important meditations on New Zealand nationhood, such as W. P. Morrell's *New Zealand* (1935). She was joining a public conversation among authors in many different genres, who sensed, like the historian J. C. Beaglehole, that in the reactions of Pākehā New Zealanders to the land, "there is glad recognition, there is love even; but there is not yet identity."[44] The currency of these ideas made them an ideal subject for a contemporary literary journalist.

Yagoda's simple definition of literary journalism is journalism that is "thoughtfully, artfully, and valuably innovative."[45] These criteria aptly describe Hyde's achievement in her railway essays. The articles are innovations on the travelogue, but they go beyond formal or stylistic cleverness to become part of the much wider contemporary debate around identity and nationalism. Hyde uses the stock techniques and ready-made audience for travel journalism to push for the same cultural transformation that her New Zealand contemporaries were urging in their more obviously literary texts. By adopting a more populist form than the novel or the poem, and by subtly weaving her message into pieces of apparently light reading, Hyde perhaps made a more immediate impact on 1930s readers than writers like Curnow, Mulgan, or Sargeson.

As Stuart Murray has proposed, New Zealand authors of the 1930s were caught in a colonial paradox in which, "as they sought to prove New Zealand's distinct sense of cultural difference," they inevitably "looked abroad for models and ideas."[46] The public discourses of the late 1930s and early 1940s typically demonstrated "the classic vocabularies of the settler colony, caught between self-aggrandizement and colonial fealty."[47] Hyde does not display that deference in her railways essays. This is not to argue with Murray's extremely compelling argument but rather to suggest that, in stepping away from conventional literary genres into the less canonical world of magazine journalism, Hyde was freed from the need to address the British paradigm for both writing and nationhood. The center is nowhere else in Hyde's essays.

NOTES

1. *New Zealand Railways Magazine,* June 1936, n.p.

2. The best discussion of this aspect of New Zealand's literary history is Jane Stafford and Mark Williams, *Maoriland: New Zealand Literature, 1872–1914* (Wellington: Victoria University Press, 2006).

3. Stuart Murray, *Never a Soul at Home: New Zealand Literary Nationalism and the 1930s* (Wellington: Victoria University Press, 1998), 12.

4. Bernard Schweizer, *Radicals on the Road: The Politics of English Travel Writing in the 1930s* (Charlottesville: University Press of Virginia, 2001), 3.

5. See Lydia Wevers, *Country of Writing: Travel Writing and New Zealand, 1809–1900* (Auckland: Auckland University Press, 2002), 140, 150.

6. Ibid., 187.

7. Further details about Hyde's life can be found in Derek Challis and Gloria Rawlinson, *The Book of Iris: A Life of Robin Hyde* (Auckland: Auckland University Press, 2002), 227. Challis is her son.

8. Gill Boddy and Jacqueline Matthews, eds., *Disputed Ground: Robin Hyde, Journalist* (Wellington: Victoria University Press, 1991), 126. *Disputed Ground* is a selection of Hyde's

journalism. It reproduces only a fraction of her work in this genre but is an extremely useful introduction to her style and preoccupations.

9. The entire run of the *New Zealand Railways Magazine* has been digitized by the New Zealand Electronic Text Center and is available at www.nzetc.org/tm/scholarly/tei-corpus-railways.html.

10. Neill Atkinson, *Trainland: How the Railways Made New Zealand* (Auckland: Random House, 2007), 118.

11. Quoted in Challis and Rawlinson, *The Book of Iris,* 227.

12. For the exact details of her itineraries, as far as they can be established, see ibid., 227, 370–91.

13. Hyde did not dissemble about her methods. In a letter to her friend Pat Lawlor, a fellow journalist who was responsible for getting her a contract with the *New Zealand Railways Magazine* following the publication of the first two railways essays, Hyde offered to produce "one about Waitomo, one about Tongariro, one about Picton and Marlborough Sounds, wildest Blenheim, etc., one about Wanganui River, one about Arthur's pass [*sic*], to all of which places I have been." May 11, 1935, Alexander Turnbull Library, MS-Papers-2425. Further correspondence between Lawlor and Hyde regarding the railways essays can be found in Lawlor's papers in the Alexander Turnbull Library, particularly the letters dated June 29, 1935 (MS-Papers-77-067-5/3), July 27, 1935 (MS-Papers-77-067-5/3), March 9, 1936 (MS-Papers-77-067-7/27), and April 15, 1937 (MS-Papers-77-067-5/3).

14. In the same letter to Lawlor quoted earlier, Hyde remarked that, in retrospect, she probably was not well enough to have undertaken the initial trip to gather material for the publicity pieces, and that even the revision of the articles for *Railways Magazine* had been undertaken at a time when she was "peculiarly seedy." May 11, 1935, Alexander Turnbull Library MS-Papers-2425.

15. Wevers, *Country of Writing,* 181.

16. Ibid., 165.

17. Robin Hyde, "On the Road to Anywhere: Russell and a Rainbow. *Dolce far niente* at Keri-Keri. Part II," *New Zealand Railways Magazine,* May 1935, 38. Selwyn was bishop of New Zealand from 1842 to 1868. He was a controversial and enormously influential figure in early New Zealand society, traveling throughout the country and becoming involved in political as well as religious affairs.

18. Robin Hyde, "On the Road to Anywhere: Acquaintance with Glow-Worms," *New Zealand Railways Magazine,* March 1936, 41 (Hyde's ellipses).

19. Robin Hyde, "On the Road to Anywhere: The Little Island of Jade Fiords," *New Zealand Railways Magazine,* May 1936, 33.

20. Wevers, *Country of Writing,* 77, 135.

21. Robin Hyde, "On the Road to Anywhere: With an Alpenstock at Arthur's Pass," *New Zealand Railways Magazine,* June 1936, 32.

22. Robin Hyde, "In Old Dunedin: A Barrel-Organ, Crab-Apples and a Castle," *New Zealand Railways Magazine,* May 1937, 67.

23. Robin Hyde, "On the Road to Anywhere: A Matter of Pipis and Kowhai. Part V," *New Zealand Railways Magazine,* January 1936, 35. Subsequent references to this work appear parenthetically in the text, abbreviated MPK.

24. Wevers, *Country of Writing,* 205–6.

25. Robin Hyde, "Ways of the North: Life in the Cabin Country," *New Zealand Railways Magazine,* August 1937, 21.

26. Robin Hyde, "On the Road to Anywhere: Northern Hospitality, and a Tawhara for Tea. Part III," *New Zealand Railways Magazine*, June 1935, 40.

27. Ibid. As Hyde explains, a tawhara is a flower that produces an edible, honey-like secretion. Tane Mahuta is the name of a gigantic kauri tree that is still a popular tourist sight; the tree shares its name with that of the Māori forest god.

28. Robin Hyde, "Old Days of Gold: Where the Streets Are Lit with Oil-Lamps," *New Zealand Railways Magazine*, June 1937, 34.

29. Robin Hyde, "On the Road to Anywhere: Snow-Men and Tussock Country," *New Zealand Railways Magazine*, July 1936, 38; and idem, "On the Road to Anywhere: In the Snow-man Country," *New Zealand Railways Magazine*, April 1936, 33, respectively. Alan Mulgan, the father of the novelist John Mulgan, had remarked, "The dry light air of Canterbury and Otago, touched ever so slightly with the scent of tussock-land, differs from the heavier balmy air—sweet with the odours of fern and tea-tree and a suggestion of the bush's richness and decay—that one breathes in the North." See Alan Mulgan, *The Pilgrim's Way in New Zealand* (London: Oxford University Press, 1935), 97.

30. Hyde, "On the Road to Anywhere: With an Alpenstock at Arthur's Pass," 32.

31. Robin Hyde, "On the Road to Anywhere: Bubble and Squeak, Plus a Grilled Trout," *New Zealand Railways Magazine*, February 1936, 25. Hyde had traveled to Australia in 1926.

32. Ibid., 27.

33. Robin Hyde, "On the Road to Anywhere: Palm Lilies and a Benedictine. 'Sweet Evening' in Opononi. Part IV," *New Zealand Railways Magazine*, August 1935, 43. In his 1895 novel *It Is Never Too Late to Mend*, Reade has one of the characters propose that in Australia "the flowers are beautiful to the eye but have no smell, and . . . the birds have all gay feathers, but no song." See *The Works of Charles Reade*, vol. 7 (New York: AMS Press, 1970), 54.

34. Robin Hyde, "Isle of the Glowing Sky: Stewart Island and a Glass Box," *New Zealand Railways Magazine*, February 1937, 34.

35. Hyde, "On the Road to Anywhere: Palm Lilies and a Benedictine," 43.

36. Robin Hyde, "The Stone in the Centre: Looking Down from Nelson," *New Zealand Railways Magazine*, July 1937, 41.

37. Hyde, "On the Road to Anywhere: Snow-Men and Tussock Country," 38.

38. Robin Hyde, "The Flying-Off Place: Stuck on Ninety-Mile Beach," *New Zealand Railways Magazine*, September 1937, 45. Subsequent references to this work appear parenthetically in the text, abbreviated F-OP.

39. Robin Hyde, "'I Hear Lake Water Lapping': The Road to Paradise," *New Zealand Railways Magazine*, April 1937, 28.

40. Ben Yagoda, preface to *The Art of Fact: A Historical Anthology of Literary Journalism,* ed. Kevin Kerrane and Ben Yagoda (New York: Simon and Schuster, 1997), 13.

41. Ibid.

42. See Paul Fussell, *Abroad: British Literary Traveling between the Wars* (Oxford: Oxford University Press, 1980), 174–77.

43. John C. Hartsock, *A History of American Literary Journalism: The Emergence of a Modern Narrative Form* (Amherst: University of Massachusetts Press, 2000), 13.

44. J. C. Beaglehole, *New Zealand: A Short History* (London: Allen and Unwin, 1936), 158.

45. Yagoda, preface, 14.

46. Murray, *Never a Soul at Home,* 13.

47. Ibid., 15.

Chapter 13

James Agee's "Continual Awareness," Untold Stories

"Saratoga Springs" and "Havana Cruise"

WILLIAM DOW

LIKE HIS *Let Us Now Praise Famous Men* (1941), James Agee's shorter literary journalism expresses the hope of trying to invent a new transforming aesthetic practice in which, as he states in his masterwork, "the reader is no less centrally involved than the authors and those of whom they tell."[1] Agee's *Famous Men,* composed of photographs by Walker Evans and Agee's narrative, began as a straightforward documentary for *Fortune*'s "Life and Circumstances" series on the daily existence of "blue- and white-collar families during the depression"[2] but soon evolved into a meditation on what Agee defines as "the nominal subject": "North American cotton tenantry as examined in the daily living of three representative white tenant families" (*FM* 8). Largely neglected in Agee criticism, Agee's short essayistic and journalistic pieces, legible through the longer, more substantial work of *Famous Men,* are essential to understanding his role as a cultural critic in the 1930s and 1940s.

While deploying *Famous Men* as a comparative backdrop for my argument, this essay will examine two of Agee's shorter pieces, "Saratoga Springs" (*Fortune,* 1935) and "Havana Cruise" (*Fortune,* 1937), for both elucidate his often problematic reader-narrator relationships, the tensions between his commitment to mimetic fidelity and his reverent or irreverent stances toward his subjects, and his attempts to fuse his "modernist project"[3] with the social implications of his art. Inverting Ella Zohar Ophir's recent claim that Agee's "modernist self-consciousness" dissolves "political clarity,"[4] I suggest that *Famous Men* demands and elicits such clarity. "The 'sense of beauty,'" Agee is compelled to admit in *Famous Men,* "like nearly everything else, is a class privilege" (*FM* 271). Agee's literary journalism never forgets such privilege, for it supports his claim of giving a "true account" of his subjects and places by presenting information that, in concrete practice, cannot be denied. At the same time, his reliance on fictional devices serves to disturb fixed assumptions and to augment his propositional claims.

Agee announces such claims in *Famous Men* by ontologically distinguishing his conception of fiction from his insistence that "nothing here is invented," that "you should so far as possible forget that this is a book," and that "disbelief should not be habitually suspended" (*FM* 214). He argues: "In a novel, a house or person has his meaning, his existence entirely through the writer. Here, a house or a person has only the most limited of his meaning through me: his true meaning is much huger. It is that he *exists,* in actual being, as you do and as I do, and as no character of the imagination can possibly exist" (*FM* 27). Agee is equally hard on journalism: "Journalism can within its own limits be 'good' or 'bad,' 'true' or 'false,' but it is not in the nature of journalism even to approach any less relative degree of truth" (*FM* 206). His plea for a kind of journalism that would not "poison the public" (*FM* 206) but would "perceive in full and . . . present immaculately what was the case"[5] has significant ramifications for his class representations in which a "reliable" and "percipient" (participant-)observer "must not be ignored."[6] Obsessed with denying the individual validity of either fiction or journalism, Agee, in *Famous Men* and in much of his other literary journalism, sees himself foremost as a cultural and social critic. Thus while expediting his "great claims,"[7] he never abandons his point of view, and his subjects rarely speak for themselves.

Agee's journalistic assignments for *Fortune, Time,* and *The Nation* in the 1930s and 1940s included stories on the Tennessee Valley Authority (a kind of conventional documentary counterpart to *Famous Men*), cockfighting, industrial pollution, a war-damaged Europe, the death of FDR, and the U.S. commercial orchid industry.[8] For my purposes, though, the most important pieces are "Saratoga" and "Havana Cruise," neither of which has received the critical attention it deserves. Preceding the actual writing of *Famous Men* by less than a year, "Saratoga" anticipates the Agee narrator of the Alabama experience: prescient yet uncertain, observing himself as much as he observes others, getting close to his subjects by giving us their world as a substitute for themselves. "Havana Cruise," published a year after Agee's most celebrated work, extends many of the techniques of *Famous Men,* revealing, most notably, his subjects through the portrayal of objects while employing strategies of address that complicate the relationship between representation and real experience. Yet while trying to discover another form of class knowledge—this time that of the "middle class"—Agee, inverting his intention in *Famous Men, de*-sacralizes his subjects, and in so doing condemns them for their non-defiance. Both pieces attempt to portray people as something more than sociological entities and to discover some of the basic patterns of 1930s American culture. To be clear, Agee was part of the 1930s phenomenon that aimed to understand, in Warren Susman's words, "the concept of culture and its implications" and the "forces operating to shape that culture into a heightened sensitivity of itself as a culture."[9] Agee's obsessive rendering of the "dignity of actuality" (*FM* 215) is in part an anxious response to this 1930s culture.

This essay purposefully focuses on these two pieces Agee published for *Fortune* magazine in the 1930s. Although the corporate-oriented *Fortune* seems an odd place for a writer like Agee, the magazine, written and edited almost exclusively by liberal and leftist writers of the period, allowed Agee to pursue his cutting critiques of American capitalism while generating "new forms of literary journalism."[10] Along with such writers as Archibald MacLeish and Dwight Macdonald, he prioritized his role of an intellectual over that of a journalist. As one historian of the 1930s has remarked:

> Writers such as MacLeish, Macdonald, and Agee can be described as interstitial intellectuals pursuing their own literary, political, and intellectual interests from the spaces they created and defended with corporate organizations. . . . They contributed to the strength and success of left politics during the decade, from a location at *Fortune*. . . . *Fortune*'s articulation of "populist, laborist, and anti-fascist" political views was part of a new landscaping of the political field, legitimating left-liberal political possibilities while undermining the assumptions that could underscore renewed business legitimacy.[11]

A cornerstone of Agee's literary journalism was an unswerving loyalty to his own understanding. Often downplayed in Agee criticism, his primary role in the 1930s was as an intellectual, pioneering new forms of cultural critique.

Rousing the Reader: Second-Person Narration

Published in *Fortune* in 1935, "Saratoga" depicts a slice of American 1930s horse-racing culture in which cultural critique, class judgments, and class distinctions predominate. Agee begins the piece by giving a brief history of the city of Saratoga Springs and then, comparing Saratoga to other American courses, argues for its distinctiveness and the "special intensity" of its horse-racing seasons (*SJ* 89). Agee then proceeds to catalogue "the sort of people who come [to Saratoga Springs] whose names you know and who are Turf and Field clubbers" (*SJ* 90) ("Marshall Field," "William du Pont," "Charles Schwartz," "Mrs. Margaret Emerson, and her son Alfred Gwynne Vanderbilt"); social relations among the wealthy regulars ("the sportsman-politician William Ziegler who for years paid Edward Ashton $7,500 for the month's use of his million-dollar turkey farm"); and "illustrious" others who "most likely have boxes at the track as they would have permanent pews if they were pillars of churches" (*SJ* 90). The narrator's focus is not on the background or personal history of these figures but rather on their social status and the hypocrisy such status suggests.

As a savvy parodic insider, the narrator then presents another side of the "crazy quilt" (*SJ* 91), which shows Saratoga's "heterogeneous clientele" (*SJ* 99). These include the famous gangsters "Little Augie," "Charlie (Lucky) Luciano," and "Dutch Schultz," "some of Manhattan's georgetted and hennaed madams," gamblers, bookies, and "hopeless small-time owners . . . that together make up America's strangest season" (*SJ* 91). Significantly, in 1935 Agee observed the results of a law that had been repealed the previous year which prohibited the open soliciting of gambling at the racetrack.[12] As the narrator explains: "Bookies and betting managed to stay very much alive in the dark age between 1908 and 1934, when they were restored to semi-legality and the right to operate openly. But we take them up only with their definite public reappearance" (*SJ* 93). The 1935 season was indeed an animated one, which saw an increase in number of the bookies, gamblers, and prostitutes (Agee supplies names and exact occupations) on whom he focuses his exposé. Strikingly, though, the narrator never deploys a first-person pronoun but instead, in this first and only instance, relies on the plural "we" to invoke the immediacy of a narrator-reader alliance so as to create a shared (visible, palpable) experience. Through this introduction ("we take them up"), followed by his comprehensive chronicling of character, the narrator wishes to establish a direct reader-narrator confrontation with the lives of the "dark" figures, their excesses, wealth, and corruption. In contrast to the narrator's reverence and engagement in *Famous Men,* however, here his dispassion presents the events with a kind of colorless air of intellectual detachment.

Nevertheless, as in "The American Roadside" (*Fortune,* 1934) and "Cockfighting" (*Fortune,* 1934), "Saratoga" most often relies on *second*-person narration, paralleling Agee's concern with reader involvement in *Famous Men.* The narrated "you" is a central aspect in the sequences of scenes that he presents—from his witnessing the "thoroughbreds . . . coming serenely awake" ("as pure unadorned running as you'll ever see" [*SJ* 93]) and methods of betting to nightlife activities (*SJ* 99), participation in a horse market (*SJ* 100), and casino gambling (*SJ* 101). Contributing to this centrality of involving the "you" in much of what the narrator witnesses, the events and actions are usually specific as regards their setting and time. For example, the narrator comments on what normally happens after the races of the day: "What you do after your supper or hot dog depends partly on who, socially and occupationally, you are, and partly on your money and day's luck" (*SJ* 99). And he describes his experiences at the "smart clubs": "Almost any tout, by the by, is optimistic enough to bring a tux to town; and at those clubs you see some pleasantly inappropriate mugs looking over their whitewashed fences" (*SJ* 102). Agee's second-person literary journalism, however, can be "open," and even arbitrary, in reference to the relationship between narration and interior monologue: he can be seen, as in *Famous Men* (388–89), as addressing himself as well as the reader.

Class Divisions, Social Disunity

Crucially, however, most of Agee's descriptions of Saratoga lifestyles and routines, while calling for various kinds of reader involvement, reflect a dichotomy of social and class divisions. These divisions apply not only to lodgings—"Far as living is concerned, they shake into position as a furnace shakes down: the dust at the bottom and the clinkers on top" (*SJ* 92)—but to several other descriptive categories as well. For example, various kinds of entertainments are contrasted: "and by now those who can afford it are on their way to the fancy clubs out in the country" (*SJ* 99) is opposed to "the poorer end of the crowd," who once flocked to the dog racing at Ballston (*SJ* 100). In descriptions of "the routine dancing and drinking" (*SJ* 101), the narrator sets up another contrast between the "chronically rich" (*SJ* 101) who frequent the more exclusive clubs and the "least moneyed people" of "Saratoga's imported Harlem on Congress Street" (*SJ* 102). Simultaneously, he preserves his point of view while never relinquishing the "you": "the brain-blinding racket you need, at this ebb of your vitality, to keep you happy the rest of the night" (*SJ* 102). Agee's narration thereby retains a public character of interaction as it constantly pulls in the "you," preventing his story from dropping into monologue or falling into anonymity. Here "Saratoga" anticipates Agee's use of direct address in the "Preliminaries" of *Famous Men* (*FM* 23–34).

Taken as a whole, "Saratoga" emphasizes, like much of the writing of the 1930s, that culture is constitutive of relations of power which may become political, in the sense that they may become contested or opposed, or may be connected to the exercise of rule and authority. "Saratoga" illustrates, in Lawrence Hanley's words, the class inequities of 1930s America and the failure of this period "to contain and to manage agents of class difference who both provoke and, ultimately, subvert 'official' boundaries between inside and outside, self and other, and order and anarchy."[13] The races provide, however temporarily, a false sense of social unity (facilitated by the power of commodity, risk, and the act of consumption) around and through which "Saratoga" negotiates its representations of "popular and elite, dominant and oppositional cultures."¹⁴ It then suggests a version of (class and social) disunity and diffusion that characterizes "national life":

> For about three hours each day, then, Saratoga's whole heterogeneous clientele is coalesced and most intensely concentrated around one single point: the swiftness of the movement of horses. It is a concentration whose essential quality is best caught in the noise a few thousand people make when first they all become aware the horses are off. . . . And then at length the last horse in the race . . . brings the day's most beautiful and most serious business to a faintly ignominious close and, with the twilight and the evening and the depth of a night ahead, thirty thousand people, more or less, are disunified and scattered at large upon the resources of the town and of the surrounding countryside. (*SJ* 99)

After commenting on "our easy twentieth-century upper-middle-class promiscuity" and the profusion of prostitution during the racing season, the narrator takes himself (and the reader) far into the "one last night": "As the ultimate parties blare and fritter towards their red-eyed end, you hear throughout the streets of Saratoga the heavy and the deliberate steady rumble, as of an army in orderly retreat, of the departing lorries" (*SJ* 102). Agee's typical visionary hope (as in *A Death in the Family*) is abandoned. As the narrative ends, all forms of social satire recede, and descriptions of "lush elms" and "wild gables" give way to images of "the pitiable slums of this curious city," where "settles, delayed a little but by no means dispelled by Saratoga's other season, the season of water, the chill and the very temper and the cold of death" (*SJ* 103). "Saratoga," in its last lines, suddenly pulls toward the reverential, the narrator concluding on an image of social tragedy, stillness, and silence for the magnitude and mystery of being.

"Havana Cruise": Agee's Wound Culture

"Havana Cruise," published in *Fortune* in 1937, the year after Agee completed *Famous Men,* relates his experience of a six-day cruise from New York to Cuba on the steamship *Oriente.* Although it is much shorter in scope, Agee intended it as a kind of inverse *Famous Men.* As he suggested in his "Plans for Work: October 1937," "related to the Alabama technique, a technique was developed part way in *Havana Cruise,* mentioned among things I have had published. I should like to apply this to the behavior of a wealthier class" (*SJ* 161). Similar to "Saratoga," "Havana Cruise" offers a panorama of class positions inflected by the narrator's criticism of the commodity of leisure, but this time he focuses more on self-contented upper- and middle-class ideals, self-indulgence on a mass scale, and the selling of consumption. Though perhaps less obviously than in *Famous Men* and "Saratoga," the narrator *is* concerned with how his text intersects with and acts upon his readers.

Agee begins by plunging the reader into a soft portraiture of the guests aboard the *Oriente* and their "forces of habit" (*SJ* 127), which he traces throughout the narrative. In fast order he introduces us to "Mr. and Mrs. B.," "Mrs. C and her feeble sister," and another "Mr. B." and "his gentle, pretty wife" (*SJ* 127), and then slowly starts his satirical fire: "For this short leisure among new faces [Miss Cox] had invested heavily in costume, in fear, in hope, and like her colleagues she searched among the men as for steamer smoke from an uncharted atoll" (*SJ* 128). A kind of male equivalent, though apparently fearless, is then forwarded: "A blond young man who resembled an Airedale sufficiently intelligent to count to ten, dance fox trots, and graduate from a gentleman's university came briskly to the dining room" (*SJ* 128). In such a way, while taking us from one scene to another, the narrator's invective increases: "His snobbishness rather flattered a number of the passengers"; "the pretentious menu"; "the hard, glassy sort of blond who should even sleep in jodhpurs, tinkered at [her] fruit and exchanged monosyllables as if they were forced bargains" (*SJ* 128). After a brief mention of the "average happily married couple," "Mr. and Mrs. L," Agee suggests that finding an "attachment" or pursuing "for one degree or another . . . a hell of a good time" (*SJ* 129) includes, most often, a certain selfishness and cruelty: "The appraisal of clothes, of class, of race, of temperament, and of the opposed sexes met and crossed and flickered in a texture of glances as swift and keen as the leaping closures of electric arcs, and essentially as irrelevant to mercy" (*SJ* 128).

The rest of the piece is devoted, however, not to romantic or sexual encounters but largely to analyzing the "creatures of a different order," that is, "the representatives of the lower-middle to middle brackets of the American urban middle class" (*SJ* 128). Agee's means of representing this class functions in at least four ways: first, through a social satire based largely on the behavior, beliefs, and language of his subjects; second, through the use of multiple strategies of address and points of view; third, through a kind of running commentary on the "self-deceit" of his subjects; and fourth, through images that suggest there will be no change in what he has critiqued but rather an "eternal sameness."[15] As it illuminates, among other things, the range of possibilities in the period regarding the successful combination of fiction and objective journalism, "Havana Cruise" takes a devastating look at the mass-mediated American culture of the 1930s.

Satire, Document to Text

What is foundational to his satirical objectives, Agee tells individual stories that are mockeries of the notion of individuality itself. The passengers and crew members he describes are of all types: "families of Cuban bourgeois on their way north for the summer" (*SJ* 139); the headwaiter, "a prim Arthur Treacher type" (*SJ* 128); the cruise director, "a professionally cute character" (*SJ* 132); "the Airedale and a duplicate" (*SJ* 131); "a gay plump woman in white shied rubber rings" (*SJ* 131). But how they unconsciously conform to, exhibit, or promote class-based beliefs is their most important trait: "Leisure, being no part of their natural lives, was precious to them; and they were aboard this ship because they were convinced that this was going to be as pleasurable a way of spending that leisure as they could afford or imagine. What they made of it, of course, and what they failed to make, they made in a beautifully logical image of themselves: of their lifelong environment, of their social and economic class" (*SJ* 129). Just as the passengers are images of their leisure, so too are they analogues to their temporary ship environment: "The T.E.L. *Oriente* is fashioned in the image of her clientele: a sound, young, pleasant, and somehow invincibly comic vessel, the seafaring analogy to a second-string summer resort, a low-priced sedan, or the newest and best hotel in a provincial city" (*SJ* 129).

Some of Agee's most acerbic satire, however, is aimed at the language of his class subjects whom he (exceptionally) grants the opportunity to speak. Intermixed with his serious "facts" ("It wasn't a very expensive outing they were taking: most of them spent between $85 and $110 for the passage" [*SJ* 129]; "Of the passenger traffic of all flags sailing from U.S. ports in 1935 the cruising passengers accounted for 10 per cent" [*SJ* 130]), the narrator continuously records this kind of indicative banter: "Mr. B. was saying that he and his wife both loved to see new places and try out new drinks, not really getting drunk of course but just seeing what they tasted like. It certainly is a lot of fun. Having Wonderful Time was saying 'I don't mind my freckles anymore but I used to be terribly sentimental about them; used to cry all the time when people teased me'" (*SJ* 133). But as Agee presents such language as belonging to the urban middle class (and does so in the form of a pastiche of characterization, dialogue, and metaphorical description), the narrator sometimes adopts the point of view and idiom of his subjects: "Between tours the *Oriente* served a goose dinner for those who mistrusted the dirty foreign food" (*SJ* 138); or "The marble floors were absolutely beautiful. The trees were just exquisite. The music every bit as smooth as Wayne King and even the native Cubans that went there seemed an awfully nice, refined class of people" (*SJ* 139). He thereby smoothly blends reports on external features and quoted speech with his discourse about a character's actions. The desires of the passengers are usually related from a single character's perspective (e.g., "the ripe redhead" [*SJ* 140]) or from a group's viewpoint (e.g., "the Vanity Fair foursome" [*SJ* 141]).

By contrast, the narrator can shift from such limited omniscient perspectives to omniscient points of view. Existing primarily outside his story world, he freely informs the reader about the moods, worries, and disappointments of a host of characters: "On the shady side of the ship a torpid husband sat under five fathoms of the Sunday Times and stuffed in the state of the world without appetite" (*SJ* 132); or "The girls knew now that none of them was going to find a husband or even an excitement to speak of" (*SJ* 139). The narrator knows that the "Ship's Card, a roguish fellow of forty[,] . . . [is] under the protection of parody" (*SJ* 134), just as he knows that "the passengers were assembling themselves toward consciousness" (*SJ* 135). In a related vein, Agee comments on responses that he believes to be representative of his class subjects. When a male passenger exclaims, "Well, I'm telling you. When you see the Statue of Liberty you're going to say this is the country for me" (*SJ* 139), the narrator interjects: "The group nodded as one. Someone threw another Cuban penny in the sewage" (*SJ* 139). And yet most of his commentary springs from such direct and intense observation, accompanied by a profusion of evidence and detail, that his versions of facts seem perfectly valid, logical, even unquestionable. So when Agee claims (even under the guise of satire) that "the high point of gayety for the cruise was reached at the rough climax of the musical-chair game" (*SJ* 135), the reader is inclined to believe him.

Directly connected to the narrator's "omniscience" is his ability to know the most persistent problem facing the guests, "the strongest and most sorrowful trait[,] . . . their talent for self-deceit" (*SJ* 129). Indeed, the narrative provides a running commentary on various forms of (class-based) self-deceit. This is why time aboard the ship, for example, is lived as a succession of discrete instants lapsing into activities, encounters, and occasions that fail to fulfill any hoped-for possibility. Not incidentally, on the last evening of the cruise "the passengers were depressed beyond even appetite, and a majority of them stayed below" (*SJ* 140). Those who partake in, appropriately, "the last supper" (*SJ* 140) have nothing "to lose and perhaps something to gain" (*SJ* 140), but despite the "tassled menus," "signal flags," "noisemakers" (*SJ* 140), and general levity, individual happiness is short-lived or illusionary. The evening's futility is emblematized thus: "A wife and a husband sat in a dark corner talking intensely: two phrases kept re-emerging with almost liturgical monotony: keep your voice down, and god damn you. And god damn you too you god damned. Quite suddenly she struck her full glass of planter's punch into his lap and they left the table walking stiffly, their whole bodies fists" (*SJ* 141).

The self-deceit, traversing through, among much else, a forced merriment ("People who had thus far only nodded and smiled began to order each other drinks and to put hands on each other's shoulders" [*SJ* 140]), troubled or irreconcilable relationships (that of the embattled "wife and husband" [*SJ* 141]), or aborted encounters (those involving the "photographer" and several of the drunken young women [*SJ* 140]), culminates in a hopeless stasis:

> The bar shut down. It was one o'clock. Everyone was troubled and frozen in the sudden silence. Life had warmed up a good deal during the evening but not enough to get on under its own steam. Tentative pacts had been hinted at but not strongly enough. The bafflement sank into embarrassment, the embarrassment into straight tiredness, and very soon nearly everyone, muted and obscurely disappointed, drained off to bed. (*SJ* 142)

The last images of the piece reinforce an atmosphere of locked-in uncontrollability and the impossibility of change. As if "it were lifted on a dream," New York is "no foal of nature, nor intention of man, but one sublime organism, singular and uncreated" (*SJ* 142). The *Oriente* becomes a ship of "ghostly movement" (*SJ* 142), immune to all other forces, following its allotted journey. Adrift, fatigued, the middle-class voyagers cannot comprehend their own meanness and sterility; they cannot free themselves from the constraints of their own class identities but instead, roughly following the endings of "Saratoga" and *Famous Men,* revert to silence and sleep.

As Robert Fitzgerald has noted, by 1937 Agee "had become grimmer about American middle-class ways and destinies and would become grimmer still."[16] And indeed "Havana Cruise" presents a deadly portrait of such varied 1930s beliefs as mass exceptionality, the extolment of middle-class democratic virtues, and the need for moderate appetites.[17] At the same time, Agee harshly evaluates the expanding cruise ship industry, a more elite form of 1930s popular culture. But a 1937 letter from Agee to Father James Harold Flye reveals another intention: "I'm glad you liked the Cruise article for I feel sure you know its cruelty was used to inspire pity in readers who never feel it when it is asked in another's behalf."[18] Agee comes back to what exemplifies so much of his literary journalism—an awareness of involving readers in what counts in his constructions of history, identity, reality, and objectivity. Following *Fortune*'s "new approach" in the 1930s, Agee had a "progressive-era faith in presenting the facts" that, combined with his emotional dramatizations, "allow[ed] them to dictate the response[s]."[19] That he wished to inspire pity and compassion in his readers is an Agee hallmark. What is perhaps less obvious is that his narrative relies on the reader's capacity to produce a sense of class completeness and actuality out of a finite set of references and descriptions.[20]

Beginning with "The Scar" (*Exeter Monthly,* 1926), Agee's literary journalism, highlighted in such 1930s pieces as "Tennessee Valley Authority" (*Fortune,* 1933), "Roman Society" (*Fortune,* 1934), and "Smoke" (*Fortune,* 1937), was still going strong in the 1940s when he turned much of his attention to film criticism. Agee's (self-referencing) journalism in "Saratoga" and "Havana Cruise," however, was part of the 1930s stream that Michael Denning has referred to as the "crisis" in "realist narrative" to which the "documentary impulse was a particular modernist solution."[21] Like other 1930s writers who were also journalists (such as John Dos Passos, Tillie Olsen, John Steinbeck, and Agnes Smedley), Agee evoked the problems in capturing the "real," bringing American culture together in a comprehensible whole, and trying to make sense of this culture by telling stories about it. But as numerous critics contend, Agee must be set apart from most other journalists of the period. W. H. Auden's much-cited 1944 letter to the editors of *The Nation* claims that Agee's articles belong "in that very select class . . . of newspaper work which has permanent literary value."[22] Using "Havana Cruise" as one of his "literary journalism" examples, Thomas Connery suggests that Agee's article "inform[s] at a level common to fiction or poetry rather than journalism."[23] Indeed, "few modernist writers," Paul Ashdown adds, "have been as earnestly prophetic as James Agee in so many forms of writing"—prophetic qualities constituting what Ashdown calls Agee's "forthspeaking journalism."[24]

In my view, however, what distinguishes Agee from his literary journalist peers is his ability to think through the physical object world: his "attempt to see or to convey even some little thing as nearly as possible as that thing is" (*FM* 204). What further distinguishes him is how he reminds us that truth is not a stable attribute but an ongoing attribution; that it is not an inherent property but rather a dynamic process resulting from the collisions and combinations of cultural "truth-values" and fictional claims to truth. He is apart in the ways that his observations elide into a participation both engaged and "un-intimate" while, vis-à-vis his readers and subjects, wishing to keep transference and identification intact.

NOTES

An earlier version of this essay appeared in my book *Narrating Class in American Fiction* (New York: Palgrave Macmillan, 2009), 207–17.

1. James Agee and Walker Evans, *Let Us Now Praise Famous Men* (1941; New York: Library of America, 2005), 28. Subsequent references to this work appear parenthetically in the text, abbreviated *FM*.

2. James Lowe, *The Creative Process of James Agee* (Baton Rouge: Louisiana State University Press, 1994), 76.

3. Janet Galligani Casey, "Focus Left: Modernist Angst and the Proletarian Camera," in *Literary Modernism and Photography,* ed. Paul Hanson (Westport: Praeger, 2002), 42. On Agee's "modernism" in *Famous Men,* see Peter Coscove, "Snapshots of the Absolute Mediamachia in *Let Us Now Praise Famous Men,*" *American Literature* 67.2 (1995): 329–57.

4. Ella Zohar Ophir, "Romantic Reverence and Modernist Representation: Vision, Power, and the Shattered Form of *Let Us Now Praise Famous Men,*" *Twentieth Century Literature* 53.2 (Summer 2007): 125.

5. Robert Fitzgerald, "A Memoir," in *James Agee: The Collected Short Prose,* ed. Robert Fitzgerald (New York: Ballantine, 1970), 29.

6. Paul Ashdown, "Prophet from Highland Avenue: Agee's Visionary Journalism," in *James Agee: Reconsiderations,* ed. Michael A. Lofaro, Tennessee Studies in Literature 33 (Knoxville: University of Tennessee Press, 1992), 60.

7. Paul Ashdown, "James Agee," in *A Sourcebook of American Literary Journalism: Representative Writers in an Emerging Genre,* ed. Thomas B. Connery (New York: Greenwood, 1992), 197.

8. See James Agee, *James Agee: Selected Journalism,* ed. Paul Ashdown (Knoxville: University of Tennessee Press, 2005). Subsequent references to this work appear parenthetically in the text, abbreviated *SJ*.

9. Warren I. Susman, *Culture as History: The Transformation of American Society in the Twentieth Century* (Washington, D.C.: Smithsonian Institution Press, 2003), 158.

10. Robert Vanderlan, "'Telling the Truth in the Headquarters of Lying': Intellectuals Writing for *Fortune Magazine* in the 1930s," *Reconstruction* 8.1 (2008): 2.

11. Ibid., 4.

12. Ashdown, "Prophet from Highland Avenue," 69.

13. Lawrence F. Hanley, "Popular Culture and Crisis: King Kong Meets Edmund Wilson," in *Radical Revisions: Rereading 1930s Culture,* ed. Bill Mullen and Sherry Lee Linkon (Urbana: University of Illinois Press, 1996), 243.

14. Ibid., 244.

15. See Theodor W. Adorno, "The Position of the Narrator in the Contemporary Novel," in *Notes to Literature,* vol. 1, trans. Shierry Weber Nicholsen (New York: Columbia University Press, 1991), 30–36.

16. Fitzgerald, "A Memoir," 40.

17. See Jon-Christian Suggs, "*Marching! Marching!* and the Idea of the Proletarian Novel," in *The Novel and the American Left: Critical Essays on Depression-Era Fiction,* ed. Janet Galligani Casey (Iowa City: University of Iowa Press, 2004), 159–61.

18. James Agee, *Letters of James Agee to Father Flye* (New York: George Braziller, 1962), 97.

19. Vanderlan, "Telling the Truth in the Headquarters of Lying," 20.

20. "Havana Cruise" encourages us to study how class, as Sally Robinson has argued for

gender, might be "produced through narrative processes, not prior to them." See Sally Robinson, *Engendering the Subject: Gender and Self-Representation in Contemporary Women's Fiction* (New York: New York University Press, 1991), 343. For a feminist "focus on gender not as a predetermined condition of the production of texts, but as a textual effect," see Robyn Warhol, "Guilty Cravings: What Feminist Narratology Can Do for Cultural Studies," in *Narratologies: New Perspectives on Narrative Analysis,* ed. David Herman (Columbus: Ohio State University Press, 1999), 342–48.

21. Michael Denning, *The Cultural Front* (New York: Verso, 1998), 119.

22. Quoted in James Agee, *Film Writing and Selected Journalism* (New York: Library of America, 2005), 3.

23. Thomas B. Connery, "Discovering a Literary Form," in *A Sourcebook of Literary Journalism: Representative Writers in an Emerging Genre,* ed. Thomas B. Connery (New York: Greenwood, 1992), 6.

24. Ashdown, "James Agee," 59, 61.

Chapter 14

Željko Kozinc, the Subversive Reporter

Literary Journalism in Slovenia

Sonja Merljak Zdovc

A LITTLE BIT of heart and sincerity can't do any harm, or so thought a small group of reporters writing for the Slovene journal *Tovariš* (Comrade), a widely circulated illustrated magazine established in 1945 that thrived in the 1960s and early 1970s.[1] These fourteen journalists and two photographers, all of them without journalistic education or experience, wrote for *Tovariš* at a time when most journalists in Slovenia saw themselves as auxiliaries to contemporary politics. These journalists, famous for their stories on social issues, soon learned an important lesson: since analytical factographic reporting was not possible in their country, they had to adopt indirect ways of commenting on the current state of affairs, such as disguising their reportages as fiction. In the 1950s and early 1960s these Slovene journalists could have learned from examples of contemporary literary journalism in the West had any been translated, but they were not.[2] Thus those who wanted to use narrative techniques had to rely mainly on a Slovene tradition of social realist writing, a tradition that dates back to the 1920s and 1930s with writers such as Ciril Kosmač, Miško Kranjec, Ivan Potrč, and Prežihov Voranc.[3] Reporters thus borrowed these writers' techniques and applied them to their own work.

Interestingly enough, their American counterparts had done something similar. In the landmark anthology *The New Journalism,* Tom Wolfe writes that such techniques had empowered social realist writing in the United States: "It only remained to be seen if magazine writers could master the techniques, in nonfiction, that had given the novel of social realism such power. . . . For journalists to take Technique away from the novelists—somehow it reminded me of Edmund Wilson's old exhortation in the early 1930's: Let's take communism away from the Communists."[4] Despite the time lag between the 1930s and the 1960s, the link with Slovenia is relevant. The Slovene journalists of the 1960s and 1970s could not take communism away from the communists for obvious reasons: they were writing in an era when any direct attack on the communist system was punishable. But just as their American counterparts had borrowed heavily from social realist writers in the United States, Slovene journalists succeeded in "tak[ing] Technique away from the novelists" and, in so doing, avoided government censorship of news coverage. Like the American New Journalists, as described by Wolfe, these Slovene journalists wrote "by trial and error, by 'instinct' rather than theory," and began "to discover the devices that gave the realistic novel its unique power, variously known as its 'immediacy,' its 'concrete reality,' its 'emotional involvement,' its 'gripping' or 'absorbing' quality."[5]

Despite the popularity of these writers in the 1960s and 1970s, Slovene literary journalism remains largely unknown and unexamined in the scholarship, both at home and abroad. One reason for this is that a theory of journalistic forms in Slovenia is itself still in a pre-paradigmatic state. According to journalism scholar Manca Košir, there is even a lack of theory of journalistic communication in general in Slovenia: "Anything of the sort usually remains on a pragmatic level, without any pretence to theoretical reflection."[6] As there is so little scholarship on the principal forms of journalistic communication (i.e., genres), Košir's textbook *Nastavki za teorijo novinarskih vrst* (Extensions to the Theory of Journalistic Species, 1988)[7] remains the landmark work. More recently, Marko Milosavljević has studied different journalistic narratives, including New Journalism and literary journalism, in *Novinarska zgodba* (*Feature Story,* 2003). In it he introduces the term *novinarska zgodba,* which is his translation of the English term "feature."[8] When he writes about the *novinarska zgodba* genre,[9] he lists works of literary journalism as examples. He fails to notice, however, the significant distinction between feature stories and literary journalism, as described by different practitioners and scholars, among them Wolfe, Walt Harrington, John C. Hartsock, and Matthew Ricketson.[10]

These advances in Slovene scholarship notwithstanding, no study has explored until very recently the use of narrative techniques of realistic fiction for an aesthetic purpose in Slovene journalistic writing, nor has anyone suggested that Slovene journalists deliberately used these techniques to avoid state censorship. Analyzing articles in *Tovariš* to find possible connections between American New Journalism and Slovene literary journalism of the 1960s and 1970s, I have discovered that, although defined as "a kind of writing that is based on facts but reads like literature"—a definition of New Journalism—this Slovene literary journalism is not really related to American New Journalism at all.[11] It had developed not as an alternative to factual reporting but as a venue for political subversion. In addition, all of the articles examined save one did not even use the four narrative techniques common to the New Journalists.[12]

None of this, however, is meant to imply that Slovene literary journalism does not exist, or that it does not owe something to its American cousins. Although Slovene writers never reached the aesthetic dimensions of America's New Journalism, theirs was a kind of golden age of journalistic writing that included the narrative techniques of realistic fiction. Neither before nor since has there been so much literary journalism published in Slovenia, especially in publications with a circulation as large as that of *Tovariš*.[13] One of the main objectives of this essay, then, is to explore the nature of and the rationale behind Slovene literary journalism, and to determine to what extent literary journalistic traditions from abroad helped to establish literary journalism at home.

By reexamining texts by one of Slovenia's foremost journalists, Željko Kozinc, I try to determine whether or not his writing could be defined as literary journalism in the broader sense of the term. Toward this aim, I analyze Kozinc's writing in light of its literary journalistic characteristics as defined by more recent scholarship. There are two reasons for employing American definitions of New Journalism here, despite my earlier claim that they are essentially dissimilar. First, there is little European scholarship on such writing; and second, the Slovene strain of literary journalism is nonetheless linked to the American tradition, albeit indirectly, through the transnational influence of the Czech journalist Egon Erwin Kisch.[14]

Fresh Winds from the East: The Influence of Egon Erwin Kisch

From the end of World War II, when Slovenia became one of the socialist republics of Yugoslavia, until its independence in 1991, the media in Slovenia served as a buttress for the socialist authorities. Journalists taught, informed, and explained events in political terms, educating readers, listeners, and viewers in the spirit of socialist self-management. They were sociopolitical workers, consciously dedicated to Marxist–Leninist ideas. The rulebooks and professional journals that provided journalists with guidelines and instructions on reporting—for example, in *Novinar* (1951, 1955, and 1958)—emphasized their role as sociopolitical workers, auxiliaries, as I noted earlier, to the politics of the day. The authorities, more specifically the Zveza komunistov (League of Communists), appointed all of the managing editors of the so-called quality newspapers, television, and radio.[15] The primary function of the communist media was propaganda and active support of the regime. Nevertheless, the media in Yugoslavia, including Slovenia, were among the freer ones in the communist bloc.[16]

The role of the Slovene media under communist rule varied according to the style and politics of the party leadership. Until the late 1940s, the political system in Slovenia was modeled on that of the Soviet Union.[17] After 1948, however, Yugoslavia introduced its own version of socialism, and this fact was also reflected in the media in Slovenia. In the 1950s, the content of the media was overtly political (that is, communist). That began to change in the 1960s, when the communist grip on the media began to loosen, and journalism started to become more democratic.

At the time, among the intellectual elite there was still a general conviction that opportunities for democratization and modernization of Slovene society should be sought within the Yugoslav socialist system, because it was a fairer society, socially speaking, than that offered by Western capitalism or Eastern socialism.[18] This view of the way news was to be reported was shared by some journalists too. In the 1960s a group of journalists, among them those writing for *Mladina* (Youth),[19] *Tedenska tribuna* (Weekly Tribune), and in particular *Tovariš,* turned away from the state's previous one-dimensional definition of journalism. At *Tovariš*—for different reasons, such as youth, bohemianism, and a wish to investigate society—narrative forms of expression were cultivated, among them feature stories and feature interviews.[20] These were the kinds of writing that were based on fact and in certain ways read like fiction but differed considerably from the conventional models of journalism, especially the hard news story. Since it was not involved in daily political events, magazine journalism was more "free" to experiment with journalistic forms. Magazine journalism began to differ from newspaper journalism, such as that of the national daily newspaper *Delo. Tovariš* did not report the news; it told stories instead.

Alenka Bibič, for example, began her article on the building of a new dam on the Drava River with a description of a scene. The scene functions, however, only as an eye-catching lead. The information it conveys is not related to the main topic of the story; it does not reveal the emotions of a character, nor does it evoke the story's universal theme.[21] Bibič writes:

> It was a nice sunny summer day. A grandpa was pushing a pram and looking for some shade for him and his grandson at Tri Ribniki. Gosposka Street was full of young people, who thought they would miss much if they did not go for a walk there every day. At Ezlek a young boy in narrow jeans was nervously looking at his watch until a young blond girl came by in her tight short skirt. From the main bridge the tourists were enthusiastically capturing the romantic scenery of Lent with their cameras.[22]

This model of traditional storytelling was thus the primary genre of the magazine *Tovariš*. But was it literary journalism?

In 1973 Wolfe defined New Journalism as a type of writing that combines the information-gathering methods of journalistic reporting with the narrative techniques of realistic fiction by means of a process he called saturation reporting.[23] The four narrative techniques common to the New Journalists are scene-by-scene construction, dialogue in full, third-person point of view, and status details.[24] American scholars would later revise this definition. Norman Sims, for instance, adds several characteristics of literary journalism to Wolfe's list: immersion reporting (an update of Wolfe's saturation reporting), accuracy, voice, structure, responsibility, and symbolic representation.[25] In *Intimate Journalism*, Walt Harrington claims that literary journalism should rise and fall on narrative structure and report physical detail, human emotion, and all that is ordinary and extraordinary in our lives.[26] Barbara Lounsberry similarly identifies four characteristics of literary nonfiction: documentable subject matter, exhaustive research (immersion, saturation), depicted scenes, and fine writing.[27] In the book *Writing Creative Nonfiction: Literature of Reality*, which she co-edited with Gay Talese, Lounsberry adds to these criteria simultaneous, sequential, and substitutionary narration; interior monologue; and the artful use of imagery, allusion, humor, and even the pyrotechnics of print itself. The nonfiction writer's goal is to enlarge our understanding of the world.[28] Their revisions expanded the definition of literary journalism, and the anthologies that followed Wolfe's *New Journalism* (for instance, Thomas B. Connery's *Sourcebook of American Literary Journalism* or Kevin Kerrane and Ben Yagoda's *Art of Fact*) included writers who were first seen by Wolfe as being "not half-bad candidates" (Stephen Crane, John Reed, George Orwell, and John Hersey).[29]

In the Slovene press, the appearance of journalistic writing that includes narrative techniques is traditionally left to the personal interests of individual journalists and editors.[30] One of these is Željko Kozinc, a key *Tovariš* reporter.[31] Kozinc, along with other journalists at *Tovariš*, lacked any formal education in journalism and didn't have much journalistic experience when he began reporting for the magazine *Mladina* in the early 1960s. Being a born writer, however, he instinctively knew that important themes had to be written about in an interesting and readable way if they were to attract readers. He felt that his articles would be more persuasive if the readers could identify with the story, and one way of achieving that goal was through the use of narrative techniques. Having no mentors at the beginning, strictly speaking, he first relied primarily on his own literary instincts and on the Slovene literary tradition, in particular the writings of the social realists Anton Ingolič, Miško

Kranjec, and Prežihov Voranc. He also absorbed influences from abroad when he tried to learn his craft by studying Serbian and Russian feature stories. His role model, however, eventually became the Prague-born journalist Egon Erwin Kisch.[32]

Kisch was the author of many stories that were "example[s] of brilliant realistic prose."[33] Yet Kisch endeavored to perfect the form of his writing. Despite writing for a newspaper, he increasingly incorporated literary elements into his pieces. His reporting technique included collecting many seemingly irrelevant details, which he would later weave into a powerful story. From his stories, for example, readers learn about the world of his time and its main concerns. They learn how people dealt with these concerns, what they were fighting for, and what caused them the most suffering. Kisch tried to find the right form for every topic, always to be innovative, and to articulate in an interesting manner what he wanted his readers to know.[34]

Željko Kozinc first encountered Kisch's writing in 1962. Browsing through the stacks of a secondhand bookstore, Kozinc came across an anthology of writings titled *Svet humorja in satire* (On Humor and Satire, 1951), which contained a piece by Kisch. The story, originally published in his autobiography *Marktplatz der Sensationen* (The Sensation Fair, 1942), was about young women who had fallen into prostitution. Kozinc particularly liked a passage in which Kisch described the dismay of his hosts upon discovering the informal form of address Kisch and the prostitutes used with each other: "He was taken around the home for fallen girls by some clergymen, who were bragging to him about their virtues, when one of the girls called out: 'Egon, do you have a smoke? They don't give them to us here.' At that moment, he lost any credibility he might have had in the eyes of those clergymen. The story he eventually wrote was thus not what was expected. However, it was better, Kischean."[35] After reading the story of the prostitutes in Prague, Kozinc decided to try his hand at Kischean writing. He liked Kisch's idea of a reporter becoming a character in his stories and assuming different roles. Thus, he too set out to write about his experiences, such as his adventures with prostitutes, cleaning shoes on the street, being an extra on a film set, selling records in a music store, and joining a work brigade. His most important story of that period, though, and one most directly influenced by Kisch, was "Dvojni obraz strašnega Pjera" (The Two Faces of Fearsome Pierre), which he published in the magazine *Mladina* in 1962.[36]

The story is about his being admitted into a reformatory in Radeče as a juvenile delinquent in order to investigate the living conditions there.[37] It opens with an image of the journalist being hit by one of the inmates:

The first evening, three youngsters sneaked into the reception room where I had been put immediately after my arrival. The smallest quite soon hit me in the face. Although I could have easily been done with him, I decided to withdraw to the corner out of concern that the bigger two would have found an excuse to beat me up. I was told to do so by another greenhorn, a young boy from the Dolenjska region, who was not careful enough and had been thoroughly beaten up before I arrived.[38]

"Dvojni obraz strašnega Pjera" resembles Kisch's story on prostitutes, "Magdalenin dom" ("The Home of the Magdalene"),[39] where there is also "a complication in which the reader will seek for a resolution."[40] Why is the journalist being hit? Where is he? What is going on? The reporter does not provide an answer immediately. Instead, the introductory scene is followed by a paragraph in which the reporter writes about how that evening all the boys in Radeče knew that he was a crybaby and not much of a fighter. Only then does he reveal the reasons for his being in Radeče.

Other narrative literary journalistic techniques are also present in the story. We find descriptive scenes (for instance, when he tells how his fellow inmates surrounded him after his conversation with the head of the correction facility, and how they all left the building and went to the banks of the Sava River, where he was questioned about his visit); immersion reporting (spending a week on a single assignment was rare then, and it is even more so now in Slovene journalism; besides, no one before or after Kozinc had had himself imprisoned for the purpose of writing a story); and voice (the first-person narrative and his trademark style of writing and structure). Although Kozinc uses narrative techniques such as these, the story is mainly expository, and thus it cannot be called literary journalism per se but is rather a conventional feature. In an article on literary journalism in which he examines the relationship between newspaper narrative and conventional feature writing, Hartsock notes that conventional style, through "descriptive scene construction[,] illustrates a discursive or expository—and thus abstract—point."[41]

In addition to being discursive, Kozinc's story is also overly sentimental and even moralistic to an extent. The reason for such a style of writing lay in the tradition of Slovene literature at the time. Social realism had a younger generation of literary adherents in the early 1950s. Peter Vodopivec writes that counter to the prevailing political optimism, its representatives portrayed the human condition more psychologically, envisaging individuals with a unique, generally tragic fate, while rejecting the public perspective and focusing on more intimate, even existentially influenced themes. This, the largest postwar literary generation, was to have a major impact on Slovene literature in the coming decades.[42] As Kozinc explains:

In the 1960s and 1970s there was already a tradition of sentimental humanism in Slovene literature. The most important subjects of my stories were the regular people who were being exploited by the system. Additionally, my colleagues and I all stemmed from the working class; we still believed in communism. Our communist upbringing imprinted in us a sense of social justice, which required a moral stance. This stance was expressed through our stories, perhaps in an oversimplistic way.[43]

In the late 1960s Kozinc finally obtained a copy of Kisch's autobiography, *Sajam senzacija* (The Sensation Fair), which had been translated into Serbo-Croatian in 1956. At the time, it was almost impossible to get Kisch's writing in Ljubljana, and Kozinc found his book by chance during one of his trips to Zagreb, Croatia. Kisch soon became his idol: "From a time which I was not familiar with, from a time when journalism was freer, Kisch whispered to me that a journalist should not restrain his heart and his sincerity."[44] He particularly revered Kisch's books *Schreib das auf, Kisch!* (*Write On, Kisch!*, 1929), *Entdeckungen in Mexiko* (*Discoveries in Mexico*, 1945), and *Abenteuer in fünf Kontinenten* (*Adventure in Five Continents*, 1948), which were all eventually translated into Serbo-Croatian or Slovene.

Kozinc began to analyze and imitate Kisch's reporting methods (what Sims would later called immersion) and his writing style, in particular Kisch's sense of accuracy, voice, structure, artful use of imagery, and humor. Kozinc especially liked the way Kisch structured his texts, and he too began introducing complex narrative techniques into his own stories. Kozinc even called himself a literary journalist. He was nevertheless not aware of literary journalism as it existed in the United States at the time because Slovene reporters had almost no access to the foreign press or Western literature.[45]

Following Kisch's lead in the selection of topics, immersion reporting, and the use of first-person narrative, Kozinc began writing stories like "Prijazna smrt predolgo se ne mudi" (Dear Death, Do Not Delay in Breaking the Spell!).[46] Here he portrayed the poverty of the region of Kozjansko, and as a result of this text an extensive humanitarian action was later launched:

> Ours was a fight for social justice. We believed that in socialism the ruling elite should not have special privileges. For us, one of the biggest sins was the devastation of the rural countryside, which was a result of urbanization. Through urbanization, the working class, which was leading the economic and social development of the time, would become more powerful. This resulted, however, in the emptying of the countryside, the consequent aging of the population in rural areas, and the changes in social strata.[47]

"Prijazna smrt predolgo, se ne mudi," which was published in *Tovariš* in 1970, was a story about elderly people dying in poverty in the depopulated region of

Kozjansko. Kozinc and the photojournalist Joco Žnidaršič embarked on the story after reading an item published in the newspaper *Delo* about a married couple found dead in Kozjansko. It turned out that the husband had died first, and the wife simply lay down beside him to await her own death. Kozinc was intrigued by the destiny of this couple and decided to investigate the situation in that region.

The story begins with Kozinc's monologue:

> Where might we find Julijana Plavčak? Perhaps at Končan's house? It is a long way to the village of Žahenberc, and who knows in which house she is warming her poor soul. It seems as if the people of Žahenberc haven't been as intrigued for many years about anything as they were by the fact that two gentlemen came looking for Julijana Plavčak. Perhaps she inherited something? No? Of course not, what could a poor soul such as her inherit?
>
> We tracked down Julijana in the end. The poor woman got so scared that she ran screaming to the attic to hide. In the cottage in which she has been a guest for the last fourteen days, she swiftly climbed up the ladder and hid among the hams which were drying there; the landlord's jaw dropped ("look at this old woman, she is not that old and useless after all"). (PS 15)

As James Agee and Walker Evans had done in the American South during the Great Depression, Kozinc and Žnidaršič spent a week among the people of the Kozjansko region, thus immersing themselves as much as was possible at that time in the lives of the local people. Kozinc then wrote the story in a narrative mode, employing scene descriptions like the following: "There it was, a cart track, wide enough for a pair of oxen to pass. In one place, ten meters long, the road was missing. A landslide had taken it away, three, four meters into the deep. 'The road has been washed away,' the farmer told us as we stood silent. 'I can see. Now what?' 'It was taken away last spring. And the community still hasn't repaired it. We need to carry everything on our backs'" (PS 17). The story also includes dialogue, such as in the following exchange:

> "Mother, what are you afraid of? Nobody wants to hurt you. They will just put your name in the paper."
>
> "They should put me in the grave, not in the paper," we heard a voice from above. (PS 15)

Finally, Kozinc tells the story in his own voice. The text even has, as Hartsock writes about similar stories, a "beginning [that] arouses expectations for the middle and end."[48] The story is accurate and told responsibly. It is also a symbolic representation of the problems facing a socialist system that did not provide adequate care for the elderly in remote areas. Presenting physical details (feverish eyes, swollen eyelids), and capturing human suffering ("Please, good man, bring me some poison. Put it in my food without me knowing. Oh, God, please forgive me this sin" [PS 17]), it is finely written and achieves the nonfiction writer's goal of enlarging our understanding of the world. All in all, the story meets several of the criteria identified by Sims, Harrington, and Lounsberry and could thus be categorized as literary journalism.

Images of Injustice: Narrative as a Vehicle for Criticism

The second and third stories from Kozinc's series on the aftermath of the socialist transformation of a formerly rural society into an urban one are the texts "Pravica vasi Rudno" (The Village of Rudno's Right) and "Topli kruh dela" ("The Warm Bread of Labor"). "Pravica vasi Rudno" was published in *Tovariš* in 1973 and "Topli kruh dela" in *Delo* the same year.[49] In mid-1973 the editor of *Tovariš*, Miro Poč, was replaced by Vilko Novak, and many reporters left the magazine, including Kozinc, who went to work for the newspaper *Delo*. There he continued publishing journalistic texts using narrative techniques. For this kind of writing he twice received a special award that was established by Mitja Gorjup, who was editor in chief at the time, in the service of promoting quality feature stories in the newspaper.

According to Ben Yagoda, narrative literary journalism can be modeled either on a novel, a movie, or a play. "Pravica vasi Rudno" follows this third strain of literary journalism, in which the reporter is on the scene and "more or less matter-of-factly relates what happens."[50] What makes it literary journalism, though, is that Kozinc structures his article in the form of a play, complete with a dramatic exposition, a climax, and an attempt at a denouement.

The story opens with a paragraph describing how the farmer Valentin Fajfar was thunderstruck to learn in a newsletter for the Alples factory in Železniki that the township of Škofja Loka had decided to build a block of houses on the farmland from which he had just collected his harvest. The second paragraph reveals that the villagers worried for a long time about what would happen to their farmland, as the news item had alarmed the whole village of Rudno. To protect their land, they pay visits to the mayor and to the managers of local factories, albeit without any positive results. Eventually they realize that they will have to fight for their farmland on their own. In the third paragraph, Kozinc writes about how they decide that their voice must be heard, and they call a town meeting in the local community.

Kozinc uses the first three paragraphs of the article as dramatic exposition, in which the protagonist, the antagonist, the basic conflict, and the setting are all presented. Again, the story begins with "a complication in which the reader will seek for a resolution."[51] What will happen to the land? Who has the right to it? Instead of being narrative-descriptive, however, the text turns dialogic, centering on one main event: a meeting between the villagers and the representatives of the factory workers. Kozinc includes descriptive scenes and dialogue in his text in order to illustrate the clash between the farmers protecting the right to hold on to their farmland and the workers fighting for a decent place to work and live.

Both sides are in the right, and Kozinc is there to witness their clash. The whole text is a detailed description of the dialogue exchanged between the two parties. The exposition is implied through this dialogue, as is the dramatic structure of the article's beginning and middle, but no conciliatory ending or resolution is offered; Kozinc could not do so, since at the time of its writing there was none. The journalist instead concludes his text with a paragraph in which he writes: "Nastran [one of the farmers] walked into the middle of the big room. He looked around and quietly asked the question that had been bothering him the whole evening: "Who can guarantee that this is my land, that nobody can chase me away?" Nobody answered his question, as the meeting had ended and with that the first act of the drama of Rudensko polje."[52]

To a certain extent this article resembles conventional journalism because its reporter covers a single event that he has witnessed, just as conventional journalists do when they report from various press conferences of a similar combative political nature. Nevertheless, Kozinc manages to transform his report from the minutes of a rather uninteresting meeting into a drama of human courage and resolve. The stage is set, the characters appear, and the conflict is presented through the extended play-like dialogue. Because of its dramatic elements and the journalist's aim of enlarging his readers' understanding of the world, the text is nevertheless closer to literary journalism than it is to conventional journalism.

By contrast, Kozinc returned to the Kischean model of a reporter in "Topli kruh dela," narrating the everyday hardships of underpaid women who work in Iskra, another factory in Železniki. The story begins by describing a conveyor belt as a "millipede." In the very lead, the reporter enters the story and addresses the reader directly. He explains how he has often met women like these from Iskra, and how they all have the same story to tell. Then he moves on to tell the story of one of these women in particular, Mara Gaser:

> As if she would like to run away, she keeps looking at the pneumatic compressors, arranged in a snail shape. There stand her co-workers with bent backs while the fat rubber of the conveyor belt silently moves near them. On the top of the belt, like scattered heaps, lie the electro-motors. A few

hand movements, the same movements performed for the last twenty years, and the heap slides away. Improved technology in the form of a pneumatic screwdriver makes her work more and because of this the millipede twinkles even faster. (T 29)

The journalist's use of metaphors ("and you do not know who drives whom—the worker the millipede or the millipede the worker") and similes ("her hands were hard as the sole of a foot" [T 29]), like his attention to detail in the scene's construction, clearly announce the article's literary aspirations.

Moreover, the journalist's reporting is accurate, with no details fabricated, and he again employs his own narrative voice. Kozinc, however, did not immerse himself in the story. (He did not spend a few days with the factory workers, for example.) Can this story be considered literary journalism, then? In the strict Wolfean sense of the term, probably not, for it lacks the aesthetic dimension of the New Journalism that Wolfe and others have privileged in the genre. Yet in comparison to literary journalism in other anthologies, such as *The Art of Fact* (1997), it might be.

In his essay "Making Facts Dance," for example, Kevin Kerrane writes that the literary touches of Victorian social reporters whose works are included in the anthology came less from artistic design than from the writers' sense of moral or political urgency, a determination to dramatize the reality of poverty, prostitution, and prejudice.[53] Kozinc is certainly determined to dramatize the reality of the factory workers' hardship—their struggle to hang on to underpaid jobs that barely allowed them to make a living, not to mention the difficulties presented by a new technology bent on increasing their work productivity—which drives this article's moral message. Their productivity will be measured according to the standards of the newly installed capitalist innovation of the "work factor system," which will render the socialist factory more competitive in the global capitalist market. The "work factor system" is not good news for the workers, however: "Before, I had to finish 790 pieces in one day, now I have to finish 1,100 per day," says Rozalka Primožič (T 29).

Despite the article's political thrust, often editorialized in its imagery, Kozinc was not allowed to criticize the general politics of the Slovene Communist Party toward, for instance, working conditions, although it was the communists who had the villages emptied and the people forced into the cities to create a more powerful working class. Such a working class would help the Zveza komunistov increase its power in Slovenia. Additionally, he could not publish data about poverty, as officially it did not exist. Such facts could be told only through metaphors, through personal stories—in short, through literary aesthetics. With his story "Topli kruh dela," he was able to introduce social and political criticisms of the socialist system in which people struggled for survival despite the state's claims of social equality. He could create an image that spoke indirectly about poverty, and this proved effective in influencing his readers' emotions.

Different Perspectives: From Anonymous Others to People We Care About

Tom Wolfe would probably categorize Željko Kozinc as a "not half-bad" candidate for the title of New Journalist.[54] Nevertheless, the reexamination of his work from the 1960s and 1970s suggests that he could in fact be called a literary journalist. Kozinc would continue to develop this style of writing throughout the 1980s and 1990s and, through his gift for reportage, is nowadays considered one of the finest Slovene reporters. In this later period, however, his career met with disruption. In 1976 Kozinc quit journalism for a decade, having been forced to resign because the border police found in the trunk of his car some illegal literature published abroad by opponents of the regime.[55] This was a time of ideological and social struggle in Slovenia. Kozinc was not a dissident, however; he was concerned with the injustice suffered by people—including the families of those people who had been on the wrong side in World War II.[56]

In 1986 he returned to work for the newspaper *Delo.* Until his retirement in 1997, he was editor of various sections of the newspaper; for the longest period he edited the "Reportaže" page, which carried predominantly feature stories. During that time he actively promoted the writing of feature stories and even started to cultivate a new generation of feature writers (for example, Mimi Podkrižnik and myself). Bored with being a pensioner, he decided to start reporting again. He published two stories that were similar in topic and in style to those he had written in the 1960s and 1970s. In these pieces he returned to a Kischean model of reporting with respect to his use of voice and imagery, his attention to structure, and his presence in the story as a character.

The first of these stories, "Obrni, kakor hočeš: tabor leti v nebo" (Turn It as You Like: The Camp Is Flying to the Sky),[57] published in *Delo,* was one of the earliest texts to point out the smoldering conflict between the Roma and local populations of the Dolenjska region. With it Kozinc tried to cast light on an otherwise ignored local problem, which—as it later turned out—would become a national problem too.

To help situate his readers within the racial conflict, Kozinc uses many different criteria of fiction writing, beginning with an extended simile that opens the text:

The Roma affair in Grosuplje is a little like boxing. The tired fighters are holding each other in a clinch to take a break from the violence, intrigues, imputation, and lies. It seems that the end of the match, which is not entirely equal, is far away: on one side is the heavyweight champion, on the other the paperweight. The first one has all the supporters on his side, the second has something that should carry a lot of weight. But it is only a piece of paper: the constitution. (O 35)

In the second paragraph Kozinc moves toward a description of the scene: "It is clearing up in the Oasis [a Roma settlement]. When I drive in, a pretty young woman runs toward me and tells me very politely that there is nobody there. Everybody is in the woods looking for mushrooms. They will be back in the evening. Can I talk to you then? *No, I am only visiting. I don't know anything; I don't care about this thing*" (O 35). Then he uses imagery and scene description to paint a picture of life in the Roma settlement that not many readers are aware of:

The walls of the Oasis are plastered so that there is no mud, the chrysanthemums are hoed, the yards swept clean, the fire logs neatly arranged; [o]n the floor there lies a ten-year-old dinar bill and many other things, collected from a scrap heap. The children play with this rubbish. Their hands are covered with the crust of snotty dirt; their faces are disheveled, scabbed and bruised. Only their eyes are clean and bright. (O 35)

In contrast to the commonly perceived notion that the local Roma are dirty, uneducated, unemployed, and a burden to the community, Kozinc portrays the settlement as self-supporting. Their habits may differ from those of the local people (for instance, they earn money by picking and selling mushrooms, and though their disheveled children may play with rubbish, the settlement is otherwise kept tidy). But these habits should in no way be used to justify the locals' resistance to the Roma settlement or, even less, their discrimination against it and its people.

The Kischean paradigm is palpable from the start here, and the reported material shows how Kozinc considered his story at once journalistic and literary. First, he demarcates the story's beginning (the conflict between the Roma people and the local community); its middle (everyday life in the Roma settlement, which enables the reader to immerse himself or herself in the Roma way of life and grasp the many related issues, such as the lack of job opportunities or the traditional racism of the local people); and its end (the failure to secure running water and electricity in the settlement, and thus an improved lifestyle). Interestingly enough, there is again no resolution.

Second, in one of his most noticeable nods to Kisch, Kozinc avoids reporting objectively. The notion that traditional "objective" journalism widens the distance between the subject of a story and its readers had been around since the late nineteenth century. According to Lincoln Steffens, the true ideal for a literary journalist is "to get the news so completely and to report it so humanly that the reader will see himself in the other fellow's place."[58] In doing so, Kozinc becomes actively involved in the story, and the dialogue between him as journalist and the characters in his story reveals this subjectivity to the reader. Indeed his narrative voice and immersion reporting, in addition to the fact that he was able to overcome what Hartsock calls an "epistemological gulf"[59] in this exchange with the Roma, are what most distinguish this piece as literary journalism in the Kischean vein.

Literary journalists are aware of the need to understand and not to judge, hoping their articles will resonate with readers because of this. Kozinc knew he had to offer his readers enough information to allow for an understanding of an act. His is one of the few stories on the topic in Slovene journalism that presented the perspectives of everybody involved. In this way, Kozinc enhanced the reader's understanding of the problem as well as his or her compassion. In this sense it is probably the best example of the potential of literary journalism in contemporary Slovene journalism.

In the second piece, "Koliko srca je v pol tolarja?" (How Much Heart Is in Half of a Tolar?),[60] Kozinc returned to the topic of underpaid factory workers, this time women at TIO, a factory that produces one of the most desirable and sexiest of objects—ladies' stockings. By beginning again with a simile, Kozinc both makes an unfamiliar and complex situation more understandable to the reader and once more shows that he considers his stories to be literary as well as journalistic in nature:

> The machine is like a spider. It twitches its extremities, it rattles and rumbles its levers and wheels, and it turns its spindle and tries to knit a web around the human. Tries to bite him. This simile is not the best one because the spider is a living being and eventually it runs out of energy; the machine, on the other hand, is always rested and always wound up. And always wound up is what a human being must also be. Only this is not possible. "I feel like I am fifty years old," said Irena Gruber, who is thirty. "On Saturdays and Sundays I can barely move."[61]

The narrative techniques in this story are even more sophisticated than in "Obrni, kakor hočeš: tabor leti v nebo." Whether posing rhetorical questions in an acerbic tone ("Sarah Lee, Are You Human?") or situating himself as a character alongside the others, Kozinc once again pays homage to Kisch's literary reportage. In addition to the scene description ("the tall columns of smoke shone in the sunlight"), the dialogue (between him as a journalist and the characters in his story), and the abundant use of metaphors (spiders for the factory machine, frogs for the stockings, and ants for the workers), there is also character development. By introducing Irena Gruber in the lead, Kozinc immediately humanizes the factory workers. A hardworking woman who fears the loss of her job, Grubar becomes for Kozinc what American soldiers killed during the Spanish-American War were to the press in the words of Stephen Crane: "a unit in the interesting sum of men slain."[62] The journalist often returns to the stories of women he mentions at the beginning. Later, for instance, he describes Irena Gruber's situation in more detail; the reader is thus able to grasp the impact of her difficult yet underpaid job on her private life. Character development of this sort is even more salient with Meta Lorenci, the head of the union, who is depicted in different, often challenging situations. Kozinc portrays her through her actions and reactions to these circumstances, and shows how she is trying to maintain her integrity in difficult situations (for instance, she has been criticized by her co-workers for her softness toward the owners of the company), as well as help her co-workers.

Again, in this story Kozinc manages to lift the shroud from a subject widely present in the press, though often reported in a dry, objectified manner. Whereas, as Hartsock notes, those stories create a distance between subject and object which necessarily alienates the reader,[63] Kozinc overcomes the "epistemological gulf" by transforming the women in this textile industry, which is rapidly heading toward being completely dismantled, from anonymous workers losing their jobs into persons with whom the reader can relate.

In the late 1990s, when both stories first appeared, Slovenia was already a democratic state in transition, well on its way to establishing the capitalist-based economy it practices today. Although the state at the time no longer censored news coverage, and journalists were free to report on any topic of their choosing, Kozinc continued to use narrative techniques in his writing. Back then, he had learned to love the genre; but by now he understood the need for it in narrowing the gap between the subject of news reporting and its object. In direct opposition to the days of socialism, when everybody was (supposedly) taken care of (for instance, everybody was entitled to housing, schooling, and employment) and at least professedly considered equal, the 1990s introduced an era of individualism. When it seemed to Kozinc that many people stopped caring about others, especially those in need, his writing maintained some of his previous subversiveness. At the end of his journalistic career, Kozinc no longer rebelled against the repressive socialist system; he now rebelled against the lack of sensitivity and moral conscience of capitalism's everyman and everywoman.

Literary Journalism's European Tradition:
Fine Writing, Socially Engaged

Literary journalism is broadly defined as journalism based on factual reporting and written with the aid of narrative techniques. The same definition could apply to nearly any feature story found in the Slovene press today. Yet in order to be defined as literary journalism, that story needs something more: a social contract of sorts between the writer and the reader. To be sure, there are similarities and differences between American and European literary journalism, especially with regard to the methods of writing. Slovene literary journalism, however, contributes another element to this definition: literary journalism as political subversion.

Željko Kozinc began using narrative techniques early in his career because he soon realized that such writing was both more attractive *and* potentially subversive. Through the wry use of elaborate metaphors, cryptic allusions, and personal stories, he was able to avoid state censorship and still deliver harsh criticisms of Slovenia's mismanaged political and social systems. Additionally, he realized that with the use of narrative techniques, he was able to "report more meaningfully."[64] In other words, his reportages could work to correct the nation's ills or help heal its gaping wounds. As discussed, Egon Erwin Kisch became his main role model in his quest for meaningful literary reportage. Inspired by Kisch's boldness in the selection of topics, his manner of reporting, and his style of writing, particularly his use of first-person narrative and textual structure, Kozinc set out to experiment with different narrative techniques in his journalistic pieces. He perhaps did not display all of the characteristics of literary journalism as later defined by American scholars, but his fine writing and his stated goal of increasing his readers' understanding of the world around them make him a literary journalist in the strict European tradition, where sociopolitical commitments are perhaps aligned more fluidly with personal ones than in the work of his American cousins.

Unfortunately, despite Kozinc's continuous efforts, literary journalism has yet to be fully recognized on Slovenia's journalistic map. Although studies from both the United States and Slovenia demonstrate how readers are demanding more well-written and sophisticated feature stories and even literary journalism,[65] few studies today reveal their presence in Slovene journalism. In other words, Kozinc remains one of the few literary journalists in Slovenia, as only a small number of Slovene journalists today are deliberately using narrative techniques in their writing, the most famous being Ervin Hladnik Milharčič.

Contemporary Slovene journalists are aware that their stories will receive more attention if they use narrative techniques in their writing, that their writing is more vivid and picturesque because of these techniques, and that elements of narrative add authenticity to their writing. They even see an added value in narratives and find them to be a more natural way of writing than the inverted pyramid of hard news stories. Nevertheless, many of these journalists also view such writing as unorthodox and thus suitable only for extraordinary events.[66]

This represents a contrast to the situation in the United States. Whereas more and more American newspaper journalists are engaging in the practice of narrative literary journalism in the pages of the dailies (not least because they and their editors sense the limitations implicit in the objectivist paradigm),[67] this trend has not yet reached Slovenia. Regardless, one thing is certain: Željko Kozinc and the rest of the writers at *Tovariš* have known since the 1960s and the 1970s that a little bit of heart and sincerity can't do their readers any harm. If anything, it helps them toward a better understanding of the world around them.

NOTES

1. In Slovenia, the golden age of journalistic writing that uses novelistic techniques started in the 1960s, was in full bloom by 1970, and ended in 1973, when *Tovariš* turned to analytical articles and published few or no feature stories. In January 1974 the magazine ceased publication; at that time it merged with the weekly newspaper *Tedenska tribuna* (both published by the same news company, ČP Delo) and formed a new illustrated weekly newspaper, *ITD*.

2. Truman Capote's nonfiction novel *In Cold Blood* (1965) was translated into Slovene in 1967, and Norman Mailer's *Armies of the Night* into Serbo-Croatian in 1971.

3. According to historian Peter Vodopivec, the more relaxed atmosphere of the 1950s encouraged not only younger artists who addressed Western artistic ideas but also adherents of prewar aesthetic movements who had continued their work after the war. In the 1950s, literature was dominated by poets and writers who followed social realism or connected themselves to its traditions, although their "former belligerence had already been replaced by a sense of solidarity with the 'little man' and disappointment with the new social political reality." See Peter Vodopivec, *Slovenska zgodovina, 1780–2004* (Slovenian History, 1780–2004) (Ljubljana: Modrijan, 2007), 310, available at www.sistory.si/publikacije/pdf/zgodovina/Slovene-History-1780-2004.pdf. All translations from Slovenian, unless otherwise noted, are my own.

4. Tom Wolfe, "The New Journalism," in *The New Journalism: With an Anthology*, ed. Tom Wolfe and E. W. Johnson (New York: Harper & Row, 1973), 31.

5. Ibid.

6. Manca Košir, "Towards the Theory of Journalistic Text Form," in *Surovi čas medijev*, ed. Manca Košir (Ljubljana: FDV, 2003), 136.

7. Manca Košir, *Nastavki za teorijo novinarskih vrst* (Ljubljana: DZS, 1988). The theory of journalistic text form as it exists in Slovene journalism originated in this textbook. Košir distinguishes among three terms: "family," "species," and "genre" (65). First, she separates journalistic

texts in the Slovene media into two broad families, the informative and the interpretative. She then concentrates on individual "species" of texts (for example, feature stories and portraits). Finally, she subdivides the latter into different genres. The feature story species—known in Slovene as *reportažna vrsta*—is thus used as an umbrella term for a text type that consists of three genres: *klasična reportaža* (classic reportage, a genre that is similar to literary journalism), *reporterska zgodba* (reported stories), and *potopis* (travelogue). The *portretna vrsta* species consists of one genre: *portret* (portrait).

8. Marko Milosavljević, *Novinarska zgodba* (Ljubljana: FDV, 2003), 6.

9. Milosavljević merges genres from two previously distinct species of journalistic writing—*reportažna* and *portretna vrsta*—into a single one, *novinarska zgodba* (ibid., 27).

10. Both types are complex, and they engage the reader's mind and emotions. News feature stories, however, are more formulaic than literary journalism. They may use some narrative techniques, such as scene description or dialogue, but these techniques are not predominant in a given text. Wolfe defines "feature" as "the newspaper term for a story that fell outside the category of hard news," whereas New Journalism is nonfiction writing that uses any literary device to "excite the reader both intellectually and emotionally." Harrington discusses the difference between news feature stories and what he calls intimate journalism, and Hartsock mentions a difference between conventional feature stories and literary journalism. Finally, Ricketson writes about a difference between feature stories and advanced feature stories which belong to literary journalism. See, respectively, Wolfe, "The New Journalism," 5, 15; Walt Harrington, "A Writer's Essay: Seeking the Extraordinary in the Ordinary," in *Intimate Journalism: The Art and Craft of Reporting Everyday Life* (Thousand Oaks, Calif.: Sage Publications, 1997), xxiii; John C. Hartsock, "'It Was a Dark and Stormy Night': Newspaper Reporters Rediscover the Art of Narrative Literary Journalism and Their Own Epistemological Heritage," *Prose Studies* 29.2 (2007): 262–63; and Matthew Ricketson, *Writing Feature Stories* (Crows Nest, NSW: Allen & Unwin, 2004), 228.

11. Those who did attempt to analyze New Journalism after Wolfe generally used his ideas as a basis; this is what I have done in my study, too. Later, scholars such as Barbara Lounsberry, Normans Sims, and Ronald Weber refined and revised Wolfe's definition on the basis of analyses of writers ignored by Wolfe—though they agreed with Wolfe's basic premise that New Journalism is more artistic than conventional journalism. See Barbara Lounsberry, "Anthology Introduction," in *Writing Creative Nonfiction: Literature of Reality,* ed. Gay Talese and Barbara Lounsberry (New York: HarperCollins, 1996), 29–31; Norman Sims, "The Art of Literary Journalism," in *Literary Journalism,* ed. Norman Sims and Mark Kramer (New York: Ballantine Books, 1995), 3–19; Ronald Weber, "Introduction: Nonfiction with a Literary Purpose," in *The Literature of Fact: Literary Non-fiction in American Writing* (Athens: Ohio University Press, 1980), 1–4.

12. Sonja Merljak Zdovc, "The Use of Novelistic Techniques in Slovene Journalism: The Case of the Magazine *Tovariš,*" *Journalism Studies* 8.2 (2007): 248.

13. Sonja Merljak Zdovc, "The Golden Age of Feature Stories: Towards the History of a Genre," in *Kraljski Dalmatin—200 godina zadarskog i hrvatskog novinarstva u europskom kontekstu* (Two Hundred Years of Journalism in Zadar and Croatia within a European Context), ed. Nada Zgrabljič (Zadar: Sveučilište u Zadru, 2007), 155.

14. In his foreword to *Sajam senzacija* (The Sensation Fair), Kisch's second work to have been translated into a Yugoslav language (here, Serbo-Croatian), Branko Kojić writes: "The history of the feature story is not long. As a special genre of journalism it appeared in the late nineteenth century in the United States of America, and from there entered the press of

European countries in a slightly different form." He continues: "An outstanding representative of such a kind of writing was Jack London; his work *The People of the Abyss,* a collection of features about life in the East End of London, is nowadays considered a classic work of this sort," adding, "In this way, a new genre of feature writing began to evolve which resembled more a short story than a piece of journalism because of its structure and treatment [of the material]; this kind of feature writing could belong to literature as well as journalism." Kojić finally links Kisch directly to Jack London: "Many writers and journalists followed his example; only a small number, however, drew the attention of the world to themselves for being great reporters of the present. Among those few who gained worldwide recognition is Egon Erwin Kisch." See Branko Kojić, "Pogovor" (Afterword), in Egon Erwin Kisch, *Sajam senzacija* (Zagreb: Novinarsko izdavačko poduzeće, 1956), 325–327.

15. Sonja Merljak Zdovc, "Slovenska revija *Tovariš* in njeni revijalni 'tovariši' v drugi polovici dvajsetega stoletja" (The Slovene Magazine *Tovariš* and Its Magazine 'Comrades' in the Second Half of the Twentieth Century), *Javnost* (The Public) 15.5 (2008): 28.

16. Owen V. Johnson, "The Roots of Journalism in Central and Eastern Europe," in *Eastern European Journalism: Before, during, and after Communism,* ed. Jerome Aumente et al. (Creskill, N.J.: Hampton Press, 1999), 31.

17. Jasna Fischer et al., *Slovenska novejša zgodovina: 1848–1992* (Recent Slovene History: 1848–1992) (Ljubljana: Mladinska knjiga, 2005), 930.

18. Vodopivec, *Slovenska zgodovina, 1780–2004,* 274.

19. The first important circle of Slovene journalists who wrote feature stories and who tried to use narrative techniques in their writing gathered at the magazine *Mladina* between 1958 and 1964. *Mladina* was something of a classroom for those who wanted to move on to more prestigious weekly publications published by ČP Delo, such as *Tovariš* and *Tedenska tribuna.*

20. Sonja Merljak Zdovc, *Literary Journalism in the United States of America and Slovenia* (Lanham, Md.: University Press of America, 2008), 83.

21. Jon Franklin, "A Story Structure," in *Telling True Stories,* ed. Mark Kramer and Wendy Call (New York: Penguin Group, 2007), 110.

22. Alenka Bibič, "Maribor ostane mesto ob Dravi," *Tovariš,* August 13, 1965, 12–17.

23. Wolfe, "The New Journalism," 15. See also Thomas B. Connery, ed., *A Sourcebook of American Literary Journalism: Representative Writers in an Emerging Genre* (New York: Greenwood Press, 1992), xi.

24. Wolfe, "The New Journalism," 31–32.

25. Sims, "The Art of Literary Journalism," 9.

26. Harrington, "A Writer's Essay," xx.

27. Barbara Lounsberry, "Introduction: The Realtors," in *The Art of Fact: Contemporary Artists of Nonfiction* (New York: Greenwood Press, 1990), xi–xviii.

28. Lounsberry, "Anthology Introduction," 30.

29. Wolfe, "The New Journalism," 45–46.

30. Sonja Merljak Zdovc, "More Stories, More Readers: Feature Writing in Slovenia," *Journalism Practice* 3.3 (2009): 319–34. This is also the case in the United States, however. According to Mark Kramer, the appearance of the feature story depends on individual journalists. See Mark Kramer, "Discovering and Redefining Narrative," paper presented at the Nieman Narrative Journalism Conference, Cambridge, Mass., November 30–December 2, 2001.

31. His oeuvre was most similar to writings of literary journalism. He started to write for *Tovariš* in 1964. Before that he was a reporter at the weekly magazine *Mladina,* and later a reporter and editor at the national daily *Delo.*

32. Most journalists did not read journalism books because they were mainly written in inaccessible foreign languages. One of the few who were familiar with Kisch's work early on was Jože Šircelj, then editor of the magazine *Mladina*. As Šircelj had studied German, he was able to read Kisch's work in the original. He brought Kisch to the attention of journalists at *Mladina*, though they could read his work only after it had been translated into Serbo-Croatian or Slovenian.

33. Kojić, "Pogovor," 328.

34. Ibid., 328–31.

35. Željko Kozinc, "Fant, tu mi širiš smrad po krepavcih" (Boy, You Made This Place Stink Like a Morgue), *Delo*, March 10, 2001, *Sobotna priloga*, 24. I have opted for a literal translation of these pieces in order to preserve and attempt to render the peculiar structure of Kozinc's sentences.

36. Željko Kozinc, "Dvojni obraz strašnega Pjera," *Mladina*, June 2, 1962, 12–13.

37. Željko Kozinc, personal interview, Ljubljana, July 12, 2008.

38. Kozinc, "Dvojni obraz strašnega Pjera," 12.

39. In Kisch, *Sajam senzacija*, 249–56. The original title of the story is "Magdalenenheim."

40. Hartsock, "It Was a Dark and Stormy Night," 263.

41. Ibid.

42. Vodopivec, *Slovenska zgodovina, 1780–2004*, 310–11.

43. Kozinc, personal interview.

44. Kozinc, "Fant, tu mi širiš smrad po krepavcih," 24.

45. At the beginning of the 1970s, when the Center for American Culture opened in Ljubljana, journalists finally had greater access to American magazines and, by reading them, came to realize that they had to get rid of the flowery lyricism, descriptiveness, and sentimentality typical of their journalism in the 1960s. They wanted to write like Ernest Hemingway and John Steinbeck, both literary journalists as well as novelists, and saw especially in the latter a kinship with the Slovene tradition of social realism. Slovene journalists found new inspiration in their work after reading Capote's *In Cold Blood* and Mailer's *Armies of the Night*. Mailer was of particular interest to them since they were aware of his rich, baroque temperament.

46. Željko Kozinc, "Prijazna smrt, predolgo se ne mudi," *Tovariš*, February 17, 1970, 15–21. Subsequent references appear parenthetically in the text, abbreviated PS.

47. Kozinc, personal interview.

48. Hartsock, "It Was a Dark and Stormy Night," 263.

49. See Željko Kozinc, "Pravica vasi Rudno," *Tovariš*, April 16, 1973, 4–7; and "Topli kruh dela," *Delo*, November 30, 1973, 29. Subsequent references to the latter appear parenthetically in the text, abbreviated T.

50. Ben Yagoda, preface to *The Art of Fact: A Historical Anthology of Literary Journalism*, ed. Kevin Kerrane and Ben Yagoda (New York: Simon and Schuster, 1997), 15.

51. Hartsock, "It Was a Dark and Stormy Night," 263.

52. Kozinc, "Pravica vasi Rudno," 7.

53. Kerrane, "Making Facts Dance," in Kerrane and Yagoda, *The Art of Fact*, 17.

54. Wolfe, "The New Journalism," 45.

55. After he left journalism, Kozinc became a scriptwriter and a novelist; in his creative endeavors he relied on the journalistic techniques and story ideas from his articles in *Tovariš*. He wrote a screenplay based on his story "Pravica vasi Rudno" because, as he explained, without the restrictions of reporting he could develop the topic more fully and give it the prominence it deserved. See Merljak Zdovc, *Literary Journalism*, 115.

56. Kozinc even wrote a story of a widow who was having difficulties securing the death certificate of her husband, who was taken away by local authorities because he was deemed to have been a local quisling during World War II. Nobody knew what had happened to him, or even whether he was dead or alive. According to the land registry, however, he was the owner of the farm. Without a death certificate, his wife was unable to carry out the legalities pertaining to inheritance. "I wrote this and the report 'flew' out of the magazine, as one of the printers informed the in-house safety and intelligence service. Somebody came, read the report, and said, 'This goes out.' Later the editor in chief even said to me, 'Kozinc, are you aware that you have two children?'" In other words, Kozinc was warned that such writing could have political consequences on the well-being of his family. See Merljak Zdovc, *Literary Journalism,* 78.

57. Željko Kozinc, "Obrni, kakor hočeš: tabor leti v nebo," *Delo,* October 25, 1997, *Sobotna priloga,* 35. Subsequent references appear parenthetically in the text, abbreviated O.

58. Quoted in John C. Hartsock, *A History of American Literary Journalism: The Emergence of a Modern Narrative Form* (Amherst: University of Massachusetts Press, 2000), 37.

59. According to Hartsock, sensationalism, too, may use literary techniques, but its purpose is not to overcome the "epistemological gulf" between one's subjectivity and the objectivity of the other person. See ibid., 141.

60. Željko Kozinc, "Koliko srca je v pol tolarja," *Delo,* January 17, 1998, *Sobotna priloga,* 35.

61. Ibid., 35.

62. Quoted in Hartsock, *A History of American Literary Journalism,* 41.

63. Hartsock, "It Was a Dark and Stormy Night," 277.

64. Ibid., 278.

65. See Merljak Zdovc, "More Stories, More Readers," 319–34.

66. For her diploma thesis under my directorship, Sabina Vrhnjak conducted a series of interviews with various journalists who used narrative techniques in their writing about a storm. A reporter for *Delo* said that although narrative is the most understandable and readable form of writing, it is probably more suitable for less serious newspapers. His answer illustrates how many reporters fail to realize the potential of narrative when writing about serious topics.

67. Hartsock, "It Was a Dark and Stormy Night," 258.

Chapter 15

Creditable or Reprehensible?

The Literary Journalism of Helen Garner

WILLA McDONALD

THE REACTIONS BY critics and the general public to the literary journalism of Helen Garner, one of Australia's leading writers, demonstrate that writing reportage with the eye of a novelist raises professional and ethical challenges. Garner's nonfiction, while masterly in its use of language, has a history of drawing heated comments from the mainstream Australian media but little attention from the academy as the subject of literary analysis. While she has many champions, Garner remains a controversial writer to many critics, such as Katherine Wilson, Matthew Ricketson, Virginia Trioli, and Inga Clendinnen, for the way she utilizes fictional techniques in the portrayal of factual situations, concentrates in her work on the subjectivity of the narrator, and, consequently, displays her personal politics.[1] It is uncomfortable territory for those who prefer their reportage straight and who distrust emotional analyses in favor of the rational.

This essay examines some of the critical reactions to Garner's writing, in particular her long-form literary journalism, and proposes that her work has provoked censure when it has refused to follow traditional journalistic conventions; chosen not to establish a clear contract of intention with its readership; privileged the exploration of the writer's emotions over intellectual frameworks; and challenged traditional notions of subjectivity and objectivity. What I hope to demonstrate is that a closer engagement with Garner's nonfiction by academic critics would be a fruitful contribution to the field of literary journalism.

An Uncommon Career

The extent of the antipathy aroused by Helen Garner's work is a testament to her abilities and influence as a writer/journalist. Her career trajectory has been an unusual one. While many writers aim toward the publication of successful novels as the pinnacle of their ambitions, Garner shifted in midlife to concentrate on writing nonfiction exclusively. Her first five books—*Monkey Grip* (1977), *Honour and Other People's Children* (1980), *The Children's Bach* (1984), *Postcards from Surfers* (1985), and *Cosmo Cosmolino* (1992)—were acclaimed works of literary fiction, her writing at the time largely supported by freelance journalism. In the 1960s she had worked by day as a high school teacher, writing in her spare time while participating in the collective that produced the alternative fortnightly magazine *The Digger*. Her future as a teacher, though, was permanently terminated in 1972. The cause was an article she wrote for the magazine about a series of impromptu sex education sessions she held with her thirteen-year-old students at Fitzroy High School. The frankly written piece, which seems relatively tame today, became part of an obscenity trial that forced *The Digger* to close in 1975.[2]

Undeterred—and perhaps encouraged—Garner continued to write journalism over the years. Though never formally trained as a journalist, she wrote prolifically for mainstream publications including the *Age* newspaper and *Time Australia* magazine. In 1993 she won her first Walkley, Australia's most prestigious journalism award, for her *Time* article about domestic violence, "Did Daniel Have to Die?"[3] The story focused on the death of a two-year-old at the hands of his stepfather, in particular the failure of the child's mother, and the twenty or so professionals and concerned individuals surrounding the boy, to take any action to protect him. The award roughly coincided with her third marriage, to the novelist Murray Bail, and her shift toward writing only nonfiction for the next fifteen years. This was so as to leave the novel-writing turf to Bail, Garner commented offhandedly at a bookshop reading in 2008.[4]

In 1995 Garner produced her first book-length work of literary journalism, *The First Stone: Some Questions about Sex and Power*. As will be discussed in more detail later in this essay, the book was highly controversial both for its politics and for its breach of journalistic conventions, with Garner adding a fictional element to the nonfiction text. Two collections of Garner's feature articles were to follow: *True Stories: Selected Non-Fiction*, which came out in 1996, winning the Nita Kibble Literary Award, and *The Feel of Steel*, which was published in 2001.[5] Then in 2004 Garner brought out her second nonfiction book, *Joe Cinque's Consolation: A True Story of Death, Grief and the Law*.[6] Although some academic reviewers remained unpersuaded about the value of her nonfiction work, continuing to distrust its personal, emotional focus, this time there were no accusations of truth twisting.[7] The piece won Garner another Walkley. Despite such professional acclaim, Garner continues to antagonize academic critics and puzzle reviewers, who flounder when it comes to categorizing her work. She chose to call her 2008 book *The Spare Room* a novel, even though it was a highly autobiographical account of the visit of a terminally ill friend. The book, typically authentic in tone, prompted a rash of reviews devoted to questioning whether or not it really was fictional.[8]

Transgressions: Conventions and Contracts

Helen Garner's early experience as a novelist shows in her journalistic style. Her control of her prose is exceptional. She arranges words like still-life paintings on the page. At the same time, her lack of formal journalism training, while stylistically liberating, may also have contributed to her running afoul of professional ethics in the writing of *The First Stone*. That book traced the events behind the criminal trial of Alan Gregory, the master of Ormond College, University of Melbourne, for indecent assault against two female students arising from incidents connected with a college party. Both women accused Gregory of touching their breasts, with one adding that in his office after the party Gregory had also told her he frequently had indecent thoughts about her. The students, failing to get satisfaction from the college administration, complained to the police, who brought charges. Garner, a public feminist of long standing, did not write the book to explore Gregory's guilt or innocence. Rather, she used the case to explore her own attitudes toward what she saw as "ghastly punitiveness" on the part of the young women, bemoaning the fact that they had failed to recognize their own power in the situation and had sought heavy-handed redress through the law.[9] Although she never interviewed the students, Garner used *The First Stone* to ruminate at length on why they had felt so helpless, why they had not used "their own weapons of youth and quick wits" to deal themselves with what she interpreted as minor sexual harassment rather than assault (*TFS* 40).

In writing this book, Garner triggered a passionate national debate about feminism, sexuality, women, and personal power. She antagonized those who said she had misunderstood institutional power and created generational stereotypes that pitted younger and older feminists against each other. She was accused of selling out women and their hard-won legal rights; of contributing to the backlash against feminism as described by Susan Faludi;[10] of feeding claims of a "victim feminism" as proposed by writers such as Camille Paglia, Katie Roiphe, and Rene Denfield in an international debate that had until then not forcefully reached the Australian public.[11] The politics surrounding the book when it came out were heated, and the arguments it engendered held the media's attention for many months.[12] Thrumming beneath the politics were also concerns among journalists and academics about the methods Garner had used in the book's research and writing. She, who as the narrator is the protagonist in this and in all her books of nonfiction, began her investigation with a sympathetic letter to Gregory. But unlike Joe McGinniss's ingratiating pleas to persuade convicted killer Jeffrey MacDonald to take part in his text *Fatal Vision,* Garner's letter was not written with a book in mind.[13] She wrote her impassioned letter to Gregory in genuine sympathy, saying of the students' complaint to the police: "This has been the most appallingly destructive, priggish and pitiless way of dealing with it. I want you to know that there are plenty of women out here who step back in dismay from the kind of treatment you have received" (*TFS* 16).

It was an unwise move. As Janet Malcolm, one of Garner's transnational influences, commented in a review of the book in the *New Yorker,* Garner did "what a journalist must never do—she showed her hand too early."[14] Gregory, not surprisingly, circulated the letter. It caused Garner to lose the trust of the two students and their supporters, creating, as she noted in the narrative, intractable difficulties for her in the subsequent research and writing of *The First Stone.* Neither the students, whom Garner was prevented from naming by Australian laws relating to sexual assault victims, nor key staff at the University of Melbourne who supported the women ever agreed to be interviewed, and much of the book is taken up with Garner's frustrations at their refusal: "Why won't you talk to me? I'm sitting here waiting to be convinced, but no one will come out of the bunker and argue it. I can write the book without your version—I can imagine it, for God's sake!—aren't I a woman?—but it's so important. If you have a case, why won't you put it to me?" (*TFS* 171).

Her protests were interpreted as arrogance by some critics (for example, Suzanne Eggins), and the book was dismissed as biased (for instance, by Wilson and Ricketson). Garner, however, is far from the first literary journalist to push a strong point of view. Pointing out the public nature of the story, especially once charges were laid against Gregory, and denying claims that the story was the private business of the young women, Garner said that she always respected their right to keep silent.[15] She also insisted on her right to discuss her own feelings surrounding their refusals. Garner, in a later essay, said that she wrote *The First Stone* to make people "not only think but feel again"—and a description of her own emotional journey while following the case was crucial to that aim.[16] Such description is indicative of Garner's style. She never presumes objectivity. It's the expression of her own reactions that is her real subject matter.

Not everyone agreed with Garner's approach. Jenna Mead, a crucial supporter of the young women, was outraged by Garner's book. She revealed in an article in the newspaper the *Age* after the book's publication,[17] and later in a speech to a conservative think tank, the Sydney Institute (shortly after Garner herself had addressed the institute),[18] that she had particular reason to be annoyed. Garner had split her into half a dozen characters, creating the impression of a conspiracy of academic feminists working to block Garner's search for the truth. While Garner revealed in her "Author's Note" to *The First Stone* that she had changed the names of all the people who appeared in the book, she did not admit to adding several people to the text. Instead, she wrote:

> At first, when I imagined this book as an extended piece of reportage, the only names I changed were those of the two young women, since our law forbids the identification of the complainants in cases of alleged indecent assault. However, I soon encountered obstacles to my research which forced me, ultimately, to write a broader, less "objective," more personal book. They also obliged me to raise the story on to a level where, instead of its being just an incident specific to one institution at one historical moment, its archetypal features have become visible. This is why I have felt free to invent names for all the characters. (*TFS* n.p.)

Mead's bombshell created a storm of criticism around Garner, who then admitted to the ruse, insisting she had been obliged to take such action by her publisher's defamation lawyers, who had advised that publication could not proceed if Mead's identity were not hidden. Said Garner later: "I did a dumb thing in *The First Stone*. . . . It was a loss of nerve, and it distorted the particular story, which I crossly regret, but I don't think it disturbed the thrust of the book's argument."[19]

Garner would indeed have been under great pressure to make the changes. As R. Thomas Berner has pointed out, the Australian defamation laws are particularly strict.[20] Changing the name of someone in a text is insufficient to protect the writer from a defamation suit if the person is still identifiable by other means.[21] This appears to be so despite the introduction of a uniform statutory code in 2006, the provisions of which are at this writing still to be tested in the courts. There is no constitutional right to free speech in Australia to ameliorate the effect of the statute and its supporting case law. This, together with the economic constraints on publishing in a country where the population is only 21 million and is geographically widespread, operates to retard the publication of serious literary journalism. In such an environment, the wishes of publishers to protect themselves against costly lawsuits can hold great sway, as they patently did in this instance.

But the legal difficulties that prompted Garner to amend the text of *The First Stone* did not exonerate her from responsibility for the changes she made. Nor did the declaration in her "Author's Note" protect her from public anger when her inventions were eventually revealed. While many critically acclaimed books in recent years have straddled the border between fact and fiction without controversy, clearly that was not the case here. W. G. Sebald famously mixed fact and invention in his novelistic travelogues, even sprinkling them with "documentary" photographs. Bruce Chatwin, V. S. Naipaul, and Paul Theroux are well known for playing with the boundary between fantasy and fact in their books. While no one went so far as to accuse Garner of literary fraud in the way writers such as Norma Khouri and James Frey have been, it is certain that many readers felt cheated by the changes she made to the facts.[22] Readers were given to understand when they read *The First Stone* that, despite its literary style, it was factually accurate. The book's tone and other encoded signals suggest it is a work of journalism. Garner herself never described the book as a novel. She always claimed it was reportage.

Writers who do successfully dance on that line between invention and fact are able to do so because their readers understand that—through the choice of subject matter and the way the texts have been constructed—the writing comes closer to fictional literature than to journalism. There is a contract, albeit sometimes a subtle one, between the writer and the reader. The temptation for a literary journalist to go beyond questions of style and storytelling to manipulate dialogue or setting or characterization can be great. But the demarcation line, as Janet Malcolm claims in *The Journalist and the Murderer,* is indelible: "The writer of nonfiction is under contract to the reader to limit himself to events that actually occurred and to characters who have counterparts in real life, and he may not embellish the truth about these events or these characters."[23] Or, as Roy Peter Clark puts it in "The Line between Fact and Fiction," writers of nonfiction should not add material that was not there, nor use the material that is there to deceive the reader knowingly.[24] While Australian readers would understand and forgive the changes Garner made to the names of the people in *The First Stone,* it was another matter when it came to splitting Mead into a range of characters. Garner not only added an invented element to the text that greatly influenced its meaning but also breached her contract with the readers that the book was factual. The ensuing controversy over *The First Stone*—exacerbated by arguments over the politics expressed in the text—was prolonged and bitter.

Privileging the Emotions

The worlds of the texts that Garner creates in her nonfiction are extremely convincing. This is as true of her second book of nonfiction, *Joe Cinque's*

Consolation, as it is of her first. *Joe Cinque's Consolation* is an account of the trials following the murder of a young engineer at the hand of his girlfriend, Canberra law student Anu Singh, and her friend Madhavi Rao. Singh drugged Cinque after a dinner party with a massive dose of Rohypnol and then fatally injected him with heroin. It took him that night and most of the next day to die. Friends knew beforehand of her plans, which were meant to end in her suicide, but no one stepped in to stop her. Singh, after a ruling of diminished responsibility, was sentenced to ten years in jail but served only four. The failure in Garner's eyes of the legal system to provide justice, and of those close to Singh to take action to prevent Cinque's killing, are the main themes of the book. Inaction by people who could prevent crimes of violence is an enduring theme in Garner's nonfiction. While *Joe Cinque's Consolation* drew praise from journalists, for example, in the *Australian* and the *Bulletin,*[25] Garner again attracted criticism from within the academy. This time, though, no one accused her of meddling with the facts; the criticism leveled against *Joe Cinque's Consolation* instead focused largely on its style.

Garner's greatest strength lies in her storytelling ability. But it is precisely her storytelling techniques that exasperate her critics. Her practice in her non-fiction is to use anecdotes that bond with the reader, advance the narrative, and evince the broader points she wants to make, as shown in this excerpt from *Joe Cinque's Consolation:*

> On the train home I opened the paper she had given me. It was a double-page tabloid spread from the *Daily Telegraph's* report of the committal proceedings: the transcript of the emergency call that Anu Singh had made to the paramedics while Joe Cinque lay dying on their bed. . . . It was the shrill blast of this dialogue that broke through my indifference and galvanized me: the killer's voice pleading, dodging, feinting; the dispatcher's desperate striving for command; and the jolting visual flashes of Joe Cinque's death throes—the close presence, behind the screaming, of a young man's body *in extremis*—his limbs, his mouth, his teeth, his heart. (*JCC* 21)

And again in this extract:

> At lunchtime, to clear my head, I went for a walk in the autumn sunshine across Garema Place, the broad pedestrian precinct in the centre of Canberra. Men and women who work in government departments stride across this square with identity cards swinging on long chains round their necks. Junkies slouch whining in phone booths. Magpies perch, warbling their absent-minded melodies, on the chair-backs of outdoor cafes. As I walked I brooded crankily on the business of the defence psychiatrists. How can an expert witness hired by the family of the accused possibly be considered disinterested?

This couldn't be right. I must have misunderstood. Why didn't the court itself appoint and pay the experts? Or was this a dumb question? (*JCC* 48–49)

Several academic reviewers, such as Eggins, Wilson, and Maryanne Dever, accused Garner of manipulation in *Joe Cinque's Consolation.* They resented Garner's maneuvering of her audience to her point of view through her use of subjective reflection and her appeal to the reader's emotions. They also disapproved of her contrived tone of authenticity and objected to her use of sweeping generalizations to include all women in her particular point of view, as demonstrated in this passage: "*Dislike of the body.* I imagined every woman in the court thinking, with an ironic twist of the mouth, *Tell me about it!* . . . Maybe only another woman could intuitively grasp the extent to which Singh, like the rest of us, was ruled by her body, imprisoned in it and condemned to struggle against it" (*JCC* 54).

In *Joe Cinque's Consolation,* as in *The First Stone,* it was said (for instance, by Eggins, Wilson, and Clendinnen) that Garner failed to give a balanced and detached account of both sides of the story. In an uncanny echo of *The First Stone,* Garner had been unable to interview Singh or Rau: "*The women won't talk to me.* Suddenly I felt very tired. Here I was, back at the same old road-block. My fantasy of a journalistic evenhandedness, long buckling under the strain, gave way completely" (*JCC* 269). Garner went on to use the absence of interviews with the plaintiffs and their supporters in both this book and *The First Stone* to throw the emphasis of the content of the text even more firmly back on her own thought processes. There were no other strong voices to counter the narrator's position. Dialogue was used only to support her authorial reflections. Garner acted as her own devil's advocate, constantly using personal revelation, and rarely flattering revelation, to create a sense that the texts were evenhanded and trustworthy.

And again, just as in *The First Stone,* the focus of the content of *Joe Cinque's Consolation* was not so much on the guilt or innocence of the defendants, but on the moral rights and wrongs within the tale,[26] with Garner using the narrative to follow her own intellectual and emotional journey:

I understand now that I went to Canberra because the break-up of my marriage [to Bail] had left me humiliated and angry. I wanted to look at women who were accused of murder. I wanted to gaze at them and hear their voices, to see the shape of their bodies and how they moved and gestured, to watch the expressions on their faces. I needed to find out if anything made them different from me: whether I could trust myself to keep the lid on the vengeful, punitive force that was in me, as it is in everyone—the wildness that one keeps in its cage, releasing it only in dreams and fantasy. (*JCC* 25)

Some critics were clearly disappointed that instead of taking the rational approach of the academic or investigative journalist, Garner used the text to explore her emotional position. Katherine Wilson praised the book for sensitively documenting "how grief can strip us of our highest ideals, as it does to Garner," but criticized it for seducing "the reader away from ideals of reason and understanding and towards impulsive judgement."[27] Similarly Inga Clendinnen, in her 2004 Lionel Murphy Memorial Lecture, wryly acknowledged Garner's exceptional storytelling skills in *Joe Cinque's Consolation,* but recommended that lawyers read it to understand the uninformed view of the general public:

> The Garner narrative is about the failure of law: of justice denied; truth abused; the virtuous injured. . . . You should read it. It exemplifies what you lawyers are up against. It exemplifies the lay person's way of "doing justice"—through appeals to moral intuitions authenticated by current popular narratives underpinned by folk psychology, with authenticity guaranteed by appeals to public or deep personal experience, and/or to mythic archetypes to give temporal depth. Garner's "heart-felt" narrative is utterly impatient of the slow business of due process and the cautious accretions of common law.[28]

Garner's involvement in Jungian psychotherapy is well known in Australian literary circles—an interest she frequently refers to in interviews. Teasing out the archetypal elements of a story is something at which she excels, appealing to the subconscious of the reader and no doubt contributing to her success as a storyteller. But here these critics charged her with going too far—with stripping the people involved of their complex humanity in order to tell a more popular story. The young female defendants, it was said, were shown as villains who took advantage of the legal system. Anu Singh was the archetypal witch who raised Garner's "girl hackles in a bristle" (*JCC* 18): "She was the figure of what a woman most fears in herself—the damaged infant, vain, frantic, destructive, out of control" (*JCC* 18). Joe Cinque, by contrast, "provoked a blur of warmth" (*JCC* 18). He was portrayed without faults—handsome, hardworking, responsible. A loving son to his mother, Rose Cinque. She in turn is shown only sympathetically in her appalling grief:

> Such power dwelt in her that others shrivelled in her presence, became wispy, insubstantial. She never grand-standed or behaved falsely; yet as their suffering and outrage intensified, there rose from the depths of her a tremendous, unassailable archetype: the mother. We recognized it. It answered to a need in us as well. Her outburst after the sentence was not a rupture of protocol. On the contrary, we had waited for her to speak, holding open a space for her to utter. It was an honoured and necessary stage of a ritual: a *pietà.* We

listened in respect, almost in gratitude. We needed to hear the sufferer cry out against her fate, although we knew that for this pain and loss there could be no remedy. (*JCC* 131)

Are accusations such as those raised by Wilson and Clendinnen entirely fair? As Brigid Rooney points out, Garner is not an academic. Nor is she a trained journalist: "Hers is the career of the freelance writer, the independent amateur, rather than the institutionally disciplined specialist. . . . [Her] literary autonomy authorizes and produces a specific node of public discourse that articulates everyday values of commonsense and direct experience. As gifted amateur, she puzzles about institutions from the outside, by virtue of which she can also divine and represent the public mind."[29] As noted earlier, no one accused Garner of getting the facts wrong in *Joe Cinque's Consolation*. It was Garner's writerly techniques—her storytelling style, her emotive appeal—that gave rise to concerns because of the *perceived* effect such an approach had on the accuracy of the story both in its telling and in its reception. This reflects a larger distrust within the Australian academy—and within parts of the profession of journalism—of literary journalism in general. It is a suspicion similar to that which Linda Hutcheon pointed to in *A Poetics of Postmodernism* regarding the commingling of history and literature—a suspicion "towards their common use of conventions of narrative, of reference, of the inscribing of subjectivity, of their identity as textuality, and even their implication in ideology."[30]

Yet the unflinching exploration of her own thoughts and feelings is Garner's signature as a writer. She is the narrator of the intimate, of the domestic, of the personal. Her self-appointed role is to investigate her own subjectivity in the hope that her honesty will resonate with readers and create a space, in turn, for their own reflections. As Andrew Riemer noted when reviewing her novel *The Spare Room*, Garner focuses on "the small scale—the larger questions are dealt with almost by implication."[31] And this is so whether she is writing fiction or nonfiction. It is this focus on the emotional—her search for an individual truth and her refusal to ground her work neatly within any particular ideology—that contributes to the controversy that surrounds it. Compounding this is the unanimous recognition that Garner is one of Australia's most gifted writers. As Robert Dessaix writes of her, "nobody's words on the page command attention quite like hers."[32] When Joan Didion was asked if she had yet read the copy of *Joe Cinque's Consolation* given to her by the Australian actress and theater director Robyn Nevin, she replied, "I couldn't put it down."[33] That persuasiveness disturbs those who disagree with her privileging of emotion—sometimes raw, ugly emotion—as her subject matter. They see dangers in the use of emotions to persuade readers, even unintentionally, to a point of view that may not support their own political stance, and in the case of criticisms of the legal system, a prevailing ideology, or the status quo.

Challenging Notions of Subjectivity and Objectivity

In 2008, with the publication of *The Spare Room,* Garner returned after a long break to writing fiction. Described on the dust jacket as a novel, the book carried the usual legal warning of a work of fiction. Yet as the extensive publicity surrounding the book's publication has revealed, its content is largely fact-based. The sixty-year-old protagonist—called "Helen"—has a terminally ill friend, Nicola, who comes to stay for three weeks in her spare room while receiving "treatments" from a clinic that practices dubious forms of alternative medicine. "Nicola," it turns out, was Garner's friend in real life, Jenya Osborne, who came to stay with the writer while she sought unconventional healing from a Melbourne clinic, although, according to Garner, the descriptions of her illness and death, and the protagonist's reactions to them, were also informed by the deaths in quick succession of others very close to the writer, including her sister and parents.[34] The storyline of *The Spare Room* is limited to tracing "Helen's" mounting anger at Nicola's denial of her impending death. The main theme of the book is grief and the guilt-ridden rage that sometimes goes with it—what that can do to our relationships, both with ourselves and with those who are dying.

Given Garner's recent practice of writing nonfiction, and given that the subject matter is so closely autobiographical, why did she choose to label this book a novel? She wanted the freedom to be more creative with the material she was working with than nonfiction allows. And she had learned caution from the critical condemnation she received in the wake of the publication of *The First Stone* and, to a lesser extent, of *Joe Cinque's Consolation.* But the labeling of the text as fictional was not straightforward either. "At first," she told Claire Scobie, "I called [Helen] by another name, Carol, I think. But at a certain point as I was writing the book, and it was first-person, I wanted to make it quite clear I wasn't inventing those ugly feelings; they were things that I've experienced. I wanted to give a stamp of authenticity at least to that. If she was called Carol or Gertrude and it's got 'novel' written on it, it's a bit slithery, and I didn't want to slither out of it."[35] Garner is nothing if not courageous. Her decision to play with the names of characters is typical of the way she uses her writing to challenge notions of objectivity and subjectivity. While the compromise was perhaps the best ethical approach she could take—and also pragmatically her safest route[36]—it still did not save her from criticism.

Dessaix, referring to earlier criticisms of Garner as a novelist who merely regurgitated her personal journals,[37] described *The Spare Room* in a review in *The Monthly* as "a hard-hitting, flinty-eyed report from the [suburban] front, not a novel."[38] To him it lacked what a novel requires: grand themes, imagination, and characters with any depth of interiority (besides the protagonist "Helen"). He agreed with those critics who, he said, regarded "a novel [as] something more sustained, more imagined, more intricately patterned, more *whole* than the sort of thing Garner writes, however much she trims and transcribes. . . . A novel is primarily a work of fiction with an architectonic quality to it that transcribed diaries just don't have."[39]

Could she, should she have called *The Spare Room* nonfiction? Garner's difficulty is that she has always been drawn temperamentally to conveying the "real." *Monkey Grip,* her well-known first novel, later a film, depicted 1970s life in a shared inner-city Melbourne household peopled by artists, musicians, and students. It focuses on the relationship between Javo, a junkie, and Nora, a single mother who is also a teacher. The "near absolute aura of authenticity"[40] of the text, and the fact that it echoes Garner's own experiences, caused it to attract mixed reviews. And her writing ever since has continued to draw conflicting responses as she has worked to find a form that allows her to express both the factuality and the emotional reality of her world.

In an essay called "I" in a 2002 issue of *Meanjin,* Garner admitted that she relies on her diaries for her published work but equally protested against those who criticized her for doing it:

> Why the sneer . . . ? It's as if this were cheating. As if it were lazy. As if there were no work involved in keeping a diary in the first place: no thinking, no discipline, no creative energy, no focusing or directing of creative energy; no intelligent or artful ordering of material; no choosing of material, for God's sake; no shaping of narrative; no ear for the music of human speech; no portrayal of the physical world; no free movement back and forth in time; no leaping between inner and outer; no examination of motive; no imaginative use of language. . . . It's as if a diary wrote itself, as if it poured out in a sludgy, involuntary, self-indulgent stream . . . [that] could have no possible relevance to, or usefulness for, or offer any pleasure to, any other living person on the planet.[41]

As Garner's words demonstrate, all writing is a "creative" act, whether it is fiction or nonfiction. And yet she wanted to go further in *The Spare Room* than is allowed in nonfiction. She wanted to change facts, omit material, invent whole scenes, and compress and transpose times. She rightly called the book fictional, but in making that earlier, cranky, impassioned plea, Garner was really calling for more open-mindedness in the critics' reception of her work as a whole—work that plays with notions of objectivity and subjectivity; work that brings literary techniques to bear on the writing of actuality.

Helen Garner's voice is unique in Australian literary journalism, a genre that arguably has a history dating back to the early days of the nation. At the turn of the nineteenth century, Henry Lawson wrote about the Australian bush for the *Worker,* the Brisbane *Boomerang,* and the recently closed *Bulletin* magazine. Banjo Patterson sent dispatches from the Boer War in prose and in poetry to the *Sydney Morning Herald* and the *Age* newspapers. In the 1950s and 1960s Charmian Clift used literary techniques to embellish her personal essays for the *Sydney Morning Herald.* And from the 1970s, long-form narrative nonfiction began to feature regularly in the pages of the mainstream media as the influence of the New Journalism was beginning to be felt here. Yet, as mentioned earlier, the genre of literary journalism as broadly defined by Tom Wolfe still struggles to be heard in Australia because of the expense and legal risks involved in producing it. Articles longer than four thousand words are rare. Many of the publications that have supported it over previous decades, such as *Nation Review,* the *National Times,* and the *Independent Monthly,* are now defunct. In spite of this, Australia currently has a number of first-rate writers who produce exceptional literary journalism, including John Birmingham, Craig Sherborne, Gideon Haigh, Malcolm Knox, and Margaret Simons. And within that field, Helen Garner's is a singular voice, carving out new ground as she uses her investigations of factual situations as springboards for her subjective reflections.

Given her stature in the field, can the neglect of Garner's nonfiction writing by the academy be solely attributed to her politics and her methods? John C. Hartsock, in *A History of American Literary Journalism,* points out that literary journalism has long received marginal attention from scholars, partly because it is so difficult to define, crossing as it does the fuzzy gray area both between and of fact and fiction.[42] The problem, he claims, has also been a political one, with long-standing biases in English departments against journalism and in journalism departments against the literary, biases that on both sides are beginning to break down. Garner's work runs afoul of this divide. While it has attracted enormous public interest in Australia over the years and, recently, substantial literary prizes, there remains a skepticism in the universities toward Garner's nonfiction work largely because it is writing that purports to be an analysis of the factual but privileges the emotional. Yet Garner's nonfiction is experimental in form. As she has developed her own approach, she has contravened established professional journalistic standards. Despite, and perhaps even because of, the controversies it has raised, Garner's literary journalism is still as deserving of serious analysis by the academy as is her fiction. Such attention would benefit our understanding of the practice of writing narrative nonfiction in general, and in particular the challenges faced in its production in a localized environment such as Australia.

NOTES

1. See Katherine Wilson, "Helen Garner's Consolation," review of *Joe Cinque's Consolation: A True Story of Death, Grief and the Law* by Helen Garner, *Overland* 178 (2005): 77–79; Matthew Ricketson, "Credibility of Other Writers," in *bodyjamming: Sexual Harassment, Feminism and Public Life,* ed. Jenna Mead (Milsons Point, NSW: Vintage/Random House, 1997), 79–100; Virginia Trioli, *Generation F: Sex, Power and the Young Feminist* (Melbourne: Minerva/Reed, 1996); and Inga Clendinnen, "Making Stories, Telling Tales: Life, Literature, Law," eighteenth Lionel Murphy Memorial Lecture, November 17, 2004, available at lionelmurphy.anu.edu .au/memorial_lectures.htm.

2. Helen Garner, "Why Does the Woman Get All the Pain," in *True Stories: Selected Non-Fiction* (Melbourne: Text Publishing, 1996), 31–37. For an alternate view of Garner's article and her influence in the school, see Rosi Braidotti, "Remembering Fitzroy High," in Mead, *bodyjamming,* 121–47.

3. Helen Garner, "Did Daniel Have to Die?" *Time Australia,* March 8, 1993, republished as "Killing Daniel," in *True Stories,* 162–68.

4. Helen Garner, unrecorded reading/seminar with Claire Scobie at Gleebooks bookshop, Sydney, October 4, 2008. See Garner's ruminations on her journalism in "The Art of the Dumb Question," in *True Stories,* 1–12.

5. Helen Garner, *The Feel of Steel* (Sydney: Picador/Pan Macmillan, 2001).

6. Helen Garner, *Joe Cinque's Consolation: A True Story of Death, Grief and the Law* (Sydney: Picador/Pan Macmillan, 2004). Subsequent references appear parenthetically in the text, abbreviated *JCC.*

7. Examples of unfavorable academic reviews include Katherine Wilson, "Helen Garner's Consolation"; and Maryanne Dever, "Hanging Out for Judgement?," *Australian Women's Book Review* 138 (2004), available at emsah.uq.edu.au/awsr/awbr/issues/138/dever.html. For a contrasting academic analysis of Garner's text, one that values her attempts at writing literary journalism but within a critical framework, see Suzanne Eggins, "Real Stories: Ethics and Narrative in Helen Garner's *Joe Cinque's Consolation,*" *Southerly* 65.1 (Spring 2005): 122–32.

8. See, for example, Deborah Bogle, "Meet the Author: Helen Garner between Two Worlds," *Advertiser,* March 29, 2008; Pamela Bone, "Unsentimental Dedication—Australian Fiction Special," *The Australian,* April 2, 2008; Libby Brooks, "False Memoir Syndrome: Trauma Hucksters' Lies Must Be Exposed, but Autobiographers Deserve Some Creative Licence," *Guardian,* March 20, 2008; Moya Costello, review of *The Pages* by Murray Bail and *The Spare Room* by Helen Garner, *TEXT* 12.2 (October 2008), available at www.textjournal.com.au/ octo8/costello_rev.htm; Kate Legge, "Truly Helen," *The Australian,* March 29, 2008; Geoffrey Lehmann, "Human Truths Revealed in Tale of Fight against Mortality," *The Australian,* March 29, 2008; Jason Steger, "It's Fiction and That's a Fact," *Age,* March 29, 2008; and Susan Wyndham, "Facts in the Fiction: Helen Garner Talks to Susan Wyndham," *Sydney Morning Herald,* March 29, 2008.

9. Helen Garner, *The First Stone: Some Questions about Sex and Power* (Sydney: Picador/Pan Macmillan, 1995), 16. Subsequent references appear parenthetically in the text, abbreviated *TFS*.

10. Susan Faludi, *Backlash: The Undeclared War against American Women* (New York: Anchor, 1992).

11. See Camille Paglia, "No Law in the Arena," in *Vamps and Tramps: New Essays* (New York: Vintage Books, 1994), 19–94; Katie Roiphe, *The Morning After: Sex, Fear, and Feminism on Campus* (New York: Bay Books/Little, Brown, 1993); and Rene Denfield, *The New Victorians: A Young Woman's Challenge to the Old Feminist Order* (St. Leonards: Allen & Unwin, 1995).

12. An analysis of media responses to *The First Stone* can be found in Anthea Taylor, *Mediating Australian Feminism: Rereading* The First Stone *Media Event* (Oxford: Peter Lang, 2008). See also her "Stones, Ripples and Waves: Refiguring *The First Stone* Media Event" (Ph.D. diss., University of New South Wales, 2005).

13. Joe McGinniss, *Fatal Vision* (New York: Signet, 1984). For a discussion of the ethics of McGinniss's approach, see Janet Malcolm, *The Journalist and the Murderer* (London: Bloomsbury, 1990).

14. Janet Malcolm, "Women at War," *New Yorker*, July 1997, 73, quoted in Mead, *bodyjamming*, 37.

15. Helen Garner, "The Fate of *The First Stone*" in *True Stories*, 170. The essay is a slightly amended version of the text of the speech Garner gave to the Sydney Institute on August 8, 1995.

16. Ibid., 170.

17. Jenna Mead, "A Player in the Ormond Drama Defends Her Cause," *Age*, August 16,. 1995.

18. Jenna Mead, "The First Stone: Feminism and Non-fiction," paper presented at the Sydney Institute, Sydney, Australia, September 20, 1995, published in the Institute's journal as "The First Stone: Feminism and Non-fiction," *Sydney Papers* 7.4 (1995): 120–31. See also Jenna Mead, "Bodyjamming, Feminism and Public Life," paper presented at the Sydney Institute, November 25, 1997, and published as "Bodyjamming, Feminism and Public Life," *Sydney Papers* 10.1 (1998): 68–84.

19. Susie Eisenhuth and Willa McDonald, eds., *The Writer's Reader: Understanding Journalism and Non-fiction* (Melbourne: Cambridge University Press, 2007), 166.

20. R. Thomas Berner, review of *The First Stone: Some Questions about Sex and Power* by Helen Garner and *Who Killed Leigh Leigh? A Story of Shame and Mateship in an Australian Town* by Kerry Carrington, *Journalism Studies* 1.2 (May 2000): 345–47.

21. For a useful summary of the current defamation law in Australia as it relates to publication in the arts field, see the Arts Law Centre of Australia website, available at www.artslaw.com.au/legalinformation/Defamation/DefamationLawsAfterJan06.asp.

22. See Norma Khouri, *Forbidden Love: Love and Betrayal in Modern Day Jordan* (London: Doubleday, 2003), published in the United States as *Honor Lost* (New York: Atria, 2003); and James Frey, *A Million Little Pieces* (New York: Anchor, 2004).

23. Malcolm, *The Journalist and the Murderer*, 153.

24. Roy Peter Clark, "The Line between Fact and Fiction," *Creative Nonfiction* 16.1 (2001): 4–15, available at www.creativenonfiction.org/thejournal/articles/issue%2016/16clark_theline.htm. See also *Poynter Online*, September 7, 2004, available at www.poynter.org/content/content_view.asp?id=3491.

25. See, for example, Diana Bagnall, "Murder She Wrote: Helen Garner Revisits the Fertile

Badlands of the Female Heart," *Bulletin,* August 17, 2004; and Emma-Kate Symons, "Inside the Skin," *The Australian,* August 21, 2004.

26. See Eggins, "Real Stories"; Wilson, "Helen Garner's Consolation"; and Clendinnen, "Making Stories, Telling Tales."

27. Wilson, "Helen Garner's Consolation," 79.

28. Clendinnen, "Making Stories, Telling Tales," para. 34.

29. Brigid Rooney, "The Sinner, the Prophet, and the Pietà: Sacrifice and the Sacred in Helen Garner's Narratives," *Antipodes* 19.2 (December 2005): 160.

30. Linda Hutcheon, *A Poetics of Postmodernism: History, Theory, Fiction* (London: Routledge, 1988), 105–6.

31. Andrew Riemer, "A Desperate Search for Hope and Dignity," *Sydney Morning Herald,* April 5, 2008.

32. Robert Dessaix, "Kitchen-Table Candour," *The Monthly* 33 (April 2008): 58–60, available at www.themonthly.com.au/tm/node/869.

33. Elizabeth Zimmer, "Journey to Joan," *The Australian,* February 23, 2008.

34. See Steger, "It's Fiction and That's a Fact"; and the unrecorded reading/seminar with Scobie.

35. Unrecorded reading/seminar with Scobie.

36. It should be pointed out here that merely labeling something "fiction" does not always protect the writer. Witness the responses to Peter Carey's *Theft: A Love Story* and Frank Moorhouse's *Martini: A Memoir* by their ex-wives (Alison Summers and Wendy James, respectively), who felt their lives and letters had been misused in the texts.

37. For a discussion of these early reviews, see Kerryn Goldsworthy, *Australian Writers: Helen Garner* (Melbourne: Oxford University Press 1996).

38. Dessaix, "Kitchen-Table Candour," para. 6.

39. Ibid., 4–5.

40. Peter Craven, "Of War and Needlework: The Fiction of Helen Garner," *Meanjin* 44.2 (Winter 1985): 209.

41. Helen Garner, "I: Helen Garner Explores the New and Different Persona a Writer Must Adopt in Each Successive Work," *Meanjin* 61.1 (March 2002): 40–44, paras. 3 and 4.

42. John C. Hartsock, *A History of American Literary Journalism* (Amherst: University of Massachusetts Press, 2001).

Chapter 16

Ryszard Kapuściński and the Borders of Documentarism

Toward Exposure without Assumption

Soenke Zehle

Even if we grant that contemporary literary journalism has many fathers and mothers, Ryszard Kapuściński was surely one of its most influential representatives. Aware of the way in which the technologies of reportage affect, structure, and transform our attentiveness to events, the Polish writer remained seemingly old-fashioned in his vision of journalism as a creative craft independent of the tyranny of real-time news and the "house styles" assumed to define and limit the expectations of established news audiences. His engaged work frequently crosses the borders of journalism understood in a narrowly documentarist sense. It is celebrated by some as an essayism successfully venturing beyond the stale realism of social advocacy, and criticized by others as an arrogant will to literariness and an abdication of authorial responsibility. These contradictions in his work offer a way to engage the practice of literary journalism in terms of an ethics of the encounter—an ethics sketched by the writer himself in his exploration of philosophies of otherness.

Writing across the Border

In addition to sending official dispatches to his governmental news agency, Kapuściński wrote alternative accounts of his experiences for a wider, increasingly international audience. His reputation as a writer is based on the later works, some of which—including book-length studies such as *Jeszcze dzień życia* (*Another Day of Life*), *Cesarz* (*The Emperor*), *Szachinszach* (*Shah of Shahs*), and *Imperium,* as well as his essay collections *Wojna futbolowa* (*The Soccer War*) and *Heban* (*The Shadow of the Sun*)—are already considered classics in the canon of contemporary literary journalism. Claiming to have witnessed almost thirty revolutions, Kapuściński developed a fascination with the long prehistory of revolutionary moments, describing in detail the Angolan war of independence, the reign of Ethiopia's last emperor, Haile Selassie, the decline of the last Shah of Iran, Mohammad Reza Pahlavi, and the disintegration of the Soviet Union.

Throughout his writings he offers metaphors—border crossing, the Other—that provide provisional unity to a work that remains largely fragmented, consisting of a vast archive of research as well as reporting. One of the last works to appear in English translation, *Podróże z Herodoten* (*Travels with Herodotus*), relates his lifelong conversation with the Greek historian-philosopher, and it is here that Kapuściński describes a mystique of the border in terms which suggest that of all of his motifs, the border and the act of border crossing is arguably the most central:

> For the closer one got to a border, the emptier grew the land and the fewer people one encountered. This emptiness created the mystery of these regions. I was struck, too, by how silent the border zone was. This mystery and quiet attracted and intrigued me. I wondered what one experiences when one crosses the border. What does one feel? What does one think? It must be a moment of great emotion, agitation, tension. What is it like, on the other side? It must certainly be—different. But what does "different" mean? What does it look like? What does it resemble? Maybe it resembles nothing that I know, and thus is inconceivable, unimaginable? And so my greatest desire, which gave me no peace, which tormented and tantalized me, was actually quite modest: I wanted one thing only—the moment, the act, the simple fact of crossing the border. To cross it and come right back—that, I thought, would be entirely sufficient, would satisfy my quite inexplicable yet acute psychological hunger.[1]

Kapuściński's writings are full of instances of border crossing; of the fear of border guards; of the experience of the border as school; of the desire to protect borders and turn them into the boundaries of a new, revived cultural and political identity in the name of postimperial self-determination; of the body, of frequent experiences of illness and incarceration. Across his writing, the border is much more than a geographical site; it is a threshold between different forms of experience. Its recognition triggers the desire to cross it, bringing into being both the message and the messenger. And while his account of border crossing can possibly be read as an artist's statement, perhaps more significantly, the centrality of this motif resonates with a growing acknowledgment of the border as key site of both contemporary cultural, economic, and political transformation and its analysis.[2] For Kapuściński, the act of border crossing is driven not only by an interest in the Other but also by a hunger for difference—a hunger, rooted in literal and metaphorical scarcity, shared by many of his countrymen as "fifty years of communist rule returned most of central and eastern Europe to a bleak isolation in which the adventures of the globetrotter—tailored by the censor—fed imaginations starving for travel and colour."[3] The experience of empire intensified a taste for the exotic, and the "acuteness" of this hunger points beyond biography, to the broader constellation of eastern European cold war writing that brought exotic accounts of distant events to audiences that received little news from the other side of the Iron Curtain.[4]

A shared experience of empire suggested to Kapuściński a commonality between his own experiences at home and those of the people he portrayed in countries struggling against colonial rule. Whereas much of postcolonial conceptualization focuses on the relationship between the First and Third Worlds, Kapuściński insists that the world behind the Iron Curtain too shared a history of colonization, expanding our sense of the contemporary "postcolony."[5] And if exoticism is integral to Kapuściński's writing, it was not simply the exoticism of the colonial travelogue, but an anti-imperialist, antiracist reworking of this tradition, pioneered by eastern European colleagues such as Egon Erwin Kisch, "who helped convert the mood of this Other-writing from uncritical awe to an anti-imperial exposé journalism with a distinctly socialist content."[6] As much as writers were part of that colonial tradition, they also mobilized it in the service of the very ethics of solidarity with "Others" whose commitment inspired political transformations that seemed possible only abroad; each report of a revolution was an act of defiance against the slow pace of change at home, culminating (in *The Emperor*) with an account of absolute power that served as a thinly disguised allegory of an ossified regime that was socialist in name only.

By placing his readers within a broader historical and geographical horizon, Kapuściński sent his dispatches to de-parochialize cultural attitudes. Again, Herodotus served as a guide, and "if one accepts that Herodotus is correct and that not only gods, but culture in its entirety arrived in Greece (i.e., in Europe) from Egypt (i.e., from Africa), then one could argue for the non-European origins of European culture."[7] For his fellow Polish journalist Wiktor Osiatyński, "Kapuściński taught us that others are no less unique. He warned that if we succumb to our obsession with our own problems[,] we risk overlooking what is really important in the world."[8] Not merely to cross a border but to write an account of its crossing—that was for Kapuściński a task far beyond the official assignment of drafting daily dispatches. By both focusing on moments of revolutionary transformation and inserting his writing within the wide horizon opened up by his conversation with the Greek historian-philosopher, giving them an almost mythological dimension, he clearly enjoyed investing his reflections with world-historical grandeur. Incorporating reams of handwritten notes (Kapuściński never used a tape recorder), he found synthesis to be the aim of his writings, in the sense of an intensity, of getting it right, of course, as the situation will pass, but also in the Herodotian sense of pre-staging (framing) individual encounters that Kapuściński knew from the start would become part of a much larger narrative, a grand narrative of contemporary human experience. At a time when philosophers were telling us that the very idea of the grand narrative had exhausted itself, having failed to attach itself permanently to notions of progress, of a progressive universalization of values of solidarity and mutual responsibility, of a cosmopolitical humanism, Kapuściński enjoyed and embraced such grandeur as he traveled, rushing from revolution to revolution to transmit by wire his terse dispatches from across the world.[9]

Hearts of Darkness

Literary journalism exists as a genre on the border between fact and fiction, as that which delineates both—their strength and limitations—but remains, of necessity, without a home, a territory of its own. Without overemphasizing this status as an aesthetic practice at (and across) the borders of documentarism, it is important to acknowledge that the idea of crossing borders (not least those of the infamous "house styles"—our readers expect stories to be told that way—assumed to stabilize journalism business models) is also at work in the general appreciation of Kapuściński's work by many of his fans and followers. Authors from Margaret Atwood to Salman Rushdie have celebrated Kapuściński's nonchalance in writing across the borders of a journalistic tradition that has foregrounded factual accuracy at the expense of aesthetic experimentation, thereby closing itself off from much of what, at least for Kapuściński, characterizes experiences of history not easily grasped from within the horizon of the house style.[10] In the eyes of his critics, however, his work reflects not only his ambition to inhabit the world differently but also his frequent failure to do so. While for some Kapuściński is a journalist turned writer-philosopher in the course of decades of an engaged essayistic documentarism, for others he is a purveyor of all too general truths about "Others" whose singularity is rendered invisible by the exoticist sweep of his writings. And no other area of Kapuściński's work has elicited more controversy than his writings on Africa.

A 2005 issue titled "Views from Africa" in *Granta,* a magazine that has done much to sustain literary journalism/literary reportage as a genre of its own, included a manifesto called "How to Write about Africa" by the Kenyan author and journalist Binyavanga Wainanina, editor of the East African literary magazine *Kwani* and winner of the Caine Prize.[11] The essay gathers the clichés of reporting on Africa into a satirical "how to" guide that reflects bitterness over how little has changed in the practice and protocols of international news coverage. Inspiration for this essay came from Kapuściński's "gonzo orientalism," a term coined by issue editor John Ryle, who had already collected the substantial criticism of Kapuściński's account of Haile Selassie's reign in *The Emperor* in his review for the *Times Literary Supplement*. Like Wainanina, Ryle fails to see in Kapuściński's tendency to generalize the poetic license of a New Journalism that Kapuściński always claimed it was: "Despite Kapuściński's vigorously anti-colonialist stance, his writing about Africa is a variety of latter-day literary colonialism, a kind of gonzo orientalism, a highly selective imposition of form, conducted in the name of humane concern, that sacrifices truth and accuracy, and homogenises and misrepresents Africans even as it aspires to speak for them."[12] For Ryle, there are limits to the extent to which literary journalism should depart from traditional fact-driven reportage:

> Here in the domain of myth, in a realm untouched by literacy, where the subject never answers back, a reporter is freed from the constraint of dates and data, the tedium of checking and cross-checking, the tyranny of documents and records. Here facts are no longer sacred; we are at play in the bush of ghosts, free to opine and to generalize about "Africa" and "the African"—and invent—without criticism from scholars, or indigenes, or self-appointed guardians of facticity.[13]

While Ryle still acknowledges the author's "often lively sympathy for the people of the countries he writes about," other writers have dismissed Kapuściński altogether. David Rieff is convinced that "if there is one thing that should be easy for supposedly enlightened Westerners in these politically correct times, it would be to look back pityingly and with a measure of shame and embarrassment on the accounts of Africa that were produced in such profusion throughout the colonial period and its immediate aftermath by generation after generation of European and American travelers."[14] Because many readers think of Kapuściński as "one of the few Western writers to approach Africa on its own terms, humanistically and without undue pessimism," there is "almost no other writer working today [who] is treated with the same veneration."[15] Rieff is all the more surprised by the enthusiasm that greeted the arrival of *The Shadow of the Sun* and troubled by "Kapuściński's apparent assumption that his lack of resources gave him more insight into the African situation than his colleagues could ever achieve."[16] In his review of

The Shadow of the Sun, Aleksandar Hemon notes that its chapters "are seldom time-specific, as if suggesting a transcendental, timeless quality of common African life," and is convinced that "Kapuściński is bent on explaining the essence of 'the African' to a Western reader," a project that "leads straight into the liberal version of neocolonial racialist discourse, suitable for a Euro-American reader routinely respectful of 'other cultures,'" but which amounts to "cultural-difference racism."[17] And writing about the controversy that followed Kapuściński's invitation to a PEN forum in 2005, Martin Kimani concludes that "there can be no African response to Kapuściński: the very concept of talking to him as an African I find to be a waste of time."[18]

As Michaela Wrong notes, "A lot of time in Kapuściński's books is spent telling the reader what 'the African' thinks, believes and feels. Try replacing the word 'African' with 'European' in these sentences—the resulting gener-alisations are so broad as to become absurd—and you begin to see why some detect a loftiness of viewpoint that is a form of racism."[19] She adds that despite Kapuściński's focus on social injustice, "he was shockingly silent on, or paid only lip-service to, many of the forces that have shaped African history: apart-heid, Aids, the IMF and the World Bank, for example," and is convinced that "Kapuściński would have helped his own case if he had been more consistent, and modest, about what he offered."[20] Because his work rarely registers such modesty, "the few African intellectuals familiar with it didn't much like it"; as a result, most African papers did not even note the writer's death in 2007. What all of these writers and critics share in their assessment of Kapuściński is the sobering sense that the tendency to cast news about the Other in clichéd metaphors and narratives has been the "house style" of too many writers for much too long—and that Kapuściński's writings do little to challenge that tradition, let alone offer an alternative approach.[21]

Unlike many of his critics, however, Wrong concedes that while "there were mistakes, misleading claims, assertions so categorical that they verged on anthropological diktats[,] . . . there was also much which rang true, truer than my sophisticated African friends will allow."[22] Kapuściński's fundamental prin-ciple is basic: to judge something, you have to be there, explore the everyday to whatever extent possible. Kapuściński offers this maxim—originally issued by the Polish-born pioneer of social anthropology Bronisław Malinowski—as a key principle of his work, as both a journalistic practice and a philosophical perspective. "In any culture, a writer who can turn the footage of our lives that hardly ever makes the final cut into the vibrant essence of his work deserves to be read," Wrong concludes, identifying in Kapuściński's attention to the banal situation, the fleeting moment, the chance encounter the defining feature of his work.[23] In fact, Kapuściński seems to pursue a higher philosophical aim in his writing from the beginning, developing an increasingly nonfactual style to frame his reports, as if his reports were a concatenation of reflections on the human condition, influenced by the situation at hand but in no way limited by it—or even, in the end, answerable to it. It is this reversal that strikes some of his readers as an abdication of authorial/journalistic responsibility. But it is also this ambivalence that offers itself as a point of departure for reflections on the ethical implications of a practice that defines itself through acts of border crossing.

Whiteness and Its Others

The drive to generalize is often the consequence of a perhaps all too eager sense of a need to translate the new into the (clichéd) accounts of the old. Kapuściński conveys little sense of self-doubt, little sense of the limitations of his sensibility, which is itself marked by the self-positioning of the writer within an anti-totalitarian horizon and moment of history that accords public intellectuals a status and their work a significance they do not have outside such contexts, culturally, geographically, and politically.[24] Yet the charge of exoticism doesn't completely grasp Kapuściński's efforts to explore, above and beyond singular encounters, something like the human condition. A contemporary of the cold war with a deep awareness of the extent to which eastern Europeans and former colonial subjects in Africa, Asia, and Latin America have shared experiences of imperial systems of rule and representation with which he thought himself to be only too familiar, Kapuściński strove to reflect on the human—that category which underlies any notion of rights (for self-determination, for instance) yet continues to elude our conceptual grasp. He understands the human mainly in terms of the experience of crossing borders, of acts of liberation that collectively have succeeded in remapping the world we live in.

It is perhaps ironic that even Kapuściński's critics find it difficult to do without generic references such as "white" and "African," but maybe such usage also serves as a reminder that journalistic accounts—literary or otherwise—which involve the negotiation of cultural difference remain enmeshed in cultural technologies of "othering" whose effective criticism requires more than narrative and stylistic experiments by individual authors. What is more, Kapuściński's frequent self-identification as "white" also indicates the ambivalence of the notion of whiteness, as it also offers a means to transcend narrow national identities and allows the Polish writer to speak no longer as Polish journalist but rather as worldly humanist from within a broader, transnational horizon—even if that kind of cosmopolitical perspective, anticipated by the colonial travelogue and adapted by contemporary observers of a politically inspiring Third Worldism, is itself the effect of violent colonial rule whose frail authority both at home and abroad called for the creation of "whiteness" as a coherent collective identity to facilitate and sustain colonial administration.[25] Kapuściński's humanism is made possible in part by this perspective, but its antiracism reaches its limits precisely in the inability to call its own conditions of possibility into question.[26]

Kapuściński's reportage also remains strangely at odds with the philosophical perspective he develops in a series of lectures on the Other, titled *Ten Inny* (2006). In these lectures he offers what could be considered an ethics of border crossing, of encounters with "Others" that do justice to their singularity. Especially in his reflections on Emmanuel Levinas, a Lithuanian Jew naturalized in France, whose work was greatly influenced by German philosophy, Kapuściński offers philosophical substantiation for his literary practice and affirms the writer's duty to cross the border, going out into the world to encounter the Other face-to-face. "In a reporter's understanding," Kapuściński writes in the first of these lectures, "a journey is a challenge and an effort, involving hard work and dedication; it is a difficult task, an ambitious project to accomplish. As we travel, we can feel that something important is happening, that we are taking part in something of which we are at once both witnesses and creators, that there is a duty incumbent upon us, and that we are responsible for something" (*O* 16). If Herodotus is the arch-reporter, Levinas is the thinker of otherness-as-responsibility, and it is from Levinas that Kapuściński derives this sense of responsibility.

The relation to the Other, Levinas suggests, involves an "exposure without assumption" that "precedes the initiative a voluntary subject would take to expose itself," an "exposure to the openness of a face," an "opening of the self to the other, which is not a conditioning or foundation of oneself in some principle, a fixity of a sedentary inhabitant or a nomad, but a relation wholly different from the occupation of a site, a building, or a settling oneself" that "reveals all its meaning only in the relationship with the other, in the proximity of a neighbor, which is responsibility for him, substitution for him."[27] Such a sense of responsibility amounts to an existential resolution, an ethical place one assumes as soon as one is in language. Levinas inserts the question of responsibility into a religious tradition, of a relationship to God, turning responsibility into the determinative structure of human subjectivity. Thus understood, responsibility is prior to representation; it has little to do with "speaking on behalf of the other" in the name of various forms of what the former BBC journalist Martin Bell called a "journalism of attachment," with a "responsibility to protect" that has become the theme of a new alliance between human rights advocacy and military intervention developed in the wake of the human rights disasters of the 1990s, or with the analytical approaches of a "peace" journalism meant to keep such humanitarian interventionism in check.[28]

Despite Levinas's emphasis, there clearly is an idea of representation implied in Kapuściński's understanding of responsibility: If I don't report, who will? Do I not have to tell the stories others would have told but no longer can? And is there an entirely different set of responsibilities that comes with the assumption of such a responsibility? This sense of speaking-on-behalf is perhaps expressed most clearly in his poetry, which often contains condensed versions of his essayistic accounts, as in the case of the soldier to whom he dedicates one of his poems:

> *On a plane to Luanda*
> *a young soldier*
> *lies on a stretcher*
> *that morning a bullet shattered his skull*
> *an IV hangs from a hook*
> *the man tosses*
> *he's delirious*
> *perhaps he's relating what happened*
> *we never found out*
> *where he flew to*
> *in the end.*[29]

The nameless soldier too has a message to deliver, and the sense of responsibility (of having to tell the story) heightened by the sight of an (unknown) Other who may no longer be able to do so speaks of the way the event of such an encounter implicates its witness into an ethical answerability toward the Other. Yet the more difficult it is to make an event visible (rather than simply show, as the professional injunction to stick to the facts might have it), the more important the author becomes in lending some coherence to the fragments collected. Maybe this is simply the essayistic paradox, but it is quite possible that Kapuściński was afraid to follow Levinas all the way. Where Levinas implies a relationship to the Other that amounts to a renunciation of selfhood, there is in Kapuściński's writing no attempt to absent himself, no letting-go of authorial certainty as a way of letting-the-Other-be, rooted in the fundamental acceptance of an ethical answerability to the Other.[30]

Paraphrasing Gandhi, one might say that "encountering the Other" would indeed be a good idea, and there is no shortage of accounts of white explorers whose selves were fortified in the course of their transnational trials and tribulations. But while it is too simple merely to assimilate Kapuściński into the troubling tradition of colonial travelogues, it is also too simple to take his reflections on otherness at face value without judging his work by the ethical standards such reflections establish. The question remains whether his uncritical canonization heightens our sense of ethical responsibility toward others, of the role of reportage in framing such encounters, and of the kind of answerability literary witnessing implies.

Kapuściński's first foreign assignment was in India, where he struggled to make sense of the language, experiencing the existential dimension of translation as an integral element of border crossing, as he virtually pieced a new world together. He taught himself English by working his way through Hemingway's narratives of male initiation, gendering and racializing his reportorial gaze more than he perhaps realized in the course of this rather particular passage to India; he then set out to describe and of course report, what he had already known, affirming an (expert's) authorial stance that he never really abandoned. Unlike V. S. Naipaul or Bruce Chatwin, Kapuściński rarely casts doubt on his reliability as a reporter, at least not in the sense of suggesting that the conclusions he draws, the narratives he develops, the arrangement of impressions he presents could or should be otherwise. Yet maybe the discomfort we sense when reading some of Kapuściński's generalizations serves as a guide to how to engage the singularity of the "otherness" that so fascinated the writer, especially when he subsumes this singularity all too quickly in the name and narrative of contemporary human experience.

Perhaps not surprisingly, given these circumstances (which are also conditions of possibility for a certain type of literary reportage or literary journalism), this is not a writer whose aim is to absent himself from his writing, in his writing. There is death, but no destitution of the author in the Levinasian sense; there is an occasional caveat, but more often in terms rather than in (intrinsic) limitations of the perspective his own approach affords. Kapuściński himself notes that "Levinas considered the I-Other relation within the bounds of a single, racially and historically homogeneous civilization," and stresses that the multiethnicity of the contemporary moment, itself rooted in the twentieth-century experience of decolonization and the migrations enabled by it, might mean that "our previous historical experience will prove to be inadequate for understanding it and being able to move about in it" (*O* 89, 91). Despite such injunctions to look beyond whiteness, Kapuściński finds it difficult to let go of the term and continues to use it as a synonym for "European." Part of this reluctance has to do with his commitment to an (Enlightenment) idea of Europe: "In this march of civilisations, Europe will be the exception, because it is the only one, right from its Greek beginnings, to show curiosity about the world and a desire not just to conquer and dominate it, but also to have knowledge of it; and in the case of its best minds, nothing but knowledge, understanding and closer relations with a view to forming a human community" (*O* 18). Kapuściński, who writes, "[When] I lived in my country I was not aware that I am a white man and that this could have any significance for my fate," becomes self-consciously white in the course of his travels, perhaps investing the sense of whiteness with significance as both an enabling aspect of his identity, literally providing him with a place from which to speak, as well as a sensitivity for the (often violent) material effects such identities are able to produce (*O* 45).

Kapuściński seems to have remained unwilling to concede that the contemporary multiethnic challenge to such constitutions of selfhood also involves a circumscription of his ability to speak about—and on behalf of—others. At the same time, there is no doubt that Kapuściński was more interested in "others" than were many of his contemporaries; the question remains how far poetic license extends when it comes to the accuracy of such engagements. Having witnessed the multiple yet mostly familiar ways in which peoples attempt to liberate themselves from (colonial) systems of rule, Kapuściński was arguably more committed to the idea of a common "world" than many of us are today. And if other worlds are possible, we need to imagine them. Often born out of a sense of solidarity, Kapuściński's essayistic writings offer a record of such an effort. But they need critical reappropriation rather than reverence.

On the Need for Literary Witnesses

For better or worse, literary journalism is an intensely subjective genre, implying an affirmation of the authorial stance it shares with the essay, notoriously difficult to define but nevertheless the subject of constant renewals as an aesthetic practice whose style is itself a way of engaging the question of its contemporaneity without necessarily lapsing into the presentism of standard news coverage. Kapuściński insisted he could not write contemporary novels, yet many of his major works have been incorporated into the canon of world literature. At the same time, their claims to the factual (real) give them a status that few works of fiction have, inspiring controversy both regarding the accuracy of Kapuściński's accounts and the scope and status of literary documentarism more generally.

Contemporary artistic practices have offered definitions of documentary essayism as a kind of relationalism necessary for better understanding the *made*-ness of cultural, economic, and social relations; and the documentary turn in contemporary visual art provides a point of reference for the way documentarism has struggled to accommodate essayistic formats (periodically exiled from documentarism proper, then reembraced as a way out of the aesthetic and political dead end of vérité-style social advocacy).[31] While Kapuściński's intensely visual style (recall the analysis of photographs that opens *Shah of Shahs*) provides some guidance even in the context of contemporary essayistic formats, he should perhaps no longer be treated as a refounder of an aesthetic practice, but as someone whose contradictory works address anew the questions raised by essayistic practices, not only in the comparatively closed context of academic inquiry but also in the fast-paced environment of international news journalism, which leaves little time for ethico-political reflection.

In her contribution to a Nobel Centennial Symposium on witness literature, Nadine Gordimer wondered "what place, task, meaning will literature have in witness to disasters which make the entire world the front line of any and every conflict?"[32] In the world of real-time crisis media, there is less and less time, or so it seems, for poetic interventions:

> Meaning is what cannot be reached by the immediacy of the image, the description of the sequence of events, the methodologies of expert analysis. . . . If witness literature is to find its place, take on a task in relation to the enormity of what is happening in acts of destruction and their aftermath, it is in the tensions of sensibility, the intense awareness, the antennae of receptivity to the lives among which writers experience their own as a source of their art.[33]

Poetic writing alone, it seems, can give meaning a temporary home, a transient act of testimony, a suggestion that stresses the responsibility of the author. Unlike Kapuściński, Gordimer approaches the practice of literary witnessing from the fictional side of what continues to operate as a divide, a dichotomy separating perspectives, places, and promises. Yet she too wonders how much poetic license testimony allows: "Is there inevitably a loss of artistic liberty for the writer in inward testimony as witness?"[34] There is, of course, no answer, but whatever practice of witnessing is, in the end, doing justice to the responsibility that comes with the act of testimony requires that

> the writer has to wrestle with all the possibilities of his medium, the Word, to find the one way in which the demands of meaning can be recited, spoken. . . . I realized, as I believe many writers do, that instead of restricting, inhibiting, coarsely despoiling aesthetic liberty, the existential condition of witness was enlarging, inspiring aesthetic liberty breaching the previous limitations of my sense of form and use of language through necessity; to create form and use anew.[35]

The question of responsibility looms large in her account, indeed an answerability to the event of crisis and its protagonists, in part because what is being witnessed is not the obvious register of violence easily captured by the ever-accelerating visual regimes of real-time news media. It is what Gordimer calls "the unspoken," that which is—demands—to be said but has yet to find its author. And in finding its author, it also shapes him or her. There is a sense in Gordimer that the event finds its—singular—witness, and vice versa; testimony is, above all, testimony to this mutual act of finding as an act that constitutes both the meaning of the event and the subject articulating such meaning by way of translating it into the means of representation available.

Considered in terms of the mutuality of literary witnessing and becoming-author, writing is less a profession than an attitude, or a gift of being in the right place at the right time. The banality of such a description takes on an additional ethical register, not far from the sense of a calling. It is the story, the genesis of writing that writes the writer into being. Criticism of his occasionally dismissive treatment of documentary material and the hair-raising simplicity of some of his generalizations notwithstanding, Kapuściński's desire to reflect on the figure of the human and develop out of each encounter something like a historical understanding of human experience is an impulse worth saving, all the more so as his works literally record many of the pitfalls and problems of such an effort. Both his poetry and his philosophical lectures stress this desire for a cosmopolitical humanism, most definitely at odds with the celebrity status that both shielded him from criticism and arguably prevented him from developing a more self-reflexive stance.

There will be no nostalgic return to an era of self-proclaimed explainers of the world, and there cannot be. The reach and resonance of Kapuściński's work were also a consequence of scarcity—the scarcity of competing accounts, of accessible local news sources, of contesting voices. He started his career as an international correspondent at a time when such reporting was done by a comparatively small team of reporters from major news agencies and networks, a (male) band of explorers that met again and again as they collectively traveled from historic site to historic site, stitching together a narrative of postwar change, of the birth of the Third World. This world has disappeared, as has the vision of tricontinentalist solidarity, having lost its hold on the utopian imagination as the space of the Third World presents itself as increasingly fragmented, its leaders less united by a common vision, its revolutionary momentum dissipated beyond retrieval into a renewed effort of transformation and tribalism.[36] Since fewer people traveled when Kapuściński and his colleagues went to report from the world's front lines, the sites we came to know as the Third World were a third world they created for us. And we trusted them; our own historical situation (especially behind the Iron Curtain) encouraged us to invest their reports with a documentary significance that news no longer enjoys today, not because of the rise of online real-time news, but because of the disappearance of readers whose situation was so fundamentally different from that of the reporters, the disappearance of an audience whose faith in the truth-telling tales from the sites of crisis and transformation also helped create the *über*-reporter as representative of an otherness we had few alternative means of relating to.

This position has disappeared, both in practice and, following the cross-disciplinary spread of postcolonial concepts and sensibilities, in theory. Instead, readers are confronted with a proliferation of general access sites whose success puts intense pressure on established news brands and the business models that sustain them, but also offers local voices from across the world unprecedented visibility.[37] Given the financial constraints of many news organizations, we may return to an age of reporting not unlike that of the early cold war, when individual reporters had to cover entire regions simply because their agencies could not afford to send more staff abroad. Again, such developments suggest that we learn from the journalistic practices and protocols developed under such conditions of scarcity, as the problems that arise with such broad beats—problems of a necessarily limited familiarity with the local, of a limited period of time spent in each location, of a limited range of languages available for local analysis—are likely to remain with us. More likely, however, are new hybrid approaches facilitated by online access—the involvement of local journalists in international news networks, and even the increasing use of "crowdsourcing" platforms to enable real-time news coverage from local actors in zones of crisis.[38]

Much of Kapuściński's later writing increasingly revolves around his own persona and occasionally amounts to a self-stylization that severely lacks the self-irony he occasionally embraced in his early work. Now considered the father of contemporary literary reportage/journalism, Kapuściński was put on a pedestal by readers and publishers alike—and while he never settled into that role entirely, he also didn't protest. History, and the history of access to media with global reach in particular, did not yet challenge such a stance, such an assumption of responsibility and representativeness. There was little chance that the actors would get out their stories on their own, as they manage to do today, and even if they did, as in the case of the inter- and postwar Pan-African publications that helped prepare a future generation of post-independence leaders, their circulation was small compared to that of a dispatch distributed by an international news agency.

Kapuściński knew that the decentralization and democratization of electronic media would begin to erode the reportorial privileges once granted those who went abroad in the name of public service—and often came back to address us with the authority of public intellectuals who spoke on behalf of those who needed representation. With the rise of general access media, such journalistic regimes of representation are less needed than before. But the disappearance of that position of privilege is also related to the disappearance of corresponding publics. As the analysis of "mass communication" built on assumptions of audience homogeneity and centralized content distribution gives way to the exploration of transnational "network cultures" driven by decentralized peer-to-peer infrastructures, the notion of a single public sphere that could serve as a platform for public intellectuals has also been called into question. Instead, journalism is faced with an ensemble of overlapping publics, and it is uncertain whether journalism can (or even needs to) create public personas that can effectively navigate all of them.

Possibly weakened by the unreliability of reporters, literary journalism is strengthened by responsible readers, and reporters remain unchallenged by readers who know less of the world than they do. In the age of real-time news media, this is beginning to change; the growing number of well-networked African bloggers, for instance, will not let colonial clichés stand, and video portals are delivering moving images from across the continent.[39] Literary journalism will be needed more than ever to provide context, to integrate fragments into broader narratives of historical transformation that in turn frame contemporary acts of literary witnessing. But more and more people will be in a position to assess—and to challenge—its factual accuracy. In the end, one element of an ethics of the encounter is the confidence that historical agency is not a privilege, granted by exceptional historical circumstances that call upon us to engage and shape a passing moment, but a constant possibility. Above and beyond facts, literary witnessing can and should render that possibility visible.

NOTES

1. Ryszard Kapuściński, *Travels with Herodotus,* trans. Klara Glowczewska (London: Penguin, 2007), 9.

2. See, for instance, Étienne Balibar, *We, the People of Europe: Reflections on Transnational Citizenship* (Princeton: Princeton University Press, 2004); and his "Strangers as Enemies: Further Reflections on the Aporias of Transnational Citizenship," a talk delivered at the Institute on Globalization and the Human Condition, McMaster University, Hamilton, Ontario, March 16, 2006, available at globalization.mcmaster.ca/wps/balibar.pdf.

3. Neal Ascherson, "Ryszard Kapuściński: from Poland to the world," *Open Democracy*, January 25, 2007, available at www.opendemocracy.net/democracy-journalismwar /kapuscinski_4286.jsp.

4. Timothy Brennan notes that the wide readership for such writing suggests an even more complex exoticism at work, as Western audiences preferred to filter their view of colonial and postcolonial difference by relating to foreign affairs through the measured otherness of their brothers and sisters from the East. See Timothy Brennan, "The Cuts of Language: The East/ West of North/South," *Public Culture* 13.1 (2001): 39–63. For Brennan, the "East of Europe is racially suspect Europe and always has been" (49), and condescending attitudes toward the East replayed "a familiar jargon of North/South colonial prejudice" (50). At the same time, this ambivalence (or displacement of colonial attitudes) offered Western readers "safe" access to difference, now in the form of foreign correspondence: "Book markets might be said again to have placed Eastern Europe resolutely at the center of an imperial problematic. After all, there is a family resemblance in media commentary about non-Western literatures and the highly publicized literary writing from Eastern Europe in the wake of *perestroika*. In the mental space of the politico-exotic enjoyed by Third World writing in the metropolitan book markets, the literatures of Eastern Europe are similarly situated, spawning new publishers' series of high production quality and yielding predictions of literary renaissance. They arrive to their audiences in the same packaging: a world literature for an age of world music. To the North American reader weighing choices in a bookstore, Eastern Europe may not be fully Europe, but it is nevertheless much more like home than is Zimbabwe or Sri Lanka. At the same time, it can claim an attractive otherness for being a version of the colonies 'at home.' As a preparation for this linkage, bridges between the two regions had long been forged by journals like *Granta* in Britain and its counterpart, *Grand Street,* in the United States, which placed writing from India, Africa, and Eastern Europe under the same marquee, as it were—Mario Vargas Llosa alongside Milan Kundera; Ryszard Kapuściński journeying through Africa" (60). In the end, even Western readers remain inside the East/West dichotomy as they reimport its displacement onto geographical "Others" for literary enjoyment: "We might say that the political dichotomy of the East/West conflict has typically been exported for the purpose of reimporting it—although now as 'foreign correspondence'" (43).

5. Kapuściński's first collection of essays was released under the title *Busz po polsku*, or *The Polish Bush*, a gesture of self-exoticization meant to place the local in a broader (post)colonial context. As Clara Cavanagh writes: "Kapuściński's writing not only expresses much of the postcolonial attitude of Polish poetry and fiction but also clarifies the possibilities for an expanded critique of colonialism than current theory offers. He demonstrates, in other words, a way of incorporating the Second World into our present theoretical frame. . . . The techniques of oppression, Kapuściński implies, are universal in our world of 'local knowledge'—and the victims and perpetrators of empire, he indicates, do not come from the First and Third Worlds alone." Clara Cavanagh, "Postcolonial Poland," *Common Knowledge* 10.1 (2004): 91–92. The term "postcolony" is borrowed from Achille Mbembe, *On the Postcolony* (Berkeley: University of California Press, 2001).

6. Neal Ascherson, introduction to Ryszard Kapuściński, *The Other,* trans. Antonia Lloyd-Jones (London: Verso, 2008), 6. Subsequent references appear parenthetically in the text, abbreviated *O*.

7. Kapuściński, *Travels with Herodotus,* 109.

8. Wiktor Osiatyński, "Ryszard Kapuściński: The Interpreter," *Open Democracy*, January 30, 2007, available at www.opendemocracy.net/democracy-journalismwar/Kapuściński _4294.jsp.

9. Noticeably, the contemporary appreciation for Herodotus includes a rehabilitation of the "digressive" features of his writing, as Peter Green writes: "That current trends in historiography echo, to a quite remarkable extent, the methods and assumptions of Herodotus is undeniable. The widespread use of social and ethnographic anthropology as an investigative tool is only the most obvious instance. Herodotus' observations about different customs and cultures—which in fact take up the greater part of the first half of the *Histories,* as he surveyed the various regions of the Persian empire—make him a groundbreaking anthropologist. Personal motivation (as opposed to abstract trends) and the influence of women in public affairs are very much back in the picture. The new understanding of oral transmission provides a satisfying answer to those who dismissed Herodotean anecdotes as mere crowd-pleasing digressions, and sheds fresh light on his careful evidential distinction between seeing (*opsis*) and hearsay (*akoê*). Many of the Persians, despite belonging to the Barbarian Other, come off with honor and dignity in his pages, even during the final narrative of Xerxes' invasion. Such insatiable and open-minded curiosity about the unfamiliar, including one's (undemonized) enemies, got him labeled *philobarbaros* by Plutarch, but today counts strongly in his favor." Peter Green, "The Great Marathon Man," *New York Review of Books,* May 15, 2008, available at www.nybooks.com/articles/21370. And while military historians and strategists continue to laud the sobriety of Thucydides, Green adds, "Herodotus has been the choice of imaginative novelists . . . and—as food for a starved soul—of an equally imaginative foreign correspondent from Iron Curtain Poland, Ryszard Kapuściński."

10. For his colleague Christopher de Bellaigue, "Kapuściński is an advocate for all who have chafed in a straightjacket called the house style, seen their lyrical phrases slashed for space, cursed the whole pedantic army of editors and fact-checkers. His slipping dates and questionable chronologies; the internal monologues that he ascribes to people who may exist or half exist, or have sprung human and beautifully expressive from his own imagination; his odd use of different tenses; these are Kapuściński's foibles, as integral to his brilliance as the profound truths that he brings. In that way, he is a journalist's writer, an example of what so many of us would love to be—if only we had the nerve." See Christopher de Bellaigue, introduction to Ryszard Kapuściński, *Shah of Shahs,* trans. William R. Brand and Katarzyna Mroczkowska-Brand (London: Penguin, 2006), xiii. Also see Joseph B. Atkins and Bernard Nezmah, "Ryszard Kapuściński: The Empathetic Existentialist," in *The Mission: Journalism, Ethics, and the World,* ed. Joseph B. Atkins (New York: Wiley-Blackwell, 2002), 217–26. Atkins and Nezmah, too, claim that Kapuściński "is arguably the world's greatest journalist" (217) and conclude their essay with a reference to Joseph Conrad, without any indication of the ambivalence ("heart of darkness") of such a reference.

11. Binyavanga Wainaina, "How to Write about Africa," *Granta* 92 (2005), available at www.granta.com/Magazine/92/How-to-Write-about-Africa.

12. John Ryle, "At Play in the Bush of Ghosts: Tropical Baroque, African Reality and the Work of Ryszard Kapuściński," *Times Literary Supplement,* June 17, 2001, available at www.richardwebster.net/print/xjohnryle.htm.

13. Ibid.

14. David Rieff, "Post-colonial Mumbo-Jumbo," *Los Angeles Times,* August 26, 2001, available at articles.latimes.com/2001/aug/26/books/bk-38349.

15. Ibid.

16. Ibid.

17. Aleksandar Hemon, "Misguided Tour," *Village Voice,* April 24, 2001, available at www.villagevoice.com/2001-04-24/books/misguided-tour.

18. Martin Kimani, "Ryszard Kapuściński: Martin Kimani Says It Is a Storm in a Teacup," April 20, 2005, available at bulletsandhoney.wordpress.com/2005/04/20/ryszard-kapuscinski-martin-kimani-says-it-is-a-storm-in-a-teacup/.

19. Michela Wrong, "Kapuściński, More Magical Than Real," *New Statesman*, February 12, 2007, 22–23.

20. Ibid.

21. Ibid.

22. Ibid.

23. Ibid.

24. Christoph Plate, "Der literarische Reporter," *Neue Zuercher Zeitung*, January 24, 2007, available at www.nzz.ch/2004/05/02/fe/article9KCJM.html.

25. The conceptual literature on "whiteness" has grown into a substantial subgenre of post-colonial theorizing. For an overview, see Steve Garner, *Whiteness: An Introduction* (London: Routledge, 2007).

26. As noted by Rieff in "Post-colonial Mumbo-Jumbo," contrary to a wide range of historical experiences of mass migration, Kapuściński remained "obsessed by the extent to which whites do not fit in" and insisted on racial difference as essential, while "the idea that race might be only one of the identities we have—biologically insignificant, and in many cultural and political contexts, not to speak of many historical epochs, comparatively insignificant—never seems to make the impression on him that it should have." Yet the writer "not only misunderstands the nature of the guilt being ascribed to him, which was almost certainly not about his oppressive actions (few Africans can have imagined this Polish journalist had participated in their colonization) but about the privileges that accrued to him, and not only in Africa, because of his race."

27. Emmanuel Levinas, *Otherwise Than Being or Beyond Essence*, trans. Alphonso Lingis (Dordrecht: Kluwer Academic Publishers, 1991), 180–81.

28. "The responsibility to protect populations from genocide, ethnic cleansing, war crimes and crimes against humanity is an international commitment by governments to prevent and react to grave crises, wherever they may occur." See www.responsibilitytoprotect.org. For attempts to spell out such a responsibility by offering concrete guidelines to good journalistic practice, see also www.reportingtheworld.org.uk and www.reportingtheworld.net. Developed from a U.K. perspective, *Reporting the World* proposes a four-point ethical checklist:

1. How is violence explained? (How does the explanation arise from the way violence is reported? Does it offer a classic "blow-by-blow" account? Or does it cover the workings of structural and cultural violence on the lives of people involved? Does it illuminate the intelligible, if dysfunctional processes which may be reproducing the violence? What are we led or left to infer about what should, or is likely to happen next?)

2. What is the shape of the conflict? (Is the conflict framed as "tug-of-war"—a zero-sum game of two parties contesting a single goal? Or as "cat's-cradle"—a pattern of many interdependent parties, with needs and interests which may overlap, or provide scope for integrated solutions?)

3. Is there any news of any efforts or ideas to resolve the conflict? (Is there anything in the report about peace plans, or any image of a solution? Must these aspects of a story wait until leaders cut a "deal"? Do the reports of any "deal" equip us to assess whether it is likely to tackle the causes of violence? Do we see any news of anyone else working to resolve or transform the conflict?)

4. What is the role of Britain; "the West"; the "international community" in this story? (Are "our" stated goals of intervention the same as our real goals? Do we get any

exploration of what the unstated goals might be? Is there anything about interventions already underway, albeit perhaps undeclared? Is there any examination of the influence of previous or prospective interventions on people's behaviour? Does it equip us to assess whether more, or less intervention might represent a solution, or to discriminate between different kinds of intervention?)

29. Ryszard Kapuściński, "A Soldier, 1975," in *I Wrote Stone: The Selected Poetry of Ryszard Kapuściński,* trans. Diana Kuprel and Marek Kusiba, ed. Daniel Wells and Stephen Henighan (Emeryville, Ontario: Biblioasis, 2008), 82.

30. The many local characters who people Kapuściński's essays are not, Rieff contends in "Post-colonial Mumbo-Jumbo," included as autonomous "Others," but are aggregated to sub-stantiate an overarching authorial perspective, "slotted into his narrative to make a point he wants to make in a voice other than his own, or, even more commonly, to illustrate a point he has already been making."

31. Maria Lind and Hito Steyerl, eds., *The Greenroom: Reconsidering the Documentary and Contemporary Art,* no. 1 (Berlin: Sternberg Press, 2008); Hito Steyerl, *Die Farbe der Wahrheit: Dokumentarismen im Kunstfeld* (Vienna: Verlag Turia & Kant, 2008).

32. Nadine Gordimer, "Literary Witness in a World of Terror: The Inward Testimony," *New Perspectives Quarterly* 26.2 (Spring 2009), available at www.digitalnpq.org/articles /nobel/321/12-09-2008/nadine_gordimer (May 15, 2009).

33. Ibid.

34. Ibid.

35. Ibid.

36. It is perhaps no accident that the rise of new ideological forces (such as religious funda-mentalism) receives comparatively little attention even in Kapuściński's later work, as its analy-sis would require an entirely new sense of post–cold war geographies. *Imperium* acknowledges the arrival of Islamic fundamentalism but does not engage it in any depth; again, however, the inability of cold war cosmopolitanisms to grasp the nature of violence in an age of terrorism not only was a task for Kapuściński but is so for a new generation of reportage writers as well.

37. See, for example, globalvoicesonline.org, whose co-founder Katherine MacKinnon worked as CNN's Beijing bureau chief from 1998 to 2001 and its Tokyo bureau chief from 2001 to 2003, but who never agreed with the double standard in international news coverage on CNN and CNN International; so she left to start Global Voices with Ethan Zukerman. See Katherine MacKinnon, "The World-Wide Conversation: Online Participatory Media and International News," Joan Shorenstein Center on the Press, Politics and Public Policy Working Paper Series (2004), available at www.hks.harvard.edu/presspol/publications/papers/working _papers/2004_02_mackinnon.pdf.

38. See, for example, www.ushahidi.com, a free crowdsourcing software developed to map post-election violence in Kenya that has already been adopted in other areas of conflict, includ-ing Gaza (a project by the Al Jazeera Media lab, labs.aljazeera.net/warongaza).

39. See www.kelele.org for a first continental conference of African bloggers. As bandwidth remains expensive, however, many providers of video portals limit access in "low-bandwidth countries" because poorer users do not generate enough advertising-based revenue—a new techno-cartography of online access that echoes the division of an earlier era. See Brad Stone and Miguel Helft, "In Developing Countries, Web Grows without Profit," *New York Times,* April 26, 2009.

Contributors

David Abrahamson is Professor of Journalism and the Charles Deering McCormick Professor of Teaching Excellence at the Medill School of Journalism at Northwestern University, where he founded and has taught a seminar in literary journalism since 1997. He is the editor of *The American Magazine: Research Perspectives and Prospects* (1995) and the author of *Magazine-Made America: The Cultural Transformation of the Postwar Periodical* (1996). He served as President of the International Association for Literary Journalism Studies from 2008 to 2010.

John S. Bak is Professor of American Literature at Nancy-Université in France, where he teaches courses in literary journalism and American drama. His articles have appeared in such journals as *Theatre Journal, Mississippi Quarterly, Journal of American Drama and Theatre,* the *Tennessee Williams Literary Journal, American Drama, Journal of Religion and Theatre, South Atlantic Review, Studies in Musical Theatre, Cercles,* and *Coup de Théâtre.* He is the author of *Ernest Hemingway, Tennessee Williams, and Queer Masculinities* (2009), and the editor of *Post/modern Dracula: From Victorian Themes to Postmodern Praxis* (2006) and *New Selected Essays: Where I Live* by Tennessee Williams (2009). He is the Founding President of the International Association for Literary Journalism Studies (2006–2008).

Peiqin Chen is Associate Professor at the College of Journalism and Communication, Shanghai Wai Guo Yu Da Xue (Shanghai International Studies University), in China, where she teaches courses on news writing, the sociology of journalism, international journalism, and literary journalism. She received her master's in English and American Literature at the College of English, Shanghai International Studies University, and her Ph.D. in journalism at the Journalism School of Fudan University in China. She was a 2006–7 Fulbright Visiting Research Scholar at the Graduate School of Journalism, Columbia University, in New York City.

Clazina Dingemanse is a researcher who focuses on the literary character of the early modern pamphlet. After studying Renaissance literature, Dingemanse wrote a dissertation on dialogued pamphlets titled *Rap van tong, scherp van pen: Literaire discussiecultuur in Nederlandse praatjespamfletten (circa 1600–1750)* (Glib Tongues, Sharp Pens: Literary Discussion Culture in Dutch Pamphlets [circa 1600–1750]). Since then she has been looking into modern incarnations of the literary pamphlet in newspapers and on the Internet.

William Dow is Professor of American Literature at the Université Paris–Est (Marne-la-Vallée) and teaches at the American University of Paris. He has published articles in such journals as *Publications of the Modern Language Association,* the *Emily Dickinson Journal, Twentieth-Century Literature, ESQ: A Journal of the American Renaissance, Critique, The Hemingway Review, MELUS, Revue française d'études américaines, Actes Sud, Profils américains,* and *Études Anglaises.* He is the author of the book *Narrating Class in American Fiction* (2009) and co-editor of *Richard Wright: New Readings in the Twenty-first Century* (2011). He is completing a book-length study on American modernism and radicalism, tentatively titled *Literary Journalism and the American Radical Tradition, 1929–1941.* He also serves as managing editor of *Literary Journalism Studies.*

Rutger de Graaf wrote his doctoral dissertation on the rise of the nineteenth-century newspaper as the primary news medium and the subsequent decline of the pamphlet at the Universiteit Utrecht in the Netherlands. De Graaf received master's degrees in both history and communication studies at the Universiteit van Amsterdam. His previous employment experience includes four years as a media analyst.

John C. Hartsock is Professor of Communication Studies at the State University of New York at Cortland. A former newspaper and wire service reporter, he is the author of two books, the critically acclaimed study, *A History of American Literary Journalism: The Emergence of a Modern Narrative Form* (2000), and a work of narrative journalism, *Seasons of a Finger Lakes Winery* (2010). He has lectured widely on the subject of narrative/literary journalism, and his articles have appeared in such journals as *Prose Studies, Genre, Points of Entry, Journal of Communication Inquiry,* and *Critical Studies in Mass Communication.* He is the editor in chief of *Literary Journalism Studies.*

Nikki Hessell is Senior Lecturer in English Literature at Victoria University of Wellington in New Zealand. She has published on the relationship between literature and journalism in the eighteenth and nineteenth centuries in *Studies in Romanticism, Romanticism on the Net, Papers on Language and Literature,* the *Coleridge Bulletin,* and the *Keats-Shelley Journal.* She is also the editor of the first complete collection of Robin Hyde's parliamentary journalism (published by the New Zealand Electronic Text Centre). Her current project is *Genius in the Gallery: Literary Authors as Parliamentary Reporters,* a book focusing on Samuel Johnson, Samuel Taylor Coleridge, and Charles Dickens, funded by a Marsden Grant from the Royal Society of New Zealand.

Maria Lassila-Merisalo is Postdoctoral Researcher in Journalism at the Jyväskylän yliopisto, Finland. In January 2009 she defended her Ph.D. dissertation on the poetics of literary journalism in Finnish magazines. She has taught courses on feature writing at the Department of Communication as well as in several open universities and continuing professional development centers, and has published several peer-reviewed articles in academic journals and publications. She received her master's in journalism in 2002 and was rewarded for the best Finnish thesis in media studies.

Edvaldo Pereira Lima is Professor (retired) at the Universidade de São Paulo and is a writer and a journalist in Brazil. He completed postdoctoral research and studies at the University of Toronto and was a guest scholar at both the University of London and the University of Florence. He helped establish the Brazilian Academy of Literary Journalism (ABJL), the first Brazilian website on the subject (TextoVivo—Narrativas da Vida Real), and the first graduate-level course on literary journalism in Brazil.

Willa McDonald is Senior Lecturer in Writing for the Media at Macquarie University in Sydney, Australia. Her publications include the edited anthology (with Susie Eisenhuth) *The Writer's Reader: Telling Stories in Journalism and Non-fiction* (2007), and the monograph *Warrior for Peace: Dorothy Auchterlonie Green* (2009).

Jenny McKay is Senior Lecturer in Magazine Journalism at the University of Sunderland in England. She has taught journalism and literature in several universities. She is the author of *The Magazines Handbook* (2006), a guide to magazine journalism and the U.K. magazine industry. She was a journalist for ten years, working in television, newspapers, and magazines. Her research interests include literary journalism, magazines, and the early journalism of Daniel Defoe. She is currently serving as associate editor of *Literary Journalism Studies.*

Sonja Merljak Zdovc is Assistant Professor at the Univerza na Primorskem in Slovenia, where she teaches a course in the theory and practice of print media. She has combined professional careers in journalism and in the academy, and is also a feature writer for the Saturday supplement of the national daily newspaper *Delo.* Her research focus includes literary journalism and journalism history. Her relevant publications include the monograph *Literary Journalism in the United States of America and Slovenia* (2008), and several articles in *Journalism Studies, Journalism Practice,* and *Journalism.*

Sonia Parratt is Associate Professor at the Universidad Complutense de Madrid, where she teaches graduate courses on print journalism. She holds an undergraduate degree in journalism from the Universidad del País Vasco and a doctorate from the Universidade de Santiago de Compostela, Spain, with a Ph.D. dissertation on the evolution of reportage in the Galician press from 1960 to 2000. She worked for several years as a television presenter, a writer of press releases, and an environmental journalist. Her research interests are news writing and reporting, and newspaper readership. Her relevant publications include the monographs *Introducción al reportaje: Antecedentes, actualidad y perspectivas* (2003), *Medio ambiente y medios de comunicación* (2006), and *Géneros periodísticos en prensa* (2008).

Bill Reynolds is Assistant Professor at the School of Journalism, Ryerson University, in Toronto. He teaches the courses Journalism and Ideas and Feature Writing Workshop to undergraduates, and Magazine and Feature Writing and Visions of Literary Journalism to graduate students. His research has been published in *Asia Pacific Media Educator* and *Literary Journalism Studies.* He won National Magazine Awards for his magazine features "Crossing the Line: How Patriotism Stifled

Freedom of Speech" (*This Magazine,* 2004), and "Geared Up: On the Road to Two-Wheeled Transcendence" (*The Walrus,* 2008). He is vice president and treasurer of the International Association for Literary Journalism Studies, and executive editor of *Literary Journalism Studies.*

Norman Sims is Professor of Journalism at the University of Massachusetts Amherst, where he teaches courses in the history of journalism, freedom of the press, writing, and literary journalism. He is the editor and co-editor of two anthologies, *The Literary Journalists* (1984) and (with Mark Kramer) *Literary Journalism* (1995). He also edited a collection of scholarly articles, *Literary Journalism in the Twentieth Century* (2008), and wrote a history of American literary journalism, *True Stories: A Century of Literary Journalism* (2007). He has been studying literary journalism for more than twenty-five years.

Isabel Soares is Assistant Professor at the Universidade Técnica de Lisboa Instituto Superior de Ciências Sociais e Políticas, the Technical University of Lisbon in Portugal. She is a Fellow at CAPP (Center for Public Administration Policies), where she carries out research on the media and communication streams and coordinates a project on urban images in early literary journalism. She is also Research Chair of the International Association for Literary Journalism Studies, of which she is a founding member, and has published an article in *Literary Journalism Studies.* She wrote the first doctoral thesis on Portuguese literary journalism, titled "The Empire of the Other: Eça de Queirós, Ramalho Ortigão, Batalha Reis, Oliveira Martins, and Victorian England" (2007).

Soenke Zehle teaches transcultural literary and media studies at Universität des Saarlandes, where he initiated a Transcultural Media Studies Project, and at the Academy of Fine Arts Saar (Department of Media Art and Design) in Saarbrücken, Germany. He has published widely on communication, media, political, and border studies.

Index